·THE·
·ROMAN·WORLD·

·THE· ·ROMAN·WORLD·

EDITED BY

JOHN WACHER

Emeritus Professor of Archaeology
University of Leicester

Volume II

LONDON AND NEW YORK

First published 1987 by Routledge & Kegan Paul Ltd

First published in paperback 1990
by Routledge
11 New Fetter Lane, London EC4P 4EE

Simultaneously published in the USA and Canada
by Routledge
29 West 35th Street, New York, NY 10001

Reissued in paperback 2002

Routledge is an imprint of the Taylor & Francis Group

© Routledge 1987, 1990, 2002

Printed and bound in Great Britain by
TJ International Ltd, Padstow, Cornwall

British Library Cataloguing in Publication Data
A catalogue record for this book is available from the British Library

Library of Congress Cataloging in Publication Data
A catalog record for this book has been requested

ISBN 0-415-26315-8 (Volume I)
ISBN 0-415-26316-6 (Volume II)
ISBN 0-415-26314-X (Set)

·CONTENTS·

CONTENTS

PART 10
·RELIGION·AND·BURIAL·

PART 11
·POST-SCRIPT·

·PLATES·

VOLUME II

vii

·FIGURES·

VOLUME II

PART 7

·RURAL·LIFE·

CHAPTER 18

·AGRICULTURE·AND· ·HORTICULTURE·

Sian Rees

'This part of Europe has a more temperate climate than we find further inland. For the winter is almost continuous in the interior.' Thus Varro introduces his reader in his work *Rerum Rusticarum* (1,ii,2–5) to the climatic benefits of Italy, and his division of the European climate into the Mediterranean and the northern European is largely true for the Empire as a whole. Within this simple two-fold division, the lands of the Empire covered a variety of climate, soils and topography, and the Romans were, of course, as dependent upon these factors as anyone else. While various facets of Roman administration in the provinces could be standardized, in the field of agriculture, Roman practice tended to be heavily based on the pre-Roman, with its inevitable accumulation of wisdom in dealing with the physical characteristics of each area. Indeed it might be said that it was largely through the non-agricultural provisions, of urbanization, communications, peace, and incentive for producing a surplus, that Roman rule in the provinces made the major contribution toward agricultural development.

The two-fold division of the lands of the Empire into the Mediterranean lands with their hot, dry summers, and the northern provinces with their cooler, wetter climate is reflected in the two quite different farming techniques practised in the respective zones: 'dry farming' in the former, 'humid farming' in the latter. This same division is largely true of the topography; the Mediterranean lands have mountain chains, low hills and alluvial plains which support different agricultural regimes: timber or summer pasture on the thin mountain soils; crops on the foothills, with olive and vine on the less rich upper parts, cereals on the lower; and stock raising and/or arable on the alluvial plains. The northern provinces have large areas of plain lands of heavier, fertile clays and loams alternating with downs of lighter but poorer chalks and limestones, with intrusions of mountain ranges. The upland areas tend to be better for stock, while the lower areas may support arable or mixed farming. They have too little sunshine, of course, to allow

481

olives, and the vine is certainly far less extensive (Stevens, 1966, 92–4).

Agricultural practices of the Roman period varied also depending on the type of pre-existing society. Many areas, such as early republican Italy were farmed by peasant agriculturalists on mixed subsistence farms, potentially, or even actually, able to make a surplus, but lacking much incentive to do so. Other areas already had highly developed agricultural systems, having been part of previous empires. Carthaginian areas of north Africa, Egypt and the Near East all had well worked out and distinctive economic and agricultural practices, with different forms of land ownership and tenurial systems, and these arrangements inevitably coloured the subsequent Roman development of their agriculture.

Of great importance as source material for this study are the works of the Roman agronomists, from Cato writing in the second century BC to Palladius in the late fourth century AD. These writers clearly benefited from the earlier treatises of Greek and Carthaginian philosophers and scientists, but unlike them, Roman agronomists wrote from first-hand agriculture experience. Cato's *De Agri Cultura,* the more systematic, practical *De Re Rustica* of Varro, written in 37 BC, and the twelve books of Columella's *De Re Rustica,* written in the mid-first century AD, describe agriculture purely in Italy, while the two volumes of agriculture in the Elder Pliny's vast *Encyclopaedia of Natural History* include material gleaned, usefully, from North Africa, the Near East and northern Europe as well as Italy. There is then a gap in the surviving material to Palladius in the later part of the fourth century. His calendar of instructions is heavily dependent on Columella, but gives us valuable insight into the agrarian recession. As well as these textbooks, innumerable references can be found to agricultural practices in non-agricultural writings: the speeches of Cicero and the poetry of Vergil, for instance. The documentary sources of the Empire outside Italy are far poorer. Reliance must be made on casual references in books such as Strabo's *Geographica,* or reference works like the *Digest,* a late, legal compilation which gives information about leases, rights and responsibilities of landowners (Part 6, Chapter 16). Papyri, surviving from Egypt because of the dry archaeological conditions, give details of sales, wills, census returns, accounts, equipment and inventories and are generally tantalizing about how much must have been lost elsewhere. Inscriptions can be useful, for instance, the series dealing with irrigation supplies in Numidia. Archaeological evidence is vital both for Italy, where it can supplement the written evidence, and for the provinces where largely it has to stand alone; knowledge of farm types, implements, fields, types of crops and their variety, nutrient value and cleanness from weeds and the growth or decline of single or groups of farms and their interrelationship is largely dependent upon information revealed by excavation, aerial photography and botanical analysis, as well as pictorial evidence on sculpture, mosaics and models.

Agriculture was of paramount importance in the economy of the Empire. References in the agronomists suggest that agriculture, unlike risky and often shady business life, was regarded as the sole respectable profession. Land remained throughout the period the only safe and permanent form of investment (Jones, 1964, 769–73) and in taxes, it provided the vast bulk of the revenue of the state. The land tax financed the main administrative needs, while other taxes paid by the land-owning classes, and rents from imperial lands, fed other departments. Rents on agricultural land were also important for the incomes of institutions such as the cities, and later the church, and the incomes of private landowners and the professional classes, who tended to invest in land, depended upon it. Investment in land tended inevitably to build up large estates at the expense of the small proprietor. The free land-owning peasant, however, while declining dramatically as a class, remained an important element in the rural population. There is evidence for considerable numbers late on in the Empire in the villages of Asia Minor, Egypt and Thrace and while it is certainly true that Italy, Sicily, Spain, North Africa and Gaul were largely populated by medium to large estates, there is, even here, evidence for the survival of the peasant proprietor.

Agriculture in early Italy was probably based on the subsistence, mixed farms of small peasant proprietors, with southern Italy and Etruria more heavily dependent on cereals, Latium on pastoralism. The olive and the vine are indigenous to the entire Mediterranean, but, while their cultivation was certainly important in republican Italy, the spread of these more profitable forms of cultivation from the first century BC was one of the noteworthy features of Italian agriculture. As Rome grew to dominate all Italy, the wine and olive-oil production of the Punic cities was severe competition, a not insignificant factor in the determination to destroy Carthage. The old Carthaginian territories were reduced to one vast area of cereal growing and Rome's early provinces of Sicily, Sardinia and the Punic parts of Spain remained what they had been for Carthage, granaries producing surplus grain for import to the City (Rostovtzeff, 1926, 195). The newly-acquired western provinces were prohibited in the early days from planting vines, so that the protected Italian production was now provided with splendid markets for the sale of oil and wine. Thus grew up the notion of commercial farming on mixed farms run by slave labour and with land as an investment that is seen in Cato. Estates, again slave-run, became increasingly important from the late republican period onward. They show considerable variety in type predominating between large-scale ranches, based on transhumance, and those based on mixed farming; by Varro's time, estates had commonly reached a size whereby trade between land-owners was viable and private estate-run services like smithies are found. Wheat growing was still part of the normal pattern of farming, though Columella in the first century AD is gloomy about its productivity and profitability. Free tenants are beginning to be mentioned alongside slaves as labour for an estate, since the supply of slaves provided by the conquest of new territories was falling away, so creating a labour shortage (Part 9, Chapter 28).

As new areas gradually became assimilated into the Empire, the characteristic development of each province would, with the establishment of peace, depend on the setting up of administrative systems based on new or existing urban centres and improved communications. The reasons for so doing were primarily fiscal, but they also resulted in a benefit to agriculture. The cities would be assigned large tracts of land for which they were responsible, and the increase of markets and of a non-productive administrative class, which had to be fed, together with improved networks of communications and the requirements of taxation, all led to the necessity to produce a surplus. In the military provinces there was also the army to be supplied. In many new provinces the earliest romanization of the countryside would have been by way of the immigration of an Italian colonist either by grant of land, to army veterans, for example, or through his own private investment. Enterprising members of the native aristocracy would have followed the lead, investing in the land but often living and working in the city. The labour on such farms would inevitably be local natives. The degree of romanization would thus depend on the attractiveness of the country to investment and also the initiative of the native land-owners. Hence in some areas such as North Africa with relatively undeveloped agriculture but fertile soils, the spread of large estates was legendary, while in other less fertile or mountainous countries, such as some of the Danube provinces, romanization was far from widespread.

By the first century AD, there had been rapid economic growth in many provinces. When, under Augustus, the prohibition on viticulture outside Italy had been removed, vine and olive growing developed rapidly, the former especially in Gaul, the latter in Spain and Africa. Inevitably there was increased competition for the markets that Italy had hitherto dominated. There are hints of gluts in the wine market, as Gallic wine of high quality won markets and Italian oil suffered from the competition of oil from Africa (cheaper) and Spain (higher quality); imperial edicts were passed as a protection for Italian producers of wine at the expense of provincials, but were only partly successful, while provincial oil production was allowed to continue unabated and many areas, North Africa in particular, developed vast olive estates.

The tendency toward larger estates owned by fewer, wealthy men who let out their land, often scattered, to tenant farmers increases both in Italy and the provinces in the second century and onwards. The largest estates were, of course, those of the imperial government and next, the estates of the senatorial classes. In the later Empire, the Church also acquired vast estates, which tended to be at the expense of the professional, urban-based classes running the medium-sized farm, as well as the landed peasant. Great landowners could either farm their land through agents, or, as became more and more the norm, lease farms on short or long term – lifetime or in perpetuity – conditions; only the home farm, at least in Italy, was left to be run by slaves under a slave manager to provide a country residence and agricultural produce for the land-owner himself. Jones thinks it unlikely that slave labour was extensively used outside Italy and Spain (Jones, 1964, 794).

The rents paid varied considerably from area to area. In Egypt a fixed payment in kind was normal, in Africa share-cropping, by which owner and tenant divided the produce according to a written agreement, was common. In Italy, money rents were usual, though part of the rent could be paid in produce, as tenants paying only money were very vulnerable to debt after bad harvests.

During the troubles of the third century, inflation, high taxation necessitated by the increasing costs of military defence, and general social and political instability, led in many parts of the Empire to a general economic depression, with a consequent decline in agriculture. Land went uncultivated and farms were abandoned, and *agri deserti* (abandoned lands) were a constant theme in the legislation, as various emperors, from Pertinax onwards, issued edicts providing incentives for private people to cultivate deserted land on long leases, either private or imperial, Italian or provincial. The few figures that are available suggest that, while in some areas such as Asia, the problem was not too bad, with about 5 per cent uncultivated, in Africa Proconsularis, by the early fifth century, the situation was disastrous with about 30 per cent abandoned. But the deterioration was uneven, and in the early fourth century there was even a certain recovery resulting from strong imperial leadership and a reorganization of administration and the currency. The villas of the Roman world show this decline and recovery (Percival, 1976, 46) though the recovery was, as Percival remarks one 'of economic stability on a lower and generally more sober level'. Some areas such as Dacia, no longer part of the Empire, never recovered at all; Britain on the other hand is peculiar in having a very vigorous recovery in the fourth century, probably largely because it had escaped invasion and civil war on anything like the continental scale (Applebaum, 1972, 228–9). But the rich tended to get richer, the poor poorer, and the lot of the tenant farmer in the later Empire was unenviable.

Turning now to actual techniques of farming practised in Italy, there is a fair amount of evidence, written and archaeological, while for the provinces the evidence is largely archaeological. In the Mediterranean, the techniques of dry farming, with its emphasis on water conservation, had certainly been worked out by Cato's time. At its simplest, this was a two-year crop-fallow system. The seed would be sown broadcast between October and December depending on the area, and the field would be harrowed and hoed throughout the winter to keep weeds down and to conserve the water from the winter rains. The grain would be harvested as early as possible in June or July, and a period of fallow would follow with weed removal by hoeing and one ploughing in late summer; there would then be at least three ploughings (Pliny advocates nine) in the following spring, with a final ploughing, often with ridging for drainage, to prepare the ground for the October sowing. This labour-intensive method of cultivation effected water conservation as much as soil replenishment, as two years' rainfall contributed towards the growth of one year's crop. The fine tilth created by the continuous ploughing minimized evaporation from the wetter lower levels, and encouraged the often heavy winter rains to soak in; constant weed removal avoided water loss by plant transpiration.

The plough was thus used as a weeding and stirring tool, and inversion of the sod was not necessary. Fallow and stubble burning would contribute to the replenishment of the soil, for, while Roman farmers certainly understood the vital nature of manuring, their problem was an acute shortage of animal dung. The shortage of permanent pasture due to the summer drought meant that only essential working animals were stall fed, and most animals were led to distant summer pastures on a transhumance basis, hence the loss of half the manure produced. Thus the climate, rather than the lack of understanding, led to the somewhat unproductive crop-fallow system.

There is evidence, however, of plenty of variations on this system. Cato refers to ground which does not require to be fallowed, implying that fertile, wetter areas like Campania could tolerate annual cropping. From the first century AD there are increasing references to partial legume rotation and combination cropping (White, 1970, 122–3). The first of them, with variations on the fallow to beans/legume to grain, is when legumes alternate with a cereal crop, the legumes providing the necessary nitrogen; the latter is the intercultivation of cereal crops with vines or, more commonly, with olives which require wide spacing, are slow to mature and which normally have a good crop only in alternate years (pl. 18.4). Intercultivation thus maximized the profit from one area of land. How far these practices were commonly used and how far they were mere textbook recommendations is difficult to say, but White suggests that rotation was not exceptional at least in Vergil's day (*Georgics* 1, 1–71 ff) while Columella mentions combination cropping as though it were quite common (V, 9.7); Pliny refers to its use in Andalusia (XVIII, 94).

As the interdependence of animal and crop husbandry was understood, and the technique of combination cropping was followed, the medium-sized mixed farm perforce remained the Roman ideal, certainly to Columella's day, despite the decline of cereal farming and the increase in vine and olive growing and large-scale ranching. Columella's ideal mixed farm would be run by a staff of slaves under a slave manager and would have sufficient variety of terrain to allow level ground for meadows, arable, willows and reed plantations, hills for grain, olive and vineyards, copses for vine props and pasture; it was preferably near a town or to sea or road communications for markets. Cattle and other domestic animals would graze the tilled land and the lightly timbered portion. However, far more space in his books is devoted to vine and olive cultivation and animal husbandry than cereals and legumes, suggesting their relative unimportance by this time. Columella is clear that he regards a slave-run farm, personally supervised by the owner, as the most profitable, but failing that, country-bred, conscientious, free tenants are preferable to unsupervised slave managers, and it would seem that the system of a home farm worked by slaves, surrounded by tenant farmers was already beginning to appear (Heitland, 1921, 255). He condemns large estates because the inevitable lack of supervision leads to decay, with lands either being overgrazed or alternatively left unworked. The main advances from Varro's day – partial legume rotation and combination cropping – require intensive labour and he is gloomy about the decline in productivity caused by bad management and carelessness.

Roman knowledge of soils inevitably depended almost totally upon the accumulated experience of farmers of the suitability of different crops to different soils – practical land use – and they knew nothing of soil classification according to structure and texture (White, 1970, 94–6). The agronomists gave advice on tests for fertility and moisture content as a guide to land purchase and selection of suitable crop, but their rough and ready methods failed to distinguish some fundamentals such as how a soil can vary in different conditions, with good management or neglect. The system of combination cropping and the tendency towards specialization laid heavy burdens on the natural fertility of the soil especially on continuously cropped land, and manuring was absolutely necessary. The evident shortage of animal manure is emphasized by the agronomists' advice to gather manure wherever possible, from poultry and all domestic animals, with the relative merits of the manure from each animal being impressively documented. Advice which conforms quite closely to modern practice on preparation, method and quantity of manuring for different crops is given, and Columella advises that irrigated gardens and orchards, which require heavy manuring for rapid feeding should be positioned so that manure-laden sewage from barnyards and house use and the lees squeezed from olives could flow there to facilitate application. Composts, made from straw, vegetable waste and chaff, leaves, ashes, sewage sludge and even house sweepings, and green manures, especially lupins, dug back into the soil while the plants are still green in May, to rot down before autumn sowing, are two substitutes for animal manures mentioned, suggesting again the shortage of the latter. There is also advice on the practice of marling and soil mixing to improve the quality of poor soils, though how often this labour-intensive technique could have been carried out is, of course, unknown. Treatment of the soil with wood ash and seaweed is referred to occasionally, though this seems to have been uncommon.

In Mediterranean countries with summer drought and short-lived but often torrential winter rains, drainage was of great importance. Large-scale drainage works to reclaim agricultural land had been carried out by the Etruscans in the north of Italy and schemes of this type were continued by Roman engineers. Some, like the Po Valley drainage scheme, were successful while others, like that of the Pomptine Marches in Campania, proved to be beyond their capacity. Normal field drainage was a matter of course and by Columella's day was quite sophisticated. Open drains on clay soils, or covered drains filled with stones, gravel or brushwood were carefully positioned to minimize soil erosion and the damage to young plants in winter storms and Pliny advocates the ridging of wetter lands while ploughing, so that while the seed is sown in the ridges, furrows were left for drainage of surface water (*Natural History* XVIII, 179). Irrigation, by channel from natural springs, or raised from wells, was used in Italy for intensively cultivated market garden plots, and in drier areas such as south Spain for fruit, olives and vines, though these could generally withstand drought without irrigation. The same was true of cereals and legumes. If farmers had no natural spring or well water they normally had to do without irrigation, though in some areas such as Tusculum near Rome, farmers could buy into the right to water from aqueducts with a strictly controlled number of hours being allowed to each user. Our knowledge of irrigation on a larger scale is greater in north Africa, Egypt, where the best systems were, and Syria (p. 497 below).

Crops grown by the Roman farmer around the Mediterranean were either sown – cereals and legumes, fodder crops and pasture for stock – or planted – olive, vine, nut, fig and fruit trees – as well as the products of the kitchen garden. Cereals were grown primarily as autumn-sown wheat and spelt, and to a lesser extent the not so highly esteemed six-row barley, while spring-sown wheat and barley seems only to have been used when the main crop had failed. Millet was grown on a large scale in Egypt, in the Middle East and Gaul but not, it seems, in Italy. Rye was considered an easy crop to grow but unpleasant to eat. Lupins, vetch and field beans were used as fodder or green manure while lucerne, alfalfa and vetches could be grown singly for cattle feed or as mixed forage crops in combination with barley, oats or emmer (White, 1970, 190–1). The soil improving qualities of these legumes, which return nitrogen to the soil, was appreciated, and they were used in rotation with cereals (p. 486 above). Their cultivation required the same dry farming techniques as cereals. In times of famine, Columella mentions that the lupin could also be used for human food, and crops such as turnips and rape, grown in wetter areas primarily for fodder, were also occasionally used for human consumption. The Roman farmer understood the necessity for selecting the best grain for the seed corn at threshing. Improvement in varieties is not specifically mentioned, but Columella and Pliny between them mention six different varieties of wheat (White, 1970, 188–9).

Cultivation of the vine and olive quickly reached very sophisticated levels, and while Cato mentioned only seven varieties of olive, Pliny knew of fifteen, and all authorities stress the importance of the selection of the right variety for different soils. A large number of varieties of vine were known, and the introduction of viticulture into western provinces eventually produced some very fine wines. The fig was also important especially, so Columella tells us, as a dried food for country folk in winter. It was grown in south-west Asia Minor, Greece and Italy, and Pliny enumerates twenty-nine varieties while Palladius mentions that it would take too long to list all the known varieties. Vegetables grown in irrigated market gardens and orchard fruits were most important for the primarily vegetarian Roman diet, with beans, turnips, rape, radish, carrots, peas and lettuce with a variety of herbs being commonly grown. The almond and hazel trees of southern Italy were famous. Apples and pears could be grown with care in central Italy, while other fruits including the cherry and peach were introduced. The market stimulus providing incentive for the development of new varieties in vine, olive and fruit growing was not so evident in the less profitable cereal cultivation. As well as these main crops, the model farm was expected to have a plantation of willows for weaving into basketry for storage, transport, collection, harvesting, winnowing, hurdles, strainers for honey and wine, matting and beehives and innumerable other purposes; willow branches were used for vine props of which a vast number were required, and its bark for vine ties (White, 1975, 51–103 and 234).

The Roman plough, vital in dry farming as a weeding and stirring implement, as well as being used for the preparation of the seed bed, was a light ard (a plough without a mould board) with wooden share or more commonly, an iron-tanged or socketed share. The actual form of the plough used is open to doubt as the only description we have is a poetic one (Vergil *Georgics* I, 169–74); the only archaeological remains of Mediterranean ploughs are of iron shares which could arguably fit either of the two main types of ard known to exist in contemporary Europe, the sole ard in which the beam is set into the sole or working part, or the bow ard where the working part is fitted into the curving beam (White, 1970, 174–5; 1967a, 123–44; Aitken, 1956, 97–106; Manning, 1964 and 1971; Rees, 1979, 65–9; fig. 18.1). Both types co-existed at somewhat earlier periods in north-west Europe (Glob, 1951) and it is not inconceivable that both co-existed perhaps for different tasks in Roman Italy though admittedly the agronomists make no reference to two types. Cross ploughing, the first to break the surface, the

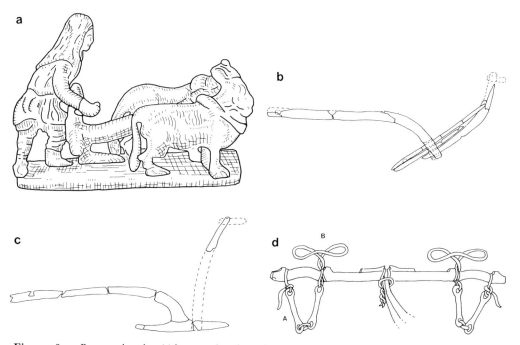

Figure 18.1   Roman ploughs: (a) bronze plough model from Piercebridge, Britain; (b) bow or beam ard; (c) crook or sole ard; (d) horn yoke with (A) neck ties and (B) noose fastenings

second at right angles to the first to break clods so finely that you could not tell the direction of the plough (Pliny, *Natural History,* XVIII, 178) was advocated for preparation of the seed bed; a third ploughing after the broadcast sowing of the seed could be carried out with ridging boards attached so as to cover the seed, or ridging could be done before sowing, the seed set on the ridges and covered by rakes or bush harrows. A team of two oxen yoked at the withers was normal, though horn yokes (fig. 18.2) were often used in the provinces but were condemned as cruel by Columella and Pliny; larger teams of oxen could also be employed for special circumstances (Rees, 1979, 72–9). Wheat was normally sown thinly to encourage bushing out and sometimes this was further encouraged by turning cattle in to browse on the young plants soon after they germinated.

The winter hoeing was done with a variety of different mattocks, hoes and rakes to suit different soils, and care had to be taken not to disturb the young cereal plants (fig. 18.3). Harvesting was done with the hand sickle, and Varro describes three different methods used in different regions of Italy (fig. 18.4). In Umbria the stalks were cut close to the ground, then the ears cut off, the straw being stacked separately; in Picenum, the ears were cut first with a saw-like implement, and the straw cut later; near Rome and generally, the stalks were cut at middle height. These differences reflect the different requirements for straw; cutting the corn half way up would leave useful litter after threshing, and stubble for the herds to graze in (White, 1970, 182); in dry areas, however, stubble would be quickly parched and rendered useless for grazing and stubble burning was clearly commonly practised. After harvesting, the corn was carried in baskets for threshing which was done by animal treading, by hand flails or by threshing sledge on a circular threshing floor with a hard, compact surface (pl. 18.3). Winnowing could be done by agitating winnowing baskets full of threshed grain so that the lighter chaff rose to the surface and was expelled, or by the winnowing shovel, using the wind to blow the lighter chaff from the mixture thrown into the air. Sieves would be used for final waste removal, and to separate the seed corn from the corn for consumption (White, 1975, 98). Grain was then stored in granaries which had to be cool and dry, with the walls, floors and ceilings treated to keep out vermin; the details which the authorities go into suggest that losses from mildew and vermin were considerable (White, 1970, 189). Grain was usually ground by the ubiquitous hand-operated, rotary quern, while larger-scale operations, near urban centres for instance, would use the far more efficient donkey driven mill (fig. 18.5). The undershot water wheel, apparently forty times more efficient than the donkey mill, was known by the first century BC, yet strangely seems never to have become widely distributed (White, 1970, 446–7).

Vines and olives would be reared in carefully prepared nursery beds for two to five years. Olive plants would then be transplanted to their permanent positions 9 m (30 ft) apart where no corn was to be sown between them, or 18 m by 12 m (60 ft by 40 ft) apart where combination cropping was practised in which case they would be

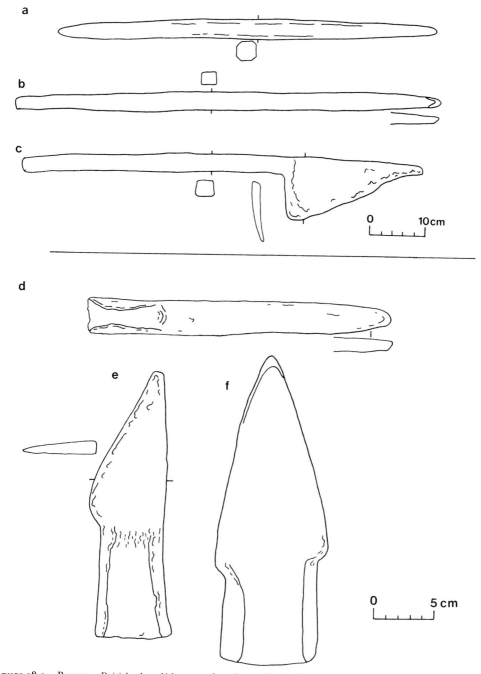

Figure 18.2 Romano-British ploughshares and coulters: (a) double-pointed bar share; (b) single-pointed bar share; (c) coulter; (d) iron sheath for bar share; (e) winged share; (f) symmetrical share

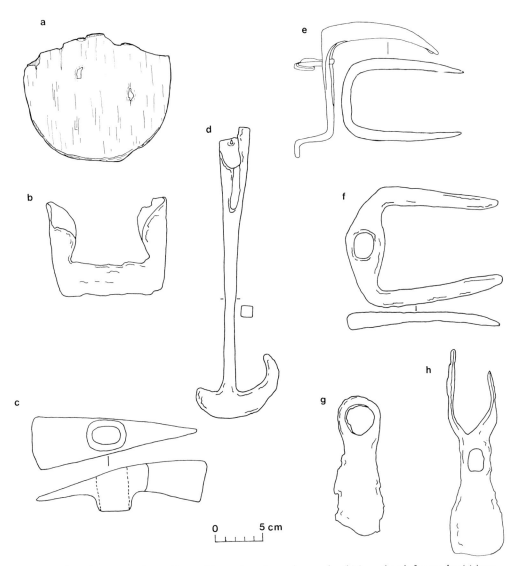

Figure 18.3 Roman spades and hoes: (a) remains of wooden spade; (b) iron sheath for spade; (c) iron mattock; (d) turf-cutter; (e and f) double-bladed hoes; (g) single-bladed hoe; (h) small weeding hoe

fenced to guard against damage from ploughing. Columella advised two ploughings a year to weed, cover the roots and drain, while manuring and pruning was also necessary. Slow to mature, the olive is a heavy investment and produces a full crop only in alternate years, hence the popularity of combination cropping, and the practice of dividing a grove into two to give an equal return each year.

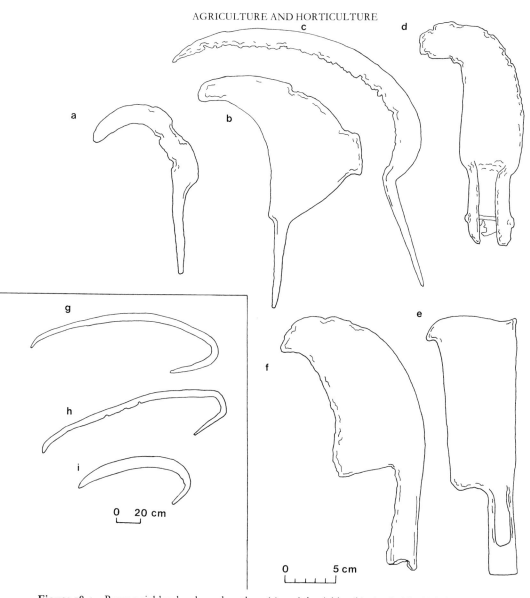

Figure 18.4 Roman sickles, hooks and scythes: (a) upright sickle; (b) vine knife; (c) balanced sickle; (d, e and f) billhooks; (g and h) long-balanced scythe; (i) short-balanced scythe

In November and December, the olives were harvested by picking, and by shaking or beating the higher branches (pl. 18.4); the produce would be pressed immediately after cleaning and softening in hot water. Four types of mill were known: the oil mill with two stones set on a horizontal axis; the revolving mill or *trapetum* (fig. 18.5) with two circular stones, plano-convex in section, which rotated against a mortar and central

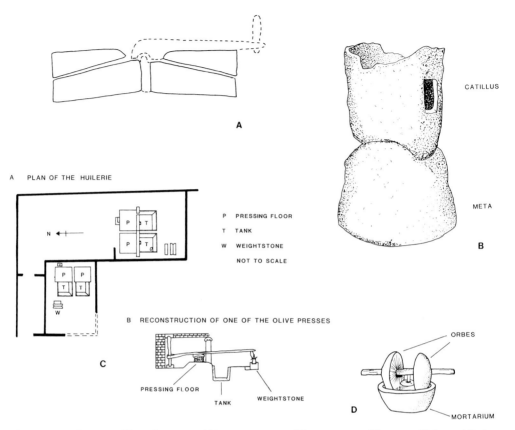

A PLAN OF THE HUILERIE

P PRESSING FLOOR

T TANK

W WEIGHTSTONE

NOT TO SCALE

CATILLUS

META

B

B RECONSTRUCTION OF ONE OF THE OLIVE PRESSES

PRESSING FLOOR

TANK

WEIGHTSTONE

ORBES

MORTARIUM

D

Figure 18.5 Roman mills and presses: (A) rotary quern of Roman type; (B) corn-mill from Albulae; (C) 'Huilerie' at Aquae Sirensis; (D) *trapetum* from Albulae (*b, c, d after Lawless*)

pillar; a simple trough for manual treading; and a *tridicula,* seemingly a type of upright grater (White, 1975, 226–8). The oil was then squeezed from the resulting mush in a press, a variety of types of which were known, worked by combinations of levers and screws (for example fig. 18.5). The oil would be collected in a tank and stored in earthenware jars. The waste lees could be used in manuring.

Vines, like the olive, are indigenous to the Mediterranean, but need a great amount of care to be successfully grown. Transplanted from the nursery beds, they were set on carefully prepared soil, preferably on a southern facing slope; they were grown either unsupported or supported on stakes, trellises, pergolas or, in Italy at least, against other trees. The unsupported vine was much commoner in the provinces. Two-bladed or short, single-bladed hoes were used for the three aerations of the vineyard soil thought essential, and pruning was done either in October after the vintage or in the spring with a specialized billhook, the *falx vinitoria* (fig. 18.4). Speed was important in the vintage, in August in dry areas like southern Spain, or September in Italy and Gaul, and the work was often put out to contract or else casual labour was hired. The pickers worked with grape-cutting knives, loading the grapes into baskets which would then be carted away either for treading or eating (pls 18.4b,c). When the grapes were trodden the remaining pulp would be pressed to extract the last of the juice, which would then be drawn into earthenware jars, proofed by pitch (pl. 18.4d), for fermentation. Columella records that discernment of the quality of a wine was an important feature of civilized life, even if it could be a little pretentious. We all know what he means!

What is known of field types on Mediterranean farms is very limited. Cato talks of vineyards of 100 *iugera* (1 *iugerum* = c. 0.3 ha or $\frac{2}{3}$ acre) and olive groves of 120 *iugera* on sloping ground with or without cereal intercultivation. Equally little is known of fields devoted to arable in villas, but with centuriation, the type of allotment where land is divided into blocks which were eventually standardized into 200 *iugerum* squares, traces of the layout occasionally survive, such as in Capua and the Lombard Plain in Italy, and extensively in North Africa.

This description of the Mediterranean farm, based on literary evidence for Italy, must form a basis for our understanding of farming in these areas in general in the Empire, though it must be appreciated that it is the advice of the agronomist that we are reading, not necessarily a description of the practical techniques. Within the same general pattern, the Mediterranean provinces developed their own distinctive features. Gallia Narbonensis, already relatively well developed, quickly acquired a sophisticated, villa-based agriculture with extensive areas of corn growing and vineyards, olive and fruit, on the belt of land between the coastal marsh and the interior hills, with perhaps more mixed-based farming in interior valleys. Spain, renowned early in the Roman world for its fertility, produced corn, wine and oil on its good land on the east and south coastal strips and its oil soon surpassed that of Italy in quality. The prosperity of Sicily and Sardinia continued with large areas of corn, grown for export to Rome, vines and fruit near the few urban centres, and pasture in the interior; there is evidence for the increase in Sicily, at least, in the growth of large estates which were devoted to profitable, large-scale ranching, matching a decline in cereal production and the consequent decline in cities which had grown up as markets for arable crops (White, 1967b, 75). Greece, moreover, was in decline and, as a general rule, cultivated land was slowly being relegated to pasture which even then was understocked (Stevens, 1966, 95). However, there was agglomeration of land into estates for olive plantations and pasture, while the cities still provided markets for the corn, oil and wine produced on the better land. Thrace and Macedonia, Upper and Lower Moesia remained relatively undeveloped, though large estates were built up; prosperous farms have been excavated, especially near the frontier, where military needs had to be met. Development of large estates and villas of considerable wealth in the plains of Pannonia was particularly noticeable and there is evidence of drainage works to create arable land, and large-scale vine planting in the later Empire, as part of an imperial policy of developing agriculture in the province, so that it was able to export grain to north Italian markets (Mócsy, 1974, 266, 272, 298–9). Pastoralism was especially important in the lower Danube provinces. In Dalmatia the coastal area and valleys, with their fertile soils, responding to the stimulus of the Roman urbanization programme, received many immigrants from Italy from an early period. Cereal growing was important in the villas of the coastal belt, mixed farming developed in the somewhat later farms of the valleys, but the vast upland, hinterland proved unattractive to Roman settlement and remained largely undeveloped, with the peasant population continuing the same mixed or pastoral farming as before (Wilkes, 1969, 337). In the Alpine provinces of Noricum and Raetia, pasture was dominant, though cereals and fruit were grown on medium-sized estates in the valleys and plains (Alföldy, 1974, 119, 107–8).

Mediterranean farming techniques were practised in north Africa, Egypt and Syria, though these also had distinctive characteristics, largely due to their earlier economic development. Within the previous Carthaginian area of northern Africa, much of the province was parcelled out to Italian colonizers and large estates quickly grew up; Pliny indeed relates that in Nero's day six men owned half of Africa. Pliny and Columella bewail the ruinous nature of the large estate, but seem primarily to be talking about Italy, and the inevitable rural depopulation that they caused. In Africa, at least, they certainly were not unprofitable (White, 1967b). Previous corn lands continued in cereal production, generally the wetter areas nearer the coast, but olive production was, with irrigation, extended to the edge of the desert. The same was true of the undeveloped areas to the west of the old Carthaginian lands; they were subject to rapid development by investors from both Italy and Africa. Some huge estates grew up, though the abundant remains of numbers of small olive farms are scattered haphazardly in the countryside; they are surrounded by hillsides carefully terraced to increase arable land and to guard against soil erosion, and are a reminder that the basic unit, as run by tenants, would not necessarily have been large, and indeed most are starkly utilitarian when compared with villas in Europe (Percival, 1976, 63, and Goodchild, 1976, 6). One of the most impressive achievements of Roman agriculture in north Africa was doubtless the distribution of olive farms with their distinctive presses, which are liberally scattered over land that is now desert (Goodchild, 1976, 8). In fact this extension of farming seems to have been a second-hand achievement, being brought about by either Roman encouragement or compulsion of the hitherto nomadic peoples to accept agriculture (settled people are easier to administer) and their consequent introduction of the olive (Tenney Frank, 1962, 450–1) into these marginal areas. Cultivation depended on the skill with which farmers terraced the wadi beds and built catchment walls along their sides to prevent soil erosion. The wadi beds could retain sufficient moisture to make possible the cultivation of cereals, dates and even vines (Goodchild, 1976, 6) while elsewhere the olive was cultivated.

The same is true of the desert margins of Syria, where the remains of olive presses survive (Hitti, 1951, 293), while Transjordan, now mostly desert, was a land abounding in crops to Josephus; the plains produced dates, grapes and olives and used reservoirs for rainfall storage. Irrigation played a part in this extension of agriculture, and a series of inscriptions from southern Numidia record a concern with the allocation of water to a large number of local farms, some of which were above the level of the flow, which implies a mechanical means of lifting water (White, 1970, 158). Small-scale terracing and large masonry dams for water control and soil retention were constructed and huge underground cisterns for rain storage still survive. The principles of irrigation were certainly recognized before the Romans, for example, in Mauretania (Lawless, 1969, 81), the Negev, and, of course, pre-eminently in Egypt where canals had been constructed to take the water from the annual Nile flood to basins bounded by dykes, and then return it at a lower level by outfall channels. Maintenance of this system was vital, and the work was carried out by compulsory peasant labour. Providing the system was maintained, the soil, irrigated and refertilized by deposition of the silt, was very productive and could tolerate an annual cropping almost unique in the Mediterranean. In the first century AD, Egypt contributed about one third of the wheat which Rome needed (Stevens, 1966, 103).

The Near Eastern provinces were divided either into city territories, some of which, such as that of Antioch, covered vast areas, or into non-urbanized lands in which there were blocks of imperial holdings and islands of private or temple lands. As elsewhere, the increased markets, the new road systems and security boosted agricultural production; the coastal belts produced cereals, mainly wheat, although rice, which requires irrigation, was occasionally grown, with the same legumes and cattle fodder as in Italy. Papyrus was grown in some areas for writing material, and flax, hemp and cotton were grown all over western Asia. The irrigated gardens of Syria were well known, producing peas, beans, cabbage and radish of high quality; Pliny also refers to the importance of Syrian trees, the plum and jujube, date, pistachio, fig, cedar, juniper, terebinth (for medical oils) and sumac (for tanning). The coastal areas produced vines and olives and Syrian wine was of high quality. Labour on the city territory and on estates was the village peasant and the Gospels give us a clear picture of the poverty of such people, whether they were free tenants or hired labourers rather than land-tied serfs, which, in theory, they were. The Gospels indicate that pastoralism based on sheep and goats was also important. It would be wrong to suggest, despite the growth of large-scale estates in Africa, Egypt and the east, that romanization spread evenly across these areas. As elsewhere, large areas of less fertile or mountain country dependent on a pastoral economy would have been largely untouched.

Outside the Mediterranean area, the northern part of Gaul and Britain with their wetter climates were free of the restrictions of dry farming, but were also, of course, out of the climatic zone of the olive; Britain in the main was also out of the optimum zone for the vine. Both Gaul and Britain, but especially Gaul were heavily populated by villas, intensively settled on the low-lying arable land (Percival, 1976, 67–82, 91–105), and all the provinces, able to sustain permanent pasture, were important for animal husbandry, especially the upland areas. Strabo mentions that Britain exported grain in pre-Roman times and Caesar notes the cereal production of Kent likening it to that of the Gallic peoples. Intensive villa settlement in Gaul hugs the fertile low lying soils suitable for cereal growing and/or vine cultivation, especially near towns and rivers, but it is markedly absent from poorer or upland areas. The medium-sized mixed farm was probably the norm with the area around Bordeaux then, as now, more specialized in viticulture, producing high quality vines. Large estates were common, and it is interesting that it is in central Gaul with its topography more conducive than the Mediterranean in general to large, flat, stone-free arable fields that we hear from Pliny of two radical inventions, the harvesting machine and the wheeled plough. The *vallus*, or *carpentum*, was a harvesting machine referred to in literature (Pliny, *Natural History*, XVIII, 296 and Palladius, *De Re Rustica*, 7, 2, 2–4) and shown on various monuments. It appears in two forms, a light version pushed by a donkey (pl. 18.2) and a heavier form pushed by an ox, and would cut the grain at mid-stalk level with iron teeth. While economical in labour, it would have been wasteful of grain, as it would inevitably miss cutting short stalks, and of straw, as the advancing animal would trample over it (White, 1967a and 1969). Of the invention of the wheeled plough it is only known that a plough with two small wheels and a spade-shaped share was in use in Pliny's day in Raetia. All the available evidence (Rees, 1979, 42–69) suggests that the north European plough of the Roman period was the beam type more suitable for the heavier and wetter soils, and finds of iron shares and coulters point to a developing sophistication and strength through the Roman era (fig. 18.2). The north European plough, unlike the Mediterranean, needed to be able to deal with a weed-covered, heavy fallowed soil; fixed, winged shares found from fourth-century contexts in Britain even suggest, but by no means prove, the use of the mouldboard to invert the sod by this period. Ploughs could certainly be 'eared' presumably for ridging or drainage, as shown on the model from Piercebridge (fig. 18.1). Other than this rather heavier plough and the invention of the *vallus*, implements were similar to those used in Italy, with a good selection of spades, hoes and mattocks, reaping and pruning hooks, rakes and scythes (Rees, 1979, passim), with the viticulture knife markedly present in south and central Gallic villas, but absent from British sites despite the possibility that the vine was grown in Britain on a limited scale (Applebaum, 1972, 103; Williams, 1977 and Jones, 1981, 97). There is some suggestion of an increased importance of stock husbandry in some areas of Britain in later periods (Frere, 1978, 274–5; Lambrick and Robinson, 1979, 136–7), and the Roman introduction of the scythe and the technique of well digging must have facilitated it, though specialized pastoral units are well attested in pre-Roman periods. The scythe and billhook are important tools in the Roman-British repertoire, the latter associated with cutting winter fodder for cattle, the former, to judge by experiments with modern reproductions (Anstee, 1967, 365), either for grain or hay cutting. Two types of scythe are known: one of normal length and one extraordinarily long type (Rees, 1979) which, appearing only in Britain, may again have been an invention in response to a desire for labour-saving implements in the northern provinces (fig. 18.4 and pl. 18.1).

Villas in Britain are concentrated on the lighter soils, especially where they adjoin fertile, but difficult, clay lands, in the south-east. Their fields are often identical to the small, squarish pre-Roman fields but larger, long, narrow fields, suggesting better ploughs and increased production, can sometimes be seen to replace them. Spelt, emmer, barley (naked and hulled), oats, bread and club wheat and rye were grown, as in the Iron Age, but later rye and club wheat appear with greater frequency and spelt becomes a principal crop (Jones, 1981). Oats were established as a cultivated grain and their particular importance in the north suggests a response to military requirements for horse fodder (Applebaum, 1972, 108–9). Beans, peas, vetch, flax, corn spurry and turnips were grown as field crops, while parsnips, peas, cabbage, mustard and herbs, and possibly radish, onions and leeks were grown in kitchen gardens with a good selection of fruits in orchards. The presence of typically spring sown and winter sown grains found together has led Applebaum to suggest that a three course rotation may have been prac-tised – winter crop – summer crop – fallow (Applebaum, 1972, 113–14), while the existence of legumes in cereal assemblages also suggests rotation (Jones, 1981, 113).

Britain and Gaul are no exception to the norm in that they seem to have had imperial estates, and had an increasing trend toward larger estates especially by the fourth century. As elsewhere it seems that it was mostly by incentive, provided by new markets, and necessity caused by taxation, rents and or requisitioning for the army, that agriculture was boosted; large-scale drainage work in the Fens to reclaim agricultural land, and an increase in the variety and number of tools available, including the rare donkey and watermill, must have helped in their different ways. The increased range of tools is also found on upland native farms and while less romanized areas probably carried on with the same mixed or pastoral farming as before, it is doubtful if they were entirely unaffected by the Roman presence. Indeed it was largely in such areas that the frontiers lay with their considerable numbers to be fed. As it is probable that much of the necessary food for the army would have been taken locally to avoid transport costs (Manning, 1974), the impact of this increased need on the local farmers must have been tremendous. Presumably the decline in demand when the army was withdrawn from an area must have been equally keenly felt.

Though the third-century decline in agriculture generally is seen in Gaul and Britain, in Britain at least there is a good recovery in the fourth century. The success of the corn-producing areas of Britain would seem to have continued, and Julian used British produce to feed the starving cities of the Rhine in 360 (Applebaum, 1972, 230). Corn-drying furnaces are found everywhere in fourth-century farms, often inserted ruthlessly into dwellings. Some of the furnaces are as early as the second century, but in the fourth they became very common, a response probably to the climate becoming somewhat wetter. The drying process makes grain easier to grind and also prolongs its power of germination (Morris, 1979, 5–22, but for a different interpretation see Reynolds, 1981, 36–43).

Finally something should be said of the part which agricultural produce played in commerce and trade (Part 8). Wheat was early imported to Rome from Sicily, North Africa and Egypt by the imperial government, but general transport of cereals was avoided because of the prohibitive costs, especially by road; Jones calculates that in Diocletian's time a waggon-load of wheat would have doubled in value over 480 km (300 miles) (Jones, 1964, 841). Accordingly, except in times of famine when extraordinary measures had to be taken, corn, fruit and vegetables were not transported long distances to markets but were grown nearer the source of need, be it urban or military. Wine and oil, however, were more valuable in proportion to their bulk and early played an important part in trade. The Italian products first dominated, but were later overtaken by Gaul, Spain and Syria in high quality wines, and by Spain and Africa in olive oil. Flax tended to be manufactured into cloth before marketing, so its value increased (Jones, 1964, 850) and linen from Antioch and Spain was exported to Italy. Apart from this, only high value agricultural goods covered long distances, such as choice wine from Palestine and Syria, dried fruits, exotic spices and medicinal and aromatic herbs from western Asia.

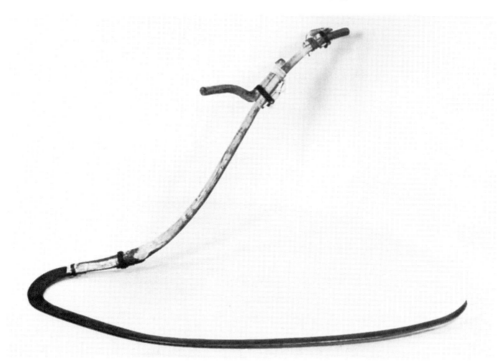

18.1   Reconstructed hafting of a copy of a Roman scythe from Great Chesterford

18.2   A harvesting machine shown on a relief from Montaubon

18.3 Animals used on a modern threshing-floor at Santorini

18.4 Representations of olive and grape harvests on a mosaic from St-Romain-en-Gal: (a) olive picking; (b) grape picking; (c) grape pressing; (d) proofing storage jars with pitch

CHAPTER 19

·ANIMAL·HUSBANDRY·

Shimon Applebaum

Our knowledge of the animal husbandry of the Roman Empire is derived from two main sources, namely, written material and archaeology. The written sources fall into three categories: Roman works on agriculture and some sources in Greek, Hebrew, Aramaic and Arabic; epigraphic material, and papyrology. The *Georgica* of Vergil and the writings of the *Scriptores Rustici* (Cato, Varro, Columella, Palladius) deal almost exclusively with Italy, but occasionally refer to agriculture outside the peninsula. Pliny in his *Natural History* pays more attention to extra-Italian farming. The geographer Strabo has useful notes on stock-farming in various parts of the Empire. The *Geoponica*, written perhaps in the seventh century, has occasional useful observations. The Mishnah and the Talmud (late second and early fifth century AD respectively) have much to say on agriculture in Judaea. Epigraphy provides inscriptions here and there which illuminate fitfully the management of livestock (most of them belong to Asia Minor and Africa). The *Edict on Prices* of Diocletian contains important notices of food and materials derived from the livestock of the Empire. Papyrology furnishes a mass of information on the agriculture of Egypt for the Ptolemaic, Roman and Byzantine periods. The Arabic *Kitab-al-Felaha* (perhaps twelfth century) was very largely based on Roman work, much of it from the *Geoponica*.

Archaeology's contribution lies mainly in the data to be derived from animal bones recovered from excavated sites; the value and problems of this area of research will be discussed below (p. 516). Other evidence furnished by archaeology includes the identification of byres and stables, and the illustration of domestic animals on coins, wall-paintings, mosaics, sculptured monuments and other forms of art.

The principal questions which this chapter will attempt to answer are: (1) what were the standards and methods of animal husbandry in the Roman period in Italy and in other parts of the Empire; (2) how far did Roman animal husbandry influence the provinces both in the Mediterranean zone and in the temperate regions ruled by Rome; (3) in what way and how were domestic animals and their products utilized by the Romans; (4) which domestic animals can be recognized in the Empire, and to what extent was improvement of livestock attempted or effected?

It will be useful to list given areas under Roman rule which were well known for the rearing of certain domestic animals. Each domestic animal, therefore, will be treated in turn, and following the brief account of its distribution in the Empire, the conduct of its branch as described by the Italian agricultural writers of the imperial epoch will be briefly recapitulated.

Cattle

Ranching of cattle was prominent in southern Italy, Etruria, Umbria and Latium, and continued in southern Italy throughout the Empire. Very large cattle ranches existed in Sicily. Cisalpine cattle were regarded by Varro as the best in Italy. Italy, indeed, owed much to the east in this sphere, particularly in the form of fodders (clover, sesame, fenugreek and lucerne) which eased the problem of winter feed; there was also benefit from the professional literature written by Carthaginian and Greek authors living under progressive hellenistic rulers.

In Greece, Epirote cows were known as record milkers and imported into southern Italy. Arcadia, Thessaly and Euboea were all well known as cattle-rearing regions. Almost every excavated site in Dalmatia has yielded cow-bells, which testify to open-range pasturing. Cattle were generally the largest group of animals whose remains were to be found in Pannonia, also in the Greek cities on the north shore of the Euxine in the Roman period. Central European investigators are agreed that the Romans introduced a larger type of cattle into Raetia, Noricum and Pannonia. In Asia Minor, Pontus, Galatia, Samos and Phrygia were known for their cattle; Pergamum had been the centre of parchment manufacture since the hellenistic period. Diocletianic inscriptions recording the census of human occupants and livestock in Asia and in some of the Aegean islands, on the other hand, do not suggest the maintenance of cattle on a large scale.

In Syria the pastures of Antioch were noted and Apamea was renowned for its cattle, as was Bashan (Batanea); Strabo refers to the large oxen bred at Petra. The importance of cattle husbandry in Judaea is confirmed by talmudic literature and has been revealed by archaeology. At Tell Heshbon (Hesbân), however, the proportion of cattle fell in the hellenistic and Roman periods, recovered in the later Roman strata, but never competed with the ovicaprids. The Mishnah gives the limit of grazing, free-range cattle as sixteen Roman miles.

Cattle in Egypt had been improved by the systematic breeding of the Ptolemies, as demonstrated in the Fayum, and herds were held in considerable numbers; the Roman conquest perpetuated these methods. In summer the stock was fed extensively on green fodder but from January to February grazed on open pasture sown the previous year. Cattle rearing was the earliest basis of agriculture in ancient Cyrene, and various ancient authors mention the country's herds, reared more particularly in the plain of Barca. The Carthaginian nobility had reared cattle; other stockmen are recorded specifically in an inscription at Sala in Mauretania. The cattle of the Spanish city of Gades were known to be rich in milk, and the bull is figured on coins of several Roman towns in Spain.

The abundance of cattle in Gaul is demonstrated by the ease with which Julius Caesar revictualled his forces with corn and cattle. On French archaeological sites cattle are often the largest group represented; Strabo states that the country was rich in beasts, emphasizing the large herds of the Belgae, yet in several Gallic villas beef was less frequently consumed than pork. Cattle, however, were predominant on Roman sites in Holland, which was administratively an adjunct of Gaul. Cattle rearing was clearly a developed branch in the early Iron Age in this area, and the Frisii paid their tribute to Rome in ox-hides.

Military concentrations along the Rhine frontier and in south Germany furnished without doubt a strong incentive to the Roman hinterland to supply beef and hides to the army. The increase in the size of cattle in this area during the Roman period is regarded by Willerding as a local development, and a number of villas such as Köln-Müngersdorf possessed generous accommodation for stalled cattle.

Cattle-rearing is generally held to have increased in Britain in the later Roman period, and is predominant on most military sites. Improvement produced animals larger than those normal in the British early Iron Age, but the smaller types persisted.

For the farmer of Italy, whether a smallholder or the owner of a large estate, the ox was the most important animal; but the former might yoke a cow or a donkey to his plough. Two hundred and forty *iugera* (*c.* 60 ha; 150 acres) needed six oxen, a vineyard of a hundred *iugera*, two oxen. The average Italian estate owner, moreover, was well aware of the importance of livestock as an integral part of mixed farming, and of its value both as an earner of income and as a fertilizer. Cattle, therefore, were valued both for work (pls 19.1, 19.2 and 19.3) and for their manure, but much less for their milk. It is generally held that meat was not widely eaten in the Mediterranean area until the later Empire, but the rapid spread of large-scale ranching in Italy in the second century BC suggests that this view requires reassessment. The estate herd was normally grazed in the fields in both summer and winter, though they might be corralled. The bulls were kept apart, and working cattle and cows in calf were generally brought in at night, and often stalled. Large-scale ranching, which developed with the rise in wealth and capitalist initiative, as Rome acquired new possessions in Africa and the eastern Mediterranean, was conducted as an independent enterprise unintegrated into the agricultural pattern, and involved extensive transhumance. It was normal practice in the 'mixed' agricultural estate to burn the grass at the end of summer to encourage fresh growth, an operation which might bring immediate advantage, but tended to destroy soil fertility. Feeding livestock in winter and early spring was a standing problem which compelled the owner, when his fresh forage and hay had given out, to feed beech mast, grape-skins and even leaves and chaff. Legumes and fenugreek, vetch and lucerne, reaching Italy from the east, did much, although apparently not enough, to solve the problem.

The Roman cattle breeder was aware of the need to improve his animals, but proceeded on the mistaken premise that the female alone determined the characteristics of her progeny. He was alert to the influence of environment, and Columella consequently advised that herds be replenished by breeds from near or similar regions. Varro and Columella mention the small white cattle of Campania, large Umbrian white cattle, the powerful breeds of Etruria and Latium, and the thick-set Apennine oxen. Carian cattle, Epirote milch stock and the small sturdy Altinum oxen of the Ligurian Alps, are known to have been imported into Italy.

Varro recommends that cows should not be mated till they were two or even four years old, and Columella rules that in the absence of abundant fodder they should be mated only every second year; if these prescriptions were applied, they would have limited the female stock to six or even as few as three pregnancies in their entire life-time.

The Roman stockman had well-worked out procedures, not all of them gentle, for breaking in oxen for ploughing or traction, but considerable care was taken to reduce injuries, whether in the field or on the road. Columella devotes a very long section of his work to veterinary remedies, and the devoted care in his treatment contrasts with the occasional folk superstitions that pass for remedies; colic could be cured by the sight of ducks, wrung withers were remedied by bleeding the hind quarters, bites by the shrewmouse were to be prevented by hanging the body of that creature round the ox's neck. The standards of Varro and Columella were high, but, even if there was much careful and systematic farming in the Empire, it must, notwithstanding, be remembered that both wrote first and foremost for the educated, even the aristocratic reader, and that their practices applied essentially to Italy and to the Mediterranean environment.

The stalling of cattle, at least of the working oxen and cows in calf, is clearly implied by Columella. Vitruvius treats of byres, and even the smallholder's humble farmhouse at Monte Forco in the Ager Capenas contained accommodation for a few head. The byre at the villa of Köln-Müngersdorf (198 head) has been referred to, and ample accommodation for wintering cattle is to be seen at Marburg (Hessen), in Germany. Systematic stalling of cattle in the Dutch farms began as early as the fifth century BC, and persisted throughout and beyond the Roman period. Byres can be identified in villas in Germany, Belgium and Britain, where the villa of Thistleton Dyer (Rutland) possessed accommodation for over fifty head approximately. Obviously the severer conditions of the northern winter made stalling more essential, but at least one of the villas studied in the vicinity of Pompeii provided planned accommodation for that purpose.

Sheep (plates 19.2, 19.4 and 19.5)

If cattle were important for the production of meat, hides and horn, and to a limited extent of butter and cheese, sheep were of fundamental importance for their wool, which provided the commonest clothing material of the entire Empire. But in contrast to today, sheep were also the chief source of milk and cheese, and, in the Mediterranean world, cows' milk was little regarded.

The great producers of wool in Italy were concentrated on the drier eastern side of the peninsula, in the south at Canusium, Venusia, also in Apulia, Calabria and Tarentum and in the north in the valley of the Po at Mutina, Padua, Brixia and Parma, at Aquileia, and Altinum in Liguria. But Sicily also ran sheep on a large scale, Sardinia and Corsica abounded in pasture, while on the westerly slopes of the Apennines, Etruria, Samnium and Campania also were known for their flocks. Apulian sheep, in fact, were driven to summer pasture in Samnium in late republican days; such long-range transhumance persisted under the Empire and was common also in Calabria, Umbria, the Abruzzi and Campania. In Diocletian's *Edict on Prices* imperial weaving mills are recorded at Rome, Aquileia, Milan, Canusium and Venusia. The finest wool was ascribed to Tarentum, famous for its sheep which, imported from Miletus, were wrapped up in winter to protect their expensive fleeces. Other imperial mills existed in Illyricum at Bassianae, Sermium, Iovia, Liburnia and Histria.

Noricum was named *regio pastorum* by Vergil, while inscribed seals from Magdalensburg named four woollen exports from that province. Poetovio (Pannonia) found similar mention in Diocletian's tariff. The most productive pastoral areas of Greece under the Empire were Argolis, Achaea, Arcadia, Euboea, Attica, and Boeotia. Achaea, indeed, was famous for its woollen cloaks (*chlainai*). Thrace also was active in this branch, producing woollen *himatia*, and the Thracian imperial mill was at Heraclea. The Dacian uplands bear ample archaeological evidence of active sheep rearing. Spain exported wool to Rome, and Columella's uncle improved fleeces by crossing African sheep imported into Gades with Tarentines. Gaul wore and exported woollen garments from a number of areas.

Britain's imperial weaving mill was at Venta, whose location is disputed (Winchester or Caister St Edmund), and Diocletian's *Edict* names rugs and capes as British exports; Eumenius praises the country's innumerable sheep 'loaded with fleeces'.

Africa possessed an active weaving industry, and Diocletian's *Edict* records African woollen covers and cloaks, also clothing from Numidia; the imperial weaving mill was at Carthage. Egypt owed the systematic development of its sheep rearing to the Ptolemies, who retained much of it as a royal enterprise and supplied stock to tenants and landholders. They also improved the flocks by importing sheep from Miletus, Arabia, Euboea and Ethiopia. Under Rome the Egyptian wool industry supplied clothing to the army as far afield as Judaea and Cappadocia, and a prime factor in the success of the branch was the planned cultivation of sown pasture.

Judaea was topographically better suited to flocks then herds, and the Old Testament alone is sufficient to establish the prevalence of sheep and goats. The Babylonian Talmud recommended the rearing of both as highly profitable. At Tell Hesbân, the only excavated site in the region, there was a decline of ovicaprids in the hellenistic and Roman periods, but they later recovered and always remained the largest group. It also seems probable that the truly fine wool so coveted in the Empire was first developed in Judaea or in the vicinity, since samples dated to the fourth century BC have been found at Wadi Daliyeh cave, and others dated to the second century AD in the refuges of the Judaean Wilderness. Strabo may be writing of this particular breed of sheep when he mentions the white-woolled sheep of the Nabataeans. The fat-tailed sheep is referred to more than once in the Mishnah. What has been said of Judaea also applied to Syria. Damascus was renowned for its textiles, an imperial weaving mill being located at Tyre. Other centres of weaving were Byblos and Beyruth.

The largest supplier of wool was certainly Asia Minor. The hellenistic kings of Pergamum, Galatia and Commagene, as well as the Seleucids, were actively interested in agriculture, and doubtless promoted sheep-breeding and wool production; it should not be forgotten that parchment was first made at Pergamum. Miletus long dominated the weaving trade, but in the Roman period lost ground to Laodicea, Hierapolis and Colossae. Bithynia, Pontus, Phrygia, Galatia, Pisidia, Cappadocia and Lycaonia were all producers of woollen goods, and several guilds of weavers, dyers and fullers are known, some of which appear to have been regarded as fundamental units of their cities' constitutions. The *Edict* of Diocletian lists hoods, mantles, short and long cloaks, undergarments and tunics, all manufactured in the above territories. Imperial weaving establishments were to be found at Cyzicus and Caesarea Mazaca.

It becomes clear that the wool industry was one of the widest and most active in the Empire, the more so if it is taken into account that many poorer families spun their own wool and that it was usual on villa estates for slaves' garments to be made on the estate itself. But where the large textile centres were concerned, it may be assumed that they were located in those areas most fitted for the rearing of sheep.

Sheep produce wool, meat, milk, hides and horn. It is therefore not surprising that there are more records of sheep in Egypt than there are of cattle, and that they were in a majority at Hesbân and Jericho, in country where ovicaprids can survive in semi-desert regions but cattle cannot. In Europe sheep tend to dominate in small native settlements and some villas, but for the most part one of the results of Roman influence was the preferred consumption of beef, especially in the towns and on military sites. It is notable, however, that the *Edict* of Diocletian lists ewes' milk but has nothing to say of the milk of cows.

Columella lists several varieties of sheep, the Milesian, the Altinum, the Apennine and those from the Po valley, but his only account of cross-breeding is that of his uncle

Marcus, who crossed African rams with Tarentine and ultimately obtained a soft-woolled sheep of the right colour, the most sought-after probably being white. In Italy sheep might be restricted to the farm, or run on a seasonal transhumant system between summer and winter pastures a hundred miles apart. A smallholder might hold a dozen head, the owner of a medium estate a hundred; long-distance transhumance was generally practised with large flocks possibly numbering thousands. The medium estate's practice depended on the ability to feed the flock in winter, and it was to the owner's advantage to graze his sheep on the stubble after harvest or in his plantations, in order to obtain manure. During the summer the flock was brought to the fold each evening. Mating time was from May to July, so that lambs were dropped between October and December. Ewes close to lambing and their offspring were kept under cover. Winter feed consisted of leaves, autumn hay, trefoil, vetch and the pods of other legumes and also barley. Lambing was followed by culling, and some of the lambs would be sold for meat if the villa was within reach of an urban market. On the other hand, long-range transhumance, run for profit by rich capitalists at the expense of the smallholder, as a practice unintegrated with productive mixed farming, tended to cause over-grazing, erosion, and soil denudation. This is probably the reason for the obstinate opposition of the Jewish scholars of Judaea to the rearing of 'small livestock' (sheep and goats) in the later first and second centuries AD. This distinctive practice, nevertheless, persisted in Italy under imperial rule. Yet archaeological survey and the excavation of a farm at Lucera revealed a successful mixed economy within a centuriated area, despite the attested long-distance transhumance between the Apennines and Apulia in the same region; this can only be explained as the result of imperial intervention and control.

Goats (plates 19.2 and 19.11)

The goat, which is capable of flourishing in rough country, is highly productive in milk because the female can reproduce twice a year; the gestation period is five months, and the milk-yield relative to the body weight is three times that of the cow and four times that of the ewe. The male is thought fit for mating at eighteen months. The goat, however, is highly susceptible to changes of temperature and to epidemics. Goats produce cheese, fat for soap, and hair from which cloaks, carpets, ropes and tent-yarns were made; skins also provided parchment. Columella's account appears to refer to the black variety, and he regards a hundred head as the optimum. Goats and sheep are normally grazed together in the Middle East, but on the classical Italian farm, at least, the goats were folded separately. The goat browses on trees and shrubs, and is consequently a destroyer of woodland cover if herded in large numbers and freely grazed; the emperor Valerian, notwithstanding, is alleged to have possessed 10,000 sheep and 15,000 goats on his estate. One of the most prolific centres for the manufacture of goat-hair products was Asia Minor (especially Cilicia), but goats were to be found in all the provinces.

The Pig (plate 19.2)

Unlike some other domestic animals, the pig furnishes nothing but meat and fat. Pork became the popular meat of the Empire and of its army, although not the most eaten; lard was an integral item of army rations, and in the third century the citizen of Rome received five pounds of free pork each month. Originally a forest animal, in Roman times the pig was still closely associated with woods, and could be kept out of doors most of the year. Although pigs are not in the habit of roving, and tend to be associated with the farmstead, they were sometimes transhumed in Italy and Spain; Varro favoured a herd of a hundred. As the pig matures in twelve months, and the sow's gestation lasts only five, it can breed twice a year, if the young are removed. Stying for fattening was certainly practised in the north-west of the Empire; sties have been identified at several villas in Britain, and at Köln-Müngersdorf in Germany. The bones of a pig which had died in the pen before its empty feeding bowl were found at the Roman villa of Lullingstone, Kent. Pig bones have also been excavated at Kurnub (Mampsis) in the northern Negev, where pigs could only have been reared in pens. Pens are required by Columella at least for farrowing, and are implicit in his recommendation to feed with grain and legumes in case of a food shortage. Pens are further mentioned in Egyptian papyri, and Egypt supplied salt pork and piglets to the army. The Cerretani and Cantabri of Spain were noted for their hams, as were the Sequani of central Gaul, the Menapii and the Belgae, also the Italian Marsi. The price of Lucanian pork sausages was listed by Diocletian, while the Po valley people sold pork to Rome. In Asia, Assos was famed for its white boars.

Horses (plates 19.3 and 19.6)

Horses played little part in the agriculture of the Roman Empire; they were used for war, for drawing light vehicles, for riding and for chariot racing. On the farm, nevertheless, they were sometimes used for threshing, and horses are illustrated drawing ploughs among the cultivators of North Africa. More important, finds of numerous horse- and cattle-bones together suggest that horses were used to round up free-range cattle, and a Gallic source supports this interpretation. If they were not extensively used for haulage, it may have been owing to the ancient method of harnessing, which constricted the horse's breathing, but some scholars object to this generalization (pl. 19.7). It also seems to be accepted that horses were sometimes used as pack animals. Mares were important as the breeders of mules, which were much favoured in the Empire. In Italy, the chief centres of horse-rearing were at Reate in the central Apennines, in the Po valley, in south-eastern Apulia, Calabria and Sicily. Elsewhere they were to be found in Greece, Epirus, Apamea of Syria, and in the Antioch region; and more especially in Arcadia and Aetolia, which contributed stock to the races at Rome. Arab horses are referred to in the Talmud, and Noricum too sent its horses to the Roman games. The imperial army drew much of its cavalry from Spain, Gaul, Illyricum, the Taurus and Thrace, while in the later Empire the famous studs of Palmatius in Cappadocia came under imperial control. Africa bred notable horses, and Cyrene, renowned for its bloodstock, was still exporting them in the late fourth century. Horse-rearing had been thoroughly organized by the Ptolemies in Egypt, assisted by the cultivation of sown pasture and green fodders. In the Byzantine period the large Apion estates maintained extensive stables for postal services and the estate inspectors.

The Roman agricultural writers distinguished between the breeding of bloodstock and the rearing of working horses. The most favourable areas were considered to be high, well-watered plainlands carrying grass pasture, for instance, the Spanish Maseta. The stock was kept out at pasture for most of the year, but stabled in cold or wet weather and fed on hay. Much attention was given to dry stabling. Columella prescribes one stallion to serve twenty mares; the working horses were grazed with the stallions, but pedigree animals were kept separate except when selective breeding was required; mating was preferably at the spring equinox; breaking-in of foals began at the end of the third year. Finds suggest that the iron horseshoe had already been introduced during the Empire, but its use may not have been common.

Mules (plate 19.7)

The mule is the offspring of a mare by an ass. The mule was used primarily as a draught and pack animal, since it is known for its pulling power and its agility in rough or mountainous country. It also possesses greater endurance than the horse, hence it served as the chief transport animal of the army. Because of its smoother gait it was utilized in Roman society to draw the coaches of aristocrats (Nero and Poppaea used them), also to bear ladies' litters. Judah the Prince, the official president of world Jewry, in the later second century, also used them to draw his carriage. In the pre-desertic zone of north Africa the mule seems to have been used for ploughing. To rear a male ass which could sire a well-bred mule, it was the practice to attach the young ass to a mare foster mother, and the young animal was sent to mate after its fourth year. The extent to which mules were utilized in the Empire is reflected in the *Edict* of Diocletian, which refers to the rations to be paid to mule drivers and to professional *muliomedici*. Arcadian mules were well-known, and Justus of Antioch (Syria) was alleged to have possessed a thousand of them. Mules were numerous in Egypt, were imported from Libya into Judaea, and are illustrated on monuments in Gaul and Pannonia. In the Black Sea cities they appear to have been commoner than horses. They were widely bred in Asia Minor, and certainly played an important part in the imperial transport service.

Donkeys (plate 19.8)

Columella lists the donkey among the animals of the highest utility. The ass can exist on the roughest natural pastures, is seldom sick, and exerts great strength in proportion to its size. It is still the combined wheelbarrow, handcart and bicycle of the Mediterranean peasant. It is reported to have pulled the plough in Baetica and Libya. On the farm, the ass carried manure to the plantations and brought back the produce to be processed. It was used to turn the grain mill, and probably also the rotating olive press. It further carried the smallholder's produce to the local market. The extensive network of ancient rural roads recently discovered in Samaria, existed in the hellenistic and Roman periods and were virtually unpaved; there is little doubt that one of their uses was the transport of local agricultural produce chiefly by mules and donkeys. Indeed, donkey-trains carried oil and wine between Brundusium and Apulia.

Donkeys were extensively bred in the central Apennines and in Arcadia; they were also part of the Ptolemaic transport organization in Egypt, where under Rome they continued to carry the *annona*, as well as operating irrigation machinery. They are mentioned frequently by the customs tariff of Palmyra as carriers of goods. The ass did not thrive in the more northerly provinces, but is found in La Tène contexts in western Gaul, and in Roman times in Britain at Newstead.

Dogs (plate 19.3)

Columella classed dogs by a broad distinction of functions: yard dogs which guarded villas, and those that herded the livestock and were also good hunters. Other Greek and Latin sources distinguished large watchdogs, hunting dogs and pets. Greece, where dog breeding was known in the fourth century, seems to have been the most prolific source of the domestic dog; in this as in other ways Italy profited from eastern Mediterranean influences in the hellenistic period, spreading perhaps via Sicily, where the dogs of Panormus, Segesta and Eryx were noted. Best known were the Molossian mastiff, the Laconian hound and the smaller hounds of Crete and Sicily. Calabria, Tyrrhenia and Umbria bred shepherd dogs and smaller types for herding and hunting. Caria, Sarmatia, Thrace, Spain, Pannonia and Libya produced their own breeds. Gaul originated the *vertragus*, renowned for speed and perhaps of greyhound type; Britain a famous mastiff credited with the strength to break a bull's neck and therefore favoured in Italy not only as a watchdog, but also for its performance in the arena. The seven formidable 'Scottish' dogs sent as a gift to Symmachus (340–c. 402) were, of course, Irish; unfortunately we have no clue as to their appearance. The fashionable cult of small lap dogs was a product of the increased leisure furnished by imperial wealth.

The camel (plate 19.9)

The camel, surprisingly, was not confined to the eastern provinces or to Africa. It only became frequent in Egypt in the hellenistic period, and did not penetrate further westward till the third century AD. It was, naturally, first and foremost a carrier of man and merchandise in predesertic areas, but also served in more clement regions; both the heavy two-humped Bactrian and the slenderer dromedary were used, the former for heavy loads. The first *ala* of *dromedarii* known was recruited by Trajan, and in the second century camel-borne troops are found attached to an infantry unit in Egypt, presumably for dispatches and scouting. In the fourth century we hear of three camel units in Egypt and two others, one in Palestine and another in Arabia. Under Severus camels were introduced into north Africa. They were also used for army transport in Roman Europe; their bones have been found at Lorenzburg, Breisgau and Vemania in Germany, at Windisch (Vindonissa) in Gaul, in Epfach (Abodiacum) in Raetia, at Vienna (Pannonia), and in the Balkans. They have also been recorded at Greenwich Park in Kent (Britain).

Poultry (plate 19.11)

Poultry, though probably important on Italian estates, was often only one of a number of species subsumed under the name of *villatica pastio*, the mass production of specialized fowl and fish for luxurious palates in a nearby urban market. Columella classifies the chief varieties of the farmyard fowl as the common or African, the Numidian and the Gallinaria. Methods of poultry breeding were evidently much influenced by hellenistic experience, and several Greek varieties are also mentioned. Cross-breeding of stock was carried out, colour being regarded as an index of fertility. Fattening of birds, sometimes by caponization, was practised, and the greatest attention was directed to the efficient and profitable production both of chicks and eggs. Columella considered 200 as the most rational flock; his account of the henhouse, to be placed east of the farmstead, is one of the most thorough in his manual. Great care was taken to provide both air and protection from marauding animals, and to prevent the sitting hen from damaging her clutch when returning to the nest, which was let into the wall. Lofts above the perches held the feed, which consisted of crushed barley, grapes, chickpea, millet, panic, bran or wild trefoil. Culling was regular, and the poultryman was enjoined to see that the eggs were regularly turned and hatching times registered. Considerable care was taken to clean and disinfect the henhouse, also to prevent the fouling of drinking troughs.

Pigeons

Breeding pigeons was almost universal in Mediterranean agriculture; they were kept for sale as a market delicacy and for their dung, which was highly esteemed. The birds were accommodated in towers or elevated lofts facing south, and cots housing as many as 5,000 are recorded. As pigeons can produce eight broods a year, they were very profitable. Turtle doves and pigeons were the most easily fattened for market, and cross-breeding of varieties (e.g. Campanian and Alexandrine) is reported. Fattened turtle doves and pigeons are listed in Diocletian's *Edict*. Pigeon rearing was carried on everywhere in Egypt, where it was usual for the birds to nest in large earthenware storage jars. In Asia, Pergamum was a well-known centre of pigeon breeding, and some temples, e.g. that of Apollo Larbenos in Phrygia, owned large numbers of these birds. Doves were sacrificed at the Temple of Jerusalem in the late Second Temple period, and Jewish scholarly literature shows that the dovecot was a normal feature of the Jewish farmstead. Finds of the bones of doves of the Roman period appear to have been few north of the Alps, but it is interesting to learn that the word for dove in British, Gallic and Breton (*colum*) was derived from the Latin word *columba*.

The goose

The goose is a northern bird which however had reached Italy by the early fourth century BC and was being reared in Egypt under the Ptolemies. The Romans preferred the white variety, but the German goose is described by Pliny. Specialists often have diffi-culty in distinguishing between the bones of wild and domesticated birds. While these seldom occur in large numbers on Roman sites, Pliny's reference to a peculiar variety, the *cheneros*, in Britain, suggests that new varieties of geese had spread to the north-western provinces. Geese were exported to Rome by the Morini of northern Gaul, who supplied their feathers for cushions, quills and the like; Belgic geese were herded on foot to Rome. They were also exported from Commagene. Flocks were reared in large enclosures, and the ganders enclosed in separate pens during laying and hatching; the birds were plucked twice a year. The *Edict* of Diocletian fixes the price of fattened geese, also of goose-down and of fattened *ducks*. These were kept together with wild specimens in enclosures which contained sheds for roosting and a pond in the centre. Their eggs

were often given to hens to hatch, so that the chicks of wild varieties became domesticated. Distinction between the bones of wild and domesticated ducks is difficult, but
the latter have been identified in Roman contexts as far north as Britain.

Peacocks

Peacocks were reared in woodland enclosures, but allowed free access to their surroundings to feed; the hens brought up their own chicks, but the eggs were often transferred
to barnyard fowl to hatch. Though not frequent in the more northerly provinces, the
bones of peacocks have been found on Roman sites in Noricum, Germany and Britain.

Turning to the contribution made by zooarchaeology to knowledge of Roman animal
husbandry, a complex situation has to be faced. The bibliography is enormous, the
amount of work done, its quality and its accessibility, vary greatly from country to
country, and there are some where, apparently, the relevant research has been lacking.
Nor, as yet, is there a standard methodology of research. What follows must be regarded
as a brief and imperfect initial essay, which must be treated with due reservation.

The contribution of zooarchaeology is to trace the spread of domestic and wild
fauna, to establish the relative proportions of species on each given site, to discover
the way the animals were utilized and, within the terms of reference of the present chapter, to determine the influence of Rome upon provincial animal husbandry. For these
purposes it is desirable to determine, among other things: (1) the maximum and average
size of the animals of each species; and (2) their sex and age at death, also their weights
in terms of meat. Results depend to a considerable extent on the efficiency of recovery
methods, which have frequently been subject to criticism and revision. Recent development has also emphasized that simple bone counts cannot reflect the relative importance
of given species, and that only a part of the bone deposited can have survived to be
excavated. The above qualifications must be remembered, and it has to be admitted
also that a great many of the reports that are bound to be utilized were written before
more recent methodological criticism.

Two further trends in this field of study should be mentioned. Recent years have
seen a tendency to avoid the attempt to classify animal bones according to fixed 'breeds'
or 'races'. More recent research has rejected a number of alleged original types and
sees the animals concerned rather as varieties. Second, an awareness has arisen of the
need to study animal remains in relation to their rural environments, and to consider
their social-economic implications. One of the most important discoveries of zooarchaeology has been to eliminate the widely-held assumption of the 'winter killing' of

livestock. It was assumed until recently that lack of winter fodder in northern Europe compelled the killing of all but working and breeding cattle in the autumn. Study of animal bones from both early Iron Age and Roman sites has now shown that a high proportion of cattle survived the initial years (Ryder and Thirsk, 1981).

On examining the problem, as to how far the expansion of Roman rule resulted in the improvement of animal husbandry, the greater part of the material likely to provide an answer is connected with two species of livestock: cattle and sheep. The raising of cattle was, in most places in Europe, the greatest support of the mixed farm and of the peasant population. Cattle composed over 50 per cent of the remains at the hill-fort of Manching (Germany) occupied both in the later La Tène and early Roman periods; it was the largest section in the villas of the central European provinces, in the Greek cities of the Black Sea, and in the Roman city of Exeter; cattle rearing apparently increased steadily in the later Roman period in Britain. That most of the forts in Germany show beef as the chief meat consumed by their garrisons may have contributed to this situation. The detachment of personnel to tend legionary cattle is indeed known both in Britain and in Germany. It has further been noted that the eating of beef and mutton was most characteristic in the rural settlements of the western Roman provinces, a phenomenon which indicates their lower standard of living in contrast to the urban populations. At Tell Hesbân in Jordan, on the other hand, sheep and goats dominated except in the later early Iron Age, the hellenistic and the early Roman period. It is accordingly in the cattle sector that we would expect to find the symptoms of improvement under Roman influence. The increased size of cattle is evident from bones studied at Manching, Xanten (Ulpia Traiana) and Münsterburg-Breissach (Germany); on Dutch sites; at Hallstatt and Oviclava (Wels), in Noricum; at Szakaly-Rieti Földek (Pannonia); at Chesterholm and Corbridge (Britain), and at various other settlements and villas in the same province. It is nevertheless remarkable that the largest known shoulder height of cattle in Roman Gaul was 154.4 cm (60 in). In Britain it was only 144 cm (56.5 in). Increase in size has further been noted and attributed to Roman influence in northern Italy at Udine, Spina and various sites in the Tyrol and north-western Yugoslavia.

It is not yet agreed how far these improvements were effected by actual import of Roman stock, by improved husbandry or by selective breeding. It should, however, be remembered that selective breeding and crossing of types were understood and practised by Roman farmers, partly as a result of hellenistic, probably also Punic influence. On the other hand, much light can be shed on the degree to which Roman influence could improve livestock conditions by the study of the outbuildings of excavated villas. A further point may be made: a comparison of British villa plans and the texts of Roman writers on agriculture has revealed a number of points in common. It may further be noted that research on Roman weaving and woollen textiles, and on ancient sheepskins has shown that the development of a fine medium wool fibre was the result of the elimination by selective breeding of the hairy 'kemps' present in the more primitive sheep.

This process was already advanced in the fourth century BC in Samaria. The 'Soay' sheep was probably the common type of the British early Iron Age, and it is likely that the Romans introduced the fine, white-woolled flocks, the 'Soay' being then crossed with them to produce the well known Roman-British wool.

There are comparatively few known Roman sites on which sheep dominated, but one was the well excavated villa of Köln-Müngersdorf in Germany; only three known excavated villas in north-western Europe have yielded a majority of sheep bones. In most villas, forts and garrisoned points in central Europe sheep took third place; in non-urban settlements they were in second place, as with some rural sites of Gaul and Holland, and also in Exeter (Britain), where this proportion was recorded from all but one site. In Gaul sheep predominated on five known rural sites. It may be noted that Köln-Müngersdorf is estimated to have maintained at least 169 head, and Bignor, a British villa, an approximate minimum of 197 head.

The evidence for the improvement of sheep in the Empire is reasonably impressive. It has been observed that in Germany strong-horned stock appear under Roman rule, and that most specimens represent larger animals with shoulder heights of 67.1 to 71.3 cm (26.4 to 28 in). In Holland a slight increase in size has been recorded; in central European villas individuals of 84 to 88 cm (33 to 35 in) shoulder height occur. A slight increase is recorded at Exeter, and a breed larger than the widespread *Ovis aries Studeri* of the lake villages, today surviving in the Soay, has been found in Britain at Bar Hill, in Cranbourne Chase, at Hemel Hempstead, and elsewhere. A long-tailed sheep identified at Sheepen, Colchester, may be a Roman introduction. A general increase in size is also noticeable at the Roman farmstead of Barton Court, Cirencester. In later Roman Britain, indeed, a numerical increase of cattle and a decline of the ovid population appears to have set in. As regards the problem of how the improvements were effected, either by import, conscious breeding or better husbandry (feeding and housing), doubtless all played a part; but it should be noted that Roman-influenced cattle and sheep were observed at the German *oppidum* of Manching *prior* to the Roman conquest, and it is hard to believe that the improvements implied could have been accomplished without the actual importation of stock from the south.

Something should be said of the purposes served by the two important branches of cattle and sheep-rearing. The chief indicators are the varying ages at which given groups were slaughtered. First, a high percentage of very young animals, more especially lambs butchered in their first year, may reflect early mortality, but it can also reflect the removal of young from the ewes in order to free the latter for milking. Where piglets are concerned, sucking pig was a favourite Roman dish, which would account for early killing. Adult killing implies fattening for the production of ham and lard. At Vindolanda 78.9 per cent of the meat cattle were killed up to two and half years, which is the age for prime beef. A preponderance of killing of old cattle, on the other hand, means that their main use had been for traction and other work. But a high percentage killed as juveniles can also imply the elimination of rams or steers not needed for breeding. A majority of sheep killed at an advanced age points to wool production, but slaughter at two years or thereabouts was frequent (Gaul, Britain, Germany, Holland, Belgium; cf. Tell Hesbân), and is recommended by Columella (VIII, 4) since at that age the young animal has been able to breed and to produce at least one satisfactory fleece.

The horse too seems to have gained in size thanks to Roman influence. Two chief type-groups have been recognized in Europe, namely: the eastern, and generally larger, group located in Russia, Hungary, Slovenia and the Balkans (withers height 121 to 149.4 cm; 47.5 to 59 in) and a western group, rather smaller in size, located in Austria, Germany and Switzerland (the 'Celtic' group), its average being 109.9 to 149.4 cm (43 to 59 in). A larger horse, developed in Italy perhaps by interbreeding with the eastern group, is found, for instance, in the Rhineland, also in south Germany, Noricum and the Danube provinces, although the smaller types survived beside them, and generally both types appear to have been of heterogeneous origin. The very large military mounts found at Gellep on the lower Meuse appear not to have been imported but to have been the products of selective breeding in the area. Horses from a knacker's yard in Roman Paris were also found to be larger (150 cm; 59 in) than the 'Celtic' type. Dutch archaeologists distinguish between large mounts introduced by the Roman army and smaller native horses. The mean withers height of horses on Roman military sites varies from 127 to 149 cm (50 to 59 in), that in villas from 125 to 145 cm (49 to 57 in); at other civilian sites from 127 to 150 cm (50 to 59 in).

The fact that the average size of all three species, cattle, sheep and horses, increased in many centres under Roman rule, but declined in western and central Europe with the destruction of the western Empire, is sufficient testimony to the effectiveness of Roman influence upon animal husbandry, so long as the Empire existed. Clearly this influence varied from region to region and from class to class of the population, but the results of a spread of Roman skills such as improved tools and water supply, protective buildings, the diversification of leguminous crops, crop rotations, efficient communications, markets, accounting, and a dependable judiciary, should not be underestimated.

Acknowledgments

My first thanks must go to those who sent me their own material, some not yet in press: these were Dr G. Barker (Sheffield), Professor A. R. Clason, Dr B. Noddle, Dr A. Riedel (Trieste), and Robert Wilson (Oxford). Professor Dr Angela von Briesch sent me on loan a number of valuable reports. Others who have assisted me with advice and bibliography are Professor D. Baatz, Professor A. Bökönyi, Professor D. Bloemers,

Professors Böhner and Weidmann of the Römisch-Germanisches Zentral Museum, Mainz, Professor Arturo Morales Muñiz (Madrid), Dr M. L. Ryder, Dr M. Shackley, Dr D. Whitehouse (the British School at Rome), and Dr S. Hellwing of Tel Aviv University. Special thanks are due to Dan Simon, Director of the Sourasky Library of Tel Aviv University, for his determined assistance enabling the completion of the present chapter, also to his staff. Equal gratitude is owed to the Ashmolean Library, Oxford.

19.1 Transport by ox-waggon in Asia; a sculptured frieze from Ephesus

(a)

(b)

(c)

19.2 A group of bronze figurines from Città Castellana, Italy: (a) oxen and plough;
(b) cows drawing a cart; (c) pigs, sheep and goats

19.3 Part of a large sarcophagus from Rome showing a road scene with an ox-cart,
horse and rider, and a dog

19.4 Sheep illustrated on the column of Marcus Aurelius, Rome

19.5 A shepherd with his flock; the tombstone of the freedman Iucundus, from Mainz

19.6 Pack-horses carrying loads over a hill; the Igel monument, Trier

19.7 A relief from Langres showing the transport of wine in bulk on a waggon drawn by a pair of mules. The disadvantage of neck-harness is apparent

19.8 Bronze statuette from Syria of a donkey with panniers

19.9 Terracotta statuette from Aphrodisias, Asia, of a camel carrying *amphorae*; the driver sits to the rear

19.10 Mosaic from a villa near Zliten, Tripolitania, showing grain being threshed by horses and oxen

19.11 Mosaic from a villa near Oudna in Tunisia showing livestock on an estate

19.12 The equestrian statue of Marcus Aurelius, Rome

CHAPTER 20

·THE·VILLA·IN·ITALY·
·AND·THE·PROVINCES·

John Percival

Although it is usually a good idea to define terms, and although studies of the Roman villa are usually prefaced by an attempt to define the term *villa* itself, there is a sense in which such an exercise is bound to be rather academic. It is very doubtful whether the Romans themselves could have agreed on a wholly watertight definition, since the word is not a legal or technical one and is likely therefore to have varied somewhat in its use by different people at different times. In practice this causes little difficulty: if it is simply a concern with identifying sites and labelling them it is only with a small minority that uncertainty or disagreement arises, and these are not likely to have a serious effect on any more general statements that may be made. There is, nevertheless, a duty to say how the word is to be used, if only to ensure that any arguments or discussions so provoked are about real issues and not simply about terminology, and this can be done quite briefly.

Essentially a villa was a place in the country: a place to live in, that is, as opposed to a temple or sanctuary, and a 'private' place as opposed to one for the use of the general public. The term is not usually appropriate for a house in a town, for which the more normal word would be *aedes*, though it could be used for a 'suburban' house, one, that is, which was strictly outside a town but was otherwise part of it in all important respects. In the great majority of cases a villa was a farm, and even with the larger ones where, it may be suspected, there were other, more important sources of wealth, it was unusual not to have some level of farming activity. Many show signs of what may rather grandly be called industrial operations, such as iron working or the manufacture of tiles, but this was usually on a fairly small scale and probably formed part of their main agricultural role, though in most provinces there are a few examples where the activity was extensive enough to see them as primarily industrial centres. There are also villas in close proximity to such things as the large-scale manufacture of pottery, and it would seem a little arbitrary to exclude them from consideration by insisting too closely on a definition in terms of agriculture.

In size a villa can be anything from a small family farmstead like Frilford in Berkshire, a house with a dozen or so rooms measuring some 22 m by 12 m (73 ft by 40 ft) overall, to a palatial establishment like Chiragan in south-west France, which, in its residential part alone, covers more than 2.4 ha (6 acres). There is some degree of uncertainty at the lower end of the scale, in that the use of the Roman word would seem to require some evidence of Roman influence in amenities or design; this clearly excludes huts and other primitive structures, but how sophisticated a building needs to be before earning the label 'villa' is to some extent a matter of personal opinion. Thus, to take the well-known example of Mayen (fig. 20.1) which lies between Coblenz and Andernach on the Rhine, most would agree that by the time of its fourth phase it was a villa as generally understood; some would be more generous, and extend the term back to the third phase, while others would be reluctant to use it until the fifth, but the uncertainty is within fairly narrow limits. It should be said also that Roman influence does not necessarily imply luxury: the word does not have this connotation in Latin as it does in more modern contexts, though many villas were of course luxurious and many were sited in particularly attractive places, such as the bay of Naples or the Mediterranean coast of France.

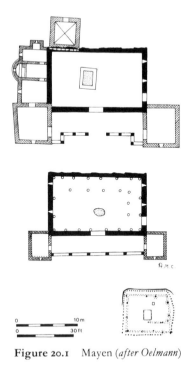

Figure 20.1 Mayen (*after Oelmann*)

The villa was common throughout much of the Empire, though most excavated sites are in the western provinces, in particular the Gallic and German provinces and Britain. Some years ago the material from Pannonia was conveniently assembled in a single volume, and more recently similar collections have been made of the villas of Spain; elsewhere it is probably not so much that villas are lacking, as that the appropriate work of exploring and collating has not been done. Even so, the number of sites is enormous: in 1956 the Ordnance Survey *Map of Roman Britain* listed 604 entries under 'Villas', 'Probable Villas' and 'Other Substantial Buildings', and the figure must by now be well in excess of 700. In Gaul there are very many more, and recent work in aerial reconnaissance has shown that the sites discovered by survey on the ground are likely to be no more than a fraction of the total. The most striking results in this connection are those of Roger Agache in the Somme basin, where something like 1,000 villas appear on air photographs in an area where only a few dozen were known before.

In broad terms, the effect of these surveys is to reveal a greater density of sites rather than to alter the notion of the overall distribution. A glance at the map of Roman Britain shows that the villa is essentially a phenomenon of the lowland zone, and this is what is to be expected in view of its primarily agricultural function, though the more romanized economy and the more stable and peaceful conditions of the lowlands might be equally important factors. There are correlations, as might be expected, between the distribution of villas and patterns in the natural environment such as soil types and river systems, and between villas and man-made features such as roads and urban centres. There is an obvious preference for the lighter and more easily worked soils, though this was by no means universal. The technique of sinking wells, with which the Romans were long acquainted, made the villa less dependent on streams and rivers for its water supply, but rivers were still important for transport. The most plentiful evidence for this is from Gaul, which was particularly well served by a natural river network, but in view of the high cost of transport by road it is likely to have played an important part in other provinces as well (Part 8, Chapter 23). This is not of course in any way to deny the importance of roads as the primary network of communication throughout the Empire, and for the villas in particular their most obvious role is that of providing the rapid and easy access to markets on which they depended. The focal points of this network, the towns, were also the main markets, though it may well be that there were other, more rural ones at certain times of the year like the fairs of the middle ages. The towns would also provide that overall experience of a romanized way of life with which the villas and their owners would increasingly be associated.

Against these very broad patterns, which might be expected to be fairly constant throughout the villa provinces, it is nevertheless possible within a given area to discern local patterns and preferences. Sometimes these are merely stylistic, indicating little more than the influence of local builders and craftsmen, but when they affect the size of villas and their overall design it is justifiable to look for more fundamental explanations, such as local patterns of land tenure or the influence of traditional methods of farming. In some cases a historical interpretation might suggest itself, such as the settling of veteran soldiers on plots of land on retirement, or the encouragement of large-scale development of new areas by wealthy investors. It is to these and similar explanations that we turn, for example, when we are confronted by the large second-century villas in south-western Gaul, or the fairly large fourth-century ones in Somerset and Gloucestershire, or again the small corridor villas that seem to predominate in much of northern France or the upper Rhine valley.

The variety of the local patterns, and the wide range of buildings to which they give rise, make generalization difficult, but it is possible nevertheless to identify a few

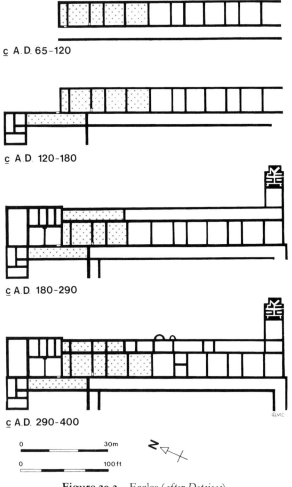

c A.D. 65-120

c A.D. 120-180

c A.D. 180-290

c A.D. 290-400

0   30m
0   100ft

Figure 20.2   Eccles (*after Detsicas*)

of the more common types of villa which recur from one province to another. At its lowest level, the villa is obviously very simple; it may consist of a single large room, as in the early phases of Mayen (fig. 20.1) already referred to, or perhaps a pair of rooms, with the segregation of human and animal occupants. Sometimes, particularly in Britain, it could consist of a row of small rooms: the most striking example of this is the early villa at Eccles in Kent (fig. 20.2), but it is found also in the first phases of Brixworth (fig. 20.5) in Northamptonshire, Frocester Court (fig. 20.4) in Gloucestershire and at a number of other places. With increasing wealth and sophistication these simple buildings developed into more complex ones: segregation continued, not only between humans and animals, but between master and servants, living rooms and workrooms, day rooms and bedrooms; new facilities, such as baths and heating systems, were added and incorporated into the design, as were corridors, verandahs, sun-rooms and so on.

The corridor, indeed, is so universal, particularly in the northern provinces, that the so-called corridor villa is not only a recognized type in its own right but by far the most common type that is encountered. Strictly speaking, what is being referred to is a verandah or portico rather than a corridor proper, and in this sense the German name of *Portikusvilla* is more accurate, or its French equivalent of *villa à galerie-façade*. Among numerous examples of it in Britain can be cited that of the 'cottage house' at Huntsham (fig. 20.5) in Herefordshire, where it is a simple addition to the front of a suite of rooms, or Great Staughton (fig. 20.3) in Huntingdonshire, where it is flanked, as in the vast majority of examples, by two symmetrically placed wing rooms to form a pleasing, and indeed imposing façade. The appeal, it may be suspected, was aesthetic as well as utilitarian, and there are many examples of villas to which it gives a deceptively grandiose appearance, presumably by deliberate design: at Hosté (fig. 20.5) in the Brabant province of Belgium, an already impressive villa is made much more so by its elongated corridor plan, and at Leutersdorf, in northern Germany, the corridor and its wing rooms have been developed into a feature apparently quite separate from the villa itself.

Such aberrations apart, there were some very impressive villas of the corridor type, particularly on the continent, and it is easy to see why it had such an appeal, even if its rather rigid overall design might at first sight seem to offer little scope for innovation and experiment. One development that became popular was to add a second corridor at the rear of the house, and sometimes another pair of corner rooms, giving the appearance almost of a military establishment rather than a peaceful agricultural one: a good example of this is Hambledon (fig. 20.3) in Buckinghamshire, and as an extreme version of it, the main residential block at Odrang in the Rhineland could also be cited. More commonly, the corner rooms at each end of the façade become extended into suites of rooms, as at Witcombe in Gloucestershire or Noyers-sur-Serein (fig. 20.3) in the northern lowlands of France. The logical conclusion of this was to extend the wings a little further, join them together by another range of rooms, and so produce a courtyard

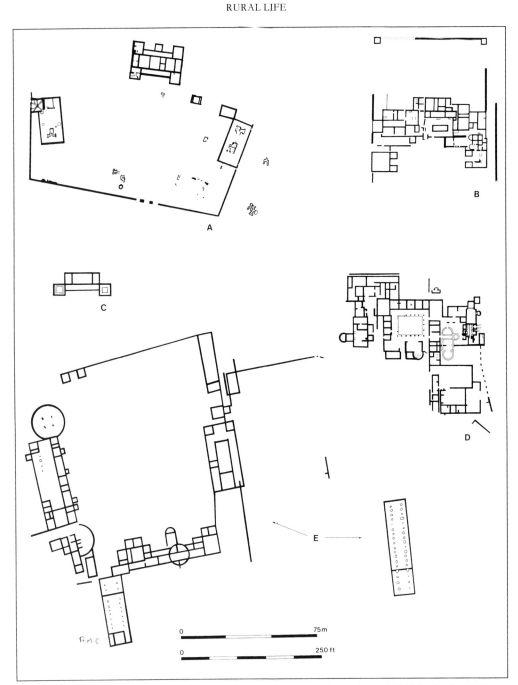

Figure 20.3 (A) Hambledon (*after Heneage Cocks*); (B) Noyers-sur-Serain (*after l' Abbé Duchatel*); (C) Great Staughton (*after Greenfield*); (D) La Cocosa, Badajoz (*after Serra Ráfols*); (E) Winterton (*after Goodburn*)

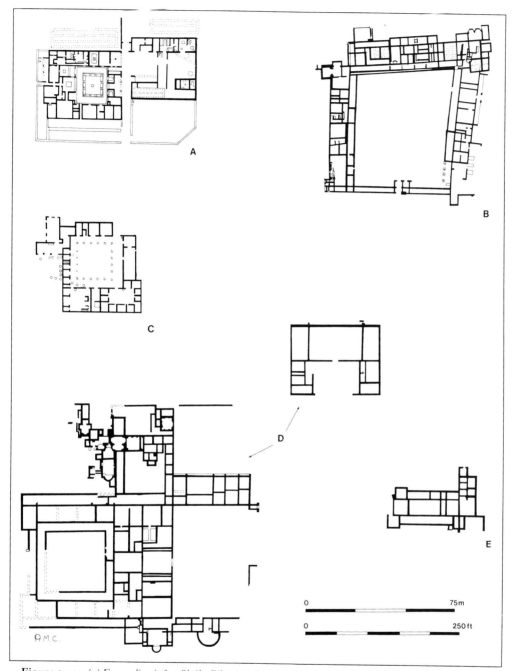

Figure 20.4 (A) Francolise (*after Sheila Gibson*); (B) North Leigh (*after Haverfield*); (C) Gragnano (*after Sheila Gibson*); (D) St Ulrich (*after Lutz*); (E) Frocester (*after Price*)

villa with rooms on four sides of an enclosed square. North Leigh (fig. 20.4) in Oxford-shire is perhaps the best example of this in Britain, and among continental examples could be mentioned Grivesnes (pl. 20.2) or Vieux-Rouen-sur-Bresle (pl. 20.1; fig. 20.6) in the Somme valley. It would, in any case, have been an obviously convenient arrange-ment to group the various buildings around a yard of some kind, and there are many 'courtyard' villas which clearly evolved in this way rather than as a development of the winged corridor type: Winterton (fig. 20.3) in Lincolnshire, Köln-Müngersdorf in the Rhineland, or even the rather 'native' looking site at Whitton (fig. 20.7) in South Glamorgan. Once this kind of grouping had been arrived at the idea could be further extended and a further courtyard added, with the advantage that a very clear separation could now be achieved between the residential part of the establishment and the parts associated with its role as a working farm. Woodchester in Gloucestershire is a striking example of this arrangement, and among the Somme valley sites already mentioned it is so common as to be almost the standard type.

How far these various types are connected in the evolutionary way which has been described is perhaps a matter for further study, but the basic scheme suggested (which is essentially that set out by Collingwood in the 1930s) is probably right, at least on a conceptual level. This is not to say that every villa necessarily evolved in the same way, nor should it be assumed that the more complex types are always later in time than the simple ones. There should be caution too about seeking to establish a single pattern of development throughout the Empire, with the various types evolving from a small number of prototypes (presumably in Italy itself) and spreading gradually to all the provinces. Such a hypothesis does not account for the very wide regional vari-ations, which are much more likely to have been the result of independent development; and there is no obvious reason at the moment why Italy should be thought of as the ultimate source of inspiration. In recent years, Italian villas have become much better known and it has to be said that, on present evidence, there is no convincing *schema* in which both they and the provincial types can be incorporated.

It would seem, from the fairly limited number of sites known, that the most com-mon simple types of villa in Italy were: first, a small enclosure with one or more build-ings, and sometimes a taller tower-like structure, grouped inside it; and second, a square or rectangular building, comprising a dozen or so rooms arranged around a central unroofed space, which might be no more than an internal passage-way but might occas-ionally merit the name of peristyle. Excavated examples of the first type are not numerous, but Monte Forco in the Ager Capenas is one, and for the second type one could point to Sambuco in southern Etruria or the rather larger site not far away at Selvasecca (fig. 20.5). For both of these, it has been argued, there are Greek prototypes, and houses on the site of Olynthus on the Chalcidic peninsula have been cited as illustra-tions. In Italy, as in northern Europe, the same factors operated as far as the development of plans is concerned: increasing wealth, acquisition of new facilities and amenities,

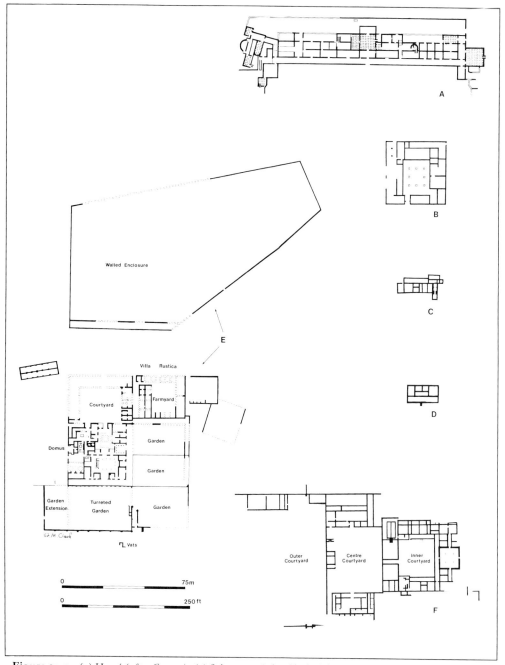

Figure 20.5 (A) Hosté (*after Cumont*); (B) Selvasecca (*after Sheila Gibson*); (C) Brixworth (*after Turland*); (D) Huntsham (*after Bridgewater*); (E) Sette Finestre (*after Sheila Gibson*); (F) Woodchester

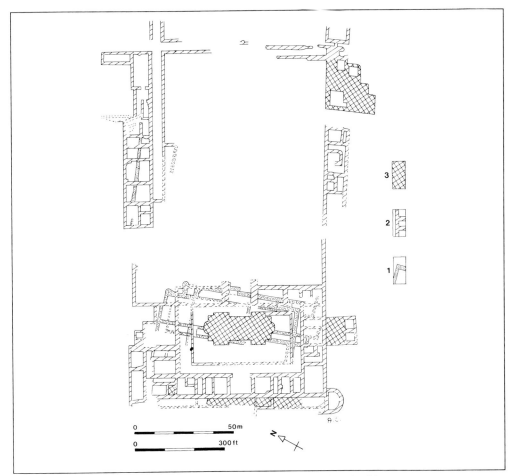

Figure 20.6 Vieux-Rouen-sur-Bresle (*after Agache*)

the segregation of people and operations. But what they lead to, essentially, is an increasingly large and complex peristyle house, such as one finds at Gragnano (fig. 20.4) in Campania or, in its more developed form, at San Rocco near Ravenna or Sette Finestre (fig. 20.5) in Etruria. These, like their more simple prototypes, are quite different from the standard types in the provinces, for which, with one exception, they would seem to provide no model.

The one exception is the peristyle villa, which is itself one of the standard provincial types: there are examples of it in most provinces and quite numerous examples in some of them. As one might expect, it is relatively common in Spain, as at La Cocosa (fig. 20.3) near Badajoz or the so-called Villa of Fortunatus at Fraga in the Huesca province;

536

Figure 20.7 Restoration drawing of the villa at Whitton (*after Jarrett*)

and in Mediterranean France, as at Montmaurin and Lalonquette in the foothills of the Pyrenees. But there are examples further north as well: Pannonia has a number of them, and at St-Ulrich (fig. 20.4), in the Moselle *département* of France, there is perhaps the most remarkable of them all. Not all of these sites are early by any means, so that it is not simply a matter of a Mediterranean type being imported wholesale in the early stages and then being superseded by local types in the course of time. But they seem to be special, in the sense that whereas the other types can be shown to be conceptually linked to one another to some extent, these are separate and outside the framework; to this extent they are an importation rather than an integral part of the local culture.

The question of villas and romanization is considered more fully below, but it is fair in general terms to say that the appearance and development of villas in a given region is an indication of the spread of Roman institutions and life-styles and, more important, of the relatively stable economy and peaceful social conditions that these imply. In an area such as Provence, where these conditions had been effectively achieved by the end of the first century BC, the villa emerged in a recognizable form in the

Augustan and Julio-Claudian period, and by the end of the first century AD it had spread through the rest of Gaul. The pattern is similar in the other Mediterranean provinces: in Africa, for example, where there was a tradition of large-scale intensive farming going back to the Carthaginian period, there were villas at least as early as in Provence and possibly earlier; and in Spain too, though evidence from excavated sites is still scarce, it is likely that many of the villas date back to the same period. Elsewhere, as one would expect, the development is rather later: the first villas in Dalmatia and Pannonia come sometime in the first century AD, and in Britain, with the exception of a few early sites in the south-east, it is the early second century before the process gets fully under way. The head start that the more southerly villas had over those further north was to have important consequences later, since the upheaval and recession of the third century caught the development of villas at different stages in the different regions. Thus in France and Spain there was ample time for the villa to reach a peak of refinement and prosperity before the troubles came, so that the Antonine and Severan periods provide us with our most splendid examples; whereas in Britain and other less favoured areas the villas encountered the crisis at a rather earlier stage in their development, and it was only in the fourth-century recovery, if at all, that they began to rival the continental ones.

Villas and the economy

A villa had its own internal economy, but it also formed part of the economy of the region in which it was situated, and a study of its remains can throw light on much broader questions than may at first appear. At the most obvious level, in their size and in the amenities they contain, the villas are indicators of wealth, both of the individual owner and of a given region at a given period of time. Of the source of that wealth they can tell us little for certain, though they can often provide hints in the form of buildings and facilities such as olive presses, grain stores, housing for cattle, or simply from their situation, in good arable land, near rich pasture and so on. There is no certainty, of course, that the wealth was derived from farming: the house and its appointments may represent the investment of capital derived from quite different sources, and in the more lavish examples this is most likely to have been the case. Lower down the scale, however, represented perhaps by a fairly modest establishment with a small bath block and a couple of mosaic pavements, it would be reasonable to assume that the refinements are the result of an agricultural surplus. This in turn implies the existence of flourishing markets and of a fairly numerous non-agricultural population requiring food. The amenities themselves imply the availability of craftsmen and of labour generally, and of a pattern of exchange rather wider than that of the immediate neighbourhood. They also indicate a degree of confidence: there are no precise figures for the cost of a mosaic or a hypocaust system, but it can hardly have been negligible, and one cannot imagine a villa owner investing in such things unless he felt reasonably secure in his tenure and in his continuing profits. Collectively, when a consistent pattern emerges from a whole range of sites, such indications are of considerable importance: it is this kind of evidence, for example, that reveals the uneven nature of the fourth-century economic recovery in Gaul, which in some areas produced quite large and lavishly appointed villas and in others more workmanlike establishments in which the luxuries of an earlier age had been in large measure abandoned.

Against this more general background the evidence for the internal economy of a villa is naturally more detailed and more precise, though it has to be said that the precision is sometimes more apparent than real. It is possible, with a fair degree of confidence, to identify rooms and buildings as being designed for particular purposes: that is, barns, byres and stables can be discovered, and the amount of grain that could be stored in them or the number of cattle or ploughing teams that they could be thought to house can, with appropriate margins of error, be calculated. Careful survey can also go some way towards reconstructing the associated field systems, and can even, by pollen analysis or from the scatter of potsherds in farmyard manure, make informed guesses about the kind of farming and the kinds of crops that were favoured. Bignor in Sussex and, more controversially, Gatcombe in Somerset can be cited as examples of villas where this kind of study has been carried out, and as useful guides to the reliability or otherwise of the techniques involved. The problem with these and similar studies is to assemble a body of evidence which is sufficiently complete and which provides an opportunity for cross-checking: clearly, if only small fragments of the field system are recovered, only very general statements about the overall management of the estate can be made; equally, if calculations are made on the basis of the fields, the figures are likely to be extremely tentative unless they can be supported by independent calculations on the basis of, for example, barns and granaries. To some extent this is a matter of archaeological technique: there are few sites at the moment which provide enough of the evidence needed, but as skills improve there is every reason to suppose that they will become more numerous and more productive. Nevertheless, there will always be questions to which archaeology alone can give no answer: for example, the cost of agricultural land at particular times in particular areas, or the cost of amenities and implements. There are questions also which, though answerable in principle, are likely to remain very difficult without the kind of statistical information which is available for later historical periods.

The great lack, of course, is documents against which the evidence of archaeology can be set, and without which it is often ambiguous and imprecise. Indeed, one of the central problems in studying the economy of the ancient world is that whereas the country, and more specifically agriculture, were at all times fundamental to it, the greater part of the evidence, in terms of documentary and epigraphic material, concerns the towns and their industry and commerce. It is all too easy to forget that the very existence of towns depended on a regular supply of food and therefore on the estates which produced it, just as the villas on those estates depended on the towns in the ways already referred to. The town and the villa were in a very obvious sense inter-dependent: the one implied the other.

This is not to say that the relationship was always the same: indeed, the subtle changes in the relationship at different periods and in different regions, though imperfectly understood in the present state of knowledge, are one of the more interesting sidelights on the evolving economy of the Empire as a whole. In broad terms, as has been said, they would be expected to rise and fall together, with flourishing markets and buoyant agricultural production, or the reverse in each case, being part of an overall pattern. At times, however, they are interestingly out of phase, as in the late first century in Britain, where it has been suggested that villas developed more rapidly than their associated urban centres, perhaps reflecting the preferences of a traditionally non-urban native aristocracy. Such situations, though, are not likely to be more than temporary, and the close interdependence of town and country should make us wary of, for example, theories of a 'flight to the country' at times of economic hardship. It can be well understood that in periods of acute economic uncertainty there might be a move towards self-sufficiency, with owners retreating to their estates and attempting to encapsulate themselves in a largely self-contained world. There is, indeed, some evidence that this happened in parts of the continent as a result of the difficulties of the third century. But if it were whole-hearted and permanent its effect would be to produce quite different establishments from the villas as they are commonly pictured; instead of the marbles and mosaics and the heating systems and all the other items which imply the interrelationship of villa and town, there would be the unspectacular evidence of the subsistence or near subsistence farming which would be all that their self-contained world could manage. Whether the term villa would still be appropriate to such an establishment is, to say the least, questionable.

Villas and society

On the social, as on the economic, level the value of the villas is partly that they illustrate and exemplify what is known already from other sources, and partly also that they modify what was thought to be known or even reveal things that were not known at all. It would be fair to say, in general, that the interpretation of villa remains from a social point of view is made more difficult by the fact that it is people rather than objects that are being dealt with, and in particular relationships between people. Such relationships may or may not be reflected in the physical layout of a villa, and the same is true of the social status of individuals or groups. If they are not, there is little that can be done unless there is evidence from other sources; if they are, they are likely to be implicit rather than explicit, and judgments about them will be correspondingly subjective.

On some matters, perhaps, there is a greater degree of assurance. If a villa is well appointed, with comfortable residential areas, good quality pavements and heating systems, it is not an unreasonable assumption that the owner either lived in it or used it fairly frequently. By the same token a villa which in other respects is large and prosperous, but is not particularly lavish in its living quarters, may be thought to be under the supervision of a farm manager on behalf of an absentee owner. A sudden decline in comfort at a particular point in the history of a villa may indicate an equally sudden change of fortune, but could also mean the departure of an owner to another home or perhaps a sale to an owner who already lived elsewhere. Even at this very simple level it is possibilities rather than certainties that are being considered; but from a number of sites collectively quite clear and reliable evidence can be obtained for the pattern of ownership at given times in given areas: the small family farms, the farms that formed part of larger estates with owners in temporary residence from time to time or not at all, the great country houses regarded by their owners as home.

There are, too, the little indications of status, often at the more humble end of the social scale: the segregation of human accommodation from that of animals, or of the owner and his family from his workmen; the provision of little verandahs and porticos; the way in which, when a villa is rebuilt and extended, it is turned back to front so that it looks away from the farmyard rather than into it. What there is, in these and similar features, is evidence for the occupants' notion of themselves and of their status in society at large. What cannot, of course, be obtained from villas is evidence for their owners' *actual* status in legal or social terms, whether they were local men or immigrants, 'Romans' or 'natives', ex-slaves, ex-soldiers or whatever. It is known from inscriptions and literary evidence that villas were regularly owned by all of them, but it is very rare to attach a particular name to a particular site, and even rarer to say with confidence that a particular villa must have belonged to this or that category of person.

There are similar uncertainties about a villa's workforce. What proportion of it was slaves and what free men? Is there evidence of a shift of emphasis from one to the other in the later Empire? How far did the status of the free worker decline towards that of a serf? On such questions the villas themselves offer little help. There are rows of small 'cells' in some Italian villas, which may or may not have been designed as slave quarters, and there are occasional items elsewhere suggesting the use of slave gangs, such as the chains discovered at the Park Street villa in Hertfordshire. But these are both rare and inconclusive, and interpretation of them probably owes too much in any case to a rather stereotyped view of the slave as a kind of superior farm animal: if he was he may not have been housed in the villa itself at all, and if he was not it is likely that he will have been largely indistinguishable from a free worker. It is known, for example, that slaves were commonly set up in dependent holdings in the same way as free *coloni*, and this alone should warn against being too hopeful of determining status by reference to buildings.

Status apart, it should at least be possible to decide whether a given villa's lands were worked directly by a labour force under centralized control or indirectly in a series of dependent farms. Even if the dependent farms themselves cannot be identified, there are possible clues at the centre: the presence or absence of living accommodation for large numbers of workers, the presence of unusually large barns suggesting storage of produce brought in by tenants, or a comparative lack of plough-teams suggesting the cultivation of the arable by contributory services. Occasionally there are other suggestive features: the apparent over-provision of bath facilities at East Grimstead in Wiltshire and Stroud in Hampshire, for example, has been thought to indicate the presence of a considerable working population in the area, though in this case perhaps the question of whether they were *coloni* or not remains unanswered.

Villas and romanization

The mention of *coloni* gives rise to a more fundamental question, and one which by no means lends itself to a simple answer: that of the extent to which the villa can be seen as an indicator of a romanized way of life in provinces which, before the coming of the Romans, had a distinctive culture of their own. At first sight, perhaps, this may seem to be an unduly cautious question: the radical difference between a villa, even a comparatively modest one, and an Iron Age hut might seem to be so obvious as not to need further discussion, while the adoption of such characteristically Roman amenities as bath suites, hypocausts, mosaic pavements and painted wall plaster, would seem to speak for itself. But it would be wrong to assume without further discussion that traditional patterns of life were wholly and rapidly abandoned in favour of Roman ones. The literary texts refer almost exclusively to the upper levels of society, who will have had most to gain from such instant conversion; there is evidence, particularly from Gaul, that not all of them showed the same enthusiasm, and one wonders in any case how far down the social scale it went. There is also an obvious danger of placing too much emphasis on material things: it is known from more recent colonial experience that a wholesale adoption of the trappings of European culture need not involve the abandonment of deep-seated traditional values and modes of behaviour, and there is no compelling reason why the ownership of a villa should in itself imply any fundamental adoption of Roman ways.

It has already been shown above that the provincial villa was not, in any case, a slavish reproduction of the Italian one, and that in spite of obvious Italian influence there were definite provincial styles of villa planning which presumably evolved to meet varying needs and conditions. In some cases there is very clear evidence of 'native' influence: the standard villa throughout much of Germany, for example, is the small corridor type with, as its central feature, a large communal room, presumably derived from the characteristic Iron Age dwelling and probably fulfilling the same basic functions. In Britain there are several features which at some time or other have been thought to indicate non-Roman social patterns, and there has in recent years been something of an upsurge in this kind of interpretation. The aisled buildings, which used to be known as 'basilican villas' and which are largely if not exclusively a British phenomenon, have seemed to many to belong to a pattern of kinship communities rather than to simple nuclear families, and it has recently been suggested that many villas which had hitherto been regarded as unexceptional were in fact occupied jointly by groups of families, sometimes with shared facilities. More generally, the absence of patterned mosaic pavements in some areas of Britain has been taken as evidence for land-holding by kinship groups rather than by individuals, the suggestion being that only under 'private' ownership would there be either the necessary capital or the permanency of tenure appropriate to such long-term investment. Much of the argument in these cases is necessarily subjective, and there seems little prospect of achieving any unanimity among scholars on the matter. What does seem clear, however, is that there is a danger of assuming too 'Roman' a picture on the basis of material possessions alone; the possessions have to be seen in context, not least in the physical context of the houses in which they were enjoyed.

This is an important point to make, because the literary and documentary sources, to which it is necessary to turn for the interpretation of archaeological evidence, come largely from the Mediterranean centre of the Empire, and may therefore overstate the 'Roman-ness' of things, if only in the sense that they will take little or no account of regional exceptions and peculiarities. Only if these are so striking as to make the normal terms and concepts inapplicable will there be any need to refer to them or to make special provision to deal with them. A possible example of this is the colonate, a dependent form of land tenure in which holdings were leased to small farmers in return for specified dues and services. The system is well documented in the legal codes, and though there is only one passage which explicitly and unmistakably connects it with Britain it is commonly supposed that it operated on at least the larger British villa estates in the late Empire, the assumption presumably being that if it did not, and a 'native' system was operating in its place, there would have been some hint of it in the sources. But this is by no means certain: the Roman administrative system was particularly good at absorbing and accommodating local practices, and there are numerous examples of Roman words being applied to institutions which were not Roman at all, such as Caesar's *equites* and *clientes* in Gaul, to mention one of the more obvious. Indeed, it may be wondered if anything short of a major disruption of the collection of taxes will have brought the details of the tenure patterns in Britain to higher official notice. So far as the documents are concerned, it cannot be inferred either that the colonate was at all common in Britain or that where it did occur it was the same colonate as that appearing in the lawbooks.

This may be an extreme case, and it should not deceive us into adopting too extreme a position. Britain, it could be argued, is something of an exception among the provinces, and it would certainly be more difficult to argue for a high level of 'native' survival over much of the continent. Even in Britain it would be hard to deny that a villa like Chedworth, let alone one like Woodchester, represents a fundamental change in the economic, social and cultural life of the people involved; and it would be inconsistent in any case to play down the importance of a villa in Britain while allowing that a similar one in Gaul, for example, is part of the romanizing process. What *must* be done is to be rid of the nineteenth-century assumption that the villas were owned and inhabited by Romans, living an entirely Roman way of life; but equally, the temptation must be resisted to see the villa owners as crude barbarians, adopting Roman amenities as status symbols only. In this, as in so many fields of study, the villas must be interpreted, not in isolation, but as part of the cultural pattern as a whole.

The end of the villa

Whatever it may imply about the 'Roman-ness' or otherwise of its owner, the villa was nevertheless, to use Professor Rivet's words, 'integrated into the social and economic organization of the Roman world', and with the passing of that world, or more accurately with the disappearance of its social and economic organization, the villa itself disappeared. The old images, admittedly, no longer carry conviction: there was no sudden and full-scale withdrawal of 'Romans' from the western provinces, and there was nothing like the total destruction of Romanity by countless hordes of barbarian invaders that is popularly imagined. But even if the drama is removed and the process drawn out it still makes sense to see the end of the villa as the result of two kinds of forces combining with, and intensifying each other: the external force of invasion by peoples outside the Empire, and the internal one of economic decline and collapse. This is not the place to go into details regarding the forces themselves, but rather to assess their impact, and chart their effects, on the villas both individually and collectively.

In a sense assistance in this task is provided by the fact that these forces, which from the late-fourth century onwards brought destruction to the villa on a massive scale, were given as it were a trial run rather more than a century earlier, so that there is a foretaste in the third century of the likely course of events later on. That many villas were destroyed in the course of the third century is indisputable, even though the precise dating of particular cases is often problematical. Many, no doubt, will have suffered accidental destruction, and it is also possible that what were seen as destruction layers in some of the early excavations may have been the result of industrial activity of some kind. Many more sites were abandoned at this time, either to be reoccupied after a gap or in many cases not at all, and there is plenty of evidence of declining standards of maintenance and a comparative lack of new building. How the blame is apportioned between the external and internal pressures will naturally be a matter for discussion, but there can be little doubt that both are involved and that each will have aggravated the other.

The survival which is evident from the late-third century onwards is by no means uniform throughout the provinces. In Britain, as has long been recognized, the fourth century saw the appearance of numerous large and luxurious villas, particularly in the west of the country, associated apparently with the incorporation of previously small estates into much larger units. A similar pattern can be discerned in the region of Trier, perhaps as a result of the town's emergence as an imperial capital, though here it is more a matter of the recovery of earlier prosperity than the unprecedented expansion achieved in Britain. Elsewhere on the continent the pattern appears to be one of unspectacular and hard-won recovery, with a concentration on the working functions of villas and a marked decline in the more luxurious aspects compared with the heyday of the late-second and early-third centuries.

This variety of response to the third-century troubles should make us wary of jumping to conclusions about the effects of the later ones. All along it has been known that the pattern of invasion was by no means uniform, either in the dates at which different regions were affected or in the intensity and scale of the invasions, or, indeed, in the character and aims of the invaders themselves. And now it is known also that the economic base was also variable from one region to another, adding a further element of uncertainty to the short-term and long-term consequences. That the vast majority of the villas went under in the course of the fifth century, or even earlier, it would be foolish to deny; the many hundreds of excavated sites which, with or without a destruction layer, yield no material beyond the period in question, are the unanswerable evidence with which to begin. But it is equally clear that the majority is not the totality, and there is increasing evidence now to suggest that a minority of sites survived the Empire, and that they are by no means negligible or insignificant.

A few may have survived intact: in the letters of Sidonius Apollinaris in the fifth century, and the poetry of Fortunatus in the sixth, there are descriptions of villas which, though they may in some cases have acquired a somewhat embattled appearance, are nevertheless recognizable as villas in the normal meaning of the term. Some of them are in the Visigothic area of Gaul, which is known from other evidence to have experienced a less traumatic transition from Roman to Germanic rule; but others, such as those in the Moselle valley, are outside it and should make the concept of uniform destruction questionable. More commonly, perhaps, the survival will have been more precarious and less complete: villas may have continued to survive as centres of settlement, losing in many cases their status as proprietary units, and evolving in due course as hamlets and later villages. The survival over much of the continent of Roman estate names in -*acum* is clearly to be interpreted in some such terms and is itself very strong evidence for survival on a considerable scale. Other villas, it seems, were converted, either immediately or after a period of abandonment and neglect, into religious sites, either because they had some religious association in the form of a shrine or something similar, or because they came to be used as the sites for cemeteries. These sites in turn might evolve into centres of settlement and so constitute a measure of continuity of a different kind.

The villa, in fact, like the Empire itself, showed a marked reluctance to die. Like the Empire, it might have looked very different in the sixth century from what it had done in the fourth; equally, both will have differed in the fourth from what they had been in the first or second, and although for the purposes of writing books and constructing syllabuses a final date has to be placed on each of them it is known nevertheless that history itself is rarely quite so tidy.

20.1   Aerial view of the villa at Vieux-Rouen-sur-Bresle, France

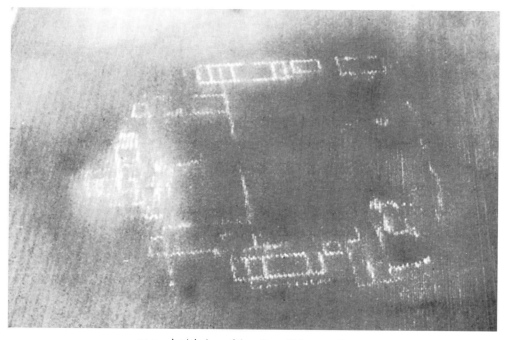

20.2   Aerial view of the villa at Grivesnes, France

·BIBLIOGRAPHY·FOR·PART·7·

Agache, R. (1978), *La Somme pré-romaine et romaine*, Amiens.

Agache, R. and Bréart, B. (1975), *Atlas d'archéologie aérienne de Picardie*, Amiens.

Aitken, R. (1956), 'Vergil's plough', *Journal of Roman Studies*, XLVI, 97–106.

Alföldy, G. (1974), *Noricum*, London.

Anstee, J. (1967), 'Scythe blades of Roman Britain', *Countryman*, Winter, 1969, 365–9.

Applebaum, S. (1972), 'Roman Britain AD 43–1043', in Finberg, H. P. R. (ed.), *The Agrarian History of England and Wales*, I, ii, Cambridge.

Barker, G. (1977), 'The stock economy of Luni', *Scavi di Luni*, II, Rome.

Blumner, H. and Mommsen, T. (eds) (1958), *Der Maximaltarif des Diocletian*, Berlin.

Boessneck, J., Von Driesch, A., Meyer-Semppenau, U. and Wechsler, E. v. Ohlen (1971), *Die Tierknochenfunde aus dem Oppidum von Manching, Ausgrabungen von Manching, Band 6*, Wiesbaden.

Bökönyi, A. (1974), *A History of Domestic Mammals in Central and Eastern Europe*, Budapest.

Branigan, K. (1973), *Town and Country. The Archaeology of Verulamium and the Roman Chilterns*, Bourne End.

Branigan, K. (1976), *The Roman Villa in South-West England*, Bradford-on-Avon.

Branigan, K. (1977), *Gatcombe Roman Villa*, British Archaeological Reports, 44, Oxford.

Brunt, P. (ed.) (1974), *The Roman Economy*, Oxford.

Clarke, G. (1982), 'The Roman villa at Woodchester', *Britannia*, XIII, pp. 197–228.

Clason, A. T. (1967), 'Animal and man in Holland's past', *Palaeohistoria* XIIIA, Groningen.

Cotton, M. A. (1979), *The Late Roman Villa at Posto, Francolise*, British School at Rome, London.

Cunliffe, B. and Grant, A. (1975), *Excavations at Portchester Castle, I, Roman*, Research

Committee of the Society of Antiquaries of London.

Fernandez Castro, M. C. (1982), *Villas Romanas en España*, Madrid.

Fouet, G. (1962), 'La villa gallo-romaine de Montmaurin (Hte.-Garonne)', *Gallia* Supplement 20, Paris.

Frere, S. S. (1978), *Britannia: A History of Roman Britain*, London.

Gabler, D., Patek, E. and Vörös, I. (eds) (1982), *Studies of the Iron Age of Hungary*, British Archaeological Reports, S144, Oxford.

Glob, P. V. (1951), *Ard og plov i Nordens Oldtid*, Jysk Arkaeologisk Selskab Skr. 1, Copenhagen.

Goodchild, R. G. (1976), *Libyan Studies: Select Papers of the late R. G. Goodchild*, Joyce Reynolds (ed), London.

Gorges, J.-G. (1979), *Les Villas hispano-romaines*, Paris.

Grenier, A. (1934), *Manuel d'archéologie gallo-romaine*, II, Paris.

Harcourt, R. A. (1974), 'The dog in prehistoric and early historic Britain', *Journal of Archaeological Science*, I, 151.

Heitland, W. E. (1921), *Agricola: a study in ancient agriculture from the point of view of labour*, Cambridge.

Hitti, P. K. (1951), *History of Syria*, London.

Jarrett, M. G. and Wrathmell, S. (1981), *Whitton, an Iron Age and Roman Farmstead in South Glamorgan*, Cardiff.

Jones, A. H. M. (1964), *The Later Roman Empire, 284–602*, Oxford.

Jones, A. H. M. (ed. P. Blunt, 1974), *The Roman Economy: studies in ancient economic and administrative history*, Oxford.

Jones, M. (1981), 'The development of crop husbandry', in M. Jones and G. Dimbleby (eds), *The Environment of Man: the Iron Age to the Anglo-Saxon Period*, British Archaeological Reports, 87, 95–127, Oxford.

Lambrick, G. and Robinson, M. (1979), *Iron Age and Roman Riverside Settlements at Farmoor, Oxfordshire*, Oxford Archaeological Unit Report 2, Council for British Archaeology Research Report 32, London.

Lawless, R. I. (1969), 'Mauretania Caesariensis – an archaeological and geographical survey', unpublished Ph.D. thesis, University of Durham.

Luff, R.-M. (1982), *A Zooarchaeological Study of the Roman North-West Provinces*, British Archaeological Reports, S137, Oxford.

Maltby, M. (1979), *Faunal Studies on Urban Sites: The Animal Bones from Exeter, 1971–5*, Huddersfield.

Maltby, M. (1981), 'Iron Age, Romano-British and Anglo-Saxon animal husbandry. A review of the faunal evidence', in M. Jones and G. Dimbleby (eds), *The Environment of Man*, British Archaeological Reports 87, 155–203, Oxford.

Manning, W. H. (1964), 'The plough in Roman Britain', *Journal of Roman Studies*, LIV, 54–65.

Manning, W. H. (1971), 'The Piercebridge ploughgroup: Prehistoric and Roman studies', *British Museum Quarterly* 35, 125–36.

Manning, W. H. (1975), 'Economic influences on land use in the military areas of the Highland Zone during the Roman Period', in J. Evans, S. Limbrey and H. Cleere (eds), *The Effect of Man on the Landscape: The Highland Zone*, Council for British Archaeology Research Report 11, 112–16.

Meates, G. W. (1979), *The Roman Villa at Lullingstone, Kent*, I, Kent Archaeological Society Monographs I, Maidstone.

Mócsy, A. (1974), *Pannonia and Upper Moesia: A history of the Middle Danube provinces of the Roman Empire*, London.

Morris, P. (1979), *Agricultural Buildings in Roman Britain*, British Archaeological Reports 70, Oxford.

Nandris, G. N. (1981), 'Aspects of Dacian economy and Highland Zone exploitations', *Dacia*, 25, 248ff.

Nobis, G. (1973), 'Zur Frage römerzeitlicher Hauspferde in Zentraleuropa', *Zeitschrift von Säugetierkunde*, 38, 224–52.

Noddle, B. (Unpubl. ms), 'A Comparison of Animal Bones of Cattle, Sheep and Swine from Ten Iron Age and Romano-British Sites'.

Painter, K. (ed.) (1980), *Roman Villas in Italy*, British Museum Occasional Papers, 24.

Percival, J. (1976), *The Roman Villa: An Historical Introduction*, London.

Percival, J. (1982), 'Recent work on Roman villas in Britain', *Caesarodunum*, 17, 305–20.

Piehler, W. (1976), *Die Knochenfunde aus dem spätrömischen Kastell Vemania*, Munich.

Rees, S. (1979), *Agricultural Implements in Prehistoric and Roman Britain*, British Archaeological Reports, 69, Oxford.

Reynolds, P. J. (1981), 'New Approaches to Familiar Problems', in M. Jones and G. Dimbleby (eds), *The Environment of Man: the Iron Age to the Anglo-Saxon Period*, British Archaeological Reports, 87, 19–49.

Riedel, A. (1979), 'A cattle horn deposit of Roman Aquileia', *Bolletino del Centro Polesana di studi archeologici ed Etnografi*.

Rivet, A. L. F. (1964), *Town and Country in Roman Britain*, second edition, London.

Rivet, A. L. F. (ed.) (1969), *The Roman Villa in Britain*, London.

Rossiter, J. J. (1978), *Roman Farm Buildings in Italy*, British Archaeological Reports, 52, Oxford.

Rostovtzeff, M. (1926), *The Social and Economic History of the Roman Empire*, Oxford.

Ryder, M. L. (1981), 'Livestock' in J. Thirsk (ed.), *The Agrarian History of England and Wales*, I, i, Cambridge.

Shackley, M. (1981), *Environmental Archaeology*, London.

Smith, J. T. (1978), 'Villas as a key to social structure', in M. Todd (ed.), *Studies in the Romano-British Villa*, 149–85, Leicester.

Smith, J. T. (1982), 'Villa plans and social structure in Britain and Gaul', *Caesarodunum*

17, pp. 321–36.

Stevens, C. E. (1966), 'Agriculture and Rural Life in the Later Roman Empire', in M. M. Postan (ed.), *The Cambridge Economic History of Europe, Volume I: The Agrarian Life of the Middle Ages*, second edition, Cambridge, 92–124.

Thomas, E. B. (1964), *Römische Villen in Pannonien*, Budapest.

Todd, M. (ed.) (1978), *Studies in the Romano-British Villa*, Leicester.

Ucko, P. J. and Dimbleby, G. W. (eds) (1969), *The Domestication and Exploitation of Plants and Animals*, London.

Weiler, D. (1981), *Säugeknochenfunde aus dem Tell Hesbân in Jordanien*, Munich.

White, K. D. (1967a), *Agricultural Implements of the Roman World*, Cambridge.

White, K. D. (1967b), 'Gallo-Roman harvesting machines', *Latomus*, XXVI, 634–47.

White, K. D. (1967c), 'Latifundia: A critical review of the evidence', *Bulletin of the Institute of Classical Studies*, 14, 62–79.

White, K. D. (1969), 'The economics of the Gallo-Roman harvesting machines', *Collection Latomus*, 102, 804–9, Brussels.

White, K. D. (1970), *Roman Farming*, London.

White, K. D. (1975), *Farm Equipment of the Roman World*, Cambridge.

Wild, J. P. (1970), *Textile Manufacture in the North-Western Roman Provinces*, Cambridge.

Wilkes, J. J. (1969), *Dalmatia*, London.

Williams, D. (1977), 'A consideration of the sub-fossil remains of *Vitis Vinefera L.* as evidence for viticulture in Roman Britain', *Britannia*, VIII, 327–38.

Yeo, C. (1948), 'The overgrazing of ranch-lands in ancient Italy', *Transactions of the American Philological Association*, 275ff.

Zeuner, F. E. (1963), *A History of Domesticated Animals*, London.

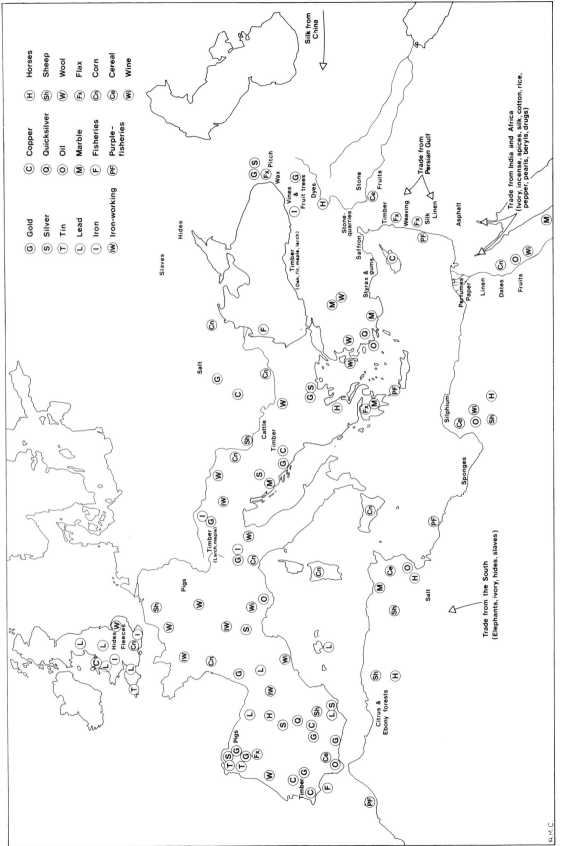

Figure 21.1 The resources of the Roman Empire

PART 8

·THE·ECONOMY·

CHAPTER 21

·IMPERIAL·ESTATES·

Dorothy J. Thompson

The primacy of land both as a measure of status and a form of investment was never doubted in the ancient world. The Roman dynasts of the late Republic were noted for their estates, and it was only natural that the emperors who followed should become the largest landowners amongst their contemporaries (Shatzman, 1975, 357–71 for Augustus). And whilst estates were only one of the sources of imperial wealth, joined for instance by quarries, mines, brickworks, salt-pans, flocks and herds (MacMullen, 1962, 277–82), they were certainly the most significant. The changing extent, nature and exploitation of these estates, which form the subject of this chapter, may therefore serve to illustrate important facets, both political and economic, of imperial power. The development, for example, from the rule of the Julio-Claudians, characterized by a tentative and personal exercise of imperial power, to the more codified and securely administered rule of the Flavians is nowhere more clearly seen than in the changing attitudes of the emperors towards their estates. What started as personal inheritance became imperial patrimony tied to office, and the reorganization of the imperial estates by the new dynasty typified this change in rule.

Imperial estates: their identification and extent

The pattern of distribution of imperial estates changed almost as often as did the emperor. The additions to the roster of imperial land and the withdrawals from it are only partially recorded in the literary, documentary and epigraphical sources that survive, and so to draw up a map of imperial land-holding at any one date is impossible. However such records as do survive give some indication of the location and changing scale of imperial estates.

'Boundary of (the estate) of our (lord) Caesar' declares, somewhat surprisingly in Latin, an undated stone from Kılıç on Lake Burdur in Greek-speaking Pisidia (*CIL* III, 6872; Bean, 1959, 82–4). Possibly connected with Nero's village of Tymbrianassos, known from Greek inscriptions to have been located at the south-west end of the lake, such explicit evidence for imperial land is rare. In Asia however it is primarily inscriptions which reveal the extent of imperial estates in the inland valleys of Phrygia, Galatia and Lydia (Strubbe, 1975; Crawford, 1976, 64–6). Sited well clear of the cities on the coast, these estates of the Roman emperor seem in part to have succeeded to the crown land of the hellenistic kingdoms (Broughton, 1934, 220–1).

Elsewhere there is other evidence. In Egypt papyri serve to supplement the more general statements of ancient historians, biographers and land-surveyors. Thus whilst Tacitus, eloquent in commenting on the greed of Nero, records how in AD 62 the emperor put Pallas to death in order to lay hands on the freedman's great riches, he gives no further details. For Egypt however papyri (Crawford, 1976, 175, note 25) record Pallas' holding in eight different villages of the Arsinoite nome with further plots in the Hermopolite and possibly Oxyrhynchite nomes; in Italy a further holding of Pallas is recorded at Sabinum by Phlegon of Tralles writing in the second century AD. Similarly with Seneca's land which Nero inherited in AD 65 on the suicide of his earlier advisor. Mentioned as significant in an earlier letter of Seneca, it is only from the papyri that the details of Seneca's land-holding in Egypt may be documented in any sort of detail. Still known in the third century AD by the name of their most prominent holder, these estates of Seneca which later, under the Flavians, were administered together with those of Nero's freedman Doryphorus as part of the holding of the emperor Titus, were located in at least thirteen different Arsinoite villages with additional land in the Hermopolite, Herakleopolite and Oxyrhynchite nomes (Crawford, 1976, 176, note 37; cf. *CIL* VIII, 23116 with Broughton, 1929, 201 for a *vicus Annaeus* at Semta in Africa). Other Egyptian estates, the earlier holdings of imperial counsellors and favourites together with members of the imperial family – Livia, for instance, Maecenas, Germanicus, Narcissus, Decius Valerius Asiaticus, Messalina or Acte – found their way back into the imperial holdings, consolidated as the estates of Vespasian or Titus. The papyri provide an unparalleled source of evidence both for their identification and exploitation. They show for instance that in Egypt, as elsewhere, imperial land, often in quite small lots, was interspersed with other types of holding (Kehoe, 1982, 137–8, note 48, Africa; Strubbe, 1975, 229 map, Phrygia).

In Africa, as in Asia, it is the epigraphical record which supplements the literary sources. For 'in Africa', as Frontinus records in a discussion of estates (*saltus*), 'the emperor owns not a little'. And Pliny's claim that, before Nero put them to death and presumably confiscated their land, six land-owners held half of the province may in part be substantiated by the epigraphical record of a *fundus* or *saltus Neronianus* (a farm or estate of Nero) in the Bagradas valley inland of Carthage which subsumed the earlier *saltus Blandianus, saltus Udensis* and areas of the *saltus Lamianus* and *Domitianus*, estates probably named after their original owners. These estates, together with other imperial holdings in the area, are recorded in a group of long inscriptions from the area which preserve rulings relevant to the land and those who exploit it (Kotula, 1952–3, 136 with map; Kolendo, 1976; Flach, 1978; Kehoe, 1982; Johne, Köhn and Weber, 1983, 309–43, 391–404). Further west, in Numidia, Theveste was a centre of imperial administration. Imperial boundary stones survive from the same area and tenants, together with imperial officials, are recorded from the countryside around Lambaesis and Thamugadi (Fentress, 1979, 134–42 with map). In Mauretania, especially in a large area southwest of Sitifis, similar boundary stones and dedications from the second and third centuries AD mark the areas of imperial ownership. Here fortified centres, *castella* or *defenciones* (like that of Matidia, the mother-in-law of the emperor Hadrian, later inherited by the Severans) formed the typical centres of exploitation. As with the *kasour* of Morocco today, these strong fortifications with their towers and battlements provided security for the imperial tenants. With their native names latinized, these tenants – *coloni Lemellefenses, castellani Perdicenses* or *coloni Kalefacalenses Pardalarienses* – repaired their walls, setting up altars and dedications to the divinity of the ruling emperor (Février, 1966). The scatter of dedications and records of imperial officials may be supplemented by the evidence of archaeology to show local settlement patterns and, with the survival of presses, the areas of olive cultivation (Lassère, 1977, 314–34 with map).

In the north-western provinces of Spain, Gaul, Germany and Britain, the epigraphical record is slighter. Inscribed *amphorae* from Spain, from Baetica and Tarraconensis, may in the third century have brought oil from imperial estates for consumption in Rome and elsewhere (Crawford, 1976, 70; Manacorda, 1977). In Spain, as in Gaul, Africa and Italy, confiscations by Septimius Severus added to the imperial holdings in the province which were already significant under Nero. Imperial procurators and other officials are recorded here, but not the boundaries of the land.

In Britain the large-scale agricultural development of some areas, especially around the Wash and in the Fenlands of East Anglia, has been ascribed to imperial initiative and ownership (Phillips, 1970, 7 and 10). Whilst plausible, such an identification which is based on archaeological evidence alone, must remain hypothetical without epigraphical or documentary support. Some imperial *saltus* or estates are known from Germany, for example the *saltus Sumelocennensis* around Rothenburg, and in Noricum, Pannonia, Raetia and Moesia the record of imperial officials is the most sure form of evidence for the existence of imperial landholding. So too from Greece imperial procurators and other lesser officials serve to indicate imperial landed interests in the province (Crawford, 1976, 66–7 and 70).

For Italy the same sorts of evidence surviving in the literary mentions of imperial estates and the epigraphical record of their staff are joined, somewhat surprisingly, by references in medieval land registers. As in Egypt land earlier belonging to members of the Julio-Claudian family and to their dependants retained this connection in the names by which the estates were later known, so too in Italy estates once of Germanicus, in the Sabine territory and at Reate, are still so named (*fundus Germanicianus* and *curtis Germaniciana*) in the medieval land register of Farfa (di Catino, 1914, xxx, *sv*; information from E. Gabba through M. H. Crawford). Other medieval cartularies may well contain such records; this source has not yet been exploited.

It is therefore from a whole range of different sources that a picture of imperial land-holding throughout the Empire begins to emerge. The picture, however, remains sketchy and incomplete.

Acquisition and alienation

When Christianity became the official religion of the Empire, Constantine (as recorded in the *Liber pontificalis*) endowed the newly established church with landed wealth, most of which came from the imperial estates. Although the growth and changing boundaries of these estates are only partially documented through the centuries, some significant periods of change and development may be noted. Whilst inheritance and confiscation formed the most regular sources of acquisition, gifts and sale featured amongst the most common forms of alienation.

In origin the Julio-Claudian estates will have been the personal patrimony of Augustus; but his extensive conquests brought significant additions. In Galatia it seems likely that Augustus annexed the lands and herds of King Amyntas, whilst the Egyptian evidence suggests a more complex origin for imperial land within that province.

In Egypt, under the personal rule of the Julio-Claudians, imperial land was used extensively to endow loyal associates of the emperor as well as members of his family (Rostovtzeff, 1957, 292–5; Tomsin, 1957; Parassoglou, 1978). Such grants were limited to the lifetime of the recipient and their return to the crown and subsequent disposal results in complicated descriptions of the plots concerned. In AD 56–7, for instance, Papos son of Tryphon, from Herakleia in the Themistos division of the Arsinoite nome, made a lease application to Euschemon, the *oikonomos* or manager of the Arsinoite estate of Tiberius Claudius Doryphorus which had earlier belonged to Narcissus. The neighbouring plots were crown land north and south, to the west another man's estate and to the east estate land which had once belonged to Maecenas and still kept his name. There are various points of interest in this document. First the favourable terms of the lease applied for suggests the land was of poor quality, a feature which frequently recurs in reference to imperial land in Egypt. In this province imperial estates (*ousiai*) predominate in the Arsinoite nome which earlier, under the Ptolemies, had been the scene of large-scale agricultural reclamation and innovation. And within this nome (the Fayum) it is more often in the outlying areas that imperial estates are found. At Tebtunis in the south Fayum no arable land occurs amongst the imperial estates of the village, and around Karanis in the north-east Fayum it is in the outlying villages that such estates predominate, in lands which were difficult to irrigate and were amongst the earliest to go out of cultivation. A group of grain receipts from AD 158–9 from the district of Karanis covers a total area of 335 arouras of which 53 per cent is in the neighbourhood of Psenarpsenesis, and from the same district at the end of the second century a total of 1847 arouras of ousiac land is recorded of which 49 per cent is from around Psenarp-senesis and 14 per cent from Patsontis. Both Psenarpsenesis and Patsontis were outlying villages which disappear from the record, presumably sanded over, after the second decade of the third century, whereas Karanis itself continued on into the fifth century. Second of note in the Herakleia lease application is the plot called after Maecenas to the east of Doryphorus' land. It would appear that earlier both plots were part of a larger tract of imperial land, part of which had been alienated under Augustus in a grant to Maecenas and which still kept the grantee's name. The location of imperial estates in Egypt therefore suggests that, rather than simply inheriting what Cleopatra had recently confiscated to finance her campaign (Dio 51.5.4–5, cf. 17.6–7; so Crawford, 1976, 40), Augustus may have made himself personally responsible for the *hypologos* land, land which was uncultivated and unproductive at the time of his conquest. The active reclamation which characterized Augustus' management of Egypt would, on this hypo-thesis, have been to the emperor's personal profit (Suetonius, *Augustus* 18.2; Dio 51.18.1; Brashear, 1979).

Whilst in Egypt, as in Asia, conquest lay at the base of imperial land-holding, con-fiscation and inheritance were without doubt the most common ways in which imperial land might grow (Hirschfeld, 1913, 544–75; Millar, 1977, 163–74). Both Tiberius and Nero were noted for their confiscations, and traces of Neronian confiscation in both Africa and Pisidia have already been mentioned. The confiscations of Septimius Severus which followed the defeat of Clodius Albinus and Pescennius Niger greatly extended the imperial land, which he laid claim to along with the Antonine name; the fall of Plautianus brought in further estates for the emperor with a special procurator to organize them.

Inheritance too increased imperial wealth. During his long lifetime Augustus acquired extensive property from bequests. In Campania for instance at Boscotrecase and in the Thracian Chersonnese he was heir to Agrippa's land. The sole heir of Maecenas and many others, Augustus set the pattern; later emperors benefited in like fashion, with Nero going so far as to require all Romans to include him in their wills.

The alienation of estates likewise took a variety of forms. The personal grants of the Julio-Claudians to their friends and family have already been mentioned; they are most easily traced in the papyrus records of Egypt. The scale of gift-giving was generous, with an expected return of unquestioning loyalty and hard work in the emperor's interest. In the one Fayum village of Philadelphia, for example, imperial land was bestowed on various members of the royal house – on Livia (Julia Augusta) and the children of Germanicus, Germanicus himself and Antonia wife of Drusus and mother of Claudius; on the *equites* Maecenas, Petronius and L. Annaeus Seneca; on the freedmen Pallas, Narcissus, Euodus and Doryphorus. Further recipients were Lurius, who may have commanded part of Octavian's fleet, Camillus, Dionysiodorus, Jucundus and Chresimus, Iucundus Grypianus, Tiberius Julius Nikanor, Decimus Valerius Asiaticus, Charmus and Philodamus (Crawford, 1976, 61 with Hanson, 1984, 116–18). Some of these men are known, some unknown, but all are likely to have had imperial connections (Parassoglou, 1978, 24–6). Nowhere is the personal approach to imperial wealth and rule more clearly seen than in these grants by the Julio-Claudians to their dependants. This system of the temporary alienation of imperial land ended with the end of the dynasty and with the financial reorganization and consolidation of the Flavians.

On occasion, when short of cash for more immediate needs, emperors might sell their estates. Following the confiscations and extravagances of Nero, Galba put much of his predecessor's land up for sale, finding many willing purchasers. Nerva too sold land when he needed revenue and Pliny mentions with approval Trajan's willingness to dispose of imperial estates by sale. Inscriptions and papyri provide further evidence for the sale of estates (MacMullen, 1976, 24). On the whole however, to judge from the scale of Constantine's donations to the church (e.g. Eusebius, *Historiae Ecclesiasticae*, 10. 6 for Carthage) and the extent of imperial estates surviving into the later Empire, the contrary tendency prevailed and overall the acquisition of estates by far outbalanced their alienation. Evidence, for instance, from AD 422 suggests that imperial holdings accounted for eighteen and a half per cent of Africa Proconsularis and fifteen per cent of Byzacena which must have represented a far larger percentage of the cultivable land within these provinces (Jones, 1964, 415–16). This may have been the picture elsewhere.

Administration and management

Like any landholder, the emperor derived profits from his estates in the rents and, outside Italy, the taxes which they produced. It was the scale of these estates which set the emperors apart. And whereas at a local level the management of imperial estates probably differed little from that of other large estates, at the provincial level the administration of these estates was closely bound in with the more general financial control of the Empire. The picture is rarely static with important changes and developments taking place over the period.

In the provinces the procuratorial system formed a framework for control and it was generally equestrian procurators who were responsible for the revenues from imperial estates. With well-staffed offices or *tabularia* these men were joined by assistant procurators, often of freedman status, with responsibility for local areas, *tractus* or *regiones*. In Africa the larger *tractus* would seem to have been subdivided into *regiones* within which lay the individual *saltus* or estates. The administrative systematization this represents was probably the work of Vespasian (Broughton, 1929, 114–15). Regional offices were centred at Hadrumetum, Theveste, Thamugadi, Thugga and Hippo Regius (Pflaum, 1960–1, 381–5, 547; Kolendo, 1968, 325). The *lex Manciana* quoted in the long inscriptions of the Bagradas valley, as regulating the norms of landlord-tenant relations, may also be a Flavian enactment (Rostowzew, 1910, 321–9).

Regiones and possibly *tractus* are also found in Asia and other provinces too (Manacorda, 1976–7, 547). And, although the evidence for this regional administration is often from a later date, as in Africa the administrative structure may date in origin from the Flavian period. So, in a hellenized form, the *region Philadelphene* in Lydia probably included the Aga Bey estate, the peasants of which appealed to the Severan emperors in the early third century AD when some of their number had been arrested:

> '. . . and so we did the only thing possible, we informed your procurator in charge of the area (*taxis* = *tractus*?), Aurelius Marcianus, and your honourable procurators in Asia. We have become suppliants, most divine of emperors that have ever been, of your divine and transcendent sovereignty, since we have been hindered from attending to the tasks of cultivation by the threats of the police agents and their representatives to put us too, who remain, in danger of our lives, and we cannot, since we are prevented from working the land, even meet the imperial payments and other obligations for the immediate future. We beg you to favour our petition and order the representative of the people and your honourable procurators to exact justice for this wrong, and to prevent access to the imperial estates and the resultant molestation to us by both the police agents and those who, under the pretext of public office and liturgies, molest and trouble your farmers, since everything we have from our forefathers belongs by prior claim to the most sacred treasury by the law on cultivation. We have communicated the truth to your divinity. And unless some justice is exacted for these wrongs by your heavenly right hand and unless aid is brought for the future, we who are left, unable to endure the greed of the police agents and their representatives under the pretexts mentioned earlier, must abandon our ancestral homes and the tombs of our forefathers, and move to private land in order to save ourselves – since those who live a life of wrongdoing are more likely to spare those who live there than to spare your farmers – and in this way we shall become fugitives from the imperial estates, on which we were born and reared and, continuing as farmers for generations, have been fulfilling our obligations to the imperial account.' (Abbott and Johnson, 1926, 478–80, no. 142.15–54)

The terms in which the peasants appeal will be discussed later, but in this context it is noteworthy that the appeal to the emperor comes only after an approach to the regional, and provincial authorities. In Lycia a *regeon Oino(andike)* is found based on Oenoanda and officials were attached to these regions. Whilst a third century regional centurion from Antioch in Pisidia is probably military, from Prymnessos in Phrygia an imperial freedman who was a *tabularius regionarius* from the *regio(nes) Ipsina et Moetana* seems likely to be an administrative official (Ballance, 1969, 143–6; cf. Torelli, 1969, 19–20 for a *servus regionarius* from Sardinia).

In Egypt the Flavians organized the *ousiai* of the Julio-Claudians into the *ousiai* of Vespasian and Titus with their own account (Parassoglou, 1978, 28–9); the lands carried the name of this imperial connection for centuries later.

The next significant development in the organization of the imperial estates would seem to belong to the reign of Hadrian. In Italy he assigned land for cultivation at Lanuvium (*Liber coloniarum*, p. 235), and in many parts of the Empire he reorganized the procuratorial system (Pflaum, 1950, 58–67). It is under Hadrian that in Egypt there first appears the category of land which is both ousiac and public (*ousiake kai demosia ge*) and the ousiac account (the *logos ousiakos*) was perhaps established in its final form in this reign. For the payment of dues corporate responsibility might be vested in a single individual. A new liturgical official, the *epiteretes*, is now found in connection with estates (Tomsin, 1964, 95–7; *P. Petaus* 75–8, introduction; *SB* X. 10761.5–6). Such officials came under the *praktores ousiakon* and were responsible for the payment of dues on palms, vineyards, pasture-land and other land which in Egypt was charged with a cash rent rather than one in kind. Generally in this reign imperial finances seem to have been overhauled and the *ratio privata* established as the imperial account (Lo Cascio, 1971–2, 87–8, 106–17).

The Severan dynasty has already been noted as a period of significant increase in the acreage of imperial estates. Large-scale confiscations were accompanied by yet further administrative reorganization (Strubbe, 1975, 249–50; Lo Cascio, 1971–2, 115–16). During the following century the Egyptian evidence shows a plethora of new officials involved in estate administration, a development which Diocletian attempted to control. One *phrontistes* with two, or at the most three, assistants chosen by the *strategos* through the *boule* was now to replace separate *cheiristai, grammateis* and *phrontistai*; unnecessary expense might thus be avoided and the estates of the treasury receive proper attention. Given the scale and importance of these estates their history is inextricably bound up with that of imperial finances, with changes in their administration reflecting changes in the central financial administration of the Empire (Jones, 1964, 411–27).

At a local level, the management of imperial estates does not differ significantly from those of private land-owners. Throughout the Roman world alongside owner-exploitation the two most common forms of exploitation were, firstly, by tenants working under lease and, secondly, by bailiff or *vilicus* management with the land worked by slaves. With a range of local variations both these forms occur on imperial estates where the type of management found would seem to differ according to the type of land, its potential productivity and traditional patterns of local labour. The variety of terms found in the Greek and Latin sources reflects this variety.

Once again the African inscriptions may serve to introduce the subject. In the Bagradas valley a two-tier system of leases appears to be the predominant pattern. A *conductor* served as head-lessee, subletting the land to the tenants (*coloni*) on the various estates. Whereas the *conductores* would seem to come from the local aristocracy, from the top stratum perhaps of the sub-curial class, the *coloni* too may have been fairly substantial individuals with the economic potential for expanding their holdings (Garnsey, 1978, 234; Kehoe, 1982, 99–103, 124). Those with responsibility for cultivating the land are mentioned at the start of the Trajanic inscription from Henchir Mettich (*CIL* VIII, 25902) which records a letter from the procurators defining the application of the *lex Manciana*. Those responsible for the land are named as *domini aut conductores vilicive* (owners, lessors or bailiffs). In the actual letter lessors (*conductores*) and bailiffs (*vilici*) are frequently mentioned, owners less so; the wording may of course reflect the scope of the original enactment rather than its current application. The letter concerns a share-cropping system with special provisions for newly planted vines and fruit trees; a money rent, as in contemporary Egypt, is specified for flocks. Those farming the estate are called *coloni*, though there is also mention of *inquilini*, native labour perhaps from outside the estate, and *stipendarii*, possibly hired labour. The letter ends with details of corvée labour, ploughing, sowing and harvesting, to be provided for the *conductor* by the *coloni*. As a group the *coloni* are represented by a *defensor*, Flavius Geminius, and by Lucius Victor son of Odilo, their *magister*, who sees to the erection of the inscription.

In the Ain el Djemela inscription from the reign of Hadrian, which may be supplemented from the Severan Ain Wassel altar with a copy of the same decision, the cultivation of marginal lands, *subseciva*, is the subject of imperial ruling. The petitioners, probably *coloni*, have complained about land taken up by the *conductores* but not exploited. Ruling through his *procurator* the emperor allows the petitioners to cultivate this land; provision is made for the payment of rent for five years (probably the normal length of a lease) to the original *conductor*, and after that to the treasury. *Coloni*, reasonably substantial individuals with the means of expanding into marginal land, are portrayed as in competition with the *conductores*. The corporate organization found here for imperial tenants occurs elsewhere in Africa and in other provinces; sharing in cult and social life these tenants formed identifiable groups with spokesmen to represent their interests, and like *coloni*, *conductores* too might come together in joint activity. In the joint record of religious dedications their shared identity of social and economic interests was boosted.

Lease arrangements might embody more general rules of cultivation; these were known and quoted. In the Commodan inscription from Suk el Khmis the *conductores* again hold a prime lease with tenants cultivating the land. The *coloni* of the *saltus Burunitanus* complain of the behaviour of Allius Maximus and other *conductores* who, they claim, are colluding with the procurator to their disadvantage. They quote a general ruling on corvée labour which had been put up on bronze and was confirmed by procuratorial decree. The rhetoric of the self-description of the *coloni*, 'mean men of the countryside (*homines rustici tenues*)', is probably exaggerated yet, unable to compete with the richer *conductores* for the favour of the procurator, they appeal directly to the emperor. They should not be constrained beyond the provisions of the *lex Hadriana* and the procuratorial rulings; this is contrary to the long-established agreement, *contra perpetuam formam*. Like the established practice of the *lex Manciana* (*consuetudo Manciana*) to which the procurators refer in the Henchir Mettich text, or the rule of cultivation (*to dikaion tes georgias*) which the Asian tenants of Aga Bey recalled (p. 563 above), such accepted practices were important in defining the rights and duties of imperial tenants. When recorded on inscriptions it is the tensions of the conflicting interests of the emperor and his representatives, of the *conductores* and of the imperial tenants, which are the focus of attention. In the provinces procurators and *conductores* might act together to their mutual advantage; direct appeal to the emperor was the most effective recourse for imperial tenants in trouble.

The African pattern of tenants-in-chief leasing imperial estates is found in other parts of the empire, in Egypt for instance under Nero, and in Asia, in Phrygia, Lycia, Caria and Lycaonia. In Greek such men were called *misthotai*. In general the systems of exploitation of imperial land differed little from those of private estates and the complex patterns repeat themselves with local variations throughout the Empire. As in the Bagradas valley with its five-year tenancies, some leases were long ones; elsewhere, as in Egypt, annual agreements were more regular. When labour is in short supply such distinctions are less significant than when it is plentiful. That the former was generally the case seems clear from the repeated threats of hard-pressed tenants to leave the land. The tenants of Aga Bey were not alone in threatening to abandon the emperor's estates.

Alongside both large and small scale tenancies of different duration, direct exploitation, through bailiffs and slaves, is found on many imperial estates. So from the *praedia Galbana* in Italy four bailiffs (*vilici*) join with the people (*pleps*) of the estate to dedicate a shrine to the *numen* of the imperial house; fifty-six names are listed in total. Of these, four were women, six or seven home-born slaves of the emperor and many others were slaves; but some of those with two names given were probably also tenants. The same combination of slave and free appears on Istrian estates likely to be imperial and in Italy where at Abella and Nola land grants were made by Vespasian to his slaves (*familia*) and tenants (*coloni*). There is more Italian evidence for bailiffs, as from Africa around Hippo, in Numidia and at Bisica. In Egypt where slaves had no role in traditional farming, exploitation by slaves never occurs. 'Those from the house (*oikos*) of Vespasian and Titus', who in the mid-third century AD are responsible for land in the Oxyrhynchite nome which was earlier private, are probably local officials representing the imperial estates. Empire-wide the patterns of management and farming of the imperial estates probably differed little from that of private land. What did differ was the status of the owner, the emperor, and the consequent ends to which this exploitation might be directed.

The emperor and his estates

Imperial interest in the best form of exploitation for imperial land may be seen in a concern both for the uses to which it was put and in the condition of those who cultivated it. According to Pliny (*Natural History*, 18. 94–5), Augustus received reports from his procurators of a four-hundred fold grain yield in African Byzacium, and a similar sample was dispatched to Nero. Whilst the details of such stories cannot possibly be genuine the imperial concern they record might just be so. In the late-second century AD, in an attempt to bring imperial land back under cultivation, Pertinax granted ten years' tax remission to be followed by the grant of possession for the cultivator (Herodian 2. 4.6–7). The Hadrianic *lex de rudibus agris* quoted by the African *coloni* on the Ain Wassel altar (*CIL* VIII, 26416. ii 10–13) is an earlier imperial ruling which perhaps had a similar purpose, and the whole tenor of the big African inscriptions suggests different imperial attempts to ensure the cultivation of the estates of the Bagradas valley. The Henchir Mettich inscription, for instance, in recalling provisions of the *lex Manciana*, defines various share-cropping arrangements for arable crops, wine, oil, honey and fruit-trees (*CIL* VIII, 25902). The lower rate of one quarter of the crop specified for beans, in contrast to the more usual third, represents a recognition of the beneficial effect on the land of this crop; such nitrogenous plants were to be encouraged. The special provision of five years' reduced rent for newly planted figs, vines and grafted olives, and ten years' for new olive trees may reflect a similar agricultural concern.

Suitable crops were one problem, labour another; and in their repeated attempts to secure a labour force the emperors fought a perpetual shortage of manpower. Unwilling to lose revenue, emperors were forced to seek inducements to keep the peasants on the land and to keep the land under cultivation. Egypt, as so often, provides the fullest evidence. Under the Julio-Claudians imperial tenants might be granted a protected status. With the label *apolusimoi* they appear to have escaped the control of the local tax collectors; liable still to poll-tax and other dues, they had the privilege of direct payment, thus avoiding the collection charges that others paid. In Philadelphia, for instance, under Claudius imperial tenants paid an annual poll-tax of forty drachmas, whilst other tenants paid forty drachmas, plus four drachmas four collection charges (Hanson, 1984, 113–18). Whether this privilege in regard to the payment of poll-tax is the same as the tax-free status (*ateleia*) of imperial *ousiai* which is recorded in several Julio-Claudian documents is not clear. Some if not all of these *ousiai* also provided protection from compulsory orders, and according to a lead tag which may once have hung around the neck of a draught animal, imperial land which had once belonged to Agrippina and Rutilia was *atelen kai anengareuton*, free from tax and compulsory orders (*SB* 4226 with Parassoglou, 1978, 18, 57).

Later emperors protected their tenants in different ways. Antoninus Pius ruled that, although lacking the right of deportation, imperial procurators were entitled to exclude from imperial estates any who might injure or harm imperial *coloni* (*Dig.* I. 19.3). Marcus Aurelius and Verus exempted *conductores* from civic obligations (*munera municipalia*) and this exemption was extended to *coloni Caesaris* under the Severans (*Dig.* L. 6.6.10–11; Millar, 1977, 180). That such rulings were not always observed is but a reflection of the realities of life.

Encouragement and inducement was one way of securing labour. Another, of course, was compulsion for which Egypt again provides evidence. The edict of Tiberius Julius Alexander in AD 68 specifically forbade the tying of farmers to cultivation – a sure sign of the practice. In the second century AD *epimerismos*, the assignment of poorer land to peasants from more profitable areas, became a regular practice.

The emperor made use of his estates in a variety of ways. The personal donations of the Julio-Claudians have already been discussed (p. 558 above) and in the fourth century Constantine's endowment of his church was on a scale unparalleled in earlier centuries. The extent of the emperor's estates was a measure of his prestige and pre-eminence. Rivals lost their land and competitors were curbed. The confiscations of a Nero (Tacitus, *Annales* 14. 65) or a Septimius Severus (SHA, *Severus* 12.3; *ILS* 1370; 1421–3; *CIL* XIV, 5344) may be understood in the context of prestige politics. In a more tangible way land well cultivated brought in rents and taxes or produce which might be used by the emperor for the purposes of imperial *liberalitas* – to feed the army or the people of Rome. Poor land might be brought under cultivation or imperial land used for the large-scale production of particular crops. And there were other uses. In Numidia in the second century AD the coincidence between imperial land and veteran settlement suggests the use of estates to subsidize the military commitments of the state. Alternatively it may reflect the employment of veterans to cultivate imperial land – a further sign of the perennial shortage of labour in this period (Fentress, 1979, 134–42 for details).

In the case of oil production, economic ends are linked with imperial *liberalitas*. The widespread extension of olive cultivation in Africa under Roman rule is well documented both from inscriptions and from remains on the ground. When after his seizure of both Rome and the Empire Septimius Severus, concerned to retain his power, instituted free oil for the people of Rome (*SHA Severus* 18.3 cf. 23.2) it was to Africa he looked for its supply. New officials appear in the *regiones* of Tripolis and Lepcis, from where Severus came. In *amphorae* produced locally, in Tripolitania and Bizacena, African oil produced on private estates (e.g. Peyras, 1975) was joined by that from the estates of the emperor newly enlarged by confiscation. Under Severus these areas flourished and Africa joined Bactica as a major supplier of Rome (Manacorda, 1976–7; 1977).

For oil, as for wine, the close study of the forms and stamps of the *amphorae* used in its transport fills out the evidence of the literary and epigraphical sources. Patterns of production begin to appear, the organization of the trade to surface (Garnsey, Hopkins and Whittaker, 1983, 27–35, 76–117, 145–62). For grain, however, the containers are lost; apart from mills and silos the archaeological evidence is scant. Yet imperial concern with the corn supply may be charted through the career records of officials both regular and extraordinary. The Trajanic official in Africa with responsibility for buying up corn to feed Rome (*curator frumenti comparandi in annonam urbis*) or the Severan procurator who looked after the provision of corn in the *tractus* of Numidia can be compared to the similar official with responsibility for buying up oil in the region of Tripolitania, a post which first occurs under Marcus Aurelius (Manacorda, 1976–7, 543–55). The evidence for such officials coincides with that for the location of imperial estates. Concentrated in Africa and Egypt, estates of the emperors are likely to have played a significant role in supplying both the capital and other large cities with the grain they required; they might similarly serve the needs of the army.

It would seem, therefore, that the character of imperial estates changed over time. The evidence suggests that they were originally regarded as personal possessions and acquired, disposed of and organized in a variety of *ad hoc* and sometimes haphazard ways. Increasingly, however, they appear to have become an important institution of the Empire. In particular, the apparent coincidence between areas of large imperial landholding and the production of key crops for the supply both of Rome and of the army suggests that the emperor as landholder played a central role in the economy of the Roman Empire.

CHAPTER 22

·THE·MONETARY·SYSTEM·

John Kent

The imperial coinage of Rome remains one of the major testimonies of the power of the Roman government in its hey-day, and to the strength of the ideal of Rome in its decline. It came into being quite unsystematically, gradually taking over the roles of its Republican precursor, and retaining for many years ambivalent, quasi-republican features.

'Imperatorial' coinages, issues struck in the provinces on behalf of generals, began in the first quarter of the first century BC. With Julius Caesar these field issues reached enormous proportions, and in 44 BC, he finally took the 'regal' step of placing his portrait on the coinage of Rome itself (pl. 22.1, 1). Much of this coinage was created to pay the swollen armies of the civil war; it therefore consisted primarily of silver *denarii*, accompanied by gold *aurei* for the higher ranks. Recognizable features of the true imperial coinage – gold and silver with the commander's name and effigy – had thus appeared. The systematic issue of related small change was still in the future; the Empire still relied upon local or regional coinages for this purpose. During the next hundred years, the 'local' bronze coinage of Rome came to supersede the mélange of colonial, municipal and tribal issues that inadequately supplied western needs. East of the Adriatic the tradition and supply of base local 'autonomous' currency was more firmly established. Not until the later third century AD did these local issues give way to an empire-wide imperial coinage. Eastern imperial coinage in silver, too, related in type and standard to the Greek tetradrachm, a practice which survived in Egypt down to 296. Most eastern issues, silver and bronze alike, were inscribed in Greek, but were assimilated to the Roman monetary system of *denarii* and *asses* (pl. 22.1, 2). Only the gold coins, which few will have handled, were fully 'Roman', 'imperial' and empire-wide from their inception.

In the early days of the Empire, the use of coin-types for the exposition of imperial ideals, aims and achievements was hesitant. Even the imperial effigy did not become an invariable feature of the imperial bronze coinage for a very long time; well into the second century, the tiny *quadrantes* lacked a portrait. The importance of the portrait is however clear enough, for on at least two occasions, the deaths of Caligula and of Geta, the *damnatio memoriae* following the fall of an emperor was associated with the attempted withdrawal or defacement of his coins.

The theoretical Roman imperial monetary system was inherited from the Republic, and may be briefly summarized here:

1 *aureus* = 25 *denarii*
1 *denarius* = 16 *asses*

In practice, things were more complicated. An inscription from Pergamum of the time of Hadrian deals with the 'buying' and 'selling' of *denarii* against *asses*, and shows that silver commanded a premium over bronze; exchange between the two metals necessitated the intervention of the moneychanger, and the payment of his commission. It is likely that gold in turn commanded a premium over silver. In times of instability or uncertainty in money supply, these exchange rates probably altered, as was known they did in the later Empire, and festivals and fairs may even have brought seasonal fluctuations, as was certainly the case in the middle ages. In the fourth century, the speculative movement of coins from one province to another was specifically prohibited, and analogies may be recognized in the trafficking in currencies so important in modern finance. In fifth-century Rome, *solidi* had to be sold to official *nummularii*, who made a living by receiving from the treasury slightly more coppers than they had given for each gold *solidus*. Coinage was therefore a commodity like any other. Its peculiar characteristic lay in being essentially a tool of government policy, being used to purchase or reward services to the state, and to exploit private resources through taxation. Its general use, by the state and others, gave coins an acceptability above that of their simple worth as ingots; this fiduciary value, too often abused by impoverished or unscrupulous governments, means that the use of coinage is inflationary by its very nature. Much of the history of the Roman imperial coinage is based on this fact.

The imperial coinage evolved in stages from the chaos of 'imperatorial' issues that followed Caesar's assassination. By 35 BC only Mark Antony and Octavian survived as contenders for power. After Actium, Octavian was in his own words *potitus rerum omnium*, and subsequent constitutional development merely formalized, refined and helped to make acceptable his absolute position. He took the name 'Augustus' at the start of 27 BC, and from that date his official personal name, 'Imperator Caesar Augustus', became an integral part of the style of almost every emperor. The reign of Augustus saw the introduction for the first time since the third century BC of a full range of denominations in all metals. Not all were struck simultaneously, but all were related metrologically and all were current together. The pattern established during the first half of his principate was to endure for almost three centuries.

During the first part of Augustus' reign, the 'local' character of his coinage remained marked. Gold and silver down to about 20 BC retained a very personal typology, with much allusion to his military triumphs of the Thirties and to the personal honours bestowed upon him. Thereafter, the emphasis changed. Reminiscences of Naulochus and Actium continued for another ten years, but were steadily and at length totally replaced by types relating to the succession. Particular emphasis was laid upon Gaius and Lucius Caesar (pl. 22.1, 3), and at the very last, Tiberius.

The location of the western imperial mints for the precious metals at this period is far from certain. Substantial series have without sufficient reason been attributed to Spain on the basis of similarities with Spanish civic bronze, while Rome was certainly used for about a decade between 20 and 10 BC. During Augustus' last twenty years the precious metal mint, guarded by a cohort, was at Lyon: according to Strabo, 'the rulers of Rome coin their money there, both silver and gold'. Bronze coinage in the

Gold (98% fine)		Silver (97% fine)		Brass (orichalcum)		Copper	
Aureus	7.85 g	Denarius	3.76 g	Sestertius	25.00 g	As	10.50 g
$\frac{1}{2}$ Aureus	3.93 g	Quinarius	1.88 g	Dupondius	12.00 g	Quadrans	3.15 g

The copper *semissis* was occasionally issued by later emperors.

		Theoretical relationships							
Aureus	1								
$\frac{1}{2}$ Aureus	2	1							
Denarius	25	$12\frac{1}{2}$	1						
Quinarius	50	25	2	1					
Sestertius	100	50	4	2	1				
Dupondius	200	100	8	4	2	1			
As	400	200	16	8	4	2	1		
Semissis	800	400	32	16	8	4	2	1	
Quandrans	1600	800	64	32	16	8	4	2	1

Figure 22.1 Comparative values of Roman coinage

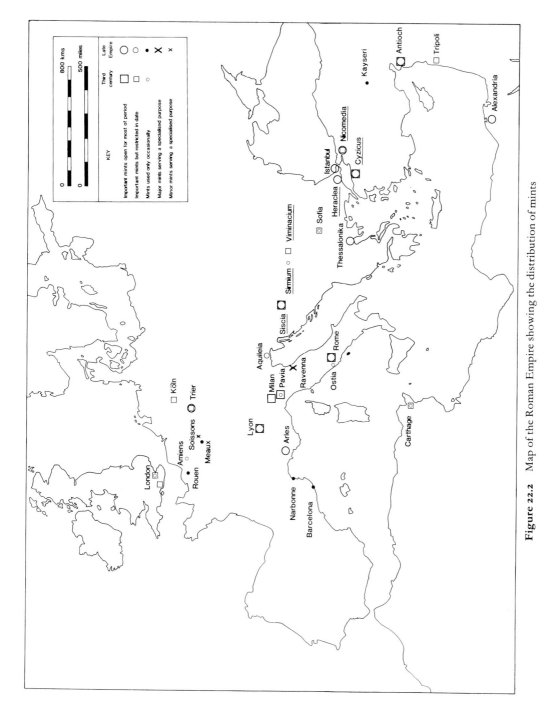

Figure 22.2 Map of the Roman Empire showing the distribution of mints

west was for long dependent on enormous issues of quasi-civic coins of Nîmes (Nemausus) (pl. 22.1, 4), probably though not certainly *asses*, which were sometimes halved. These were supplemented by brass and copper issues of Rome, bearing the names of the Roman moneyers. Their most notable feature was the letters SC, dominating one side; though this massive coinage came to circulate freely all over the west, the emphasis on the Decree of the Senate gives even these issues a somewhat 'civic', or at least regional look. Only *asses* bore Augustus' head, and some denominations did not even carry his name (pl. 22.1, 5). The *asses* of Nemausus were replaced in Gaul towards the end of the first century BC by more sophisticated issues from Lyon, whose provincial character is emphasized by the type of the altar of Rome and Augustus. 'Imperial' provincial bronze coinages of restricted currency were also struck in Asia, Syria and Egypt, but apart from the latter, made comparatively slight impact on the mass of local issues.

Much of the coinage of Augustus is poor in style and experimental, almost makeshift, in character. By the end of his reign, something like stability had been achieved, and this was reinforced by the well-known conservatism of Tiberius. The latter's issues show a tendency for types to be extremely conventional, and to remain unaltered for years on end; there is however a marked improvement in style and technique. Imperial coinage in the western half of the Empire was concentrated at two centres: Lyon, for gold and silver; Rome, for brass and copper. At Lyon, a single type, the enthroned figure of Pax, served for *aurei* and *denarii* throughout most of the reign; the ROM ET AVG bronze coinage, so important in Augustus' later years, virtually ceased. Brass and copper issues of Rome were not produced continuously; *asses* were struck in 16, *sestertii, dupondii* and *asses* in 23 and again in 35–37. As under Augustus, the presumptive successor, Tiberius' son Drusus the Younger, received much attention. There is however a developing use of a face of the coin for 'propaganda'. A specific illustration of the beneficence of the imperial government may be seen on the *sestertius* celebrating the emperor's generosity to the cities of Asia, ruined in the earthquake of 17. The personified virtues of Justice, Well-being, Mercy, Moderation, Good Fortune and Piety are representative of the many qualities of the emperor and his heir which future coinages were to exploit; the gods themselves were as yet absent, with the exception of the deified Augustus, founder of the dynasty (pl. 22.1, 8).

Succeeding reigns followed a similar pattern of regular, though much scarcer, gold and silver from Lyon, and sporadic brass and copper from Rome. Precious metal types of Gaius are almost exclusively dynastic, the uncontroversial commemoration of his dead father and mother, and of the deified Augustus. The lower denominations were more adventurous, including his dead brothers and living sisters. A massive issue of *asses* without imperial name celebrated Agrippa. The reason for its issue on so vast a scale is not known, particularly since Caligula is said to have disliked mention of his grandfather; its date however is certain.

Under Claudius, the precious metals and those of copper alloy retained their separate styles and techniques. It has been thought that the Lyon mint ceased to produce gold and silver, and was merged with that of Rome during Gaius' reign. Be this as it may, it is not until the end of Nero's reign that any real rapprochement between precious and base metal coins can be detected. Claudian gold and silver continue the dynastic theme, honouring the emperor's parents Drusus the Elder and Antonia, his wife Agrippina and adopted son Nero. Brass and copper coins follow the same pattern, adding the emperor's late brother Germanicus. Many types are personal to the emperor and his achievements, such as the *sestertius* SPES AVGVSTA – Claudius was born on 1 August, sacred to Spes – and the precious metal DE BRITANN, celebrating the successful invasion of Britain.

A severe contraction of the money-supply seems to be characteristic of the years following AD 40, and it is no doubt in this context that forgery and countermarking flourished. Particularly vulnerable to forgery were the common *dupondii* of Antonia and the *asses* of Agrippa and Claudius (pl. 22.1, 6, 7). There was also a large output of false *denarii*, silver-plated surfaces on base cores, which copied not only the rare current issues, but also the abundant coinages of Augustus and Tiberius. Countermarks were freely applied to official base-metal coins, particularly those circulating on frontiers. Occasionally their meaning is clear: thus, DVP on a *sestertius* or AS on a *dupondius* evidently halved the face value of coins so stamped; PROB presumably gave the coin a validity that it would otherwise have lacked. The effect of the numerous imperial initials (pl. 22.1, 8) and cyphers cannot be determined, but it is likely that they asserted the continued acceptability and value of coins that might otherwise have been refused or heavily discounted.

The reign of Nero marks the transition from the experimental days of the early Empire to a norm that prevailed down to the mid-third century. During his first ten years, the existing situation continued to deteriorate. No brass and copper was struck at Rome, and the gold mint, though its location at this date is disputed, produced a steadily decreasing output. The earliest of these coins are interesting for their association of Nero with his mother Agrippina, but her effigy was used only briefly.

In 64, Nero carried out a comprehensive and lasting reform of the coinage. Gold and silver coin was reduced in weight, the silver also in fineness. *Aurei* began to be produced in very large numbers, sufficient to dominate the currency for the next hundred years. *Denarii*, though more abundant than their predecessors, were not particularly numerous, and certainly failed to oust the large existing issues of the Republic and early Empire, which circulated down to the end of the first century. It is likely that the occasion of the reform was used to remove the coinage of precious metals from Lyon to Rome. The initial reform of the bronze coinages seems to have involved producing all denominations in brass (*orichalcum*), from the *sestertius* of *c.* 27.00 g down to the tiny *quadrans* of *c.* 2.00 g. To facilitate their recognition by the public, the new *dupondii, asses* and *semisses* received marks of value, ⊤⊤, ⊤ and S respectively. This elegant and logical arrangement soon reverted to the former bimetallic system, and the *dupondius* and *as*, now almost the same size once more, were distinguished by the addition of rays to Nero's head on the *dupondius* (pl. 22.1, 9). The Lyon mint continued active, producing a large output of brass and copper coins; its products can be recognized by a distinctive style, and the presence of a small globe at the point of truncation of the emperor's head. Artistry rises to considerable heights on issues from both mints, and there are many interesting topical and architectural types. The care lavished on the coinage may well reflect Nero's own artistic tastes.

Nero's fall in 68 was followed by a year and a half of confusion, during which three emperors rose and fell. The successive coinages of Galba, Otho and Vitellius were supplemented by ephemeral issues for Clodius Macer in Africa, and anonymous coinages in Gaul. The latter were, as Tacitus (*Histories* IV.36, 58) seems to imply, acceptable Roman donatives which usefully left open the identity of the donor at a time when the outcome of the civil wars seemed doubtful.

With the establishment of the Flavian dynasty, the coinage settled down to the norm which had evolved under Nero. Main issues were, naturally, in the name of the reigning emperor; subsidiary coinages naming other personages were of greater or lesser importance, at the emperor's will. We have already seen the extensive commemoration of ancestors, not necessarily deified, by the Julio-Claudians. Living and dead relatives such as wives, sons and daughters now found a regular place; sometimes, as in the case of Faustina I (pl. 22.1, 10), this was out of genuine affection, in other cases, such as Sabina, the unloved wife of Hadrian (pl. 22.1, 11), to emphasize her husband's insistence that she be given the honours due to her. Sons are displayed on the coinage to advertise the hope of dynastic stability. As sons of reigning emperors, they bore the name of Caesar, and only acquired the *praenomen* Imperator if they were adult and with military experience. Thus, Titus, son of Vespasian (pl. 22.1, 12), and Carinus and Numerian, sons of Carus, appear with the laurel wreath and title of an Imperator; Marcus Aurelius on the other hand, and the many little third-century boys without military command, lack the title Imperator, and appear bare-headed (pl. 22.1, 13). By the fourth century, Caesar had become a mere title, and its holders seem invariably to have received a salutation as Imperator on appointment. The style of an emperor's son, daughter or wife was now 'Nobilissimus, –a', an epithet that probably reached back to the second century (pl. 22.1, 14). Into the third century, acclamation by the army as Imperator was an authentic reaction to military success by the emperor or his legates. By the end of the century this in turn had become formalized, the emperor being acclaimed on his accession, and thereafter on the anniversaries of his *dies imperii*, the number of acclamations thus denoting the year of the reign. Coins attest the annual salutations down to the middle of the fifth century (pl. 22.1, 15), but it was a logical step for Justinian to abandon them for a plain regnal year.

Policy over reverse types and inscriptions varied. Some emperors, such as Trajan, proclaimed an unchanging message, SPQR OPTIMO PRINCIPI, using a vast range of designs to illustrate the imperial 'excellence' – scenes of conquest, buildings, figures of gods and personified virtues (pl. 22.2, 16, 17). By the second quarter of the third century, however, the constructive use of coinage to convey imperial policy was largely at an end, and reverses are mainly devoted to personifications of an emperor's ideal qualities. No doubt the specific choice was often topical; in the later Empire, there is some evidence for pageants in the Circus in Rome, perhaps a normal part of the *Pompa Circensis*, at which the crowd was edified by inscribed tableaux, dwelling upon military valour and imperial victory (Eunapius, frag. 78). The *pompa* described by Ovid for example included Victoria as well as gods. These occasions may well have provided opportunities for loyal demonstrations, and form an obvious link with coin design. A specifically Roman origin also goes far to account for the parochial character of some of the designs, which appear unintelligible and devoid of significance to anyone beyond the capital. In spite of the care taken over both obverses and reverse for a century and a half after Nero's reform, it has been doubted whether the 'message' of the imperial coinage reached, or was even directed to a particular public, or indeed served any purpose but the boosting of the imperial ego. Certainly the third-century emperors seem to have lost interest in the reverses, and as will be seen below, the late Empire had very different notions about coin design.

The effigy of an emperor was sacrosanct; to deface or reject it was treason, the repudiation of his authority; to accept an emperor's coin was, on the contrary, to acknowledge his rule. The importance of the name and likeness is a natural corollary. During the first three centuries of the Empire, much care was taken in all branches of representational art to create a consistent, characteristic and easily recognizable official portrait. It is impossible to say whether realism was the aim, but it is inevitable that likenesses will have flattered the vanity of their subjects, however strange it may seem that the portraits of Nero (pl. 22.1, 9) and Caracalla (pl. 22.2, 18), for example, should have pleased those emperors. Dio in fact tells us that the latter cultivated a ferocious expression, a habit that would have shocked Marcus Aurelius, from whom he took his official name. The late Empire, with its very different concept of the ruler, rejected anything more than the most basic concessions to individuality. Had 'market research', or perhaps the advent of emperors from lower strata of society, brought the realization that trouble taken over a characterized portrait and a carefully thought out reverse type was just a waste of time and effort? Between the accession of Vespasian and that of Severus, changes in the coinage were gradual at first, then accelerated during the last half of the second century. The silver content of the *denarius* steadily declined. From an approximate fineness of 90 per cent under Nero, the figure had sunk to 70 per cent by the death of Commodus. During the same period, the base metal coinage also suffered; the zinc content fell from around 20 per cent to 5 per cent, being largely replaced by lead. Lead was also used increasingly to adulterate the copper *asses*, and the result was to create a softer and more corrodible alloy.

The reigns of Severus and Caracalla marked a critical stage in the development of the coinage. The former reduced the silver content of the *denarius* to 50 per cent, without alteration to the *aureus*, thus fatally imperilling the relationship between the two denominations. Under Hadrian, the basic relationship of 25:1 will still have been valid, assuming gold to have been ten times more precious than silver, and Dio Cassius implies that it still existed under Marcus Aurelius. Sixty years later, the *denarius* had lost a third of its silver, while the *aureus* remained unchanged, and it is very likely that Severan *denarii* were, legally or otherwise, discounted in commerce. This is the most likely explanation for the creation in 215 by Caracalla of a new and large denomination of silver coin (pl. 22.2, 18, 19), alongside a slightly lighter *aureus*. It is generally called the 'antoninianus', borrowing the name from one of the innumerable imaginary coins cited by the *Scriptores Historiae Augustae*; it is a harmless convention, provided it is recognized as having no ancient authority. Its nominal value is harder to determine. With a weight around 5.20 g it may have restored a piece tariffed at twenty-five to the new *aureus*, and have been specifically designed for military pay. This solution may imply that the market discount on the *denarius* had been officially recognized, and that the latter now passed at the rate of, say, thirty-six to the *aureus*. It may also have been accepted that not all *denarii* were equal, and the moneychangers can be imagined having a busy and profitable time working out the market rates for the numerous surviving first- and second-century issues. Other solutions have been proposed. Some have seen the new coin (which is about half as heavy again as a *denarius*) as a grossly inflationary double *denarius*, others as a *denarius* and a half to a *denarius* of unchanged value. Both theories assume a greater control of market forces than seems possible for an ancient government, and the hoarding of antoniniani together with various qualities of *denarius* suggests that, at least in practice, natural relationships determined by silver content were in operation.

The antoninianus had a very distinctive appearance. Emperors' heads were radiate as on the *dupondius*, but a novel feature was the crescent moon behind the shoulders of empresses (pl. 22.2, 19). The new denomination was struck side by side with the *denarius* for about five years, and then was abruptly discontinued; presumably the requirements of military pay will have been met by increasing the output of *denarii*. Strangely, the crescent bust was not immediately adopted for the *dupondii* of empresses. This logical step was not taken until the reign of Severus Alexander, some years after the antoninianus had ceased to be struck.

However, the continuation without rival of the *denarius* through the reigns of Elagabalus, Alexander and Maximinus I proved to be its swan-song. Although it maintained a vestigial existence, in 238 it was replaced for all practical purposes by the antoninianus, revived at a lighter weight, and at an ever-decreasing silver fineness. By 250, debased antoniniani had sunk to the metallic equivalent of Severan *denarii* many of which were now overstruck by Decius (pl. 22.2, 20) and Gallus. Since 238, the weight of the *aureus* had fallen *pari passu* with the decline of the silver coin, and into the reign of Gallienus, when the smallest *aurei* weighed no more than 1.25 g. Corresponding antoniniani contained little more than 10 per cent silver. The virtual impracticability of striking smaller gold coins now led to the abandonment of the old stable relationships between gold and silver coin. Credit for recognizing and acting upon this necessity belongs to Postumus, rebel emperor of Gaul, but Gallienus speedily followed suit, and large gold coins became once more the rule. In the late Empire, the relationship of gold coin to the others varied according to government edict and market rates, and this system must have its origin at this time. Actual weight standards varied from reign to reign, and it is not possible to say what factors determined them.

Between its creation in 215 and the end of Gallienus' reign, the antoninianus had lost getting on for 95 per cent of its metallic worth, and no doubt also of its purchasing power. The results of this inflation were dramatic. A vast increase in production was necessary, if a monetary economy was to continue at the same level. This was tackled in two ways; first by the doubling of the establishment of the mint of Rome itself, second by the permanent setting up of provincial imperial mints. The mint of Rome was divided into six work units, called *officinae*; these are known from inscriptions, but are first indicated on the coinage in 248. The number was doubled under Gallienus, and the slap-dash style of his later coins illustrates the pressure under which they worked. From the reign of Gordian III, provincial mints increasingly supplemented the supply of coin. Antioch, Milan (pl. 22.2, 21), Trier and (?) Viminacium had all come into existence by 260; Lyon, Siscia and Cyzicus followed in the next decade. Of the old Greek imperial mints, only Alexandria survived, its tetradrachms (pl. 22.2, 26, 27) as poor-looking and base as the antoniniani.

The brass and copper currency, and the related city issues in the east, collapsed in the 260s. An antoninianus of Gallienus was the approximate metallic equivalent of an *as*, and there is no reason to believe that it was worth any more. After a brief attempt to upvalue the old bronze coinage in the early 260s, suggested by Postumus' restriking of old *sestertii* with his new radiate types (pl. 22.2, 22), the entire weight of the currency was borne by the debased antoniniani. Abundant as these coins are, it may be questioned whether output was really sufficient. And with each successive issue of the 260s being struck in an inferior alloy and poorer style, it is not surprising that forgery became rife (pl. 22.2, 23, 24); who could be sure how small, how base or how bad in style the latest official coins might be? Many of the counterfeits were illiterate and tiny, no more than a quarter of the size of the prototypes, and this is a reminder that, common as these coins appear to us, there were levels of society that handled coin so infrequently as to have but little idea of the aspect of an authentic imperial antoninianus. The fineness of coins was in any case very difficult to determine, since even the basest issues were so treated as to present a silvery surface.

A partial resolution of the crisis came under Aurelian. A bloody insurrection involving the moneyers in Rome doubtless marks a stage in the progress of that formidable emperor towards putting the empire to rights. There followed a reform, in which the mints of Rome, Pavia (newly transferred from Milan) and Siscia received dies with a common style, and in which the radiate base silver coin was increased in weight to about 4.25 g and was often marked XXI (pl. 22.2, 25). As the eastern mints were brought into the system, a Greek equivalent, KA, was used as an alternative. Analyses make it certain that this formula denotes twenty parts of alloy to one of silver. The coin was thus approximately metallically equal to two early imperial *asses*. It is often represented as a deflationary step, but this is unlikely. The contemporary alteration in the Alexandrian tetradrachm involved a reduction in weight of about 20 per cent (pl. 22.2, 26, 27), and this would suggest that in terms of *denarii* of account, the reformed radiate of Aurelian was tariffed at about double that of his first year, perhaps four or five *denarii*. The reform was intended to reintroduce other denominations, at least at Rome. A smaller laureate coin is not uncommon, and is sometimes inscribed vsv, perhaps an indication that it was worth half the piece with xxi. A larger laureate coin of some 8.0 g has no silver content at all, and may represent the *denarius* itself. Still larger bronze pieces are very rare and may be donative in purpose. The radiate alone survived Aurelian's reign in regular currency. Later reigns occasionally produce pieces inscribed ia or x et i, or with a double tier of rays from the emperor's head. These contain 10 per cent of silver and so were worth double the ordinary coin. They are very rare, and must have been exceedingly difficult for the general public to recognize.

Coinage remained outwardly stable for twenty years after Aurelian's reform. Inflation of the *denarius* was doubtless tackled by periodic revaluation of the actual coins, and the principal interest of these lies in the steady evolution of the system of mint-marks and in the exotic portraiture. Each mint still produced its own range of reverse types, and even the obverse portraits and titulature were very far from uniform. The imposition of explicit mint-marks was therefore not essential, and remained somewhat random down to the time of Diocletian's reform. However, many of the features that were later to become standard make their appearance; the initial of the mint, sometimes preceded by the formula sm (*Sacra Moneta*: 'Imperial Mint') and accompanied by a numeral denoting the *officina*; sometimes a symbol, such as wreath, star, palm-branch or crescent, or a letter or group of letters, defining particular issues. The tentative introduction of such marks between Philip and Gallienus (pl. 22.2, 21) has already been noted. In the time of the latter begins the use of unusual effigies and titulature. Gallienus introduces armed, helmeted and consular portraits, and remarkable legends: GALLIENAE AVGVSTAE (a 'hypercorrect' form of the vocative), GALLIENVM AVG SENATVS (recalling some honour bestowed by the Senate on its ruler). Postumus, his contemporary, brings in the facing bust, and also has himself represented as Hercules, with lion-skin and club. Armed and consular effigies enjoyed a particular vogue at the mints of Pavia (pl. 22.2, 25) and Siscia.

The mint of Serdica was fond of grandiose titulatures, derived from the language of acclamation:

BONO IMP C PROBO P F INVICT AVG
DEO ET DOMINO PROBO INVICTO AVG
PERPETVO IMP C M AVR PROBO AVG

Regularly associated with the armed effigies we find VIRTVS POSTVMI or FLORIANI or PROBI or CARI or DIOCLETIANI AVG, the personification of the emperor by his own valour. The personified qualities of the rulers gave rise naturally to association, if not identification, with particular gods. In the second century, it was still regarded as monstrous that Commodus should identify himself with Hercules (pl. 22.2, 28), and Caracalla specifically rejected such an identification. But when Postumus followed the example of Commodus, it seems to have passed without adverse comment, and from this time dates the systematic start of the use of quasi-divine *praenomina* as cult replacements for the regular *Imperator Caesar*, though they are little used on coins.

The mint-organization of the early Empire came under the emperor's *a rationibus*, who controlled a *familia monetalis* administered by a procurator. It is doubtful if the senatorial *tresviri* who figure on the 'local' Roman coinage of Augustus retained even a nominal connection with the mint. The *familia* was, as its name suggests, servile or semi-servile and hereditary in character. Inscriptions show that it included specialized workmen, and some of its operations were so disagreeable that criminals could be condemned to work there. As imperial mints were established in the provinces, this organization was set up in the favoured cities; the *monetarii* of Cyzicus are said to have formed one of the principal classes of the city. Supervision of the mints remained with the retitled *Rationalis Summae Rei* in the third and early fourth centuries, and passed to the *Sacrae Largitiones* when this was defined under the sons of Constantine.

The late imperial coinage begins suddenly, with a reform executed by Diocletian in and after 293. As befits a plan of that great organizer, the reform was of majestic scope, empire-wide, deeply thought out and seminal to all later developments. It swept away the last traces of local coinage, introduced fundamental changes in the denominations, style, typology and organization of the coinage, points which will be considered in turn. In the first place, it was a coinage stable in gold and for long periods also in silver. Diocletian stabilized the weight of the *aureus* at one-sixtieth of a pound, about 5.20 g, early in his reign; under him and his immediate successors coins were often marked with the Greek numeral $\equiv$ (60) to denote this. Constantine the Great reduced the standard of his gold coin to one-seventy-second of a pound, about 4.45 g, in 309, and his successive victories over rival emperors meant that by 324 it had become the standard for the whole empire. This coin which is known as the *solidus* (pl. 22.2, 29), originally a generic name for any stable gold piece, remained virtually inviolate until

579

the eleventh century. It was regular for imperial donatives to be made in *solidi* and this explains why they are so much more abundant than gold coins of the early Empire. From the beginning, half-*solidi* (*semisses*) were produced in small numbers, and, rather puzzlingly, three-eighths of *solidi*; the latter, which must have served some special purpose when introduced, gave way about 385 to the more logical thirds of *solidi* (*tremisses*). *Tremisses* became very much more abundant in the fifth century; perhaps, like third- and quarter-guineas in eighteenth-century England, they were useful in an age when little silver was struck. Gold coin in the late Empire was of a high standard of fineness, except for a brief period in the late 350s and early 360s, when control briefly slackened, and a few light-weight issues were struck by the usurper Magnentius.

Although third-century radiates were struck with a silvery surface, however base their alloy, no Roman 'silver' coin since the second century, apart from Carausius' emergency issues in Britain, had actually contained more silver than base metal. Diocletian revived a true silver coinage in 293. It reproduced the Neronian *denarius* in both weight and fineness (pl. 22.2, 30), but its name and valuation are unknown, and it ceased to be struck before 310. Down to 324 a motley series of more or less base pieces of widely varying weights and fineness, all struck by Constantine I, presents a picture of confusion. Thereafter, there was lasting improvement. Constantine revived the Diocletianic piece, and supplemented it by multiples. A new silver piece of about 2.00 g, was introduced *c.* 358 and was an immediate success. Metallically, it will have been worth about thirty to the *solidus*. Very large numbers of these coins were struck, particularly in the west, down to the beginning of the fifth century (pl. 22.2, 31), when the coinage of silver was drastically curtailed; it has been thought that cessation of the supply of the metal from Britain was a major contributory factor to this collapse of the silver currency. Nevertheless, there was no consequential debasement, and small issues continued to be made from time to time in both halves of the Empire.

The base metal coinage, which continued to be issued with a silvery surface down to the middle of the fourth century, is very complex, and its development can be no more than outlined. Diocletian retained a nominal 5 per cent silver alloy for a substantial coin of about 10.00 g, sometimes marked XXI (pl. 22.2, 32). This would be the approximate equivalent of five or six imperial *asses*, and is about the size of an old penny. It is often referred to conventionally as the '*follis*', but there is no ancient authority for this. It bears a laurelled head, the radiate effigy being kept for a piece of 4.00 g, but devoid of silver. It was short-lived, and may have been worth as little as one-tenth of the larger denomination. The fate of the older radiates is uncertain, but immediate devaluation and subsequent demonetization is probable. Values in terms of *denarii* of account are known, but inflation was still in full swing, and the *follis* might have started with a value of fifty and the radiate at five *denarii* as suggested for the latter by the Aphrodisias inscription. The latter shows that even within Diocletian's reign substantial revaluation of the more important denominations took place, no doubt as inflation rendered official tariffs impossible to sustain. Later rulers reverted to the earlier practice of debasing the coin, though revaluations must have continued. By 318 the *follis* had fallen to a piece of 3.5 g, with a silver content of little more than 1 per cent, worth metallically no more than a twentieth of the Diocletianic coin, though probably tariffed at many hundreds of *denarii*.

A reform in 318 was based on the correspondingly debased Diocletianic silver piece. This should have been tariffed at about five times the value of the *follis* of 296, and the maintenance of this differential in Constantine's dominions is suggested by base (25 per cent silver) pieces of 310–311, contemporary with *folles* containing a theoretical $2\frac{1}{2}$ per cent silver and weighing about 4.5 g. The *folles*, of whatever standard, seem to have co-existed happily; no doubt larger, finer issues were appropriately revalued. Now, all disappeared together, leaving only the new issues, perhaps called *centenionalis*, supplemented by considerable numbers of forgeries. The new currency period lasted for thirty years, with several reductions of weight and/or silver content. A complex reform in 348 created a three-denomination system, with coins varying in weight, fineness and type based on a *pecunia maiorina* of 5.2 g and $2\frac{1}{2}$ per cent silver. It was ruined by civil war and massive forgery, and in 354 Constantius II seems to have recognized that the day of the base billon coin was over. Apart from a brief revival under Julian, base metal coins were from now on made exclusively in a copper alloy, though they were so over-valued that it paid forgers to overstrike the old demonetized billon coins with false dies, rather than extract the silver. After Constantius II, every emperor seems to have had his own ideas as to what denominations were required. Other than Julian's 8.25 g coin containing 3 per cent silver, only modest coppers not exceeding about 5.2 g were struck (pl. 22.2, 33). By the end of the fourth century, coins in excess of 2.5 g were unusual, and the vast majority of fifth-century pieces were little 'nummi' weighing about 1.25 g, and valued at around 7000 to the *solidus* (pl. 22.2, 34). Such coinage continued in the east down to its total reform by Anastasius. In the west, it largely died out towards the end of the reign of Valentinian III, and was only sporadic thereafter. The movement towards the revival of larger coins operated in the west, too, where Rome under the Ostrogoths produced archaizing pieces of forty nummi in the name of Zeno.

Coins of the fourth century are with few exceptions neatly and competently made, in low relief, but well modelled. On the whole, the base metal coins are much smaller than early imperial pieces, though until the 350s their silver component must have given them an enhanced purchasing power, comparable at least with *dupondii* and *asses*. After 400, style and technique decline. Gold and silver pieces remain competent, though increasingly crude. Coppers, especially in the west, sink to a very low standard, and the student is often baffled by the large proportion of more or less illegible pieces. In Valentinian III's later years, his coppers cease to be fully literate (pl. 22.2, 34), and after about 460, eastern pieces show the same defect. Anastasius revived literacy at his reform, but seems to have been totally indifferent to the artistry of his money, an unfortunate characteristic that was to persist through much of the Byzantine coinage.

After a brief transition, the reform of Diocletian imparted to the coinage completely new concepts of typology. The image of the ruler underwent a total rethink. Instead of a 'realistic' portrait, a symbolic effigy was displayed with ever-decreasing emphasis on personal characteristics. Under the Tetrarchy, ruthlessness is the impression mainly conveyed, but Constantine I and his successors preferred to stress their aloof, quasi-divine position. To the end, the western emperors maintained, at least on their *solidi*, a vestigial distinction between sovereigns who were old, young, stout or lean; but in the east the effigy became totally stereotyped soon after 400, and did duty for all emperors of whatever age or size, a single bust even coming to serve for a pair of joint rulers. Obverse inscriptions rapidly became disappointingly terse and uninformative. After 350 there were few legends that differed significantly from the banal D(ominus) N(oster) CONSTANTIVS (for example) P(ius, later -erpetuus) F(elix) AVG(ustus). Reverses, too, underwent a profound change. In the first place, it was now usual for contemporary issues at all mints under a single emperor to exhibit the same types. Such concord some-times even extended to mints in east and west alike. Typology was little related to early imperial practice, and strictly topical reverses, such as those of Arles celebrating the arrival of the mint from Ostia, are very seldom seen. Pagan gods disappeared in the west in 318, in the east in 324; their place was filled by an already well established, but limited range of symbolic types, complemented by an appropriate inscription. The old-style personification, defined by its accompanying legend, appears in a very restricted manner, such as VICTORIA AVG, with a figure of Victory. Victory, almost the sole survivor of her class, though as common as ever, is more characteristically linked with such legends as SECVRITAS or SALVS REI PVBLICAE (pl. 22.2, 33). The emperor is no longer defined on the reverse by additional titles; rather, he is GLORIA ROMANORVM, RESTITVTOR or SPES REI PVBLICAE. His *vota*, the quinquennial expressions of loyalty, play an increas-ingly prominent role. Roma herself is as likely to be accompanied by VIRTVS ROMANORVM (pl. 22.2, 31) or CONCORDIA AVGGG as to be specifically named. The language of late Roman coins is thus limited, but allusive rather than descriptive. Its expressions are closely related to the extravagance of acclamation; the emperor as guarantor of *Salus Rei Publicae*, for example, goes back at least to Vespasian. With the fifth century comes the start of immobilization of types. Immobilization was never quite complete, but the drastic restriction of theme and treatment testifies to the limited interest of the later Romans in their coin-types.

The organization inherited from the third century continued at first without change. The reform of Diocletian involved the creation or relocation of some mints, the main-tenance of others. All indicated their identity by the minimum number of letters; gener-ally just initials e.g., R = Rome, L = Lyon, T = Ticinum (Pavia), S = Siscia, etc. Ambiguities were recognized and resolved, by the junior foundation expanding its signature e.g., LON = London, TR = Trier, SD = Serdica. Three mints began with the letter A; Antioch, the senior, used A for its gold, but ANT for billon, in distinction from AQ = Aquileia and ALE = Alexandria. In the course of the fourth century, mint-marks became ever more explicit, with elaborate series-marks (e.g. pl. 22.2, 33). During the fifth century, the mints of the western Empire rapidly fell away; Rome is the only significant producer of bronze after 420. In the east however, Heraclea is the only mint to disappear during the fifth century, and the late imperial system did not break down until the seventh century.

Down to 365–6, all coinage was produced at the ordinary public mints, though the peripatetic character of the imperial courts led inevitably to coinage in the precious metals tending to move from mint to mint with the court. Complaints about the corruption of the officials who brought coin to the Treasury from the provinces, and, it might have been added, evidence that the moneyers were surreptitiously adulterating the gold coin, led Valentinian I and Valens to concentrate the minting of gold, and probably silver, too, in a special mobile Treasury department, and to accept gold from the provinces only in the form of refined bars. These reforms led to the placing of the letters OB (*obryzum* = refined gold) and PS (*pusulatum* = refined silver) on coins made under this system. It is fortunate that after a brief period of anonymity, it was decided to reinstate the name of the appropriate city (pl. 22.2, 29). But far into the Byzantine period the *moneta auri* in a capital city such as Constantinople with its Treasury staff, remained quite separate from the *moneta publica* with its hereditary and semi-servile workers.

It has often been said that the Roman Empire 'fell' in a limited sense only, and the coinage well illustrates this theme. Imitative coins in the name of Honorius and even bearing the putative mint-mark of Ravenna, were being produced by the Visigoths in south-western Gaul in the emperor's own life-time. When at length the Roman army of Italy turned itself into a kingdom in 476 and the last western emperor died in 480, there remained the eastern emperor as an acceptable symbol of unity. Gold coinage was in his name alone well into the sixth century, and only as the fifth drew to its close did Vandals, Goths and Burgundians venture to place their names on the silver and bronze. The Roman Empire indeed lived on in its coins, and in the shilling and penny, Germanic translations of *solidus* and *denarius*, can be said not to be quite extinct yet.

22.1 Coins of the Republic and Empire discussed in the text (pp. 568–74)

22.2 Coins of the Empire discussed in the text (pp. 574–83)

CHAPTER 23

·INDUSTRIAL·GROWTH·

W. H. Manning

In modern usage there is a clear distinction between craft and industry. Industry implies the mechanical mass production of a limited range of standardized products, often by semi-skilled workmen, whereas a craft involves the individual production of a range of related goods by a skilled worker using relatively few mechanical aids. In the Roman world there was no such distinction and industry in the modern sense scarcely existed, the nearest approach to it being concentrations of workshops, some of which might employ several score of workmen, producing very similar goods; and it is in this rather loose sense that the term is used in this chapter.

The Roman Empire was not a monolithic unit with a uniform culture. It had been formed by the fusion of many states and tribes with cultural heritages of great diversity. Those in the eastern Mediterranean had a long and complex history which had culminated in the relative cultural unity of the hellenistic period. In matters of craft and technology Rome had little to teach and much to learn from them. What the Roman government was able to do, however, was to bring prolonged peace and a reasonably just administration which resulted in a considerable rise in both private and public wealth, as well as a more *laissez faire* approach to economic matters which led to the ending of most of the royal monopolies of the hellenistic kingdoms. It would be difficult to argue that the great prosperity of this area, which reached its apogee in the late first and second centuries AD, did not find its reflection in a corresponding growth in the crafts and trades which together formed ancient industry. The lavish expenditure on public works alone would have given employment to thousands of craftsmen and put very large sums of money into circulation within the cities. Under such conditions the industries which serviced these communities flourished in a way rarely seen before; for while there had been periods of prosperity in earlier centuries they had tended to be more localized whereas now a whole range of provinces benefitted.

The normal form of industry in these areas, and in Italy and the older Graeco-Roman areas of the western Mediterranean, was very uniform. The basic units were almost all small; even the largest factories rarely employed more than a few score of men, and their main, indeed usually their only, market was the local one. The more necessary an article was for the life of the masses the greater would be the demand for it and the higher the likelihood that it would be made locally; thus clothing was normally produced in the home, and every village might have a baker, blacksmith and potter. On the other hand it would have been necessary for the villager to have to go to town or to a fair, or be visited by a peddlar, if he wanted something which was less basic. But a large city, and there were many around the Mediterranean, would have supported almost all the industries needed to satisfy its own requirements, although much of the raw materials must have been imported. The manufactured goods imported into these cities, and through them into the smaller communities around them, varied considerably and were by no means confined to the more luxurious items. No doubt all the usual factors of reputation, prestige and simple snobbery were involved in determining why imported goods were preferred to essentially similar ones produced locally, but to obtain a share of this market was one of the few ways in which an industry could hope to expand beyond its local area, although in fact few actually did so. In reality many of the factors which made such an expansion possible were outside the control of the producers themselves, most notably, perhaps, their position on the existing trade networks, and in particular on those carrying the agricultural produce which formed the major part of all ancient long distance trade. For most industries, even in the wealthier provinces, when expansion came it was as a consequence of the rising prosperity of the early Empire which meant that more people could afford to buy more of their products. When growth occurred in an industry it appears to have taken the form of an increase in the numbers of productive units rather than a substantial enlargement of individual firms. Very large industrial concerns were extremely rare in the Roman world.

By contrast the history and culture of the European provinces were quite different. If Rome could bring little that was new in the manufacturing field to the hellenistic world she had much to offer the peoples of western Europe. Technologically Rome was not a great deal more advanced than many of the native cultures of those areas, although the tendency was for the general level of technology to fall as one moved farther from the Mediterranean. Britain, in particular, was surprisingly retarded in some ways; the potter's wheel had only been introduced at the end of the first century BC although it had been in use in Gaul for the previous four centuries, and the potter's kiln had arrived even later. Similarly the shaft furnace used in the classical world for the smelting of metals, first appeared in Britain at about the time of the Roman conquest. But in other crafts, such as fine metalworking which were related to the requirements of aristocratic patrons, the native craftsmen were quite as competent as their Roman counterparts.

With the incorporation of these areas into the Empire there came a series of fundamentally important changes. Some were certainly technological, but upon the whole these were probably the least significant, and many of the more important operated on industry indirectly. First there was the *pax Romana*, not universal and not unbroken, but sufficiently so to convert a normal condition of war into one of peace; the consequences of this alone on the pattern of trade and the growth of population and markets will have been profound. Similarly what had been a series of divided tribes were now united into single provinces, a fact which over a period of time must have destroyed many of the older cultural barriers to the movement of goods and craftsmen. Although large areas of Iron Age Europe had shared a basically common culture they were divided politically into a large number of independent tribes often at war with their neighbours. Their economies were basically agricultural, and although crafts flourished many were geared to the demands of the tribal aristocracies rather than any larger market. Most of the population lived in the countryside and such concentrations as occurred in the hillforts and *oppida* were small by comparison with the great cities of the Mediterranean world, and the markets which they created will have been correspondingly small. All of the more advanced areas, including the south of Britain, had developed some form of monetary economy, but in many areas this did not involve the widespread use of low value copper coins and without them the system was incapable of coping with the small transactions of everyday life. The introduction of the Roman monetary system (Chapter 22) which had a graduated coinage suitable for almost every transaction, will have had a revolutionary effect on the economy, the more so as it appeared together with a developed, if by our standards primitive, banking system with facilities for loans. Finally, the acceptance of all of this was no doubt encouraged by the imposition of the elaborate system of Roman taxation.

The rapid development of an extensive network of roads, particularly necessary for the short distance movement of raw materials and manufactured goods, will have been of great importance, and it is probable that the facilities for river traffic will also have been improved (Chapter 26). Finally it should not be forgotten that the Roman government deliberately encouraged the romanization of the tribal aristocracies, as Tacitus' life of Agricola makes clear. The acceptance of such a concept would have involved not only wearing a *toga* and taking baths, but of an appreciation of the advantages of urban life, and of the idea that it was the duty of the wealthy citizens of a city or state to contribute to the public good by spending part of their fortune on public works. Taken together these various factors totally changed the economic face of western Europe in a remarkably short time. In particular they led to the appearance of true cities which will have provided the markets necessary for the development and growth of industry.

As observed above, the normal pattern of trade and industry was one of local needs being satisfied by local production, and any city, together with the area around it, will have provided the market necessary for the development of industry. In the main these industries were concerned with the basic necessities of life, such as the processing of food, including milling and baking; the production of clothing, weaving, fulling and dyeing, and the tanning and working of leather; the manufacture of domestic utensils, equipment and tools, potters, and smiths working with silver, copper alloys and iron; and all of those many trades which formed the building industry, limeburners, brickmakers, plumbers, carpenters and so forth. In those provinces which had a long history of urban life, particularly in the eastern Empire, such industries already existed, and their growth probably did little more than reflect the increasing population and wealth of the earlier centuries of the imperial period, but in most of the western provinces many were new introductions. In Britain, northern Gaul and Germany, as well as in most of the Danube provinces there was little or no tradition of building in stone or brick and much of the construction industry will have been a fresh development, while many existing industries, such as the pottery industry in Britain, saw a massive expansion to cope with the new demand.

It was probably in the interim period between the development of a taste for romanized products but before the local industries had developed the capacity to satisfy it, that the established producers in the older provinces had their greatest chance to establish export markets. The industries which were best placed to take advantage of this were those in adjacent provinces, or if more distant, those able to move their products to the new markets by water. The products most likely to achieve a firm place in those markets were mainly in the middle price range, glass, fine pottery, copper-alloy vessels and other metalwork, and fine cloth. Coarse pottery, iron tools and other cheap goods were usually produced locally, although in some cases, such as pottery lamps, foreign exporters were sometimes able to obtain a share of the market. Inevitably the success of these imports led to local imitations, as happened in Britain with the glass industry which had a firm but scarcely distinguished place in the local economy, and with samian ware which totally failed to establish itself.

Although the cities were largely self-sufficient the Roman world contained one major group for which this was only partially true, namely the army. When the vast area of the Empire is considered, the size of its army was surprisingly small, perhaps some 350,000 men in the second century AD. Its economic effect, however, was considerable, partly because it was not distributed evenly through all the provinces but concentrated in a few key ones, usually near the frontiers. A Roman legionary fortress with its associated settlement formed a substantial market, and while most of its basic requirements will have been satisfied by the industries which grew up around it, it was still a huge potential market for exporting industries. Much of the basic military equipment was supplied by the state either from its own factories or by bulk purchase, although the soldier probably had to pay for it, but other equipment of a more personal nature may have been left to individual choice. Obtaining a state contract must have been the making of many firms in the Roman world; indeed it may have been sufficient to have established some provincial industries which had the advantage of being closer to the military bases than were the older industries of Italy. This factor will have applied most fully in the western provinces where the armies lay on the frontiers far from the Mediterranean; in the east they were more often associated with existing cities which could supply their needs. In the west too, most of the fortresses were situated on navigable rivers; a policy probably intended to make provisioning easier but a great bonus for any industry wishing to break into the military market or gain a military contract. One result was that some of the contractors were surprisingly far from the armies which they supplied. Thus much of the coarse pottery used on Hadrian's Wall came over four hundred miles by sea from southern Dorset, an arrangement which led to substantial growth in the pottery industry there.

The question which arises is why were some industries able to build up a considerable export market while others, producing very similar goods, failed to do so? To find the answer attention must be turned to what was undoubtedly the largest of all the productive industries of antiquity, namely agriculture. Not only did this employ the vast majority of the working population and absorb the major part of all investment, but it was one of the few areas of commerce which was socially acceptable to the Roman patrician and probably by custom and imitation to many of the native provincial aristocracies as well, in whose hands the greater part of the wealth of the ancient world was concentrated. Partly because agriculture was a suitable occupation for a gentleman there existed a large body of specialist literature which leaves little doubt that the Roman agriculturalist regarded farming as a commercial enterprise. Indeed no nineteenth-century industrialist could have expressed a harsher view of the need to obtain a sufficient return on investment than Cato. The impression given by the literature is fully confirmed by the archaeological evidence. The facilities of the Boscoreale villa near Pompeii (fig. 23.1), which perished in the eruption of AD 79, included storage vats for 104,550 l (23,000 gal.) of wine and 18,180 l (4,000 gal.) of olive oil. This villa cannot have been the centre of a very large estate, for land prices on the lower slopes of Vesuvius were probably too valuable for that, but it is known that elsewhere in Italy and in many of the other provinces there existed *latifundia*, great estates run as productive units, where the facilities for processing the produce will have been on a correspondingly large scale.

The great cities of the Roman world had an almost insatiable appetite for the basic agricultural products of their time: grain, olive oil and wine. In many cases the quantities needed were so great that they could not be provided locally and had to be brought from distant sources along well-defined trade routes. A study of the inscriptions left by the *mercatores* and *negotiatores* who handled the bulk trade of the Empire makes it clear that most were concerned with foodstuffs, metals and timber, cloth and pottery. The Mediterranean in particular was criss-crossed by sea routes along which grain, oil and wine were carried from the producing countries – Asia, Syria, Egypt, Africa, Spain

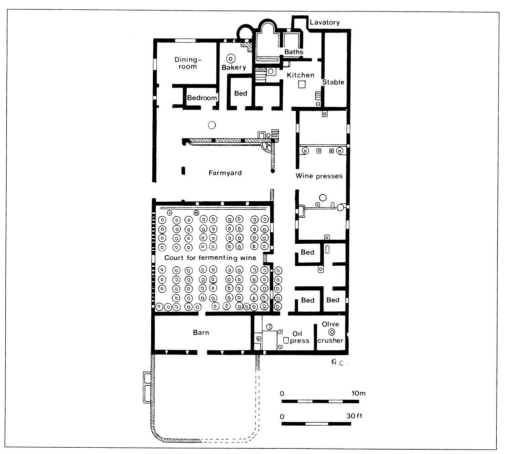

Figure 23.1 Plan of the villa at Boscoreale (*after Grant*)

and Gaul – to the consuming cities, and above all to Rome. This is not the point for a detailed discussion of this commerce (Chapter 25) but there is no doubt that it dominated Roman trading patterns and that all other forms of long distance commerce were of minor importance by comparison (Chapter 26). Lucian, on seeing one of the great grain freighters which plied between Alexandria and Italy, in the harbour of Athens, where it had been driven by storms, was told that it carried enough grain to feed the whole of that city for a year; and although this was a considerable exaggeration, the dimensions which he gives for it indicate that it could have carried over a thousand tons of grain. Such ships carried the exports of Egypt as supercargo, and although Strabo noted that they carried little on their return journey from Pozzuoli, this is a comparative statement, for all the workshops of Capua would not have produced sufficient bronze vessels to have filled one such freighter let alone a fleet of them. The Alexandria to Pozzuoli or Ostia route may have been the most important but it was unique only in the volume of trade which it carried, and almost all of the major maritime cities of the Mediterranean were either exporters or importers of foodstuffs, often on a very considerable scale. The existence of this traffic offered an immense advantage to the manufacturers of the ports involved for products which would never have formed a viable cargo on their own could be carried as supercargo by vessels laden with grain or oil. Other prime exports which probably formed a base on which small industries could build their own export trade included metals and timber. It is noticeable, for example, that the celebrated fish-sauce (*garum*) industry of Cartagena exported its dubious product through the port which handled the output of one of the largest and richest of all the Spanish mining areas.

An industry which had to rely on overland transport for the movement of its products, even for quite short distances, was placed at an immense disadvantage by the very high cost of such transport. All transport was relatively expensive, but road transport was easily the most expensive of all, and sea transport the cheapest. Cato, writing in the mid-second century BC, gives two examples which make the cost of moving heavy goods overland very clear. The first concerns the transport of an olive press bought at Suessa, some 40 km (25 miles) from his estate, for a total of 425 *sesterces*. Fetching it, however, took an ox-cart and six men, with six boys to drive the oxen, no less than six days, at a cost of 72 *sesterces*, or some 17 per cent of the original price of the mill. Another press, bought this time at Pompeii 120 km (75 miles) from his estate, for 384 *sesterces* cost no less than 280 *sesterces*, or 73 per cent of its initial cost, to transport to his farm. There is no information on the cost of sea transport at this time but Diocletian's Price Edict of AD 301 provides figures for both sea and land transport. Using these, and the calculations of A. H. M. Jones and R. Duncan-Jones, the haulage of a 550 kg (1,200 lb) waggon load of wheat cost 20 *denarii* per Roman mile, which, if the price of wheat quoted in the Edict is used would have increased its final cost by about 33 per cent for every 100 Roman miles it was carried. By contrast the cost of moving the same load of grain the 1,250 miles from Alexandria to Rome was 960 *denarii* or 76.8 *denarii* per 100 Roman miles which would raise the cost of the grain by 1.3 per cent for every 100 Roman miles it was carried. This figure might be thought abnormally low, and may indeed reflect the great size of the freighters used on that particular run, but other prices quoted for sea carriage, such as 72 *denarii* for transporting a similar quantity of grain from Alexandria to Byzantium, or 1560 *denarii* from Syria to Lusitania are not much higher. River transport, which was of great importance in the Roman world, is not mentioned in the Edict but Duncan-Jones quotes figures from Egypt in the first century AD which give an increase of *c.* 6.4 per cent per 100 Roman miles, making it more expensive than sea transport but less than one-fifth of the comparable charge for carriage in an ox-waggon. None of these figures should be taken too literally; they must have varied with the nature of the goods, the type of voyage and the period, but the general relative costs are valid and make the advantages of carriage by water quite obvious.

This is almost certainly one of the reasons why the Roman army so often sited its major bases on navigable rivers such as the Rhine and Danube, and it is noticeable that many of the great cities of the Empire lay by the sea: Alexandria, Caesarea, Tyre, Sidon, Ephesus, Carthage, Syracuse, Pozzuoli, Cartagena, Cadiz, Narbonne, and Marseilles, while many others stood on navigable rivers which gave direct access to the sea and were capable of receiving sea-going vessels: Antioch, Cologne, Lyon, Arles and London all being obvious examples. Still more lay only a few short miles from the coast, as with Pergamum and Rome itself, which had the advantage of having a river capable of carrying barges if not larger vessels from its port at Ostia. Not all of these developed a major exporting industry, Rome and Antioch, for example, remained essentially consumers rather than exporters, but many of the others did so, in some cases on a very large scale. When this was the case there can be little doubt that one of the key factors, probably often the key factor, was the relative cheapness with which raw materials could reach them and their products be shipped out. Indeed it is debatable whether an export trade in manufactured goods usually developed unless there was also a considerable trade in raw materials and in particular in agricultural produce. Clearly there were exceptions, especially among the luxury items, but as a generalization it is true and presumably indicates that the total trade in manufactured goods from any one area was rarely enough to generate a viable trading pattern of its own. The corollary is that certain cities became major exporters largely because they had access to water transport and were centres for the bulk movement of agricultural products, and that without adequate access to such transport industry was usually incapable of expanding beyond its local markets. But it would be unwise to assume that most of these exporting industries were of great size, or that their exports formed a dominant part of the economy of their area, for in most cases this is unlikely to have been the case. Rather the local market was the basis of their success and what was sold elsewhere was a desirable bonus. Obviously any such generalization is not universally true. The specialized pottery industries of Arretium and later of Gaul produced on a scale which must have made their local sales of minor importance, and the same was certainly true of the mining areas of the Empire, particularly of Spain, although here for rather different reasons.

The production of metals is probably the great exception to most of these generalizations, for, apart from iron which is a widely distributed metal, workable deposits of ores are found only in restricted areas. Although mining is discussed in detail elsewhere in this work (Chapter 24), it must be noted here that if agriculture is excepted, it was almost certainly the most concentrated and largest of all the industries of the ancient world. Strabo writing at the beginning of the first century AD, tells us that some 40,000 men were employed in the silver mines at Cartagena in Spain, and this was only one of several large mining areas in that province. Similarly the mining regulations from the Vipasca (Aljustrel) region of Portugal indicate a degree of organization which can only have applied to a massive industrial enterprise, although they also make it clear that the mines themselves were divided up among a number of lessees. In the Roman period, and for many centuries after, it was normal for the ores to be smelted as close as possible to the mine in order to reduce the weight to be transported. But smelting on a large scale requires equally large quantities of charcoal, the production of which is notoriously destructive of timber. In at least one case, the Island of Elba which was famous for its iron mines, the early exhaustion of the timber on the island itself necessitated transporting the ore to Populonia on the Italian mainland for smelting. The blooms produced at Populonia, aptly described by Diodorus as being 'like large sponges', were then taken by sea to the smiths of Pozzuoli from whence the finished tools and weapons were exported, in Diodorus's words again, to 'every port in the world'. In both cases the movement of the raw material was by sea, as was the export of the finished products; had Pozzuoli not been a major port this export industry would probably not have existed.

Quarrying, although allied to mining in its techniques, was generally a far more localized industry. Where suitable stone was easily available it was used, but it is heavy and the cost of haulage was high even when it could be moved by water, which limited the distances it was carried. But there were factors which overrode this simple economic principle, in particular the desire for private and public display which demanded that important buildings should be constructed of stone and decorated with fine stone veneers and sculpture (pl. 23.4); the more exotic the stone, the more prestige it carried. The result was that certain desirable and fashionable stones were quarried on an enormous scale and moved over great distances. Even the *basilica* of such a minor provincial town as Silchester could boast veneers not only of Purbeck marble but also of Italian and Pyrenean marble. But while no doubt a source of local pride this achievement becomes insignificant when compared with the feats of conspicuous display seen in some of the Mediterranean cities, and in particular in Rome itself. To quote a single example, the sixteen columns of the porch of the Pantheon, each weighing about sixty tons, came from Egypt, and these were by no means the largest blocks produced by the quarries of that country in the Roman period (pl. 23.4). Feats such as this may have been immensely impressive but they contributed little to the real growth of the stone-working industries which was brought about by the thousands of more modest buildings which required stone for their fabric and decoration. When it is remembered that in most of the western provinces there was no pre-Roman tradition of building in mortared stone, then the great expansion of these industries becomes obvious. Quarries which were either on the sea, as at Thasos and Proconnesus, or were close to it as in Thessaly or on the Isle of Purbeck, were much appreciated as they reduced the distance that the stone had to be hauled overland; but if the stone was desirable enough it was likely to be quarried no matter where it was found. Most of the quarries producing the finer stones were imperial property but many others were private enterprises. In either case their products were usually exported in standardized blocks, as ready-cut veneers or roughed-out sculpture, all intended to reduce the cost of transport by eliminating unnecessary weight. This is the reason for the unfinished sarcophagi which are found in areas far from the source of their stone. The quarryman, the mason and the sculptor had all been important trades before the Roman period but their expansion under the Empire was dramatic, especially in the first few centuries of the Christian era when costly and magnificent buildings became a matter of civic pride, and decorative sculpture and statuary were used on a scale unparalleled before. The sheer quantity of marble statuary which still survives from this period shows that its production was an industry, even if the individual workshops were probably relatively small.

As the mining of metals was controlled by the distribution of the ores rather than of the markets, it is not surprising that large-scale manufacturing industries were not sited near the mines themselves. Instead the smelted metals were taken to the industries. All cities appear to have received the metals necessary for their local requirements, but large-scale metal-working industries tended to develop in certain favoured areas which had good access both to the raw materials and the markets. Two examples may suffice to make this point. In the late Republic and early Empire the most important area for the manufacture of copper alloy vessels was Capua. The scale of this industry may be debated but the wide distribution of its products shows its success. Capua lay only a relatively short distance from what was then the greatest of the Italian ports, Pozzuoli, itself a major centre for the production of iron tools and implements, as mentioned above. In both cases there can be no doubt that it was accessibility to sea transport, for bringing in the raw materials and carrying away the finished goods, which was the key to their success in more distant markets, and that this success was firmly based on the large local market of Campania which was one of the wealthiest and most populous regions of Italy. The second example comes from the north-east of Italy. The city of Aquileia lies at the head of the Adriatic where the roads across the mountains from Noricum reached the sea. In imperial times it became one of the major industrial centres of Italy with much of its industry dependent on iron from the mines of Noricum less than 160 km (100 miles) north. Norican iron was regarded as second only to the legendary Seric iron, which was actually pure steel and imported at great expense from India, and it too was a form of steel. Nor was iron the only metal worked at Aquileia for at the other end of the scale the city was famous for its silver ware, as well as having an important and flourishing glass industry, both catering for the export market to the Danubian provinces.

Metalwork in general was among the most widely traded of manufactured products, although with the exception of a few unusual areas such as Elba and Noricum, iron was probably too widely found to be carried very far. For other metals Spain was the *El Dorado* of the Roman period, producing gold, silver, copper, tin, lead and iron in great quantities. An appreciable amount no doubt was used in that province but the greater part was exported to provide the raw materials for the metal industries of the western Mediterranean area and even further afield. The success of Capua and other cities in Campania in producing copper alloy vessels is well known, but the same area was probably equally successful in the production of silver ware. Hoards such as those from the Boscoreale villa or the House of the Menander in Pompeii, both containing over one hundred pieces, show how widely silver plate was in use among the upper middle classes of the period. Syria, Alexandria and Italy were especially famous for their silver ware, but all major cities will have had their silver-smiths. The production of silver plate is one of the few areas where there is reasonably firm evidence for the development of the factory system. Most pieces no doubt, were produced in small workshops, probably often using material provided by the customer himself, but casual comments by Pliny the Elder and inscriptions from Rome, which was a centre of silver-smithing, suggest that the larger scale, a factory system was not uncommon, with skilled craftsmen specializing in particular aspects of the work. Thus men are found, usually either freed-men or slaves, who are referred to as casters, embossers, engravers, gilders and polishers, suggesting a degree of specialization more consistent with the factory system than the small workshop (pl. 23.5). And what applied to silver plate must have applied with equal force to the bronze industry.

Another industry which has left sufficient traces to make some comments on its structure and growth was that producing fine pottery. The knowledge of it is based mainly on archaeological evidence and is probably fullest for the red-gloss wares produced from the Augustan period onwards, first in Italy at Arrezzo (Arretium) and then successively in southern, central and eastern Gaul. The sheer quantity of this pottery found throughout the Roman world and far beyond it indicates the success of these industries but says relatively little about their structure. The location of the production sites was partly controlled by sources of suitable clays, but Arrezzo had been a major industrial centre for centuries before this industry became important (pl. 23.6). Other parts of Italy, including Pozzuoli, produced essentially similar wares, and the arretine products were not inherently better than their rivals, some of which were exported in considerable quantities. However, the success of the arretine industry was on such an immense scale as to suggest that it owed much of that success to its production and marketing techniques. The industry seems to have been divided among a number of separate firms usually owned by Roman citizens, apparently commonly of servile origin, with the work being done by slaves. The largest number known are the fifty-eight of P. Cornelius; but these are the named men who worked on the actual production of the pots and they must have been supported by a large number of anonymous slaves who did the more menial tasks, such as preparing the clay or stoking the furnaces. If allowance is made for them the larger producers may have employed upwards of one hundred people, although the average establishment was probably smaller. Within each firm there were specialists producing the moulds in which the pots were made, the *poincons* with which these moulds were decorated, and the pots themselves. Although arretine was probably the largest of the Italian pottery exporting industries it was not the only one. The potters ACO and SARIUS working in northern Italy under Augustus were exporting fine beakers and bowls. ACO also began production at Lyon in Gaul, where pottery very similar to that produced at Arrezzo was made early in the Augustan period. Whether this reflects the founding of branches by the main arretine firms, or an attempt to found a rival industry using craftsmen from Arrezzo cannot be decided, but clearly the reason was the increasing importance of the Gallic market. The great intrinsic wealth of Gaul was becoming increasingly obvious as the first century BC drew to its close, and its attractiveness as a market was made even greater by the large army active in Germany as Augustus' plans for the conquest of that country progressed. The choice of Lyon for these industries was logical and indicates what the Roman entrepreneur regarded as the main requirements for the creation of a successful new industry – excellent communications by road, access to most parts of Gaul and the Mediterranean by water, and a sound home market provided by the rapidly growing capital of Gallia Lugudunensis, which was soon to become the richest city in all of Gaul. If, as seems highly probable, this marks a deliberate attempt by arretine manufacturers, who were then hardly threatened by any competition, to establish branches closer to their developing markets, it indicates a dynamic approach which suggests that the decline later seen in the arretine industry, and many others in Italy, may be as much the result of their own success in establishing branches as a simple failure to adjust to provincial competition. In saying this a concerted effort by 'the arretine industry' must not be envisaged. Such industries consisted of many firms, some of which were expansionist no doubt, while others were not. The survivors were those who were the most dynamic and adapted most rapidly to changing circumstances. Lyon itself turned out to be but a short and passing phase in the development of the Gallic samian-ware industry, but it was a significant one. More successful was the industry producing fine cups and beakers which retained an important share of the markets of Gaul, Germany and Britain until late in the first century AD.

A somewhat similar situation appears to be detectable in the glass industry. In the hellenistic period the main production centres had been on the Syrian coast and in Egypt, particularly at Alexandria. Undoubtedly one of the reasons for the industry being in those areas was the availability of the fine sand and natron, or alternatively plant ash, necessary for the production of the glass, but probably more important was the fact that they were also the largest markets in the hellenistic world. Until the end of the first millennium BC almost all glass vessels were produced either by dipping a core into molten glass, by casting, or by fusing multicoloured rods to form the highly prized mosaic glass; all time-consuming and relatively expensive techniques. In the first century BC however, a complete revolution took place in the industry which led to its rapid expansion both in the areas of production and in the quantity produced. The cause of this was the invention of glass-blowing by Syrian workers, a method of production which so increased the speed with which glass vessels could be made as dramatically to reduce their cost. Overnight what had been a product for the luxury market became available to all, and the only problem in building up a mass market was that the cost of transporting the fragile product might make its price too high. In the event this was largely overcome by the producers moving closer to their markets, and in particular to Italy. Such a movement was no new thing. It must have been the method by which the Alexandrian industry had itself been founded, and as the Italian market had grown some Alexandrian workmen or firms had already moved to Campania and Rome, probably in the first century BC. The Campanian industry was fortunate in having suitable sand available on the coast, but it can scarcely be a coincidence that it was established close to the port of Pozzuoli with its excellent communications both with the east and with the largest of all markets, Rome itself. The introduction of the technique of glass-blowing into the western provinces appears to have been the work of Syrian craftsmen who established workshops initially in northern Italy, where a small industry already existed, and then in Gaul, once again probably at Lyon. Subsequently glass houses appeared in all of the newer provinces, including Britain, although in most cases the finer pieces appear to have remained a monopoly of a limited number of specialized centres. The northern markets came to be dominated by the huge industry centred on Cologne, which continued to produce on a considerable scale throughout the Roman period, having the immense advantage of being on one of the greatest navigable rivers in Europe with direct access to the sea. Another major centre was at Aquileia, no doubt producing as much for the Danube provinces as for Italy and the Adriatic region.

The expansion of the glass industry is particularly well documented, but it is probable that the process by which it and the fine pottery industries grew, namely by the movement of workmen closer to the new markets created by the initial success of their products, was the normal one by which such industries developed in the Roman world. Such expansion will have been particularly characteristic of the western provinces where industries on this scale had not existed before their incorporation in the Empire, and where there was often a marked difference on the levels of technology between the native cultures and that of the Roman world. In the eastern provinces the basic development had occurred during the hellenistic period if not before, and while the industries may have expanded in the favourable climate provided by the early Empire it was from a well established foundation. In some cases the existence of developed industries may even have retarded the adoption of new ideas. Thus the glass industry in Egypt failed to introduce the mass-production of blown glass until the second century AD, by which time the technique was in use throughout the rest of the Empire.

Without question one of the largest and most labour intensive of all ancient industries was that producing cloth (pl. 23.5). The evidence of spindle-whorls, loom-weights and the like makes it clear that spinning and weaving were practised on a large scale throughout the Empire, and it need not be doubted that local needs were satisfied locally

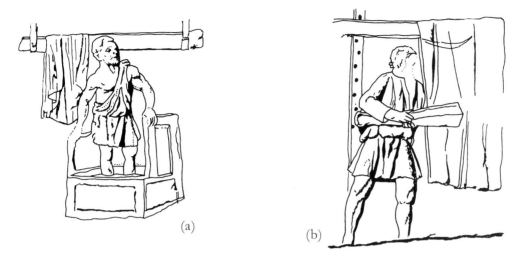

Figure 23.2   (a) Tombstone from Sens, France, showing a fuller at work; (b) tombstone from Sens, France, illustrating the use of cropping shears for trimming the knap (*after J. P. Wild*)

and that only exceptionally was either the cloth or finished clothing transported for any distance (fig. 23.2). But, while the rural areas and smaller, agriculturally-dependent settlements may have been self-sufficient, the greater cities were not and will have provided large and profitable markets for the producers of suitable cloths. Even in those areas which were largely self-sufficient there will have been a market for the finer and more luxurious cloths. Certain centres had a high reputation for such fabrics; Sicily and Malta were two, but most were in the eastern provinces where both woollen and linen cloths were produced in great quantities. At Hierapolis in western Turkey, where the local spring water is particularly suitable for the processing and dyeing of cloth, we find references to woolwashers, woolworkers, fullers and dyers, but not to spinners, and to weavers only of special fabrics; a fact which tends to confirm the evidence from other areas that the spinning and weaving of the common fabrics was a domestic industry. The trade in cloth and clothing is most fully illustrated by Diocletian's Price Edict where they form a group second in size only to foodstuffs. Clothing is listed from all over the Empire, including the oft quoted *birrus Britannicus*, although in some cases it may be suspected that the regional name refers to the area from which the type originated rather than its sole place of manufacture in AD 301. The largest groups of cloth came from the east and the names of Scythopolis, Tarsus, Byblus and Laodiceia occur with monotonous regularity. Nor were all their products intended for the luxury market; many types are quoted in three distinct grades and priced accordingly. The evidence from Egypt, thanks to the survival of so many papyri, is a great deal fuller than for other provinces. There linen rather than wool was the staple product and there are references to guilds of weavers in various cities. Under the Ptolemies almost all industry in Egypt had been a state monopoly, but the Roman government preferred to encourage private enterprise and linen-weaving, along with glass-making and the manufacture of papyrus, became one of the major exporting industries of the Roman period. Within the industry various districts specialized in different weaves, and many are known by the name of the area from which the model was derived. Thus are recorded Spanish, Italic and Dalmatic garments, and Lodix, originally a speciality of Laodiceia, being woven at Arsinoe. Some of these fabrics, along with the other products of Egyptian industry, as well as goods imported into the country such as arretine pottery, were exported through the Red Sea ports to Arabia and India.

Pompeii is the city which provides the most complete view of a major cloth industry in action at the time of the eruption of AD 79. The reason for this development probably lay in the fact that, as Strabo noted, Pompeii was the port for the produce of the southern part of Campania and for some considerable distance inland. Other important exports from the city were wine, oil, fish-sauce, and millstones. Much, perhaps most, of the cloth will have arrived in the city along the river Sarno having been woven in the towns and mountains behind the city, where the flocks which produced it were pastured. Relatively little is likely to have come as raw wool although there is sufficient evidence to show that both spinning and weaving were done there, as in all Italian cities at that time. The major processes undertaken in Pompeii, however, were fulling and dyeing, particularly the former. The scale of this industry and its importance in the economic life of the city is shown by the large and splendid market building which was provided for the fullers on one side of the forum. No other trade had facilities of this type, but it is informative to contrast this building with the converted houses in which the fullers and dyers worked, with their tanks built into formerly elegant peristyles. Such establishments were typical of the Roman world; small, individual units only became important in the mass, and the contrast between such workshops and the grandiose building in which their goods were sold is an effective symbol of their combined weight.

Baking was the only industry in Pompeii which surpassed fulling in size (pls 23.2 and 23.3). As was normal in the ancient world the Pompeiian baker was also a miller and even today the bakeries are immediately recognizable by the large hour-glass shaped millstones and by the ovens. The number of these establishments and of the taverns, which were even more common, is a reminder that even in an exporting town most of the commerce was actually concerned with local needs. But if these were the major trades of Pompeii they were not the only ones and others are known from the remains of their workshops, and from inscriptions and graffiti, particularly those announcing that candidates for local offices had the support of one or another of the craft guilds. Trades known in the town include goldsmiths, gem engravers, bronze workers, blacksmiths, and tanners; while the well-known paintings showing cupids at work provide invaluable visual evidence of fullers, goldsmiths, perfumers, shoemakers and carpenters (pl. 23.5a and b). No doubt in most cases their products were sold directly to the public from the workshops which also served as showrooms, as was normal in the ancient world. This is the arrangement in the fine altar from Rome of the cutler L. Cornelius Atimetus where is seen on one face the smith and his assistant at work in the forge, and on the other the shop with the owner, who is in the process of selling a knife to a customer, standing in front of a rack laden with reaping hooks, chisels and knives (pl. 23.1a and b).

Although this information comes from one Campanian town it would have been equally applicable, no doubt with some local variations, to many thousands of others scattered throughout the Empire. Indeed a similar picture emerges from the papyri concerned with town life in Egypt. In the unimportant village of Tebtynis for example, an astonishing array of crafts – dyeing, fulling, wool-carding, weaving, garment-making, stone-working, cobbling, gold and bronze smithing, strigil-making, plumbing, tin-smithing, milling and baking, potting and brick making, carpentry, making arms and breastplates, are to be found, as well as a host of trades which were not industrial; few if any of this formidable list can have been concerned with anything other than local trade.

The election posters of Pompeii and inscriptions from throughout the Empire show that most of the crafts and industries of a city were united in a series of specialized *collegia*, membership of which appears to have been restricted to the owners of firms. Most of the labour force of the industries of Italy and the more Italianized provinces were slaves, particularly in the early Empire, but it is clear that the abler ones might often hope for manumission and the opportunity to set up in business on their own. Roman society might frown on the patrician being involved in commerce, but there was no stigma attached to his acting as the financial backer and patron of his freedmen, and much, perhaps most, of Italian industry in the late Republic and early Empire was in the hands of freedmen or their descendants. In Asia Minor on the other hand the industrial workforce appears to have consisted largely of poor freemen, while in the Celtic areas, where slavery had played little part in pre-Roman society, most of the workers will also have been freemen.

The political, military and economic problems which beset the Roman world in the third century inevitably led to profound changes in its social and economic structure from which industry was not exempt. Volumes have been written on this subject, but all that needs to be said here is that by the fourth century the social structure of the Roman world had hardened, and that state intervention and control was on an ever-increasing scale. No doubt in practice many crafts had always been hereditary but this was now a legal requirement, with a considerable degree of state control being exercised through the existing trade *collegia*. At the same time there were attempts to control the prices of goods and services throughout the Empire, the best known being the price edict issued by Diocletian in AD 301. What effect these changes had on industry is not known; all the archaeological and much of the literary evidence suggests that most industries continued to flourish, and that it was only during barbarian invasions and civil wars that they suffered any real setbacks. The structure of Roman industry with its multitude of small units will have increased its resilience, as no doubt did the fact that most produced necessities rather than luxuries.

In two fields, however, the state became directly involved for it took control of the armaments works and certain weaving mills and dye-works. The Roman government had always been understandably concerned to ensure that its armies had an adequate supply of equipment, and as early as Cicero, he mentions the wealth made by a man in charge of arms factories during the Social War. Although firm evidence is largely lacking it appears that in the early Empire the government was content to ensure a supply of equipment by the use of contracts supplemented by some production by the army itself. Inevitably specialized armaments manufacturers tended to be concentrated in certain cities and it was probably by nationalizing them that the state armaments factories were created. In the eastern provinces there were fifteen such factories, mainly producing shields and general arms, but including three specializing in the armour for heavy cavalry and one each for shields and lances. In the west there were more; five in Illyricum, six in Italy and nine in Gaul, a pattern which must reflect their earlier distribution and the current strategic requirements. Of these, six were general producers, one made breast plates, six made shields, two made swords, two made arrows, one made bows, and one made *ballistae*. In addition there were three factories in the west and two in the east making the elaborate armour worn by officers.

The workmen in these establishments were equated with soldiers, receiving the same rations and being branded like them to make recapture easier should they desert, although the evidence suggests that it was actually a popular employment. By contrast the state weaving mills were staffed with slaves. The details are known only of those in the western provinces where there were two linen mills and fourteen woollen mills, probably because linen had always been a speciality of the eastern provinces; of these the largest number was again in Gaul. There were also nine dye-works. The output of them all will have been intended for the army and other government services. How large these factories were is not known with certainty but the evidence suggests that each had a considerable work force, although if their internal structure reflected the fact that they had been formed by the nationalization of many separate firms it may have been much divided. Even so one other state industry, minting, appears to have employed a massive workforce; at least that is if credence can be given to the alleged loss of 7,000 soldiers when Aurelian stormed the mint in Rome.

Inevitably the gradual collapse of the western Empire wrought profound changes in, and a considerable contraction of, its industries, but it should be remembered that this was not the case in the eastern provinces where industry continued unabated into the Byzantine period.

The final conclusion of any discussion of Roman industry must be that its growth was largely the result of economic and social factors. It grew because its markets increased with the rising population and the urbanization of the western provinces, but with only a handful of exceptions, it was usually concerned with supplying local requirements. To take one example, research has shown that the products of even the more successful coarse pottery industries rarely travelled more than a few score kilometres from the kiln sites, and there is no reason to suppose that this industry differed from most others. The main exporting industries were those which provided the raw materials without which Roman civilization could not have survived, such as foodstuffs, metals, timber and cloth; or, much more rarely, were monopolies, as was the papyrus industry of Egypt. Other exporting industries were largely dependent on being able to send their goods along routes and in ships which existed primarily to carry food and raw materials. It was for this reason that so many of the industrial centres of the Roman world lay on the coast or by one of the great navigable rivers.

The advantages which the Roman manufacturer had were immense when they are compared with those of his predecessors and successors. He worked within an efficient financial system, often in periods of prolonged peace when trade could flourish unhindered; he traded in what was probably the largest common market that the world has ever seen, with only a few minor taxes to pay on crossing provincial boundaries; communications both by land and sea were better than they had ever been before or were to be again for many centuries; and he sold his goods in a world in which there was immense private and public wealth. When all these factors are considered, it is necessary to ask why industry only expanded sufficiently to fulfil the increased demand rather than transforming itself and creating a true industrial revolution? Regrettably, of course, the question is largely rhetorical with no certain answer, but it is possible to define a number of factors which would have had to be overcome if such a revolution was to have occurred. Perhaps the key one is the fact that industry was socially unacceptable to the upper classes who effectively controlled the resources of the Empire. Only agriculture was a suitable occupation for them and while they were not loath to obtain their share of the profits of trade and industry they could not become openly involved in it. Without their direct interest change, if not impossible, was far less likely. The Roman legal system made it difficult to create the type of limited liability company with a multitude of shareholders which has proved particularly well suited to financing industrial concerns, and which ensures continuity through more than one generation. In consequence most Roman industry remained in the hands of individuals or small groups. Raising capital was usually a personal matter, for although banks existed the main source of loans remained the wealthy individual, which is why so many firms were owned by freedmen who had received the backing of their former owners. Nor was industry a fashionable field of investment; land was always preferred.

Finally there was an almost total lack of technical innovation and invention; a fact which cannot have been helped by the absence of patent laws. The industries of the fourth century were those which had existed at the end of the Republic and they were still using the same techniques and processes. What could happen when a revolutionary new technique was applied was shown by the explosive growth of the glass industry after the invention of blowing, but this stands almost in isolation in all the centuries of Roman industrial history. The result was that growth could only be produced by scaling up technical processes of limited capacity, which meant that above a certain point production could be increased only by multiplying the number of units and not by changing to other processes better suited to large scale production. Undoubtedly the greatest limitation in this field was the almost total failure to utilize any sources of power other than those provided by animals and man. When it is remembered that the water-mill was invented in the hellenistic area in the first century BC this failure becomes even more surprising. The evidence suggests that the Romans used both the undershot and the more efficient overshot wheel, as well as devising a system of gears which converted the vertical rotation of the mill-wheel to the horizontal rotation of mill-stones (fig. 23.3). But this most important invention was only applied on a large scale to the grinding of corn. Admittedly there is one tantalizing passage in a late Roman poem which appears to indicate that a water-wheel on the river Ruwer, a tributary of

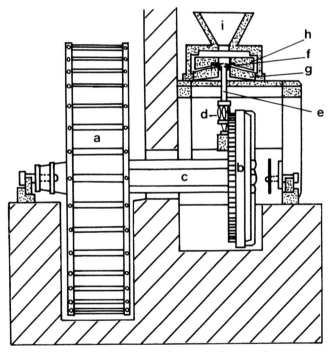

Figure 23.3 Reconstruction drawing of a water-mill for grinding cereals, as proposed by Vitruvius: (a) water-wheel; (b) vertical drum; (c) axle of a and b; (d) horizontal drum; (e) axle of d; (f) iron dovetail; (g, h) millstones; (i) hopper (*after White*)

the Mosel, was being used to power a saw for cutting stone, in which case it is possible that a cam was being used to convert the rotation of the wheel to the reciprocating motion of the saw. If so the failure of Roman industrialists to apply this to such similar processes as driving the bellows of furnaces, working the hammers of forges and fulling mills, or pumping water from mines becomes even more incomprehensible; had they done so they might have achieved a true industrial revolution. A hint of the power available to them is provided by the complex of sixteen mill-wheels arranged in two parallel rows which ran down the hillside at the Barbegal near Arles in Gaul (pl. 23.7). Built in the late third or fourth century with its own aqueduct to supply it with water, it was capable of grinding enough grain to feed many thousand people. Yet while it is perhaps the most impressive industrial monument to survive from the Roman period, it exemplifies the point made above: any increase in production was obtained by using a number of similar units rather than by taking an entirely new approach to the problem. Given the failure to make even the obvious uses of water power it is hardly surprising that the other sources of power hinted at by such inventors as Hero of Alexander, who designed both primitive windmills and steam engines, went quite unnoticed. Roman industry was trapped in its own technical inertia and there it remained until the system of which it formed but one part finally collapsed in the west of Europe in the fifth century AD.

23.1a   The first face of the funerary relief of L. Cornelius Atimetus,
showing the forge on one side

23.1b The second face of the funerary relief of L. Cornelius Atimetus,
showing the shop on the other

23.2　Pompeiian bakery with millstones

23.3　Relief from Rome of a donkey-powered
flour mill

23.4　Relief from the monument of the Haterii, Rome, depicting a building
under construction with a crane

23.5   Frescoes from the *triclinium* of the House of the Vettii, Pompeii, showing cupids acting as (a) perfumers; (b) goldsmiths; (c) fullers

23.6 Arretine crater by M. Perennius Tigranus, decorated with scenes showing four pairs of lovers in different attitudes; second half of the first century BC

23.7 The sequence of water-mills at the Barbegal, near Arles, France

CHAPTER 24

·MINING·

Ann Woods

With the expansion of Roman influence and power during the Principate and early Empire, new areas rich in mineral deposits became available for exploitation and the Romans were quick to take advantage of them. Their mining techniques display a degree of expertise which has been largely unappreciated until relatively recently: most reports on Roman mining methods have concentrated on the more obvious shaft-and-gallery system (with its associated equipment) that was employed in underground mining, with the result that the rather more impressive surface techniques have remained in the background.

Evidence of mining can be found in many provinces of the Empire but probably the most spectacular remains have been found in Spain, first in the hard rock regions of the south which were exploited from an early period, and second in the auriferous country of the north-west. In these two geologically very different areas the full range of skills involved in Roman mining can be seen: although possessing little geological knowledge by modern standards, they were adept at suiting mining techniques to the immediate conditions, particularly in the latter region. In recent years, this has been the subject of much research, and systematic recording of the sites, aided by literary evidence, has enabled convincing interpretations to be made.

This contribution attempts to present a general survey of the many and varied mining techniques employed by the Romans. It is not intended as an exhaustive treatment, but rather as a summary of certain specific techniques, with emphasis being placed on the results of recent research. The descriptions of mines and techniques recorded herein largely represent the results of mining on a grand scale. It is worth remembering that smaller, less organized ventures were probably just as common but have left less impressive or obvious remains. Many mines cannot be accurately dated and existing descriptions and interpretations of much mining evidence must be approached with

611

caution. Many sites were mined by successive generations throughout antiquity, ore extraction continuing until the source was exhausted. Similar techniques and tools were used from prehistory through to the medieval period, and later mining activity may have obliterated all traces of earlier endeavours. In addition, there was a tendency during the late nineteenth and early twentieth centuries to attribute all traces of mining to the Romans and it is only recently that the accuracy of such reports has been questioned. In so far as early work is concerned, the value of the extensive survey provided by Davies (1935) must not be underestimated: fifty years after publication it remains the standard work on the subject. This, and the recent work by Healy (1978), provide far more detail than it is possible to include here on the ore deposits exploited by the Romans at various sites throughout the Empire. They also deal with aspects, such as administration of the mines, which are beyond the scope of the present paper.

The primary mining techniques employed by the Romans were dictated, not by the type of mineral being mined, but rather by the geological and geographical conditions in which it occurred. Primary ore deposits, such as veins, occur in hard-rock formations; the usual method for mining these deposits was by the digging of shafts and galleries to follow the mineral vein through the rock. In contrast soft-rock deposits, particularly the ones from which gold was extracted in north-west Spain, were mined by surface techniques: such deposits are too soft or too shallow to be tunnelled into and the ore or metal is distributed through them in such a way as to make that type of mining impracticable.

In contrast, methods used for the final collection of the ore were determined by the nature of the mineral concerned. Because of the high specific gravity of gold itself, and of cassiterite and galena, the most common ores of tin and lead respectively, all can be retrieved after mining or crushing by techniques involving the use of flowing water: they will settle out while lighter material is washed away. Such methods will be classified here as secondary mining techniques, as opposed to primary techniques used to obtain the ore from the environment in the first place.

In their early papers dealing with gold mining techniques, Lewis and Jones (1969; 1970) used a classification system based on the occurrence of the mineral deposits and postulated two basic categories, alluvial and placer, the distinction between them being largely based on the position of the mined mineral deposit. Consequently, they distinguished between 'low-level placer deposits' in rivers and river valleys and 'high-level alluvial deposits' (1970, 169), the latter supposedly being better stratified (1969, 245) and of greater age (1970, 169). These definitions were also followed by Jones and Bird (1972) and Bird (1972). Such a distinction is, however, geologically invalid in that alluvial deposits are in fact typical placer deposits and, moreover, there are various other types of placers, such as eluvial-, beach- or bench-placers, and not just the stream-placers that Lewis and Jones have used as their placer deposit. A fuller description of these can be found in Read and Watson (1968, 608ff.) or as summarized by Healy (1978, 30ff.).

Healy (1978, 87–90) has lumped the alluvial and placer mining techniques of Lewis and Jones together under the title of placer mining but has introduced another category of opencast mining in which he includes shallow, and often not extensive, opencast mines which appear to have been merely excavated, and the ore-bearing material collected, without the use of any water-based mining technique. This second category, however, also appears invalid: the most obvious signs of Roman workings are the huge opencasts that are the result of their mining techniques, particularly in soft-rock deposits, involving the use of water.

Unfortunately it is not possible to place all these categories of deposit and their associated mining techniques under the one classification of soft-rock mining: the methods normally associated with soft-rock deposits have also been used for hard-rock mining at Braña la Folgueirosa, Iboyo and other sites in north-west Spain (Bird, 1972) where the more usual hard-rock techniques – the shaft-and-gallery system – were little utilized.

Therefore, as the same mining method could be, and sometimes was, applied to totally different types of site and mineral deposit, a distinction based on the occurrence of the ore does not appear to be the most appropriate. The classification used here is accordingly based on the type of mining method used, and two main categories can be seen to exist: surface and underground mining. The mining methods applied to ore deposits described by earlier writers (Lewis and Jones, 1969; 1970; Jones and Bird, 1972; Bird, 1972) as alluvials and placers, together with Healy's opencast and placer mining, will all here be described as surface mining techniques. The shaft-and-gallery system, and immediately related techniques, usually associated with hard-rock deposits, will fall under the category of underground mining and will be described first.

In general, Roman underground mining was based on a shaft-and-gallery technique: they used shafts, adits and galleries to locate, follow and extract an ore-bearing vein. Most Roman shafts were square or rectangular and Davies (1935, 21) has described, with examples, the methods used to make both types. Circular shafts were used less frequently but have nevertheless been recorded from Rio Tinto (Palmer, 1926–7, 310). The shape of the shaft would largely have been determined by the type of rock it was being dug into and not, as suggested elsewhere (Healy, 1978, 91) by the type of lining material: whereas the latter could be easily adapted to the shape of the shaft (stone for round shafts, wood for angular), making an inappropriately-shaped shaft (such as a circular shaft in a strongly fissile rock like schist) would have been extremely difficult.

Entry to the mines via the shafts was often achieved by foothold notches cut in the side walls, as at Rio Tinto (Palmer, 1926–7, Fig. 83 or Healy, 1978, pl. 19) or by ladder. In some instances wood was hammered into holes cut in the shaft walls to form a more permanent and substantial ladder. These were usually set towards the side of the shaft, as at Linares, or even close to the corner, presumably to leave room for the removal of buckets from the mines. In some instances the spacing between these beams

Figure 24.1 Spain, showing provincial boundaries and principal mining sites mentioned in the text

was so great that it is thought that workers sat on them to pass the buckets of ore (or possibly water) to the surface; rock-cut steps in sloping adits may have been used for a similar purpose.

Many of the Roman adits are extremely long and in some cases have been hacked through barren rock: at Centenillo, Rickard (1927, 921–2) recorded several lengthy adits, one of them over 1000 m (1,100 yd.) before it reached the ore body. He also (1928, 132) commented on the small size of the Roman levels at Rio Tinto, stating that this (around 1–1.2 m; 1.1–1.5 yd.) and their arched roofs made them distinguishable from other workings. Size, however, appears not to be a criterion for distinguishing Roman workings from those of other periods: Davies (1933–4, 16–17) records a great variety of sizes for Roman galleries. Neither, it seems, can shape be used as a distinguishing feature: square, rectangular, arched and trapezoidal adits and galleries are all known. Many of the last are wider at the top than at the bottom, the extra width supposedly being to allow for the miners' shoulders, especially if buckets of ore or tools were being carried. A similar technique, producing what are known as coffin levels, was employed in more recent times in the lead mines of Derbyshire. The lower gallery at Dolaucothi (Wales) is 2.5 m (2.7 yd.) high, 1.2 m (1.3 yd.) wide at the bottom and 1.9 m (2 yd.) wide at the top (Boon, 1974a, 486 and Fig. 17). In comparison with Spanish galleries of similar shape, the one from Dolaucothi is much larger and this has led Boon to suggest that beasts of burden, possibly pit ponies, were used to remove debris from the mines.

Fire-setting was probably the method used to drive adits and galleries in the harder rocks and evidence has been reported from many sites. However, burnt wood in mines is not always indicative of the use of this process: fires may have been lit at the bases of shafts to create draughts for ventilation, and burnt remains and blackened walls may therefore be a result.

In fire-setting, a fire is lighted against the rock face; the heat from the fire causes the rock to expand which may be sufficient to crack it. In most cases, however, the hot rock is quenched with water, the resulting rapid contracting ensuring even greater disintegration. This process has been used since prehistoric times and was presumably particularly effective on siliceous rocks. Quartz has a high co-efficient of thermal expansion, increasing in volume quite rapidly when heated, especially at the temperatures that might be attained during fire-setting. These large expansions would make it particularly susceptible to cracking by heating and, if temperatures in excess of the inversion point were reached, the corresponding rapid reduction in size brought about by sudden quenching and lowering of the temperature would achieve even more effective results.

There is literary evidence for the use of fire-setting in antiquity: amongst others it is described by Pliny (xxxiii, 71) and described and illustrated by Agricola (v, 118–19) (fig. 24.2). Pliny mentions the use of vinegar for the quenching of siliceous rocks. Such a suggestion is strange for it could not have had a chemical effect on such rocks, but he specifically mentions it in this context and not in relation to calcareous rocks where

Figure 24.2 Fire-setting as depicted by Agricola

its action might have been employed to accelerate disintegration. This passage from Pliny has been much debated elsewhere (for example Davies, 1933–4, 20; 1935, 22; Howat, 1939, 239–40; Forbes, 1963, 203) without really arriving at a satisfactory explanation. Forbes, however, does include a helpful anecdote: 'The method is still in use in Northern Italy in road-building. There the author was assured that the vinegar was "a very cold substance", which would strengthen the water's effect, for did not a drop of strong vinegar on the top of the hand cause an icy feeling?'

Arched galleries and adits may well be the result of fire-setting. Howat has illustrated the typical elliptical cross-section due to 'the manner in which the flames licked the roof of the passage' and Collins has noted the tendency of such passages to slope upward because of the heat being more intense on the roof than on the floor. He also drew attention to the characteristic rounded or conchoidal depressions left after thin flakes of rock are removed by fire-setting and to the readily recognizable rock debris that results from the use of this method.

Owing to the relatively small size of most of the galleries and adits, little shoring was needed, but examples of wooden props have been found at various sites. At Tharsis the walls of the passage, as illustrated by Stevenson (1876), were lined with circular wooden posts supporting recurrent beams. In one of the galleries at Dolaucothi remains of wooden posts and slabs used to support the roof have been found (Boon, 1974a, 483).

Numerous tools of wood, stone and metal have been found associated with Roman mine workings. These too, like the actual excavation method employed, would have varied according to the rock type. Stone hammers and picks, many of them grooved for hafting, have been found in practically every mine in southern Spain (see, for example, Sandars, 1905; Rothenberg and Blanco-Freijeiro, 1981) and have been assigned to Roman mining operations. Recently, however, some doubt has been expressed over this; research by the Huelva Archaeometallurgical Project indicates that many of these tools may not have been found *in situ* or may represent secondary use (Rothenberg and Blanco-Freijeiro, 1981, 165).

Iron tools have also been found, again primarily from the Spanish mines, and must be considered the main tool for hard rock mining. Adit, shaft and gallery walls reveal imprints of the tools used on them, allowing conclusions to be drawn concerning the actual mining methods employed. The workings at Timna in the Arabah provide plentiful evidence of pick marks in the soft white sandstone from which the Romans extracted copper (Rothenberg, 1972, pl. 118) and some to be seen in the walls at Dolaucothi show that the galleries were dug from the outside inwards (Boon, 1974a, 487). Chisel and wedge marks have been found in many other workings. Davies (1935, 20) notes that the absence of tool marks in one of the galleries at Linares suggests the use of wooden wedges; these were hammered into the face and, when wetted, would expand and crack the rock.

In general, careful working of the rock face is a characteristic of Roman mining techniques; this must, in many cases, have been difficult to achieve given the relatively low levels of illumination available to the miners. Lighting appears to have been provided almost entirely by small ceramic oil lamps. Examples have been found in many mines where they were placed in niches cut in the walls. At Sotiel Coronada, lamp niches were found less than a metre (3.3 ft) apart near the roof of adits, and occasionally containing clay which had been used to ensure stability of the lamps (Davies, 1935, 121).

Ventilation must also have been a problem, particularly in the deeper mines. When vertical shafts are used, two or more are often necessary to ensure ventilation; this may account for the frequent occurrence of pairs of shafts at sites such as Rio Tinto and Laurion. The lighting of a fire at the base of one shaft would create increased draught down the other and so provide fresh air. Some shafts are reported as showing grooves down the sides so that they could be divided in half with timber partitions to perform the same function (Davies, 1935, 24). Further ventilation problems may have been created by the use of fire-setting. Although the fire itself would have helped to promote a draught, the smoke, and the fumes brought about by dowsing and quenching the hot rock face, coupled with any gases given off by heated ores, must have made the atmosphere in mines extremely unpleasant. Sulphide ores in particular must have been a problem in this way: the fire would have caused partial roasting of some of them and the evolution of sulphur dioxide. If Pliny's description of the use of vinegar is accurate, the additional smell must have made the mines absolutely unbearable, and it would have taken some time for the air to clear sufficiently for work to resume. McCarthy (in Davies, 1933–4, 40) states that after fire-setting was used in a Gold Coast mine he visited, some three days had to elapse before the mine could be entered comfortably. Agricola's illustration of the use of fire-setting (fig. 24.2), showing a miner apparently suffering from the atmosphere in the mine, is likely to be an accurate representation.

Probably the greatest problem in the European mines, however, was water. Difficulties were always encountered when mining at depth as the Romans were not able to alter the height of the water table. They solved drainage problems by three main methods: first by bailing, second by cutting cross adits and drainage channels, and third by the use of mechanical water-raising devices such as the screw pump and the water-wheel.

Pliny, in his description of silver mining, mentions (xxxiii, 97) the use of bailing for draining the mines. He also records the use of human chains (xxxiii, 71) for removing the ore from the mines. Slave and convict labour probably provided the workforce for both these activities. Numerous examples of copper-alloy and esparto grass buckets, the latter made watertight by a lining of tar or pitch, have been found in Roman workings, especially at Cartagena and Mazarron (Davies, 1935, 25 and Fig. 23). Their capacity was about 15 litres ($3\frac{1}{4}$ gal.). They are similar in appearance to examples of ore-haulage baskets that have been found, also being strengthened by four or six wooden ribs (see Healy, 1978, pl. 32c), but have a pointed base and a V-shaped cross-bar for a handle; such a shape would tilt of its own accord when placed in water and thus fill more easily. Davies also suggests (1935, 25) that the five bronze rings found at Rio Tinto may have been frames for similar buckets.

Copper or copper-alloy buckets, which could have been used for carrying both ore and water, have been recorded from several sites in southern Spain. The one from a mine near Posadas (Sandars, 1905, Fig. 15) has a handle that would have allowed the bucket to tilt when dipped into water. Most writers, however, record that this bucket has dents in its side, probably caused by its being bumped against the side of the shaft while being hauled to the surface by rope, the inference being that it is an ore, rather than a bailing bucket.

The second method for drainage was the cutting of trenches and cross adits down which water could flow to a sump whence it could be removed by bailing. Diodorus Siculus records the use of this process (v, 37, 3):

And now and then, as they go down deep, they come upon flowing subterranean rivers, but they overcome the might of these rivers by diverting the streams which flow in on them by means of channels leading off at an angle.

Such a system appears to have taken time to develop: few such adits have been found, for example, from the early workings at Cartagena. Davies (1935, 24) records the presence of deep cross-cuts at Madenokhorio, Dolaucothi, Rio Tinto, Centenillo and Minas dos Mouros. At the last site, a narrow channel 5 metres (5.5 yd) deep was cut in the floor of the adit, carefully following the line of the side walls (Harrison, 1931, 143 and Fig. 4). This may have been to increase drainage facilities although the somewhat confusing account provided by its discoverer does not indicate this, stating instead that it was 'to permit of the deepening of the whole open-cut'. In view of the fact that this adit was only 7 metres (7.6 yd) above the level of the nearby river and that there were three specially made circular chambers along it, each containing a granite block and showing tracks that were most probably worn by animals driving machinery, it seems likely that the channel was in fact intended for drainage rather than as a preliminary step in deepening the adit.

The most effective drainage was accomplished by the use of machinery and there is abundant evidence for the use of both screw pumps and water-wheels. The Archimedean or Egyptian screw consisted of helical vanes wound around a central core encased in a barrel of wooden planking. It was rotated to raise water from one level to another. The method of construction is described in some detail by Vitruvius (x, 6, 1–4) and Diodorus Siculus (v, 37, 3) describes the use of such screw pumps in the Spanish mines:

> they draw out the waters of the streams by means of what is called by men the Egyptian screw . . . and by the use of such screws they carry the water in successive lifts as far as the entrance, drying up in this way the spot where they are digging and making it well suited to the furtherance of their operations.

Several examples have been found to support Vitruvius' description and the screws appear to have been used in the Spanish and Portuguese mines during the first and early second centuries. Five were found at Centenillo; that from Level 10 (fig. 24.3) was 4.27 m (4.6 yd) long and consisted of a wooden core some 20 cm (7.7 in.) in diameter, to which a copper helical vane was attached, in a wooden barrel 50 cm (20 in.) in diameter. Iron spigots were fixed at each end for pivoting and it was rotated by means of cleats attached to the exterior of the barrel about half-way along its length.

Other screws were longer: that found at Beaune (Haute Vienne), for example, made of chestnut, measured 8 m (8.7 yd) in length and 30 cm (11.8 in.) in diameter (Forbes, 1963, 215). The three screws found at Sotiel Coronada were 3.6 m (3.9 yd.) long and 48 cm (19 in.) in diameter. The helix of one of these oak screws, clearly illustrated by Healy (1978, pl. 24b) is composed of small slabs of wood nailed and glued on top of each other; Davies has suggested (1935, 27) that wooden vanes would swell in the presence of water and therefore leak less, but that copper would cope better with the weight of the water. A lead barrel for a screw has also been found in a Spanish mine

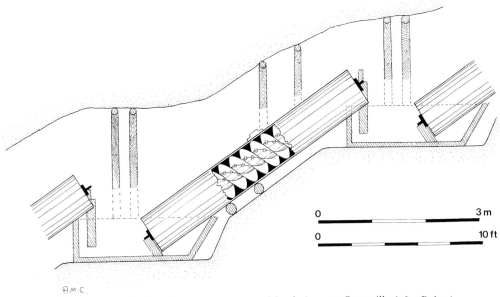

AMC.

Figure 24.3   Archimedean screw-pump used for drainage at Centenillo (*after Palmer*)

but there is no proof that it dates from the Roman period.

The screws were mounted in series, raising water from one sump to another which was emptied in turn by the next screw. Some, such as the example from Centenillo (fig. 24.3), were turned by the cleats featured on the outer barrel while others, for example at Alcaracejos (Portugal), were probably turned by the use of a crank handle. The latter method was employed in Japanese mines of the seventeenth century and illustrated on a scroll dated to 1840 (Bromehead, 1942).

The lift obtaining by a screw pump is a result of the length of the pump itself, its angle of inclination, and the pitch of the spiral vane. Vitruvius (x, 6, 4), using the Pythagorean triangle as his basis, suggests an angle of about 37 degrees as the required inclination for the mounting of such screws and, although his original illustration has been lost, later (usually medieval) depictions commonly show such an angle of inclination. However, this would have made the screw extremely difficult to turn by means of human power treading on the barrel cleats but may, as Landels suggests (1978, 61), represent a compromise, being chosen to give maximum lift at the cost of reduced output. Other illustrations, however, show a much smaller angle of inclination: a wallpainting from the Casa dell'Efebo at Pompeii (illustrated by Forbes, 1963, 213) and which may show a screw pump in use, shows only a very slight angle of tilt, as does a terracotta relief from Alexandria (Healy, 1978, pl. 25). Increased efficiency may have been obtained by using a greater angle of inclination than in these depictions or by turning the screw with a crank handle. At Sotiel Coronada, the screws were mounted at an angle of 15–20 degrees, similar to that shown on the terracotta model, but at Centenillo the angle was closer to 35 degrees (fig. 24.3).

It has been calculated (Landels, 1978, 63) that a screw pump 2.4 m (2.6 yd) long and 33 cm (12 in.) in diameter, mounted at the 37-degree angle suggested by Vitruvius, could raise between 9,600 l (2,100 gal.) and 14,000 l (3,000 gal.) of water, depending on its efficiency, to a head of 1.16 m (3.8 ft) in one hour. Obviously, the screws were

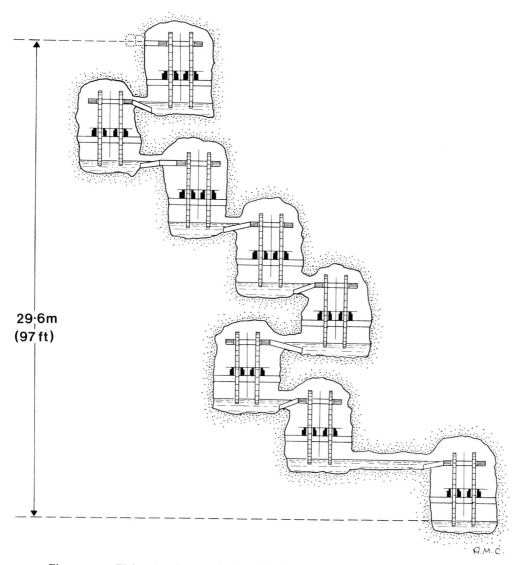

Figure 24.4 Eight pairs of water-wheels used to drain one mine at Rio Tinto (*after Palmer*)

Figure 24.5 Water-wheels used to raise water to a higher level at the Terme del Mithra, Ostia
(*after Schiøler*)

not as effective for water-raising as wheels but they had the advantage of providing a more even flow of water.

There is no evidence for the use in mines of the simple *tympanum*, described in some detail by Vitruvius (x, 4, 1–2) and by Landels (1978, 63–6). Abundant evidence does, however, exist for the other main type of drainage machine, the water-wheel: wheels or fragments have been found in many of the Spanish and Portuguese mines as well as at Dolaucothi.

These, basically undershot wheels in reverse, could raise water to a much greater height than could the screw pump and, although requiring more manpower for operation, appear to have been the main agency for mine drainage, particularly during and after the first century AD. They were presumably only employed in mines where the expected ore yield was sufficiently great to justify the expense as, for example, at Rio Tinto, where remains of eight pairs have been found in one mine (fig. 24.4) and where traces of some forty wheels in all have been located. Surviving fragments indicate that they were provided in pre-fabricated kits: spokes or side-pieces of the rim buckets, for example on the wheels from Tharsis (Stevenson, 1876, 280) and one from Rio Tinto (Boon and Williams, 1966, 124), were marked with letters or numerals to assist in their assembly underground.

The wheels were openwork, of wood (usually pine), and had compartments for

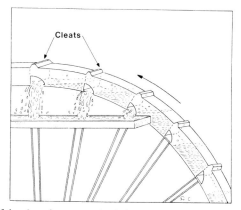

Figure 24.6 Section of the rim of a water-wheel showing the cleats used for rotating the wheel and the compartments in which the water was raised (*after Landels*)

raising water incorporated in their circumference. A brief but adequate description is provided by Vitruvius (x, 4, 3), emphasizing that these wheels were capable of raising water higher than the ordinary *tympanum*. The wheels were turned by men treading on the cleats on the outer rim, balancing themselves by means of ropes or possibly by support bars, as in fig. 24.5. Water was raised in the compartments and deposited in a launder (figs 24.5 and 24.6) at the top of the rotation whence it flowed into a sump which would be emptied by the next wheel. Figure 24.5 also shows how this would have been done; even though it is a reconstruction of water-wheels being used to raise water in the Terme del Mithra at Ostia rather than to drain mines, the principle is the same. Each compartment had an opening in the side of the wheel-rim, roughly quadrant-shaped, through which the water entered from the sump and flowed out into the launder at the top. The wheel was turned so that the straight edges of these openings were on the leading end of the compartment (fig. 24.6) in order to reduce spillage.

The wheels were frequently used in pairs (fig. 24.7); in some cases, as at Rio Tinto (fig. 24.4), they were employed to lift water through a series of separate but connected levels, while at others they were arranged in series along sloping galleries. When worked in pairs, the wheels discharged their contents into the same launder; if two launders were used turbulence would have occurred in the water at the junction of the launders and this was avoided by rotating the wheels in opposite directions, thus propelling the water in the same direction along the launder (fig. 24.7).

At São Domingos, nine wheels were found, arranged up a gallery sloping at about 40 degrees. An illustration of one of these wheels (Cross Brown in Palmer, 1926–7, 319) indicates that, unlike the Rio Tinto wheels, it was used on its own for it is provided with a launder on each side and, presumably, with openings on both sides of the rim compartments. Most other wheels, however, have only one opening, indicating that they were part of a pair: Landels (1978, 70) considers that the second opening, as well

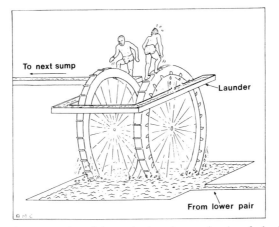

Figure 24.7 Reconstruction of the method used to work pairs of wheels (*after Landels*)

as requiring the provision of a second launder, would double the spillage. As a result of this, and the fact that the system of numbers marked on the spokes of the wheel from Rio Tinto was ignored when it was restored in the British Museum, he considers the reconstruction to be inaccurate. He levels similar criticism at the reconstruction drawing of the Dolaucothi drainage wheel (Boon and Williams, 1966, Fig. 6): the fact that this has been reconstructed from just one board, less than 1 metre (1.1 yd) in length, may account for inaccuracies and suggests that to attempt such a reconstruction on so little evidence was perhaps optimistic.

As with screw pumps, extant remains of the wheels indicate that they varied considerably in size, presumably dictated by the size of the gallery in which they were required to function and by the amount of water that needed to be removed. The Dolaucothi wheel has an estimated diameter of 3.6 m (3.9 yd) but is illustrated at rather less than this in the reconstruction drawing, two from São Domingos were 3.65 m (3.95 yd), while another eight from that site measured 4.87 m (5.2 yd). The average size of the Rio Tinto wheels was 4.5 m (4.9 yd), while that reported from Logroño was 4.57 m (4.95 yd). Other reports have included a wheel from Léon province in northern Spain which had a diameter of over 6 m (6.5 yd) (Holmann in Davies, 1933–4, 43).

The height that water can be lifted by such wheels is related to the diameter of the wheel, and the amount is determined by the number and size of the rim compartments. Palmer's calculations (1926–7, 302–4) indicate that a wheel *c.* 4.65 m (5 yd) in diameter could raise about 86 l (19 gal.) per minute over a height of 3.65 m (4 yd). Following on from this, it has been calculated that the nest of sixteen wheels found at Rio Tinto (fig. 24.4) could have raised nearly 11,000 l (2,420 gal.) in an hour over 29.6 m (32 yd), the total height attainable by the eight pairs. Palmer's estimated 61 per cent efficiency may not appear spectacular but the sheer amount of water that could be raised relatively large distances for comparatively little expenditure of energy made them far more effective than any other method employed for mine drainage.

Water was a major factor in surface mining techniques too. In contrast, however, the problem was not one of removal but of supply: the characteristic techniques employed in surface mining involved the use of millions of litres of water per day and, as most of the sites where these methods were employed were situated in elevated positions, extensive aqueduct and tank systems had to be constructed to supply and store the vast quantities required.

Until relatively recently less study had been undertaken of surface mining techniques. The existence of most of the gold mines in north-west Spain was known, but little had been done in the way of systematic recording and interpretation; over the last decade or so, however, this area in particular has been the subject of several long-term research programmes (for example, Lewis and Jones, 1970; Jones and Bird, 1972; Bird, 1972; Domergue and Hérail, 1977; 1978) and the surface features at Dolaucothi have also been subjected to some close scrutiny (Jones et al., 1960; Lewis and Jones, 1969; Jones and Lewis, 1971; Boon, 1974a). This increased research has resulted in detailed planning and recording of the sites but has also, as in the case of los Castellones/Luyego I, produced rather different interpretations (Bird, 1980; Domergue, 1984).

The most characteristic feature of Roman surface mining techniques is the extensive use of water as a mining agent. The two main methods were hushing (also called booming) and ground sluicing. For the former large tanks, fed by aqueduct systems, were constructed; when a sufficient head of water had collected, it was released in a wave to pour down over the deposit. It could have been used for three purposes: first to clear overburden and expose mineral deposits, second to wash the latter down to pools or tanks from which the ore could be extracted later by a variety of washing techniques, or third to remove mining debris. The result of the long-term use of hushing is an opencast. In contrast, ground sluicing is a method that can be used when a continuous flow of water is available and where ore deposits occur nearer to the surface. As with hushing, it may be used to remove overburden and to wash out ore but is generally employed on a much smaller scale. Archaeological evidence for the use of such a technique is limited as it can be used to clear areas down to bedrock and may thus remove all traces of the actual mining method itself. By analogy with more recent gold-mining practices, such as those employed in the nineteenth-century booms in California and Australia, it is reasonable to assume that this method was employed even at sites where no traces remain. Evidence of its use has, though, been detected at several sites in northern Spain, along the Rio Duerna.

One oft-quoted method that the Romans did not use, however, was hydraulicing. This term, *sensu stricto*, should only be applied to 'excavation . . . by streams of water under press from nozzles' (Peele, 1963, 10–550). Vertical faces of opencasts or other surface deposits are hosed with water under pressure, either to wash the material down or to undercut banks to bring about their collapse. The flow of water back from the face carries the washed-down material to sluice boxes where separation of the ore particles can be effected (for fuller details see Griffith, 1960; Harrison, 1962; Peele, 1963). Although now not much in evidence for mining, the technique can be seen in use at St Austell, Cornwall, where it is the principal method employed for the extraction of china clay.

The term hydraulicing was unfortunately adopted by Lewis and Jones (1969, 269) and defined as 'The use of a continuous flow of water to break down soft beds.' Later (1970, 177) they elaborated on this when, in their description of las Medulas, they stated that

> it [water] was played directly on to the deposit itself in a continuous stream, in exactly the same way as ground sluices were used in the nineteenth century. The stream has thus cut the numerous gullies in the northern half of the site, as already described. This type of work is known as hydraulicing by analogy with the modern practice of mining metalliferous gravels and placer deposits with jets provided with a head of water.

It is immediately obvious that they are confusing the two different types of mining: they are describing ground sluicing but then calling it hydraulicing. The great difference between the two methods is that hydraulicing is a high-pressure technique. Some subsequent writers (for example Healy, 1978, 88), following the definition given by Lewis and Jones, also state that this method was used by the Romans. Even greater confusion is evident in a recently published resumé of Roman mining in which, for a change, hushing is correctly described and named but then conflated with modern hydraulicing techniques:

> the water was directed into a number of large storage tanks, from which it was discharged in a series of waves, to remove the overburden. This latter process, known technically as 'hushing', is still used, and for exactly the same purpose, in modern tin mining, with the greatly increased velocity provided by jets of water discharged from 'monitors'. (White, 1984, 116–17)

In that there is absolutely no evidence for the use of such a technique by the Romans and the fact that they were, it seems, incapable of obtaining the kind of pressure necessary for its successful employment, any suggestion of the use of hydraulicing must be dismissed. The term was not used by Bird (1972) or by Jones and Bird (1972) who have described ground sluicing and called it just that, and it is to be hoped that the term will not appear in future discussions of Roman mining techniques.

Evidence for the use of hushing is available from nearly all the sites in north-west Spain, as well as from Dolaucothi, and tanks or remains thereof can still be seen posi-

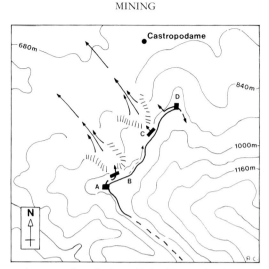

Figure 24.8 Castropodame, a soft-rock site, with hushing tanks above the opencasts (*after Bird*)

tioned above and slightly to one side of the opencasts (figs 24.8, 24.9, 24.10). In most cases, there are several tanks grouped around each opencast: los Castellones, for example, has three at the main U-shaped opencast, constructed in a stepped pattern up the hillside (Jones and Bird, 1972, 64), while at las Medulas a cluster of five tanks is situated between two opencasts on the south ridge. At other sites, however, such as Fresnedo and Castropodame (fig. 24.8), only one hushing tank was used to work each opencast.

There appears to have been no standard size or shape for the tanks and great variations exist. As far as shape is concerned, some are square but most are rectangular, and examples of both long narrow and shallow wide tanks are known. Shape appears to have been largely determined by the position of the tank on the site and the size was presumably dictated by the expected extent of the ore deposit and the amount of overburden that had to be removed to expose it. The tanks at las Medulas mentioned above measured about 100 × 20 m (109 × 21 yd.) (Lewis and Jones, 1970, 175) while the three from los Castellones measured 57 × 16 m (62 × 17.5 yd.), 65 × 20 m (70 × 21 yd.), and 50 × 18 m (57 × 19.5 yd.) (Jones and Bird, 1972, 64). At the latter site, hushing also appears to have been done with water from the dams to the west of the site; these were semi-circular, with two sluices, and were used during what Jones and Bird have interpreted as the later stages of the site (1972, 68–70).

The above sites are examples of soft-rock sites where one would expect hushing to be the principal mining method employed, but numerous examples of hushing tanks have also been found at hard-rock sites such as Iboyo, Fresnedo, Puerto del Palo, Braña la Folgueirosa (Bird, 1972) and Dolaucothi. The main purpose for hushing at sites such as these would have been to remove overburden and expose the ore-bearing veins. Lewis and Jones have provided good evidence for changes in function of hushing tanks at

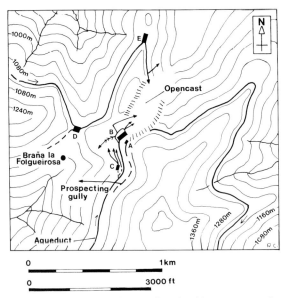

Figure 24.9 Braña la Folgueirosa, a hard-rock site, where hushing appears to have been used (*after Bird*)

Dolaucothi (1969, 255) and indeed this is to be expected. Examples are known of the conversion of such tanks for subsequent use as reservoirs for water storage in general or for providing water for functions such as sluicing and ore washing.

At Puerto del Palo, a tank measuring 55 × 5 m (60 × 5.5 yd.), with walls over 3.5 m (3.8 yd.) high, is positioned some 15 m (16.5 yd.) from the present edge of the larger opencast (Lewis and Jones, 1970, 179). Tank B at Braña la Folgueirosa (fig. 24.9) measures 61 × 10 m (72 × 11 yd.), survives to a height of over two metres (2.2 yd.), and probably had a capacity of 1,300,000 l (286,000 gal.) when full. It was constructed by digging into the hillside and using the excavated material for the outer bank (Bird, 1972, 41). Several of the tanks at Dolaucothi have been excavated and have yielded evidence for the methods of construction employed as well as of changes in function of the tanks. The larger tank fed by the Annell aqueduct at this site measured 27.5 × 12 m (30 × 13 yd.) and was also built by cutting back into the hillside. Tank C, approximately 24 × 6 m (26 × 6.5 yd.), originally had an outer wall 7.9 m (8.5 yd.) across constructed of laminated clay and shale, strengthened on the interior by a clay layer over 3 m (3.3 yd.) thick, and further reinforced on the outside by turf layers and a timber beam (Jones and Lewis, 1971, 294).

Water was released from the hushing tanks via sluices controlled by gates. A timber gate has been excavated from tank E (a reservoir, rather than a hushing tank) at Dolaucothi, but examples of stone gates are also known, for example from las Medulas. The water flowed down huge V-shaped sluices (see Lewis and Jones, 1970, pl. XXIIIc) to the edge of the opencast and poured over, washing all before it.

Pliny's description (xxxiii, 75) of hushing, in which he records the use of five sluices, is well known. Bird (1972, 42), however, considers that such a number would have been unlikely as a much stronger rush of water would have been achieved by using fewer sluices. Most tanks do in fact seem to have had only one, but these probably divided into numerous smaller channels as they neared the edge of the opencast. At Dolaucothi for instance, the two channels leading down from the larger tank mentioned above divide into at least eight smaller ones at the head of the opencast (Lewis and Jones, 1969, 266) though these may well have been used for ground sluicing rather than hushing.

It must also be remembered that the remains that are visible now represent the final stages of working. Obviously hushing tanks were originally situated some distance back from the edge of the opencasts, the water pouring large distances down the sluices before it reached the edge: this would have given the water more force and also meant that mining could be continued until the face of the opencast was worked back close to the hushing tank. At Dolaucothi the larger tank above Area I opencast is still 35 m (38 yd.) from the edge. Conversely, many tanks are now perched right on the lip; further use of hushing would almost certainly have resulted in their collapse into the mine. Jones and Bird (1972, 70) have found evidence in the Duerna valley of an incompletely worked site in which the tanks are placed at a much lower level than at other mines; on this basis they suggest that work on the sites began at the base of the auriferous deposit and was gradually worked back and upwards by combined hushing and ground sluicing.

At some sites, such as la Leitosa (fig. 24.10), the vast amount of unwanted material shifted by hushing has resulted in the build-up of huge alluvial fans in the river valleys below the sites. At las Medulas, a section cut by a stream through the plain has revealed alluvial material some 30 m (32 yd.) deep that is the result of Roman exploitation of this vast mine.

Naturally, since it is a most effective way of clearing overburden, hushing was also used for prospecting: hush-gullies have been identified at las Medulas, Puerto del Palo, Braña la Folgueirosa, and Castropodame, which include both hard- and soft-rock sites. Such evidence obviously indicates unsuccessful prospecting: if it had been successful, all traces of the hush-gully would have been removed by subsequent mining to create an opencast.

The second type of primary surface mining technique was ground sluicing, involving the use of a more controlled, continuous flow of water. It could be employed in two ways: firstly and more commonly, after hushing, to wash out ore-bearing material which had been exposed by that method or, secondly, on its own, as a way of clearing overburden and washing out the ore. Identification of this technique, as with hushing, has been largely as a result of comparison with nineteenth-century mining methods. Ground sluicing, as described by Paul (1947, 151–2), involved the excavation of a shallow

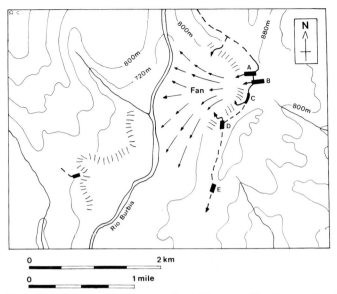

Figure 24.10   Plan of la Leitosa showing the vast alluvial fan created by the use of hushing (*after Bird*)

trench down the slope that was to be worked into which a stream of water was directed. The miners then picked and shovelled material from the nearby paddock into the flowing water. Lighter material was washed away but heavier particles (gold in this case) settled on the bottom and could be removed later when the water supply was closed off.

As far as Roman mining techniques are concerned, the steep nature of many of the sites, particularly in north-west Spain, would have precluded any human involvement in ground sluicing and it was probably achieved by relying on water action alone to wash down the sought-after auriferous material. Long gully systems running down from tanks at sites such as la Leitosa and las Medulas (Bird, 1972, 57–8), sometimes crossing each other do, however, provide evidence of the use of this method.

Although few traces usually remain in the opencasts themselves, it seems safe to assume that ground sluicing was used as an adjunct to hushing and that the two methods are responsible for creating the opencasts. Obviously, these two methods overlap to a certain extent and evidence for them may be confusing, especially because the basic equipment, a tank or dam and one or more sluices, may be the same. The example from Dolaucothi, where the sluice leading from the larger hushing tank divides into eight smaller channels as it nears the opencast, has already been mentioned; it is not, by any means, a unique case.

Definite evidence has been provided by several sites in the Duerna valley (Jones and Bird, 1972, 16–2) and las Omanas (Bird, 1972, 53). At these sites, overburden is shallower and the gold-bearing deposits closer to the surface than in most of the other northern Spanish sites. After preliminary hushing to remove the top of the overburden,

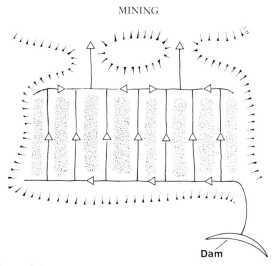

Figure 24.11   Ground sluicing as employed at various sites in the Duerna valley (*after Bird*)

the deposits were worked back in steps by a more recognizable form of ground sluicing. At the back of each step was a leat; sluices ran down from it at regular intervals to a gully below (fig. 24.11). Water was released from a dam at the top of the site, flowed across the top leat and was channelled into the sluices, each probably being worked in turn. Ore-bearing material from the surrounding paddock would have been shovelled in, and the gold retrieved from the lower gully. Similar methods of ground sluicing have been practised in more recent times (for example, Griffith, 1960, 120–1; Peele, 1941, 10–542).

Use of this technique can result in the clearing of quite large areas down to bedrock, but evidence can often be seen on the Spanish sites in the form of large rock piles. Jones and Bird (1972, 60) have suggested that large rocks would have been removed from the sluices at an early stage; some may, however, have been left there to act as natural riffles (as described by Paul, 1947, 152) behind which the gold could collect. Either way, these mounds, composed of rocks extracted at some stage from the sluices, are characteristic of many of the sites in north-west Spain and prove that ground sluicing was used.

At a few other sites, signs of other mining techniques can be detected. These are, as yet, isolated examples but as such provide more proof that the mining methods employed by the Romans were devised in response to the different conditions, both geographical and geological, of the sites they were exploiting. At Fucochicos (Jones and Bird, 1972, 71–3), also in the Duerna valley, there is a large horseshoe-shaped opencast with an aqueduct leading to it, but no traces of any tank or dam are to be seen. A ridge of alluvial material, 4 m (4.4 yd) high, follows the shape of the opencast (fig. 24.12); water was channelled between this ridge and the face of the opencast, thus undercutting the cliff. The water would also have washed debris through to the end

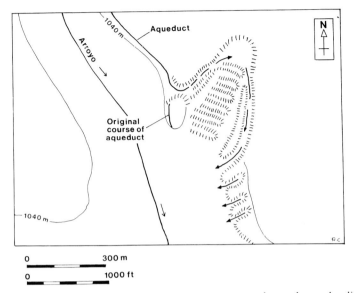

Figure 24.12   Plan of Fucochicos where a channel of water was used to undercut the cliff (*after Jones and Bird*)

of the channel between the ridge and face where the gold would have been removed, presumably by sluicing.

It appears that at at least one site, Montefurado in the Sil valley (fig. 24.13), there is some evidence for the damming and diversion of the river so that the auriferous stream-placer deposits in the exposed riverbed could be extracted. It has been suggested (Lewis and Jones, 1970, 171–4) that at this site a tunnel was cut to work a hard rock vein deposit; later the river was diverted through the tunnel, thus cutting off a loop in the river from which gold could be mined. As yet there is no irrefutable proof and nothing at the site is dateable; it is, however, the only site where there is sufficient evidence even to propose the use of such a method and it seems not unreasonable to expect that the Romans employed such a technique: they clearly had the required technical competence.

Finally, secondary mining techniques should be mentioned. In this category are included such methods as the use of washing tables, sluice boxes, perhaps even panning: that is, all the methods that were used to extract ore-bearing material either after it had been washed out by hushing and ground sluicing or, of course, after it had been obtained by the underground mining methods described earlier: the methods for finally collecting and concentrating the ore are applicable to mined material from both hard and soft-rock deposits.

As previously mentioned, such methods are practicable because most ores are heavy and will settle out of flowing water while lighter waste will be carried away. Unfortu-

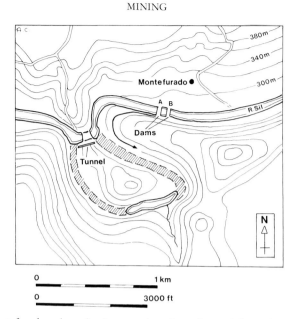

Figure 24.13   Montefurado, where the river may have been diverted through the tunnel in order to
facilitate mining of the river bed thus exposed (*after Lewis and Jones*)

nately, except in the case of stepped washing tables cut into the ground, actual evidence
for the use of these methods is virtually non-existent and again reliance must be placed
on analogy with more recent mining methods, particularly those of the nineteenth-
century gold rushes.

Stepped washing tables, connected to a water supply have, nevertheless, been identified at several sites, notably Dolaucothi (Lewis and Jones, 1969, 256–8; Jones and
Lewis, 1971, 294) and Braña la Folgueirosa (Bird, 1972, 43). When cut into the ground,
they represent an extension of ground sluicing techniques, the same technique in fact,
on a smaller and more precise scale, employed to extract the ore particles after most
of the gangue has been washed away by hushing and ground sluicing or removed by
crushing.

Although no actual remains have been found, it is to be expected that wooden
sluice boxes (fig. 24.14) or long toms (fig. 24.15) were also constructed. As with other
sluicing techniques, the heavier ore particles are caught behind the riffles and unwanted
material is washed away. Pliny makes it clear that the Romans were familiar with sluicing
techniques and although his description (xxxiii, 76) seems to refer more specifically to
the use of stepped sluices or washing tables cut into the ground, both types were probably
used.

In summary, the mining techniques employed by the Romans were, in almost every
instance, the most appropriate for the type of deposit being worked: they were adapted

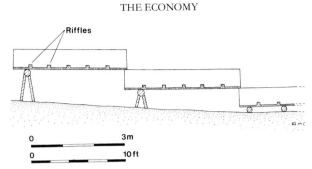

Figure 24.14 Wooden sluice boxes as employed in modern mining (*after Griffith*)

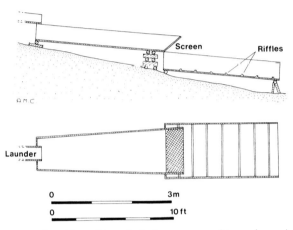

Figure 24.15 Another type of washing table, called a long tom, used in modern mining (*after Griffith*)

to the site rather than to the particular mineral being sought. Although it is generally believed that they had little geological knowledge, they were obviously aware of the problems created by various environments and adapted their mining methods accordingly. While not denying their achievements in underground mining, particularly in dealing with drainage problems, their surface techniques are probably of greater importance: the size and extent of these workings, in both hard- and soft-rock deposits, and the engineering and organization involved, first, in providing the water necessary for the methods used in their exploitation and, second, in actually carrying out these techniques on such a vast scale, must rank as one of the most outstanding, if relatively unglamorous, achievements in the ancient world. It is worth remembering that many of the sites mined during the period of Roman domination, particularly in north-west Spain, have not been worked since: few subsequent civilizations have had the expertise to exploit these sites at all, let alone on anything like the scale achieved during the first and second centuries.

CHAPTER 25

·TRADE·WITHIN·THE· ·EMPIRE·AND·BEYOND·THE· ·FRONTIERS·

A. J. Parker

Trade was regarded as ungenteel by the land-owners and literati of ancient Rome, just as it was by the aristocracy and gentry of more recent times. The ownership of land lay at the centre of the traditional Roman view of society and status, as may be seen in the census qualifications required for membership of the governing classes (Part 9). However, the use of land was not confined to recreation or feeding the owner's household; profits, whether from rents or from the sale of produce, were intentionally sought, with the aid of labour (slaves, hired labourers or tenants), agents, equipment (for processing and packaging produce), wagons and boats, etc., as appropriate. Commercial services as such were relatively undeveloped, but links of kinship or friendship between landed families in Rome and in the provinces enabled agents, servants, couriers and shippers to be called upon according to need. Such people must also have been the ostensible providers of loans and guarantees which could often have come originally from senators who remained in the background (D'Arms, 1981).

Such was the picture in the second and first centuries BC. The officers' share of the profits of Roman conquests was devoted in part to the production and export of wine and other commodities, in part to the importation of luxury goods and works of art from overseas, particularly from Greece. Under the early Empire a different picture emerges. The pacification of the Mediterranean, and of an increasing number of outlying areas, enabled a boom in commercial exchanges. Manufactures such as pottery, lamps or glass, many of them made at first in Italy, found their way to the furthest frontier provinces; the extremely frequent occurrence of exotic objects in both urban and rural sites throughout the Empire can only reflect a fully-developed commercial economy (Cotton, 1979; Riley, 1981). Government taxes, levied on goods which crossed a provincial boundary, were for the most part relatively light, but none the less very likely contributed to state income and indirectly to development in general (Hopkins, 1980).

On the other hand, there were limits to the freedom of trade under the early Empire (cf. Hopkins, 1983). Corn and olive oil, and on occasion wine and other goods, were obtained by imperial officials for distribution, free or at a cheap price, to citizens living at Rome. The frontier armies, even though many of their supplies were purchased for cash, rather than exacted by taxation or requisition, consumed value without contributing to investment or production (cf. Breeze, 1982). Land-owners, especially in Africa, grew rich through the efforts of local labourers, but returned benefits only irregularly in the form of donations to public works or feasts.

However the early imperial economy is characterized, of the vigour of general commercial activity there can be no doubt. Whether economic development was a conscious policy in the emperors' minds may be doubted, though they were, of course, constantly asked by communities or individuals to help provide facilities. Usually one assumes that any imperial involvement in building roads, bridges or harbours, especially in the newer provinces, was strategic in intent; however, the same developments could not but favour trade. Thus, Lyons (Lugudunum) grew within two decades from practically nothing in *c.* 30 BC to be, not only the seat of Augustus' administration in Gaul, but also a busy commercial and manufacturing city (Walker, S., 1981; Lasfargues *et al.*, 1976). At Bordeaux, Cologne, Avenches, and elsewhere, inland ports were constructed in this period, a remarkable development of transport facilities, whether imperially inspired or not (Drinkwater, 1983; Anon., 1984; Bonnet, 1982).

In the Mediterranean region, on the other hand, the story of Roman imperial trade perhaps begins rather with the suppression of the pirates by Pompey in 67 BC, which, after a period of civil war, was followed by a lasting peace; two fleets, with headquarters at Misenum and Ravenna, kept piracy at bay until at least the third century AD. All on board a ship from Alexandria, standing in to Puteoli late in Augustus' reign, justifiably cheered the old emperor and said that he was responsible for their prosperity.

The largest ships were, of course, those engaged in the transport of bulky goods, such as grain, wine, or, in some cases, stone. The involvement of emperors (by command) or senators (by agents) in such shipments would likely produce the guarantees needed to assemble them. Both the stakes, and the losses or winnings, of investment in bulk cargoes were high, as it seems from the fictional Trimalchio's experience in the mid-first century AD. Such large risks may have been the exception, for, in the case of olive oil, grain, and other cargoes in the imperial period, evidence exists that the goods of several merchants were loaded aboard. Naturally, too, small consignments, for example drinking-glasses, pins, or metal ingots, are attested archaeologically even on board ships carrying a main bulk cargo of more than 400 tons. None the less, the number of large cargoes, predominantly of one commodity, distinguishes the hellenistic and imperial period in Mediterranean shipping from earlier and later periods. Probably, too, the Mediterranean must be pictured in those periods as dotted with thousands of sails: both the number of shipwrecks discovered by divers, and the casual nature of ancient references to travel by ship, indicate that traffic was generally frequent and, on important routes, intense (Casson, 1970).

The result, as archaeological finds testify, is a scene of vigorous commercial exchange; from Caesarea in Palestine to Pompeii in Italy or Londinium in Britain, imported lamps, pottery, glass and metalware are found in significant quantity. Obviously some people, and some sites, were better able than others to acquire the goods they desired. In the Mediterranean regions, Roman colonies, such as Knossos or Corinth, with their population of well-off settlers, tend to produce an especially wide range of imported objects (cf. Wright, 1980); in the frontier provinces, army garrisons, and their associated settlements, as well as commercial centres such as London, had inhabitants with similarly cosmopolitan tastes. But such places also served as centres through which objects were traded with barbarians beyond the frontier; Toulouse, for example, in the first century BC evidently constituted a centre for the export of Italian wine to Gaul (Tchernia, 1983), and this was true also of Cologne and Aquincum in the Empire (Kunow, 1980). The effects of romanization can be seen in the distribution of trade goods beyond the imperial frontier (cf. Todd, 1975, 35–42); there is, in northern Europe, a strip about 200 km (125 miles) wide in which Roman pottery, ornaments, and even coins were clearly in regular use. Further afield, more 'prestigious' items were in demand by chiefs, who, to judge from literary and other non-archaeological evidence, collected skins, amber, slaves, etc. from their people (Hedeager, 1978). In some cases Roman goods may have been gifts, made in exchange for tribal friendship or the supply of troops; in others, Roman objects might have been plundered from frontier settlements, or, more likely exacted as tolls or protection money from traders and caravans (cf. Al-Ansary, 1982). In any case, Roman goods which found their way to these economically less-developed societies had a social and political function which went well beyond their use in the Roman imperial state.

Within the Empire, the most important trade was certainly that in grain. Large quantities of wheat were constantly on the move, sometimes for great distances. At Rome, anyway, the acknowledged objective of free or rationed corn distribution was to ensure *quies*, good order (Rowland, 1976). The avoidance of shortages and the prevention of price increases were obviously vital, especially as many inhabitants of imperial Rome were essentially unemployed, and there was no public cash relief. By constructing granaries, and having officials who were responsible for keeping them full, the emperors gradually took the staple of the citizens of Rome out of the hands of merchants, so that 'corners' could not be made. In the provinces, governors acted similarly, if they could; in Pisidia, for example, about AD 93 the governor took measures to force merchants not to hoard corn at a time of shortage but to bring it out for sale, and also fixed a maximum price (McCrum and Woodhead, 1961, no. 464). Even here it may have been principally the city of Antioch that was thus protected; in times of famine, countryfolk had to eat what they could find.

The imperial system refrained from taking over the supply of the capital altogether; although regulations were made affecting the principal supply routes (e.g. from Alexandria to Rome, by the Flavian period, four months' supply in each year came to Rome from Egypt), the actual provision of corn and of ships was normally left to merchants and shippers (Rickman, 1980). In the early Empire, shippers were left free agents, albeit sometimes rewarded by inducements (Rougé, 1966, 465–74; Pomey and Tchernia, 1978). In the late Empire, a more centralized system was operated in the west, especially after the foundation of Constantinople, to which Egyptian grain was diverted; a tax in kind was now regularly collected and will normally have produced a surplus from provinces such as Sicily or those in north Africa. Shippers, too, were required by imperial edict to undertake regular voyages with corn.

The corn trade is the principal example of trade which was regular, often long-distance, and involved large quantities. Another example is that of preserved fish and fish-sauce. In the Mediterranean region, fish, both fresh and preserved, and fish-sauce were a normal part of the diet, at any rate in places within reach of the sea. Dried or salted fish, processed in quite distant regions where fish of appropriate kinds were plentiful, was a convenient object of trade for supplying distant cities. 'Bread and sauce' were the two elements of a Greek dinner, the sauce normally being understood as fish, and such was the usual diet of ordinary people in Roman times, too. Tunny was a favourite salt fish; it was caught and processed in Bithynia, Africa, Baetica and elsewhere. Archaeological evidence from the Roman period suggests that mackerel and sardines were also widely consumed; mackerel from the south coast of Spain, and sardines from the southern and central parts of Lusitania, were transported in *amphorae*, common in the first century AD, less frequent in later centuries. Romans also had a passion for salty sauces made by steeping fish in vats packed with salt. The sauces, which went by various names such as *garum* or *allec*, were used in cooking or as a condiment at table; greatly in demand by gourmets at Rome, they were also consumed widely in the frontier provinces, where they may have served a dietary need, but certainly provided a tang of home, or of high life. The distribution of first-century southern Spanish fish-sauce *amphorae* reflects this; they are found particularly in Roman garrisons in Germany and Britain, and also to some extent in civil settlements of the period. It would be absurd to suppose that fish sauce was supplied in response to some kind of official order, or a regular arrangement for ordering soldiers' rations; it can only have been bought, supposedly as a relatively expensive commodity, by those with money, who at this time were principally the soldiers. Here, then, is an example of long-distance trade stimulated, as far as can be told, purely by the consumers' demand.

The conditions of southern Spain and Portugal were obviously particularly favourable for fish-preserving and sauce-making; plentiful fish and ample sunshine made production simple. However, the distance from the Mediterranean to the north-west frontiers must have made Spanish fish sauce expensive, and it is thus no surprise to find that in the second and third centuries AD fish-sauce factories were set up in Brittany, and even in London (Galliou, 1983, 125–35; Bateman and Locker, 1982). As with manufacturing industries (p. 643 below), the trend was for production gradually to move towards the consumer. In some cases (e.g. *terra sigillata*) this may have been due to a decline or collapse in the production centres; in Lusitania, however, if not other parts of Spain, fish preserves were still being exported to Mediterranean consumers as late as the first decades of the fifth century AD. Therefore the reason for the decline in provincial finds, which is marked from the end of the first century AD, must be a drop in demand for the exotic product. However, the provincialization of the culture of the frontier provinces in the third and fourth centuries affected this trade, too; fish-sauce merchants (*negotiatores allecarii*) are recorded on inscriptions of the late second and early third centuries from the shrines of Nehalennia at the old mouth of the Rhine, but after *c.* 275 there is little evidence of any kind for this trade outside the Mediterranean region (cf. Hassall, 1978).

Within the Mediterranean region, fish sauce was produced almost everywhere. In the first century AD in Pompeii, fish products were imported from southern Spain, but there was also a local industry; Pompeian fisheries had a certain repute, and some Pompeian fish-sauce jars, a distinctive type of narrow-necked flagon, have been found at Rome, but they are almost completely unknown elsewhere. Such industries existed in many coastal areas, but only in special circumstances can they have exported much. A rather different picture emerges in the case of two other Mediterranean products, wine and olive oil. Although both are thought of as characteristic of Mediterranean agriculture, their production on an economic, as opposed to a household, scale was localized, at least, in the early Empire. Moreover, for whatever reason, viticulture and wine making spread slowly to areas such as Gaul, and olives remained at all times a specialized crop.

Wine that was good enough to travel had been shipped in *amphorae* from Syria, Greece, Etruria, Carthage and elsewhere from pre-classical times onwards. In the third century BC, exports from Campania, Latium, Etruria, and possibly from Spain began to assume a noticeable frequency, to judge from finds of so-called Graeco-Italic *amphorae* (Will, 1982). From the mid-second century onwards, great quantities of Italian wine were exported, to Africa, Spain, and, above all, to Gaul, in *amphorae* of Dressel form 1, strongly made and securely stopped and sealed to stand up to long-distance carriage (pl. 25.1). Much of this wine was of fine quality, such as the Caecuban wine lost in the wreck of la Madrague de Giens (pl. 25.1) in the period 60–35 BC; it came from vineyards in southern Latium, and the corks were sealed with merchants' marks to authenticate the contents (Tchernia *et al.*, 1978). The *amphorae* from this site do not preserve their painted labels, but finds elsewhere show that the estate, the variety of grape, and the date were often indicated, just as they are on a modern good-quality wine label. Roman and Italian land-owners doubtless took pride in the production of fine wine, but they also regarded its sale as a valuable source of profit. Substantial invest-ment was of course required, not only in the land, equipment and staff needed to produce the wine, but also in ships and even harbours; although such affairs are largely concealed by Roman gentlemanly reticence, there is little doubt that rich, landed families such as the Sestii of Cosa were involved, often through servants or agents, in all aspects of wine export (D'Arms, 1981; Will, 1982).

Surprisingly, this trade seems not to have survived on any scale into the Empire. During the first part of Augustus' reign, Italian amphora-makers changed from the tradi-tional Dressel form 1 to a lighter, more economical form, the Dressel 2–4. This form, which imitated the Greek *amphorae* of Cos, began to be made, not only in Italy, but also in Spain and Gaul, and, in the first century AD, it is *amphorae* from the provinces at least as much as from Italy which are found in wrecks and on land (Tchernia, 1980; Arthur, 1982). Several explanations can be advanced for this change; one must be the peaceful conditions of the Augustan period, which permitted free competition between production areas, but it may also be that, for unrecorded reasons, Italian producers ceased to make the high-tannin wines, chemically similar to modern claret, which had been bottled in the Dressel 1 *amphorae* and commanded a market as far afield as Britain and Palestine in the first century BC. Besides Spanish and Gallic wine, Rhodian wine *amphorae* are also found in mid-first century AD provincial sites, showing that consumers were still prepared to meet the cost of transporting wine from distant areas of production. However, during the late first and the second centuries, wine production spread north-wards through Gaul, and Gallic *amphorae* and Rhenish barrels form the archaeological record of wine imports to Britain. In the later period, wine was still transported around the eastern Mediterranean region in *amphorae*, but in most of the western provinces drinkers seem to have relied more on local products – at Rome, Italian wine, and, in the frontier provinces, very probably mostly beer (Whitehouse, 1981; Boon, 1974c, 286).

Whereas wine remained an unessential, albeit enjoyable, ingredient of life, olive oil must have seemed indispensable, since it was used not only for cooking but also for lighting and personal hygiene. In the first, second and third centuries AD there is scarcely a site, no matter how humble, in the western provinces which has not produ-ced at least one sherd of the Spanish oil amphora, Dressel 20 (fig. 25.1). From archaic Greek times onwards, *amphorae* used for olive-oil transport were made of coarse, porous clay and had a generally bulky, rounded shape; such were the Apulian and Tripolitanian *amphorae* of the first century BC, and so were the Baetican Dressel 20. No certain example of this form exists earlier than the closing years of the first century BC, yet by the Claudian period they were being widely exported (Colls *et al.*, 1977). At Rome, Spanish oil jars, broken and dumped after decanting, form a large proportion of the Monte Testaccio, a great mound of sherds near the Tiber quays; there are indeed Tripolitanian and other *amphorae* in the Testaccio as well, but, in the mid second century, a period whose remains have been particularly thoroughly examined, Spanish *amphorae* were certainly the most

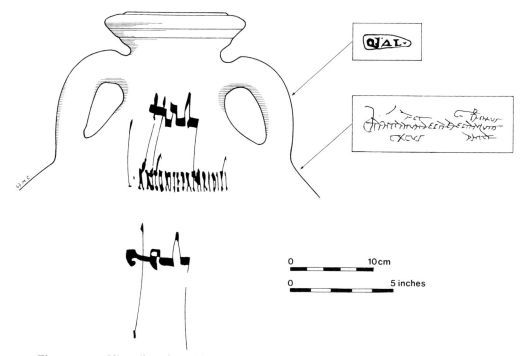

Figure 25.1 Olive-oil *amphora* with stamped and painted inscriptions giving the manufacturer and merchant, and dated to the mid-second century. Found in a shipwreck off the south of France (*after Liou and Callender*)

numerous. In this period, perhaps the peak of prosperity at Rome, care was taken to secure a regular supply of good quality oil; imperial agents were stationed both in Baetica and at Ostia to arrange shipping contracts.

The extensive spread of Baetican oil exports is documented not only by anonymous sherds but also by the stamps, which were applied, apparently on a minority of *amphorae*, by potters as a maker's mark. The stamp illustrated (fig. 25.1), Q.I.AL, was found in a mid-second century AD shipwreck at l'Anse Saint-Gervais, Fos-sur-Mer (ancient *Fossae Marianae*, at the canalized mouth of the Rhone). In the same cargo were similar *amphorae*, stamped L.S.A.R. These stamps, which must represent the abbreviated name of the owner of the pottery, with an added initial or control mark, have been found in Baetica itself, at Rome (several examples), at Arles, Orange and Vienne in Southern Gaul, at Heddernheim in Germany, and at Wroxeter in Britain – a typical distribution for Spanish olive-oil *amphorae* (Callender, 1965, nos 925d and 1460b). Those in the Saint Gervais shipwreck still bear their painted labels; the illustration shows (a) XXCVS: $85\frac{1}{2}$ pounds, the weight of the empty *amphora*: (b) L. ANTONI EPAPHRODITI: the oil merchant responsible for shipping the oil, Lucius Antonius Epaphroditus; (c) CXCVS: $195\frac{1}{2}$ pounds, the weight of the oil – 64 kg, i.e. 71.3 l ($15\frac{1}{2}$ gal) of oil; (d) *ac(cepi)t g primus charitianum aeliae aelian(ae) luiis cxcus anice[t(us)]*: 'received by Primus, oil from the Charitianus farm, owner Aelia Aeliana; 57½ [unexplained]; 195½ (pounds) weighed by Anicetus'. Other *amphorae* in the same cargo were also shipped by Antonius Epaphroditus, but contained oil from a different estate; there was also some oil shipped by Antonius Melissus and Antonius Peregrinus, who may have been freedmen in the service of the same house as Antonius Epaphroditus. Documents such as these show how much of western imperial trade was run on a family basis; the family might be based in Baetica, or southern Gaul, but a son or a trusted freedman would be posted to Ostia or Rome to act at the far end of the main despatch route (Liou, 1980).

The trade goods so far discussed have been bulky and heavy, and consignments took up most or all of a ship. Smaller consignments might be added, by the shipper or by individual crewmen, to use up space, and in some cases, logically enough, these could be of goods which complemented the main cargo. Thus, ships bearing a wine cargo sometimes carried drinking cups as well, especially where, as in Campania in the third and second centuries BC, high quality pottery was made in the same area as the wine (Morel, 1981). In the wreck at la Madrague de Giens (p. 639 above) there have been found numerous coarse-ware pots, including over 200 vessels in a red ware made, like the main cargo of wine *amphorae*, in Italy (pl. 25.1). However, small consignments of this kind need not have been loaded in their area of origin, but were doubtless often acquired from dealers at the quayside or direct from other ships in port. Thus, aboard the ship wrecked at la Madrague de Giens, there were more than 300 cups and other vessels of black-gloss ware, many of them apparently of non-Italian, albeit western, fabric (Morel, 1981, 64 and 96). The point remains, though, that much of the impetus towards trade in Roman manufactured goods was due, not merely to the political and other background situation of the late Republic and early Empire, but also to the spread of Roman customs and the demand from provincial subjects for both the consumable supplies and the equipment which such customs required. Such must also be true of oil-lamps. The glossy, red, moulded pottery lamps made in Italy in the first and second centuries AD are found at most provincial sites, at least in forts and towns; the use of such lamps to burn imported olive oil, while it may have been more pleasant and efficient than that of locally-produced dips or candles, must have been rather expensive and due principally to a desire to be 'stylish' (Bailey, 1974). In any case, whole cargoes of lamps are unknown; the largest known consignment, from which 2,300 lamps have been recovered (though there were certainly more on board originally), from a ship wrecked at Gruissan in southern Gaul *c.* AD 130, can have been only a complement to the other cargo, including *mortaria*, of what was apparently a large vessel (Solier *et al.*, 1981, 85–114). For such complementary or 'piggy-back' consignments to be worthwhile, a regular flow of bulk goods was obviously necessary. In the case of fine-wall pottery drinking cups, made in southern Spain and exported in small numbers to pre-Flavian sites in Britain and elsewhere, the substantial movement of olive oil and fish sauce provided opportunity for some cases of pottery to find their way to retailers in the far-off provinces (Greene, 1979, 134ff.). Clearly, such trade was threatened, not only by decline in demand or a crisis among suppliers, but also by any change or interruption to the 'host' traffic. At all events, neither Italian lamps nor Spanish cups reached the frontier regions for long; by the third century, if not before, most British homes must have been using locally made lights, as imported pottery lamps are practically unknown, and many types of pottery and glass drinking cups supplanted cups from the south from the late first century on. By contrast, oil-lamps were made and used, often in huge numbers, in the Mediterranean region throughout antiquity; though many were of local origin, some centres (such as Cnidus) exported special types of lamp, and in the case of Africa (if not elsewhere) both tableware and lamps found widespread buyers (see below).

In the case of the manufactured goods so far discussed, distinctive characteristics and circumstances of discovery indicate the place of production, and thus permit the movement of goods to be traced from findspots. Advances in archaeological techniques have already enabled many types of pottery or *amphorae* to be ascribed to a source, and much work of this kind remains to be done (Peacock, 1977). Some classes of object, however, are harder to identify in these ways; most metals, and also glass, may include no characteristic elements related to their origin, and glass in particular was normally made with at least some recycled material. In the case of oil-lamps, the very method of manufacture, using a pattern to create moulds from which the actual lamps were made, not only limited the opportunity for distinctive marks to be applied by the potter but also encouraged imitation and 'pirate' production (Bailey, 1976). Thus, lamps such as the widespread type of plain lamps bearing the mark FORTIS must have originated from many points of production which makes discussion of such industry and its products of limited value in present circumstances (Bailey, 1980, 96 and 275; but cf. Harris, 1980a). Moreover, not only were products imitated, but producers often set up branch factories, travelled about, or even migrated, taking their designs and even their actual moulds with them. Such migration of production is a recurrent and significant theme in the period of the Empire. Three examples are the production of *terra sigillata*, glass vessels, and *mortaria*.

The red-gloss ware of central Italy, generally known as arretine ware, began to be made at Arezzo in Etruria in the decade following 50 BC (Goudineau, 1968). The finest products (pl. 23.6) were elegant, moulded cups and jugs, with decoration created by modelling punches in the shape of figures and floral patterns which were impressed into the mould from which the body of the cup was made. Plain vessels were, of course, made in great numbers and exported, but even figured pieces occasionally turn up in the provinces (e.g. Brown, 1968, no. 25). The factories of the arretine masters such as Marcus Perennius (fig. 25.2) were at first established at Arretium, or not far away; by 15 BC, however, workshops were set up nearer the coast, at Pisa (which was on the

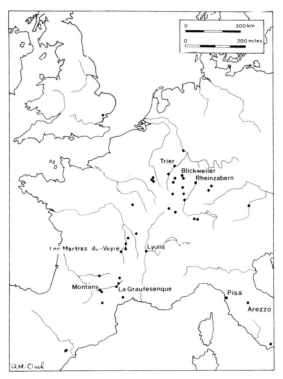

Figure 25.2 Map showing the development of samian factories (*after Marsh*)

sea in antiquity), presumably to make export to Gaul easier, and, indeed, by the same period at least one master, Cnaeus Ateius, had opened a branch at Lugudunum in Gaul (fig. 25.2). The political and commercial importance of Lugudunum, and its relative closeness to the frontier areas where high-quality wares were in demand, must be the explanation. Thereafter the chief exporting centres of red-gloss pottery were, in turn, southern Gaul in the first century, La Graufesenque and Montans; Central Gaul in the late first and second centuries, Lezoux, Les Martres-de-Veyre, etc., and then eastern Gaul, Trier, Blickweiler and Rheinzabern, in the late second and early third centuries. This rise and fall of successive producers may have been due, not to changes in the requirements of the distant customers, but to a decline in demand close to the factory for high-quality pottery (Marsh, 1981); however, the general trend, outwards towards the regions where fine wares of this kind were infrequently made, fits the picture of a centrifugal movement seen in other industries.

Such an industry was the manufacture of vessel-glass. Drinking cups and other vessels, made by the traditional cast-and-ground technique, but in increasing number and, doubtless, cheapness, were produced in the first century BC in the eastern Mediterranean region (Asia Minor, Syria and Egypt); however, archaeological finds, especially at Rome, show that production spread also to Italy by the last quarter of the century – doubtless in response to the Augustan Peace (Grose, 1977). Meanwhile, in Syria and Palestine, a revolutionary innovation, that of blowing glass vessels, took place apparently in this period. Free-blown glasses are hard to group or attribute; however, during the Augustan period some Sidonian glass-makers used moulds to shape their blown vessels. They often included their signature in the mould, and that of Ennion is especially well known (pl. 25.2). Since many glasses signed by Ennion have been found in the area of Aquileia, it is likely that Ennion either established a branch at Aquileia, or, more likely, moved there from Sidon; Aquileia was well placed to supply markets, not only in the Po Valley, but also across the Julian Alps in the Danube provinces. These migrations continued during the first century AD, and, by Flavian times, glass-making had probably spread throughout most of the western provinces. The qualities of blown glass were exploited especially in Germany and northern Gaul, notably at Cologne; from this area comes a class of long-necked jugs, their precise origin unknown, but found only in central and northern Gaul, Germany and Britain (pl. 25.3). These accomplished products show how rapidly provincial schools could develop in response to demand.

The identification of production centres and trade patterns is made more difficult by the fact that craftsmen may have been peripatetic. Jewellers, mosaicists, metalworkers and even glass-makers could have carried their materials about with them, or re-worked customers' scrap; potters and tilers, too, could have set up away from home in many circumstances. Even so, where a special quality or finish of the product was required, there were advantages in working at a single site, where the right materials and fuel were to hand. This was so with *mortaria* – large, heavy bowls for general kitchen use; a good *mortarium*, resistant to wear or breakage, could evidently find a buyer even at a long distance from the kiln, and the frequent use of prominent stamps with the maker's name (at least on *mortaria* of the mid-first to mid-second centuries) suggests that a good factory could soon acquire a reputation. Thus, in the mid-first century AD, *mortaria*, some from Rome and others from Aoste found their way to the north-west frontier regions (Hartley, 1973a; 1973b). Once more, a series of migrations took place; in the Neronian-Flavian period, by several masters including two with the name Quintus Valerius from northern Gaul to south-east Britain; again in the second century from midland to north-east Britain by the master Sarrius (Hartley, 1977a). In these examples, there is no doubt that the potters actually shifted operations; the incentive must, again, have been to get closer to reliable markets (Hartley, 1975). Moreover, as with glass-making, the wares of provincial manufacturers soon became predominant; by the end of the second century, few *mortaria* were being imported to Britain. The chief exception was a number of large vessels of distinctive shape, made in Germany and shipped by sea to London for distribution; the product itself, and the ease of delivery, in this case overcame the disadvantage of distance (Hartley, 1977b; Haupt, 1981). Elsewhere in the Roman world, Roman and Italian *mortaria* enjoyed similar appeal in the early Empire

(Riley, 1981), but cooks seem to have made do, as time went by, with less robust bowls of ordinary coarse fabric. A curious exception is found in the stamped *mortaria* made at Ras el-Basit on the Syrian coast (fig. 25.3). In the third and early fourth centuries, potters who applied stamps, not only in Greek but also in Latin, made *mortaria* which were exported principally to southern Anatolia, Cyprus, Palestine and Egypt, despite the fact that *mortaria* are relatively rare in the Mediterranean region, and stamped examples rare anywhere, by this period. It is likely enough that the Latin stamps are earlier than the Greek (fig. 25.3), and provide, therefore, a further example of the migration of craftsmen, in this case, from west to east (Hayes, 1967).

The objects of trade so far discussed have been foodstuffs or manufactured items which ended by being bought by private individuals. In the case of 'heavy' goods, however, such as timber, stone and bricks, much never reached a shop-counter but was used by professionals (Darvill and McWhirr, 1984). Moreover, both timber and the best stone were often, especially in the Mediterranean region, in short supply, or difficult to reach and transport. Trade in such goods, therefore, was more likely to remain within the control of the highest level of economic and physical power in the state, that is, under the Empire, the emperor, and, to a lesser extent, the army.

The timber requirements of the Roman world were divided into that for long, straight pieces for ships and buildings, and that for firewood. There were also special needs, e.g. for fine woods for furniture, but these must have been small compared with the others. For firewood, fruit-tree prunings and coppice wood from lowland estates would go a long way, but the demands of a large Roman city, for household cooking and heating, for workshop furnaces, and for the public baths, must, in prosperous periods, have outstripped normal sources of supply. For long timbers, on the other hand, it was necessary to climb the mountains of Lebanon, Cyprus, or Calabria, or bring trees from the distant European forests. Forest resources, especially of fir for warship

Figure 25.3 *Mortarium* manufactured at Ras el-Basit, Syria (*after Hayes*)

construction, had been tightly controlled by pre-Roman rulers, and the emperors, too, kept a grip on such strategic forests as the Lebanon range (Meiggs, 1982). The imperial peace reduced pressure on warship timber supplies, but increased all kinds of other demands, for merchant ships, for roof beams of public buildings, for quays and bridges, and so on. Curiously, there is no specific evidence that any Roman forests were regularly replanted, and there must have been a progressive shortage of good timber and even some deforestation of the landscape.

In the northern provinces, timber supplies were presumably less of a problem. However, the concrete and brick structures characteristic of Rome and parts of the Mediterranean provinces must have been hard to re-create in many parts of northern Europe; in Britain, at any rate, there are very few recorded brick-built buildings – bricks were used mostly for hypocausts and levelling courses – and tiled roofs are mostly a feature of the first and second centuries; in the later period, 'home-grown' stone tiles became normal instead. There is no provincial parallel for the tile industry of the city of Rome, where many of the tileries, by the mid-second century, were owned by members of the imperial family, their high-quality products identified by stamps giving full information about their origin; the tiles were used by the thousand to create a strong, fire-proof skin for the great concrete public buildings of Rome and the extensive commercial and domestic structures of Ostia (Steinby, 1981). By contrast, even one of the best-known provincial factories, at Minety, in southern Britain, produced tiles with a range of stamps which offer no explicit information; the map (fig. 25.4) shows the distribution of seven different tile-stamps, comprising the letters TPF and a further series-letter or initial (McWhirr and Viner, 1978). This is one of the most widely distributed British stamps, but, even so, detailed study of the stamped tiles suggests that not all the tiles were transported from the kilns at Minety, where some of them were certainly made, but that some were made at other sites, even at the place where a building was being erected, by a peripatetic tiler who carried his stamp around with him (Darvill and McWhirr, 1984). There was thus a diversity of modes of manufacture and distribution of these products; at one extreme, army units or local magistrates set up tileries to provide roofs for their buildings, and, at the other, individual tilers must have hawked their services round villa-owners who planned to improve or extend their property.

As already explained, fine stones, known to Romans and archaeologists as marble, but including granite, diorite, breccia, etc., were likely to be obtained and used principally by the emperor. Many marble quarries, by the second century AD, were imperial property, acquired by conquest, legacy or confiscation, though the actual extraction could be contracted to companies (Ward-Perkins, 1980; Pensabene, 1983). Imperial freedmen and slaves supervised operations, and the labour was done at least partly by condemned criminals, but there must also have been scope for free enterprise in cutting or transporting stone. The city of Simitthus in Numidia, established as a *colonia* in *c.* 27 BC, was peopled mostly with immigrants, attracted to the opportunity offered by exploi-

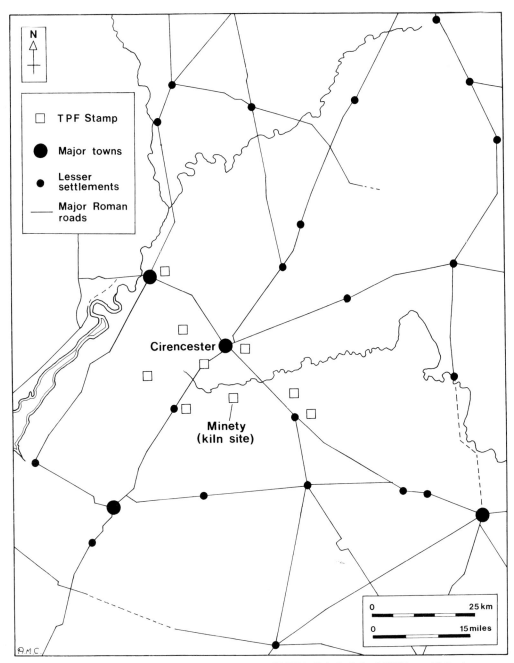

Figure 25.4 Distribution map of tiles stamped TPF in Britain (*after McWhirr and Viner*)

tation of the yellow marble of the Jebel Chemtou (Lassère, 1980). This marble, together with a dozen or so other kinds of white or coloured marble from Italy, Greece, Anatolia and Egypt, was eagerly sought after, not only because of its beautiful colour, but also because it was free from flaws and so could be relied on for columns and large architectural elements. It also provided useful quantities of veneers for floors and walls for which it was extensively used. A curious aspect of the marble trade was that very large quantities were cut in the late first and early–mid second centuries, but by no means all was used at once (Ward-Perkins, 1951; 1971). It seems as if, having set up an organization to extract and transport the stone, the emperors kept it working to provide a reserve, without paying attention to current needs. Of course, there were always opportunities for them to display generosity, by giving columns away for some new building in the provinces.

Only the base survives of a column of pink Egyptian granite which was set up to commemorate Antoninus Pius (fig. 25.5). The inscription records that the column

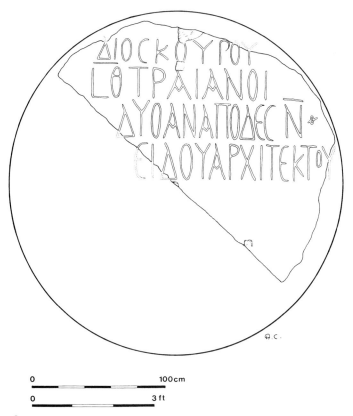

Figure 25.5   Quarry inscription on the underside of the Column of Antoninus Pius, formerly in the Campus Martius, Rome: red Egyptian granite, quarried in AD 106 (*after Ward-Perkins*)

649

was one of two, fifty Roman feet long, extracted and listed in the ninth year of Trajan's reign (AD 106) under the quarry supervisor Dioskouros and the engineer (*architektos*) Herakleides, whose name can be restored from other quarry marks of the same period. Something about the inscription suggests the pride which was taken in the successful extraction of this great monolith; even so, not quite the tallest column, nor yet the heaviest block, known to have been extracted and transported to Rome. It may indeed have been a 'spare', left over from the temple built at the head of Trajan's Forum, rather than just unallocated stock, but the fact that such a piece was available at all half-a-century later is an indication of the great quantity of stone at Rome. Moreover, the weight of such pieces (117 tons) testifies to the resources expended on their transportation. The columns of the porch of Hadrian's Pantheon (pl. 25.4), likewise of Egyptian granite, both pink and grey, suggest the scale, though they are mere forty-footers weighing 84 tons. The lintel of the porch, of Pentelic marble from Attica, must weigh 120 tons, which had to be hoisted into position, not just hauled upright. However, not all marble, even from imperial quarries, was restricted to such use; veneers and small pieces did find their way, presumably through some form of commercial distribution, to the provinces (e.g. Crummy, 1983, 107 and microfiche 3).

In the examples discussed so far, therefore, one can see a variety of trade patterns. Interest, naturally, focuses on distinctive, non-perishable items which travelled long distances, and are thus clearly identifiable in the archaeological record. However, many of the daily requirements of life were locally obtained, and of perishable substances. Most foodstuffs have left little trace; animal bones have been studied thoroughly only in parts of the Empire, and in any case are largely mute as to their origin; the serious collection and study of fish and bird bones and shells from Roman sites are still in their infancy. Vegetables were certainly part of most Romans' diet, as recipes and other written sources make clear, and flowers were grown and sold, not just for personal and household use, but to decorate shrines and victims at religious festivals (Loane, 1938); almost no actual remains of these survive. Household and farm implements, and pots and bowls, whether of normally perishable wood, or of iron, must also have been made for the most part locally, if not in the house or on the farm. On the other hand, items such as silverware, gems, or statuettes have been thoroughly listed and discussed, but, even if their findspot is known, they can have affected only a small minority of the population, and the extent to which they were really distributed by trade, as opposed to manufacture to order, and transport in their owner's baggage, is very uncertain.

Not all desirable materials could be found within the Empire, even at its greatest extent. A substantial frontier tax and other charges added to the considerable expenses incurred by what could be a very long and dangerous journey, with many tolls along the way, for exotic imports (Raschke, 1978, 670). Naturally, therefore, imports of this kind, at any rate those which had to come overland, tended to be of luxuries which could command a high price. Ivory, for example, was much used for statuettes and inlays; elephants and elephant tusks were well known as a symbol of Africa in general, but it seems likely that by the imperial period both ivory and perhaps animals were normally obtained from east Africa via Nubia (cf. Huntingford, 1980). Roman contact with west Africa seems to have been very limited (Sutton, 1983). The near eastern deserts, on the other hand, were themselves the source of some types of precious stones which were an ideal object of trade in such conditions, and which were crossed by caravans, at least at some periods (cf. Bowersock, 1983). Thus, the relatively fertile regions of south Arabia exported incense and myrrh, partly by ship to Egypt and thence to Rome, partly across the southern edge of the Arabian Desert and onward to Petra (Groom, 1981). A parallel kind of traffic was in amber from the Gdańsk (Danzig) area of the Baltic coast, which reached Aquileia normally by an overland journey (Strong, 1966, 9–10). Roman merchants made direct contacts with native suppliers on the Baltic coast in the mid-first century AD, and it was only from then until the late second century that amber was in ample supply in the Mediterranean region. Here, as elsewhere, Roman enterprise played an important part in developing external trade, and improved navigational techniques doubtless enabled more to be carried on by sea (cf. Kunow, 1980; Raschke, 1979). Many goods, including amber, were imported in a raw state, and re-worked on arrival at cities such as Aquileia and Alexandria. Gems, however, and perhaps ivory, were transported on and sold to carvers at Rome or in the further provinces. Silk, on the other hand, which had one of the longest journeys, from China via north-west India to the eastern provinces, was conveyed both as yarn and as woven fabric; expensive though it was, genuine Chinese damask was not an exorbitantly priced luxury and reached even the far north-western provinces (Crummy, 1983, 148; cf. Wild, 1984).

Such imports tended to be of small items; a more bulky trade was in pepper. In the Roman period, black and white pepper was obtained from the Malabar region of south India, modern Kerala (another type, 'long pepper', used in medicine, came from north-west India). Peppercorns, though light, bulk large, and must have been transported wherever possible by ship. Leaving either Muziris, on the south-west coast, or Barygaza, on the north-west coast, large, well-found Roman vessels ran before the winter monsoon and up the Red Sea to Egyptian ports, for transhipment to Alexandria and so onwards to Rome (Raschke, 1979; Casson, 1980). Here a whole range of warehouses, the Horrea Piperataria, was devoted to its storage, and, perhaps, sale at the emperor's profit (Loane, 1944). The pepper warehouses, divided into courtyards containing pools of water, with their evocative, appetizing fragrance, conjure up an image of the resources which could be summoned up in imperial Rome. Just as the great marble blocks could be won from distant mountains and deserts within the Empire, so too even whole warehouses could be filled with rare goods from far beyond the frontiers; as late as AD 408, Alaric could demand 3000 pounds of pepper and 4000 silk garments (according to Zosimus, 5.41.4) as part of the city's ransom. These dramatic, exotic aspects of imported goods were picked out for political use by magistrates, and above all by the emperor himself, in the case of animals. Great numbers of animals were captured, especially in the frontier areas of north Africa and Anatolia; elephants, big cats, and ostriches were particularly valued for the fine spectacle they gave when hunted or fought in the arena, but strange beasts such as the hippopotamus were also brought for exhibition. The mosaics of several late Roman villas in Sicily vividly illustrate the almost military organization involved in rounding up the beasts and getting them rapidly by oared ship to exhibition; those involved in such a business would naturally hold a special place, especially in the ceremonial atmosphere of fourth-century Rome and Constantinople.

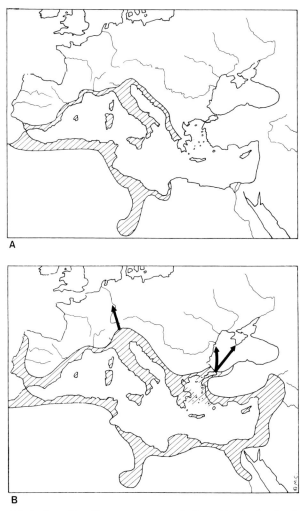

Figure 25.6   Marketing of late Roman pottery, as indicated by its distribution (*after Hayes*)

In any case, animals crossed the imperial frontier regularly, and in great numbers, for, especially in Africa, the *limes* to some extent followed an ecological boundary, and thus cut across transhumance routes (Fentress, 1979). The towers, gates and walls or ramparts which guarded and blocked valleys leading from lowland, winter grazing to upland, summer territories were no doubt constructed mainly to prevent disorder among drovers and infiltration by raiding bands (Part 4, Chapter 10; Brogan, 1979/80), but perhaps more deliberately to collect taxes (Fentress, 1979, 184; cf. Shaw, 1981, 59–60). Surviving tariffs show that nothing was forgotten (Fentress, 1979, 208–9), and humans, too, had their price, as importation must normally have been one of the main sources of slaves (cf. Harris, 1980b).

In general, the picture which can be drawn of Roman trade is of active but rather specialized development in the late Republic, followed by a boom under Augustus, which lasted, in some areas till the Flavian period, in others to the end of the second century. The disturbances and crises of the third century certainly affected trade, and, indeed, the very success of the economy of the early Empire might have contributed to its subsequent decline (Groenman-van Waateringe, 1983); however, by the third century, much of the long-distance traffic in manufactured goods and processed foodstuffs had already faded away. In many parts of the Empire, the later third century and the fourth century saw industries flourish which served a group of provinces, a province, or part of a province, but commercial contacts between, say, Germany and Rome were now much rarer than contacts between Germany and Britain. In the central Mediterranean, there appears to have been a move towards self-sufficiency; it seems that fourth- and early fifth-century Romans drank mostly Italian, indeed Latin, wines (Whitehouse, 1981). Against this background there stands the extraordinary success of the potters of Byzacena (North Africa), whose plates, dishes and lamps were widely traded in this period (fig. 25.6). From modest beginnings in the first century, African pottery exports became widespread in the second, but were essentially confined to the nearer coastal regions of the Mediterranean; in later centuries, however, they reached to the east Mediterranean and the Black Sea, and penetrated inland in many parts (Hayes, 1972). Simultaneously, as recent excavations at Carthage and other Mediterranean cities have shown, many eastern provincial centres were engaged in what was probably a relatively small-scale exchange of products which lasted almost until the Arab Conquest in the seventh century.

25.1 (a) and (b) The shipwreck at Madrague de Giens, southern France, with its cargo of *amphorae*

25.2   Glass jug from the workshop of Ennion

25.3   Glass jug found at Enfield (Middx.), Britain

25.4   The Pantheon, Rome, showing the size of the columns in the portico

CHAPTER 26

·TRANSPORT·BY·LAND·
·AND·WATER·

Alan McWhirr

As the Roman Empire expanded the need for rapid communication between distant parts and its centre became increasingly important for good government. Events in each province needed to be known in Rome, particularly those occurring in areas where detachments of the Roman army were on duty. The efficient deployment of troops necessitated both the construction of good roads in each province, and the use of ships if the army was moved from one part of the Empire to another.

Gradually military roads came to be used by the civilian population for the movement of goods throughout the Empire. With the use of boats and an efficient road system, trade flourished and goods were often transported thousands of miles. Equally important for the economy of a region were the scores of local roads, rivers and even canals which were used to move goods to market.

The map of the Empire which can be drawn today represents a palimpsest of roads built for a variety of reasons over many centuries and it is certainly far from being a complete record of those used throughout the Empire during the period under discussion (fig. 26.1). The history and development of the road network differs in each province although it is possible to identify a number of common elements. Literary and epigraphic evidence is available for some parts of the Roman world, but its quality is variable and it is not always apparent whether these references are applicable over the Empire as a whole.

As the major road network was laid out originally to facilitate the movement of troops the direction of roads and their mode of construction was governed by strategic considerations and by the type and volume of military traffic which was expected to use them. Later, when military rule was replaced by civilian authorities, the need to move from one settlement to another prompted new roads to be built, mainly to facilitate trade.

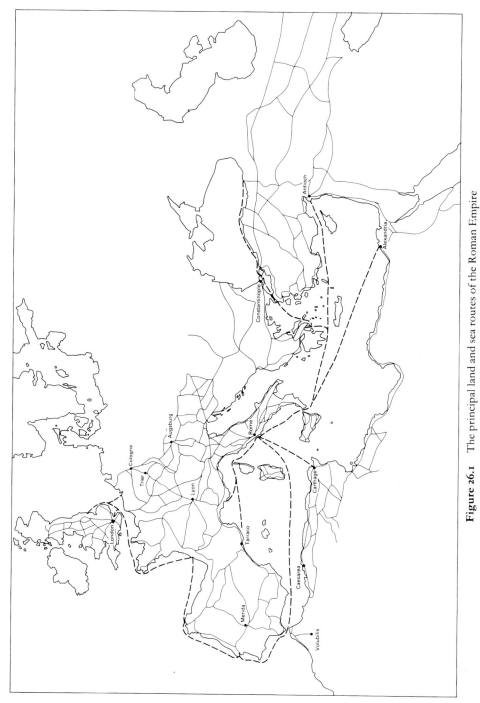

Figure 26.1   The principal land and sea routes of the Roman Empire

The major roads were built with care to withstand regular use by wheeled vehicles, but the main cross-country tracks, mainly used by traders, never developed into highways for general use and so no attempts were made to provide firm road surfaces. These tracks are difficult to locate and would not have been recorded on any of the official lists which were produced. As well as traders' tracks each rural settlement must have been linked to the major road network, but again by unmade roads, similar to those which linked modern farms to main roads before it became necessary to lay hard surfaces to enable bulk milk tankers to drive directly into the farm. They remain difficult to detect archaeologically.

There were, then, a number of different types of road ranging from those built by the army to military specifications, to those unmade tracks used by local populations for travelling to and from market. Such a range necessarily means that building methods varied. In addition, the materials from which they were constructed would have been dug nearby and so reflect the local soils and geology. The terrain through which roads passed also dictated how they were built. Low-lying and marshy land frequently required a bigger causeway than usual and sometimes it was even necessary to lay down a timber framework resting on wooden piles to give support. Galen, writing in the second half of the second century AD, comments on the fact that many roads were covered in mud or flooded by rivers and that this was corrected by raising them on high embankments. Roads cut through mountains may not have required additional surfaces to make them usable by pedestrians and vehicular traffic and in such regions are often not built in straight alignments. Clearly there is no standard Roman road; they varied both in their method of construction and, despite what has been written in the past, in their width. There are, however, one or two general points which relate to road building. Where possible the most direct route was chosen giving rise to miles of straight roads, but for topographical or other reasons roads did not always adhere to such precise alignments. During construction soft material such as topsoil was dug away and a rammed base of small stone or gravel built up to the appropriate height to facilitate drainage; this height varied from one area to another. The final surface depended upon the materials available; it might have been crushed limestone, pebbles or regularly cut slabs. The edge of the road was sometimes marked by a line of kerb stones. Ditches were frequently dug adjacent to roads to help remove water, but were not always present.

The construction of roads frequently required the skills of the civil engineer to solve specific problems such as the crossing of rivers or ravines. Architects had for some time incorporated the arch into the design of buildings and so it was a natural development for it to be used in bridge building (pl. 26.1). On navigable rivers sufficient headroom had to be left to enable boats to pass beneath as well as to support the road; both could be achieved by using the arch. On wide rivers it was necessary to build piers in the river bed thus producing a multispan bridge; whenever possible, however, single span bridges were built so as to avoid this hazardous operation. The bridge at

Narni which carried the Via Flaminia over the Tiber, originally had four arches; the survivor has a span of 32 m (105 ft) and an overall height of 30 m (98 ft) (White, 1984, 98). Not all bridges were built of stone as at Narni; there were many timber examples (pl. 26.2) and possibly bridges containing both stone and timber. Although undoubtedly some rivers were forded, bridges were erected when major roads crossed even quite small rivers. This can be clearly seen at Cirencester where a bridge was constructed over the river Churn outside the Verulamium Gate (Wacher, 1975, 302) to carry the road over a fairly insignificant stream.

Land surveyors, *agrimensores*, were capable of laying out the land with considerable accuracy and used surveying instruments such as the *groma*. Such surveyors were, no doubt, responsible for centuriation, but how far they became involved in surveying roads is not clear. The literary evidence for road construction is sparse. There are some details in a poem by Statius who was writing about the *via Domitiana*, a short stretch of road completed in AD 95 which ran from Mondragone in Campania to the port of Pozzuoli. In this poem Statius speaks of marking out the limits of the land required for the road with furrows and of the excavation of a trench which was in turn filled with foundation material. He also speaks of kerbing and of the many different groups of workmen involved, some cutting down trees, others working and fetching stone, lime burners and navvies. This brief literary account does no more than give a general picture; the detailed military manuals on road building which were, no doubt, produced for the army are lacking. Roads were in need of constant maintenance work and inscriptions often record the fact. A Spanish milestone dated to AD 79 notes that Vespasian 'rebuilt the *via Augusta* from Janus to the Atlantic, building new bridges and restoring old ones'. Another milestone from Moesia mentions the rebuilding and extending of the *Iter Scrofularium* by Domitian in AD 92–3 which was described as 'dilapidated by old age and the encroachment of the Danube'. Similar milestones note the repair of roads as far afield as Cyrene and the Lebanon.

A number of documents have survived in one form or another which provide information about the road network in the Empire. The Peutinger Table (*Tabula Peutingeriana*) is a medieval copy of a map found at Worms in the fifteenth century. The date of the original map is unknown, but it appears to be a late classical document. The surviving medieval scroll (*rotulus*) was 6.75 m (12 ft) long and 34 cm (13½ in.) wide and the map was produced in five colours. Although not drawn to scale it provides useful information about roads and settlements along them by including over 500 small 'pictures' of the settlements. The Antonine Itinerary (*Itinerarium Provinciarum Antonini Augusti*) is a much quoted work and the subject of some debate as to its origin and date. It contains 225 routes or itineraries each of which includes the starting and finishing places and a list of stopping-places along it. In addition the total mileage is given and the distance between each named place on the route. It has been noted that few of the individual *itinera* actually take the shortest route between the two named places at the head of the itinerary. This makes it most unlikely that it represents a list of routes used by the *Cursus Publicus*. Other variations within the itinerary suggest that it was not a single compilation, but a 'collection of journeys which were made or planned at different dates by different people' (Rivet, 1970, 67) and probably brought together during the reign of Caracalla. The itinerary also includes a short section on sea routes.

Mention has already been made of milestones which were erected along the principal roads of the Empire, and over 4,000 have been recorded. Generally these stones were cylindrical in shape and 2 m to 4 m (6½ ft to 13 ft) high. The inscription contains the name of the builder or restorer of the road and an indication of the distance travelled. In addition to the milestones there were also signposts probably made of wood. They are mentioned, for example, in an inscription found near Forum Popillii in Lucania and dated to 130 BC which speaks of building a road from Regium to Capua and placing on that road bridges, milestones and signposts.

Such a road network enabled people and goods to move freely. People walked, rode on horseback (pl. 19.3) or made use of a range of horse-drawn vehicles in order to travel, but the choice of transport for those engaged in trade depended to a great extent on the commodities they were carrying. All-purpose carts were used to move a wide range of goods, but there were also purpose-built carts such as that shown on a bas-relief from Langres in northern France which shows a solidly-built, four-wheeled waggon carrying a single large barrel for moving liquids in bulk (pl. 19.7). Large heavy loads of stone are likely to have required specially designed waggons or carts so that awkward shaped blocks could be moved from the quarry, not all of which were conveniently situated close to water to make use of boats. Pack animals were extensively used to transport goods particularly across rough terrain and their use in the Roman world has, in the past, probably been underestimated (pl. 19.6). In parts of the world today pottery is taken to market by mule or donkey without undue problems with breakage. Varro, in *De Re Rustica*, writes about trains of 'panniered asses' which traders formed to move oil, wine or grain (pl. 19.8). A wide variety of goods could have been carried by pack animals and no doubt many of the small rural craftsmen as well as the long-distance traders made use of them.

Larger operations, some of which were working on an industrial scale, needed to transport goods in quantity and this was achieved by using animals to haul waggons and carts. Oxen were used to pull heavy vehicles, and the design of such vehicles can be seen in sculptured reliefs from around the Empire (pl. 19.3). Transport by ox-drawn carts was not quick, travelling between thirty to fifty kilometres (20 to 30 miles) a day, and if long distances were involved it was almost certainly cheaper to go by sea.

There are many references to sea journeys in Roman literature and details of some of the boats that were used on these journeys can be seen on stone reliefs and mosaics. In addition the recent interest in underwater archaeology, in which wrecks have been examined, has provided further information about the type of boats used and how they were propelled. Merchant vessels were mostly powered by sail as teams of rowers would have taken up valuable cargo space. A representative selection of boats can be seen on mosaics from the Piazzale delle Corporazioni at Ostia (pl. 26.5). Roman boats were built by first laying down the keel, sternposts and stern, then the hull was made and the frames or ribs inserted. Outer timbers or 'wales' were fitted to give greater strength to the hull and a mixture of pitch and wax applied to joints. The design and position of the sails which were then added determined how the vessel could be manoeuvred and whether it could sail into the wind. It had been thought for a long time that Roman ships only carried a square rig (a single, or sometimes multiple, square sail) and, with such an arrangement, could not tack and so sail into the wind. However, it is now clear that various designs of fore-and-aft rigs were in use and this enabled them to sail closer to the wind. With such boats and good seamanship and navigation it is not surprising that a great deal of trade around the Empire involved the use of sea-going cargo vessels.

Rivers also played their part in providing a means of transporting goods. Undoubtedly sea-going vessels could enter some rivers and sail upstream to docks and wharfs such as those on the banks of the Thames at Londinium (pl. 26.3). On other occasions it may have been necessary to transfer cargo to river boats as was the case at Ostia. The extent to which shallow draught boats or barges were used to move produce around within a province is unclear. Today such boats can be seen in parts of the world carrying loads of pottery on quite small rivers and there is no reason to doubt that this happened in the Roman period. If rivers were situated conveniently close to where a commodity was being made then river transport would have been considered, but if goods had to be loaded on to carts and then taken to a river and transferred to boats, with the reverse process happening at the other end, then this would have been a costly and cumbersome exercise.

With so much maritime trade being carried out it was necessary to have ports and harbours where the boats could berth to load and unload. The recent interest in 'waterfront archaeology' has revealed a growing number of places where boats could berth. Not all places built sheltered harbours as at Ostia or Carthage, since they were not always necessary, but many docks were developed alongside rivers which were capable of receiving sea-going vessels. The wharfs found at London and Xanten are probably typical of the many places which existed around the Empire where ships could transfer their cargoes.

Large harbours were of course built not only to meet the demand of merchants, but also as bases for the navy. Piraeus consisted, to begin with, of a naval harbour, docks and ship-sheds, but by the fourth century AD it had become the chief commercial port of Greece with many quays and warehouses. The two harbours at Carthage have in recent years been intensively studied by a multi-national team of archaeologists (fig. 26.2). The site has been identified with the Punic naval and commercial harbours which

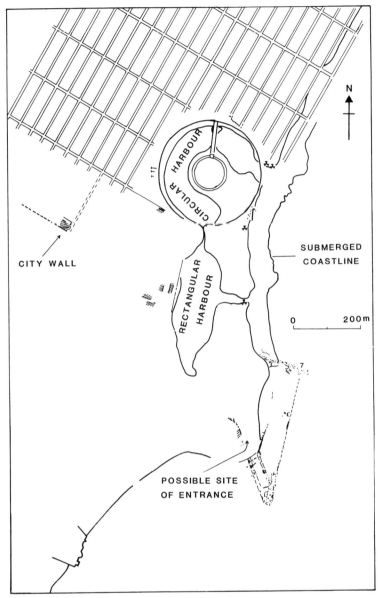

Figure 26.2 Plan of the harbour area at Carthage (*after Hurst*)

Appian described in *Libyca* (VIII, 96) and excavations on the island of the circular harbour have revealed a series of building phases dating from about 400 BC to the end of the seventh century AD. Stone-built Punic ship-sheds existed in the second century BC, but by the Augustan period they had gone out of use. At some places it is still

Figure 26.3 The harbour at Ostia (*after Meiggs and White*)

possible to see remains of harbour installations. The warehouses and porticos beside the quays at Lepcis Magna covered over 10 ha (25 acres) and parts of the 1200 m (1,350 yd) long quay still survive.

One of the best documented examples of the impact of trade in an area is at Ostia (fig. 26.3). Trade with Rome was extensive and as the city was situated 25 km (15 miles) inland the import of goods generated a thriving port and city on the sea coast at Ostia, the mouth of the Tiber, linked with Rome by roads and by the Tiber itself. The features that have been discovered on the coast may be exceptional, being the port of Rome, but they serve to illustrate a thriving community centred on a port. Initially a river harbour was sufficient to meet the needs of Rome, but by the beginning of the first century AD the size of merchant ships and the growing number began to accelerate overcrowding problems at the harbour, which had been developing for nearly a century. In addition, the silt brought down by the Tiber was causing problems both in the harbour and further out to sea, thus preventing large boats with a deep draught from entering port. A contemporary account by Dionysius of Halicarnassus gives a clear impression of what Ostia was like in the first century BC:

> The river widens considerably as it reaches the sea and forms large bays, like the best sea harbours. . . . Ships with oars, however large, and merchantmen with sails of up to 3,000 (*amphorae*) capacity enter the mouth itself and row or are towed up to Rome; but larger ships ride at anchor outside the mouth and unload and reload with the help of river vessels.

Other accounts, notably one by Strabo, refer to problems of silting and speak of Ostia being harbourless with boats having to anchor far out in the surge. Caesar planned to divert the Tiber and drain the salt marshes as well as build a harbour, but it was left to Claudius to take the initiative and begin this bold engineering venture. Suetonius tells us that:

> at Ostia, Claudius threw out curved breakwaters on either side of the harbour and built a deep-water mole by its entrance. For the base of this mole he used the ship in which Caligula had transported a great obelisk from Heliopolis . . . and finally crowned with a very tall lighthouse that guided ships into the harbour at night by the beams of a lamp.

Work on this new harbour began in AD 42 some 3 km (2 miles) north of the Tiber and by AD 46 new canals were cut to connect it directly with the Tiber and Rome. The construction of buildings around the harbour continued for at least the first ten years of Nero's reign. The next major work was initiated by Trajan who built an hexagonal inner harbour with sides about 360 m (390 yd) long around which stood a whole range of buildings including baths, temples, a theatre and a palace. The need for this inner harbour was vividly demonstrated by a disastrous storm in AD 62 when 200 ships were wrecked within the Claudian harbour. Now the inner basin afforded shelter to large ocean-going ships which could unload their cargoes safely into the warehouses around the harbour or into river-going vessels for Rome.

Some goods were stored at Ostia until they could be moved upstream to Rome, or sent by road if this was more practicable. The buildings at Ostia, therefore, reflect this involvement with trade. There are a considerable number of *horrea*, many of which were used to store grain, but perhaps the building which best illustrates the city's close involvement with trade and commerce, and particularly the use of boats for this purpose, is the Piazzale delle Corporazioni. Built at the time of Augustus this rectangular structure measured about 80 m by 110 m (87 yd by 120 yd) overall and consisted of a large open space around which was a double colonnade linking sixty-one small rooms, each of which was about 5 m by 4 m (16 ft by 13 ft). In the central open space was a temple possibly dedicated to the goddess Ceres. Of particular interest are the mosaics which were laid in front of each one of the small rooms depicting the occupation of the room's owner. The building is clearly a meeting place of traders where business was done, each room representing an office. A number were shippers as indicated by the mosaic inscriptions such as, NAVI NARBONENSES and the accompanying picture of a boat. On some of the mosaics depicting shippers a lighthouse is also seen, presumably the one which stood at the entrance to the harbour. Traders from Carthage, Alexandria, Narbonne, and Sardinia are recorded and represented are tanners, rope sellers, timber merchants, corn dealers and animal importers.

Ostia was not the only port to have been equipped with a lighthouse. They existed at Alexandria, Coruña (north-west Spain), Dover (pl. 26.4), Boulogne and Lepcis Magna and were designed not only to warn of dangers, but to guide ships safely to port.

The port of Ostia also provided another example of a type of engineering work which was to be found elsewhere in the Roman world, namely, the canal. Most canals were constructed to facilitate transport by boat, but some were cut to drain areas of land and to control rivers which might flood. The engineering problems in constructing such canals were considerable and great skill was required to maintain sufficient water to enable boats to move freely, involving the use of locks, barrages, sluice gates and weirs. Two literary references mention the movement of goods by canal. Tacitus speaks of a plan to connect the Rhine and Saône so that merchandise could pass from the Mediterranean along them and into the seas beyond (*Annals* 13.53.3). The Younger Pliny wanted to connect a lake in the province of Bithynia with the sea (10.41).

The success of the communication system can be judged by the extent to which goods were traded within the Empire, something referred to elsewhere in this volume (Chapter 25). Although many roads and harbours were originally constructed to facilitate the movement of troops, they were later used for trading purposes and so were maintained. It is not surprising, therefore, that the Roman road network has left its mark on the modern landscape.

26.1   Roman bridge at Rimini

26.2   South-west corner of the late first-century timber quay and possible abutment (in the background) of the contemporary bridge over the Thames, at Pudding Lane, London

26.3 Late first-century timber quay backed by an open-fronted warehouse.
The drain is second-century: Pudding Lane, London

26.4   The *pharos* at Dover

26.5   Mosaic from the Piazzale delle Corporazioni, Ostia, showing a grain ship from Sicily.
The inscription refers to the *naviculare et negotiantes Karalitani*, shipowners and merchants from Cagliari

·BIBLIOGRAPHY·FOR·PART·8·

Abbott, F. F. and Johnson, A. C. (1926), *Municipal Administration in the Roman Empire*, New York.

Agricola, G. (1950), *De Re Metallica* (translated H. C. Hoover and L. H. Hoover), New York.

Al-Ansary, A. R. (1982), *Qaryat al-Fau. A Portrait of Pre-Islamic Civilisation in Saudi Arabia*, Riyadh.

Anon (1984), 'L'îlot Saint-Christoly, arrière port de Burdigala', *Archéologia*, 192–93, 62–5.

Arthur, P. (1982), 'Roman amphorae and the *Ager Falernus* under the Empire', *Papers of the British School at Rome*, 50, 22–33.

Bailey, D. M. (1974), 'Six Roman lamps from London', *Antiquaries Journal*, 54, 292–5.

Bailey, D. M. (1976), 'Pottery lamps', in D. E. Strong and P. D. C. Brown (eds), *Roman Crafts*, London, 93–103.

Bailey, D. M. (1980), *A Catalogue of the Lamps in the British Museum, 2, Roman Lamps made in Italy*, London.

Ballance, M. H. (1969), 'Regio Ipsina et Moetana', *Anatolian Studies*, 19, 143–6.

Bastien, P. (1967), *Le Monnayage de bronze de Postume*, Wetteren.

Bastien, P. (1984), *Le Monnayage de Magnence* (second edition), Wetteren.

Bateman, N. and Locker, A. (1982), 'The sauce of the Thames', *London Archaeologist*, 4, 204–7.

Bean, G. E. (1959), 'Notes and inscriptions from Pisidia, Part I', *Anatolian Studies*, 9, 67–117.

Bean, G. E. (1968), *Turkey's Southern Shore*, London.

Bird, D. G. (1972), 'The Roman gold-mines of north-west Spain', *Bonner Jahrbücher*, 172, 36–64.

Bird, D. G. (1980), 'Review of works by C. Domergue', *Britannia*, XI, 434–6.

Bogaers, J. E. (1983), 'Foreign affairs', in B. Hartley and J. S. Wacher (eds), *Rome and her Northern Provinces*, Gloucester, 13–32.

Bolin, S. (1959), *State and Currency in the Roman Empire to AD 300*, Stockholm.

Bonnet, F. (1982), 'Les ports romains d'Aventicum', *Archäologie der Schweiz*, 5.2: 127–31.

Boon, G. C. (1974a), 'Aperçu sur la production des métaux non-ferreux dans la Bretagne romaine', *Apulum* 9, 453–503.

Boon, G. C. (1974b), 'Counterfeit coins in Roman Britain', in P. J. Casey and R. Reece (eds), *Coins and the Archaeologist*, British Archaeological Reports, 4, Oxford.

Boon, G. C. (1974c), *Silchester, the Roman Town of Calleva*, Newton Abbot.

Boon, G. C. and Williams, C. (1966), 'The Dolaucothi drainage wheel', *Journal of Roman Studies*, LVI, 122–7.

Bowersock, G. W. (1983), *Roman Arabia*, Cambridge, Mass.

Brashear, W. (1979), 'Before the penthemeros: government funds for the canals', *Bulletin of the American Society of Papyrologists*, 16, 25–9.

Breeze, D. (1982), 'Demand and supply on the northern frontier', in P. Clack and S. Haselgrove (eds), *Rural Settlement in the Roman North*, 148–65, Durham.

Brogan, O. (1979/80), 'Hadd Hajar, a *clausura* in the Tripolitanian Gebel Garian south of Asabaa', *Libyan Studies*, 11, 45–52.

Bromehead, C. N. (1942), 'Ancient mining processes', *Antiquity*, 16, 193–207.

Broughton, T. R. S. (1929), *The Romanization of Africa Proconsularis*, London.

Broughton, T. R. S. (1934), 'Roman landholding in Asia Minor', *Transactions of the American Philological Association*, 65, 207–39.

Brown, A. C. (1968), *Catalogue of Italian Terra-Sigillata in the Ashmolean Museum*, Oxford.

Cadoux, C. J. (1933), *Ancient Smyrna*, Oxford.

Calder, W. M. (1912), 'Colonia Caesareia Antiocheia', *Journal of Roman Studies*, II, 79–109.

Callender, M. H. (1965), *Roman Amphorae*, Oxford.

Callu, J.-P. (1969), *La politique monétaire des émpereurs romains de 238 à 311*, Paris.

Carson, R. A. G. (1964), *Catalogue of Coins of the Roman Empire in the British Museum, Volume VI, Severus Alexander to Balbinus and Pupienus*, London.

Carson, R. A. G. (1980), *Principal Coins of the Romans, Volume II, The Principate, 31 BC–AD 296*, London.

Carson, R. A. G. (1981), *Principal Coins of the Romans, Volume III, The Dominate, AD 296–498*, London.

Carson, R. A. G., Hill, P. V. and Kent, J. P. C. (1960), *Late Roman Bronze Coinage, AD 324–498*, London.

Carson, R. A. G. and Sutherland, C. H. V. (eds) (1956), *Essays in Roman Coinage Presented to Harold Mattingly*, Oxford.

Casey, P. J. (ed.) (1979), *The End of Roman Britain*, British Archaeological Reports, 71, Oxford.

Casey, P. J. and Reece, R. (eds) (1974), *Coins and the Archaeologist*, British Archaeological Reports, 4, Oxford.

Casson, L. (1970), *Ships and Seamanship in the Ancient World*, Princeton.

Casson, L. (1980), 'Rome's trade with the East: the sea voyage to Africa and India', *Transactions of the American Philological Association*, 110, 21–36.

Catino, G. di (1914), *Il regesto di Farfa*, volume I, Rome.

Chalon, G. (1964), *L'Édit de Tiberius Julius Alexander: étude historique et exégétique*, Bibliotheca Helvetica Romana 5, Lausanne.

Chevallier, R. (1976), *Roman Roads*, London.

Collins, A. L. (1892), 'Fire-setting: the art of mining by fire', *Transactions of the Federated Institution of Mining Engineers*, 5, 82–92.

Colls, D. *et al.* (1977), 'L'Épave Port-Vendres II et le Commerce de la Bétique à l'époque de Claude', *Archaeonautica*, 1, Paris.

Cotton, M. A. (1979), *The Late Republican Villa at Posto, Francolise*, London.

Crawford, D. J. (1976), 'Imperial estates', in M. I. Finley (ed.), *Studies in Roman Property*, Cambridge, 35–70 and 173–80.

Crummy, N. (1983), *Colchester Archaeological Report, 2: The Roman Small Finds from Excavations in Colchester, 1971–9*, Colchester.

D'Arms, J. H. (1981), *Commerce and Social Standing in Ancient Rome*, Cambridge, Mass.

Darvill, T. and McWhirr, A. (1984), 'Brick and tile production in Roman Britain: models of economic organization', *World Archaeology*, 15, 239–61.

Davies, O. (1933–4), 'Roman and medieval mining technique', *Transactions of the Institution of Mining and Metallurgy*, 43, 3–54.

Davies, O. (1935), *Roman Mines in Europe*, Oxford.

Dilke, O. A. W. (1971), *The Roman Land Surveyors*, Newton Abbot.

Domergue, C. (1984), 'Mines d'or romaines du nord-ouest de l'Espagne – Les Coronas: technique d'exploitation ou habitats?' in T. F. C. Blagg, R. F. J. Jones and S. J. Keay (eds), *Papers in Iberian Archaeology*, British Archaeological Reports, S193, (ii), 370–83, Oxford.

Domergue, C. and Hérail, G. (1977), *Une Méthode pour l'étude des mines antiques en alluvion: l'exemple des mines d'or romaines de la Valduerna (Léon, Espagne)*, Paris.

Domergue, C. and Hérail, G. (1978), *Mines d'or romaines d'Espagne: le district de la Valduerna (Léon)*, Toulouse.

Drinkwater, J. F. (1979), 'Local careers in the three Gauls', *Britannia*, X, 89–100.

Drinkwater, J. F. (1983), *Roman Gaul. The Three Provinces, 58 BC–AD 260*, Beckenham.

Duncan-Jones, R. (1974), *The Economy of the Roman Empire*, Cambridge.

Elmer, G. (1941), 'Die Münzprägung der gallischen Kaiser in Köln, Trier und Mailand', *Bonner Jahrbücher* 146.

Erim, K. T., Reynolds, J. and Crawford, M. (1971), 'Diocletian's currency reform: a new inscription', *Journal of Roman Studies*, LXI 171.

Fentress, E. W. B. (1979), *Numidia and the Roman Army*, British Archaeological Reports, International Series, 53, Oxford.

Février, P.-A. (1966), 'Inscriptions inédites relatives aux domaines de la région de Sétif', in R. Chevallier (ed.), *Mélanges d'archéologie et d'histoire offerts à A. Piganiol*, volume I, 217–28, Paris.

Finley, M. I. (1973), *The Ancient Economy*, London.

Flach, D. (1978), 'Inschriftenuntersuchungen zum römischen Kolonat in Nordafrika', *Chiron*, 8, 442–92.

Flam-Zuckermann, L. (1972), 'Un exemple de la genèse des domaines impériaux d'après deux inscriptions de Bithynie', *Historia*, 21, 114–19.

Forbes, R. J. (1963), *Studies in Ancient Technology*, volume VII, Leiden.

Galen, *On Methods of Healing*, IX, 8 (Ed. Kuhn, Volume X) 632–3.

Galliou, P. (1983), *L'Armorique Romaine*, Braspars.

Garnsey, P. D. A. (1978), 'Rome's African empire under the Principate', in P. D. A. Garnsey and C. R. Whittaker (eds), *Imperialism in the Ancient World*, Cambridge, 223–54, 343–54.

Garnsey, P. D. A., Hopkins, K. and Whittaker, C. R. (1983), *Trade in the Ancient Economy*, London.

Gilliam, J. F. (1965), 'Dura Postes and the Constitutio Antoniniana', *Historia*, 14, 74–92.

Gnoli, R. (1971), *Marmora Romana*, Rome.

Goudineau, C. (1968), *Fouilles de l'École Française de Rome à Bolsena (Poggio Moscini) 1962–1967, IV, La Céramique Arétine Lisse*, Paris.

Greene, K. T. (1979), *Usk: the Pre-Flavian Fine Wares*, Cardiff.

Griffith, S. V. (1960), *Alluvial Prospecting and Mining*, second revised edition, Oxford.

Groenman-van Waateringe, W. (1983), 'The disastrous effect of the Roman occupation', *Roman and Native in the Low Countries*, 147–57, Oxford.

Groom, N. (1981), *Frankincense and Myrrh. A Study of the Arabian Incense Trade*, London.

Grose, D. F. (1977), 'Early blown glass: the western evidence', *Journal of Glass Studies*, 19, 9–29.

Gsell, S. (1932), 'Esclaves ruraux dans l'Afrique romaine', *Mélanges Gustave Glotz*, volume I, 397–415, Paris.

Hammer, J. (1908), 'Der Feingehalt der griechischen und römischen Münzen', *Zeitschrift für Numismatik* 26, 1.

Hanson, A. E. (1984), 'Caligulan month-names at Philadelphia and related matters', M. Gigante (ed.), *Atti del XVII Congresso Internazionale di Papirologia*, 107–18, Naples.

Harris, W. V. (1980a), 'Roman terracotta lamps: the organization of an industry', *Journal of Roman Studies*, LXX, 126–45.

Harris, W. V. (1980b), 'Towards a study of the Roman slave trade', *Memoirs of the American Academy at Rome*, 36, 117–40.

Harrison, F. A. (1931), 'Ancient mining activities in Portugal', *Mining Magazine*, 45, 137–45.

Harrison, H. L. H. (1962), *Alluvial Mining for Tin and Gold*, London.

Hartley, K. F. (1973a), 'The marketing and distribution of mortaria', A. Detsicas (ed.), *Current Research in Romano-British Coarse Pottery*, Council for British Archaeology Research Report, 10, 39–51, London.

Hartley, K. F. (1973b), 'La diffusion des mortiers, tuiles et autres produits en provenance des fabriques italiennes', *Cahiers d'Archéologie Subaquatique*, 2, 49–60.

Hartley, K. F. (1975), 'Mortarium stamps', in A. Robertson, M. Scott, and L. Keppie (eds), *Bar Hill: a Roman fort and its finds*, British Archaeological Reports, 16, 142–7, Oxford.

Hartley, K. F. (1977a), 'Two major potteries producing mortaria in the first century AD', *Roman Pottery Studies in Britain and Beyond*, British Archaeological Reports, S30, 5–17, Oxford.

Hartley, K. F. (1977b), 'The mortaria from New Fresh Wharf', in B. Hobley and J. Schofield, 1977.

Hassall, M. (1978), 'Britain and the Rhine Provinces: epigraphic evidence for Roman trade', in H. F. Cleere and J. du Plat Taylor (eds), *Roman Shipping and Trade*, Council for British Archaeology Research Report, 24, 41–8, London.

Haupt, D. (1981), 'Von Birgel nach Silchester', *Bonner Jahrbücher*, 181, 383–91.

Hayes, J. W. (1967), 'North Syrian mortaria', *Hesperia*, 36, 337–47.

Hayes, J. W. (1972), *Late Roman Pottery. A catalogue of Roman fine wares*, London.

Healy, J. F. (1978), *Mining and Metallurgy in the Greek and Roman World*, London.

Hedeager, L. (1978), 'A quantitative analysis of Roman imports in Europe north of the Limes (0–400 AD) and the question of Romano-Germanic exchange', *New Directions in Scandinavian Archaeology*, Copenhagen, 191–216.

Herrmann, P. (1959), 'Neue Inschriften zur Landeskunde von Lydien und angrenzenden Gebieten', *Denkschiften der österreichischen Akademie der Wissenschaften*, Philos.-hist. Klasse, 77, 1.

Hirschfeld, O. (1913), 'Der Grundbesitz der römischen Kaiser in der ersten drei Jahrhunderten', *Kleine Schriften*, 516–75, Berlin.

Hobley, B. and Schofield, J. (1977), 'Excavations in the City of London. First Interim Report, 1974–5', *Antiquaries Journal*, 57, 31–66.

Hopkins, K. (1980), 'Taxes and trade in the Roman Empire', *Journal of Roman Studies*, LXX, 101–25.

Hopkins, K. (1983), 'Introduction' to *Trade in the Ancient Economy*, Garnsey, Hopkins and Whittaker (eds), London.

Howat, D. D. (1939), 'Fire-setting', *Mine and Quarry Engineering*, 4, 239–45.

Huntingford, G. W. B. (1980), 'The Periplus of the Erythraean Sea', Hakluyt Society, Second Series, 151.

Johne, K-P., Köhn, J. and Weber, V. (1983), *Die Kolonen in Italien und den westlichen Provinzen des römischen Reiches*, Berlin.

Johnson, A. C., Coleman-Norton, P. R. and Bourne, F. C. (eds) (1961), *Ancient Roman Statutes*, Austin, Texas.

Jones, A. H. M. (1964), *The Later Roman Empire 284–602*, Oxford.

Jones, G. D. B., Blakey, I. J. and Macpherson, E. C. F. (1960), 'Dolaucothi: the Roman aqueduct', *Bulletin of the Board of Celtic Studies*, 19, 71–84.

Jones, G. D. B. and Lewis, P. R. (1971), 'The Dolaucothi gold-mines', *Bonner Jahrbücher*, 171, 288–300.

Jones, R. F. J. and Bird, D. G. (1972), 'Roman gold-mining in north-west Spain, II: workings on the Rio Duerna', *Journal of Roman Studies*, LXII, 59–74.

Kehoe, D. P. (1982), 'The Economics of Food Production on Roman Imperial Estates in North Africa', unpublished Ph.D. dissertation, University of Michigan.

Keil, J. and v. Premerstein, A. (1914–15), 'Bericht über eine dritte Reise in Lydien', *Denkschriften der österreichischen Akademie der Wissenschaften*, Philos.-hist. Klasse, 57, 1.

Kent, J. P. C. (1956), 'Gold coinage in the late Roman Empire', in R. A. G. Carson and C. H. V. Sutherland (eds), *Essays in Roman Coinage presented to Harold Mattingly*, Oxford.

Kent, J. P. C. (1978), *Roman Coins*, London.

Kent, J. P. C. (1979), 'The end of Roman Britain. The literary and numismatic evidence', in P. J. Casey (ed.), *The End of Roman Britain*, British Archaeological Reports, 71, Oxford.

Kolendo, J. (1968), 'La hiérarchie des procurateurs dans l'inscription d'Aïn-el-Djemala (*CIL* VIII 25943)', *Revue des études latines*, 46, 319–29.

Kolendo, J. (1976), *Le colonat en Afrique sous le haut empire*, Annales littéraires de l'Université de Besançon, Centre de recherches d'histoire ancienne, Volume 17, Paris.

Kotula, T. (1952–3), 'Roswój terytorialny i organizacja latyfundiów w rzymskiej Afryce w okresie wczesnego Cesarstwa', *Eos*, 46, 113–39.

Kunow, J. (1980), *Negotiator et Vectura. Händler und Transport im freien Germanien*, Marburg.

Landels, J. G. (1978), *Engineering in the Ancient World*, London.

Lasfargues, J. and A. and Vertet, H. (1976), 'L'atelier de potiers augustéen de la Muette à Lyon', *Notes d'Épigraphie et d'Archéologie Lyonnaises*, 61–80, Lyon.

Lassère, J.-M. (1977), *Ubique populus: peuplement et mouvement de population dans l'Afrique romaine de la chute de Carthage à la fin de la dynastie des Sévères (146 a.c.–235 p.c.)*, Editions du centre national de la recherche scientifique, Paris.

Lassère, J.-M. (1980), 'Remarques sur le peuplement de la *Colonia Iulia Augusta Numidica Simitthus*', *Antiquités Africaines*, 16, 27–44.

Lewis, P. R. and Jones, G. D. B. (1969), 'The Dolaucothi gold-mines I: the surface evidence', *Antiquaries Journal*, 49, 244–72.

Lewis, P. R. and Jones, G. D. B. (1970), 'Roman gold-mining in north-west Spain', *Journal of Roman Studies*, LX, 169–85.

Liou, B. (1980), 'Les amphores à huile de l'épave *Saint-Gervais 3* à Fos-sur-Mer: premières observations sur les inscriptions peintes', *Producción y Comercio del Aceite en la Antigüedad*, Madrid, 161–75.

Loane, H. (1938), *Industry and Commerce of the City of Rome (50 BC–200 AD)*, Baltimore.

Loane, H. (1944), 'Vespasian's spice market and tribute in kind', *Classical Philology*, 39, 10–21.

Lo Cascio, E. (1971–2), 'Patrimonium, ratio privata, res privata', *Annali dell'Istituto Italiano per gli studi storici*, 3, 55–121.

McCrum, M. and Woodhead, A. G. (1961), *Select Documents of the Principates of the Flavian Emperors, AD 68–96*, Cambridge.

MacMullen, R. (1962), 'Three notes on imperial estates', *Classical Quarterly*, new series, 12, 277–82.

MacMullen, R. (1976), 'Two notes on imperial properties', *Athenaeum*, new series, 54, 19–36.

McWhirr, A. and Viner, D. (1978), 'The production and distribution of tiles in Roman Britain with special reference to the Cirencester region', *Britannia*, IX, 359–77.

Manacorda, D. (1976–7), 'Testimonianze sulla produzione e il consumo dell'olio tripolitano nel III seculo', *Dialoghi di Archeologia*, 9–10, 542–601.

Manacorda, D. (1977), 'Il *Kalendarium Vegetianum* e le anfore della Betica', *Mélanges de l'école française de Rome*, 89, 313–32.

Marsh, G. (1981), 'London's Samian supply and its relationship to the development of the Gallic Samian industry', *Roman Pottery Research in Britain and North-West Europe*, Oxford, 173–238.

Mattingly, H. (1923), *Catalogue of Coins of the Roman Empire in the British Museum, Vol. I Augustus–Vitellius*, London.

Mattingly, H. (1930), *Catalogue of Coins of the Roman Empire in the British Museum, Vol. II, Vespasian–Domitian*, London.

Mattingly, H. (1936), *Catalogue of Coins of the Roman Empire in the British Museum, Vol. III, Nerva–Hadrian*, London.

Mattingly, H. (1940), *Catalogue of Coins of the Roman Empire in the British Museum, Vol. IV, Antoninus Pius–Commodus*, London.

Mattingly, H. (1950), *Catalogue of Coins of the Roman Empire in the British Museum, Vol. V, Pertinax–Elagabalus*, London.

Mattingly, H. and Sydenham, E. A. (eds) (1926), *The Roman Imperial Coinage, Vol. II*, London.

Mattingly, H. and Sydenham, E. A. (eds) (1927), *The Roman Imperial Coinage, Vol. V.1*, P. H. Webb, London.

Mattingly, H. and Sydenham, E. A. (eds) (1930), *The Roman Imperial Coinage, Vol. III*, London.

Mattingly, H. and Sydenham, E. A. (eds) (1933), *The Roman Imperial Coinage, Vol. V.2*, P. H. Webb, London.

Mattingly, H. and Sydenham, E. A. (eds) (1936), *The Roman Imperial Coinage, Vol. IV.1*, London.

Mattingly, H. and Sydenham, E. A (eds) (1938), *The Roman Imperial Coinage, Vol. IV.2*, London.

Mattingly, H., Sydenham, E. A and Sutherland, C. H. V. (eds) (1949), *The Roman Imperial Coinage, Vol. IV.3*, H. Mattingly, London.

Mattingly, H., Sutherland, C. H. V. and Carson, R. A. G. (1953), *The Roman Imperial Coinage, Vol. IX*, J. W. E. Pearce, London.

Mau, A. (1899), *Pompeii: Its Life and Art* (translated by F. W. Kelsey), New York.

Meiggs, R. (1973), *Roman Ostia*, Oxford.

Meiggs, R. (1982), *Trees and Timber in the Ancient Mediterranean World*, Oxford.

Millar, F. (1977), *The Emperor in the Roman World (31 BC–AD 377)*, London.

Milne, G. and Hobley, B. (eds) (1981), *Waterfront Archaeology in Britain and Northern Europe*, London.

Morel, J.-P. (1981), *Céramique Campanienne: les formes*, Rome.

Palmer, R. E. (1926–7), 'Notes on some ancient mine equipments and systems', *Transactions of the Institution of Mining and Metallurgy*, 36, 299–336.

Parassoglou, G. M. (1978), *Imperial estates in Egypt*, American Studies in Papyrology, 18, Amsterdam.

Paul, R. W. (1947), *California Gold*, Cambridge, Mass.

Peacock, D. P. S. (1977), *Pottery and Early Commerce*, London.

Peele, R. (ed.) (1941), *Mining Engineers' Handbook*, third edition, London.

Pensabene, P. (1983), 'Osservazioni sulla diffusione dei marmi e sul loro prezzo nella Roma imperiale', *Dialoghi di Archeologia*, (3) 1, 55–63.

Peyras, J. (1975), 'Le fundus Aufidianus: étude d'un grand domaine romain de la région de Mateur (Tunisie du Nord)', *Antiquités Africaines*, 9, 181–222.

Pflaum, H. G. (1950), *Les Procurateurs équestres sous le haut-empire romain*, Paris.

Pflaum, H. G. (1960–1), *Les Carrières procuratoriennes équestres sous le haut-empire romain*, Institut français d'archéologie de Beyrouth: Bibliothèque archéologique et historique, 57, Paris.

Phillips, C. W. (1970), *The Fenland in Roman Times: studies of a major area of peasant colonisation with a Gazetteer covering all known sites and finds*, Royal Geographical Society research series 5, London.

Piganiol, A. (1962), *Les Documents cadastraux d'Orange*, Gallia Supplement 16.

Poethke, G. (1969a), *Epimerismos: Betrachtungen zur Zwangspacht in Ägypten während der Principatszeit*, Papyrologica Bruxellensia, 8, Bruxelles.

Poethke, G. (1969b), 'Epimerismos von Bodenflächen verschiedener *OYEIAI* der drei Bezirke des Arsinoites', *Archiv für Papyrusforschung*, 19, 77–84.

Poethke, G. (1976), 'Der Berliner Epimerismos-Papyrus von Jahre 139 (P 11529 + 16015)', *Archiv für Papyrusforschung*, 24–5, 101–9.

Pomey, P. and Tchernia, A. (1978), 'Le tonnage maximum des navires de commerce romains', *Archaeonautica*, 2, 233–51.

Price, J. (1977), 'The Roman glass', in Gentry, A. *et al.* 'Excavations at Lincoln Road, London Borough of Enfield, November 1974–March 1976', *Transactions of the London and Middlesex Archaeological Society*, 28, 101–89.

Price, J. (1978), 'Trade in glass', H. F. Cleere and J. du Plat Taylor (eds), *Roman Shipping and Trade*, Council for British Archaeology Research Report, 24, 70–8, London.

Raschke, M. G. (1978), 'New studies in Roman commerce with the East', in H. Temporini (ed.) *Aufstieg und Niedergang der römischen Welt*, II 9.2, 604–1384, Berlin/New York.

Raschke, M. G. (1979), 'The role of oriental commerce in the economies of the cities of the eastern Mediterranean in the Roman period', *Archaeological News*, 8 2/3, 68–77.

Read, H. H. and Watson, J. (1968), *Introduction to Geology, Volume I: Principles*, second edition, London.

Reynolds, J. (1982), *Aphrodisias and Rome*, London.

Rickard, T. A. (1927), 'With the geologists in Spain', *Engineering and Mining Journal*, 123, 917–23.

Rickard, T. A. (1928), 'The mining of the Romans in Spain', *Journal of Roman Studies*, XVIII, 129–43.

Rickman, G. E. (1980), 'The grain trade under the Roman Empire', *Memoirs of the American Academy at Rome*, 36, 261–75.

Riley, J. A. (1981), 'Italy and the Eastern Mediterranean in the Hellenistic and early Roman periods: the evidence of coarse pottery', *Archaeology and Italian Society*, Oxford, 69–78.

Rivet, A. L. F. (1970), 'The British section of the Antonine Itinerary', *Britannia* I, 34–82.

Robertson, A. S. (1962), *Roman Imperial Coins in the Hunter Coin Cabinet, University of Glasgow, Vol. I, Augustus–Nerva*, Oxford.

Robertson, A. S. (1971), *Roman Imperial Coins in the Hunter Coin Cabinet, University of Glasgow, Vol. II, Trajan–Commodus*, Oxford.

Robertson, A. S. (1977), *Roman Imperial Coins in the Hunter Coin Cabinet, University of Glasgow, Volume III, Pertinax–Aemilian*, Oxford.

Robertson, A. S. (1978), *Roman Imperial Coins in the Hunter Coin Cabinet, University of Glasgow, Vol. IV, Valerian I–Allectus*, Oxford.

Robertson, A. S. (1982), *Roman Imperial Coins in the Hunter Coin Cabinet, University of Glasgow, Vol. V, Reform of Diocletian–Zeno*, Oxford.

Rostovtzeff, M. (1957), *The Social and Economic History of the Roman Empire*, second edition, Oxford, by P. M. Fraser.

Rostowzew, M. (1910), *Studien zur Geschichte des römischen Kolonates, Archiv für Papyrusforschung*, Beiheft 1, Leipzig and Berlin.

Rothenberg, B. (1972), *Timna*, London.

Rothenberg, B. and Blanco-Freijeiro, A. (1981), *Studies in Ancient Mining and Metallurgy in South-West Spain*, London.

Rougé, J. (1966), *Recherches sur l'Organisation du Commerce Maritime en Méditerranée sous l'Empire Romain*, Paris.

Rowland, R. J. (1976), 'The "very poor" and the grain dole at Rome and Oxyrhynchus', *Zeitschrift für Papyrologie und Epigraphik*, 21, 69–72.

Roxan, M. M. (1978), *Roman Military Diplomas, Vol. I*, University of London Institute of Archaeology.

Roxan, M. M. (1981), 'The distribution of Roman military diplomas', *Epigraphische Studien*, 12, 265–86.

Roxan, M. M. (1984), 'Observations on the reasons for the changes circa AD 140', in W. Eck and H. Wolff (eds), *Proceedings of the Colloquium on Roman military diplomas, held at Passau 1984*.

Sandars, H. (1905), 'The Linares bas-relief and Roman mining operations in Baetica', *Archaeologia*, 59, 311–32.

Schiøler, T. (1973), *Roman and Islamic Water-lifting Wheels*, Odense.

Shatzman, I. (1975), *Senatorial Wealth and Roman Politics*, Bruxelles.

Shaw, B. D. (1981), 'Rural markets in North Africa and the political economy of the Roman Empire', *Antiquités Africaines*, 17, 37–83.

Sherwin-White, A. N. (1973), *The Roman Citizenship*, second edition, Oxford.

Skinner, B. J. (1966), 'Thermal expansion', in S. P. Clark (ed.), *Handbook of Physical Constants*, Memoir 97, Geological Society of America.

Solier, Y. *et al.* (1981), 'Les épaves de Gruissan', *Archaeonautica*, 3, 7–264.

Steinby, M. (1981), 'La diffusione dell'opus doliare urbano', *Società Romana e Produzione Schiavistica*, 2, 237–45 and 292, Bari.

Stevenson, A. S. (1876), 'Roman wheel from Tharsis, in Spain', *Archaeologia Aeliana*, 7, 279–81.

Strong, D. E. (1966), *Catalogue of the Carved Amber in the Department of Greek and Roman Antiquities*, London.

Strubbe, J. (1975), 'A group of imperial estates in central Phrygia', *Ancient Society*, 6, 229–50.

Sutherland, C. H. V. and Carson, R. A. G. (1966), *The Roman Imperial Coinage, Vol. VII*, P. M. Bruun, London.

Sutherland, C. H. V. and Carson, R. A. G. (1967), *The Roman Imperial Coinage, Vol. VI*, C. H. V. Sutherland, London.

Sutherland, C. H. V. and Carson, R. A. G. (1981), *The Roman Imperial Coinage, Vol. VIII*, J. P. C. Kent, London.

Sutherland, C. H. V. and Carson, R. A. G. (1984), *The Roman Imperial Coinage, Vol. I*, 2nd edition, C. H. V. Sutherland, London.

Sutherland, C. H. V. and Kraay, C. M. (1975), *Catalogue of Coins of the Roman Empire in the Ashmolean Museum, Part I, Augustus (31 BC–AD 14)*, Oxford.

Sutton, J. E. G. (1983), 'West African metals and the ancient Mediterranean', *Oxford Journal of Archaeology*, 2, 181–8.

Tchernia, A. (1980), 'Quelques remarques sur le commerce du vin et les amphores', *Memoirs of the American Academy at Rome*, 36, 305–12.

Tchernia, A. (1983), 'Italian wine in Gaul at the end of the Republic', *Trade in the Ancient Economy*, London, 87–104.

Tchernia, A., Pomey, P. and Hesnard, A. (1978), *L'Épave Romaine de la Madrague de Giens*, Gallia Supplement 34.

Todd, M. (1975), *The Northern Barbarians, 100 BC–AD 300*, London.

Tomsin, A. (1957), 'Notes sur les *ousiai* a l'époque romaine', *Studi in onore di A. Calderini e R. Paribeni*, 2, 211–24.

Tomsin, A. (1964), 'Le recrutement de la main d'oeuvre dans les domaines privés de l'Égypte romaine', *Studien zur Papyrologie und antiken Wirtschaftsgeschichte Friedrich Oertel zum achtzigsten Geburtstag gewidmet*, 81–100, Bonn.

Torelli, M. (1969), 'Contributi al supplemento del *CIL* IX', *Atti della Academia Nazionale dei Lincei*, 24, 9–48.

Wacher, J. S. (1975), *The Towns of Roman Britain*, London.

Walker, D. R. (1976), *The Metrology of Roman Silver Coinage, Part 1, Augustus–Domitian*, Oxford.

Walker, D. R. (1977), *The Metrology of Roman Silver Coinage, Part 2, Nerva–Commodus*, Oxford.

Walker, D. R. (1978), *The Metrology of Roman Silver Coinage, Part 3, Pertinax–Uranius Antoninus*, Oxford.

Walker, S. (1981), *Récentes Recherches en Archéologie Gallo-Romaine et Paléochrétienne sur Lyon et sa Région*, Oxford.

Ward-Perkins, J. B. (1951), 'Tripolitania and the marble trade', *Journal of Roman Studies*, XLI, 89–104.

Ward-Perkins, J. B. (1971), 'Quarrying in antiquity. Technology, tradition and social change', *Proceedings of the British Academy*, 57, 137–58.

Ward-Perkins, J. B. (1980), 'The marble trade and its organization: evidence from Nicomedia', *Memoirs of the American Academy at Rome*, 36, 325–38.

Ward-Perkins, J. B. (1981), *Roman Imperial Architecture*, Harmondsworth.

Weaver, P. C. (1972), *Familia Caesaris: a social study of the emperor's freedmen and slaves*, Cambridge.

West, L. C. (1958), *Gold to Silver Standards in the Roman Empire to AD 300*, New York.

White, K. D. (1970), *Roman Farming*, London.

White, K. D. (1984), *Greek and Roman Technology*, London.

Whitehouse, D. B. (1981), 'The Schola Praeconum and the food supply of Rome in the fifth century AD', *Archaeology and Italian Society*, Oxford, 191–5.

Wild, J. P. (1984), 'Camulodunum and the silk road', *Current Archaeology*, 93, 298–9.

Will, E. L. (1982), 'Greco-Italic amphoras', *Hesperia*, 51, 338–56 and po. 85.

Wright, K. S. (1980), 'A Tiberian pottery deposit from Corinth', *Hesperia*, 49, 135–77 and plates 28–34.

PART 9

·SOCIETY·

CHAPTER 27

·ROMANS·AND· ·NON-ROMANS·

Mark Hassall

And as they bound him with thongs, Paul said to the centurion that stood by, 'Is it lawful for you to scourge a Roman and uncondemned?' (*Acts* 22, 25)

Paul's status as a Roman citizen (*civis Romanus*) on this occasion won for him immunity from summary corporal punishment – immunity that he would not have enjoyed as a non-Roman, a mere provincial or *civis peregrinus*. Roman citizenship, like American or British citizenship today, carried with it certain privileges irrespective of the holder's ethnic origin. As far as the centurion was concerned what mattered was that Paul had Roman citizenship. It was irrelevant that he was a Greek-speaking Jew from southern Asia Minor who had never set foot in Italy, let alone Rome, and whose knowledge of Latin was probably no better than the centurion's.

The institution of Roman citizenship, something to which even the humblest provincial could aspire, was one of the great open secrets of the Roman Empire, and perhaps more than any other factor contributed to internal stability among the provincials. Through the award of citizenship (*civitas*) to the more intelligent and ambitious of the *peregrini*, the most influential sections of provincial society came to identify their own interests with those of the greater body of the Roman state. First generation provincials, particularly in the less civilized western provinces, might yearn for their independence, and indeed, on occasion, fight for it; but the wonder is not so much that the isolated revolt did in fact happen among Rome's most recently acquired provinces, but that such revolts did not happen more often and continue to happen. It was only when the security of the frontiers broke down in the course of the third century AD, coupled with the collapse of the economy, that in some areas sectional interests drove the provincials to revolt. And even when this did happen the rebellions were almost invariably attempts to gain a more favoured place in comparison with other regions, rather than to break away from the Empire. The Roman Empire, unlike the British Empire, did not collapse through the growth of nationalism within its borders, but through internal economic difficulties and external military pressures.

Before turning to examine more closely the whole question of Roman citizenship as opposed to provincial status, it is worth while drawing one other contrast, this time between the Roman Empire and the Greek World. If a Roman citizen could be ethnically a Greek, a Celt, Italian or Semite, whose first language was that appropriate to his origin, a Greek besides being ethnically a Hellene, also *spoke* Greek. In the very few cases where this was not so, for example at Side where the colonists, ethnically Greeks, adopted the local Anatolian language, it was a cause of acute embarrassment: as regards the Sidetans the claim was even made that, on their arrival, they suddenly started speaking an alien, and unique, language, rather than simply 'going native'. To be a Greek was furthermore to share in a common culture whose finest flowering is usually reckoned to have been at Athens in the fifth century BC, but which existed in all the cities of the Greek *diaspora*, from the colonies in the Black Sea to those in the western Mediterranean. From Panticapaeum in the Crimea to Massilia at the mouth of the Rhône, the colonists shared a common devotion to the epic poems of Homer and the cult of the Olympian gods. This cultural unity was in stark contrast to the lack of political harmony that existed in the Greek world; near neighbours among the city states of mainland Greece were more often than not deadly enemies, while rivalry might even spring up between mother cities and daughter colonies as happened in the case of Corinth and Corcyra (Curfu). In the Roman Empire on the other hand the imposition of the Roman peace created a world state in which internal warfare had no part, but one which embraced a large diversity of languages, religions and cultures.

There was however one concept that the Romans had, from the days of the Republic, shared with the Greeks: the notion that the natural way for a man to live was in a city-state, even if, in the case of Rome, this meant that any Italian south of the Po was counted as a citizen of Rome after the Social Wars of 90–88 BC, a privilege that was extended by Caesar to inhabitants of the whole peninsula in 49 BC. This was hardly surprising since the normal polity for most of the more advanced Mediterranean races including Greeks, Romans, Etruscans and Phoenicians, was the city-state. The Latin word for the political entity that encompassed the totality of citizens (*cives*) of any one community was the same that was used for citizenship, *civitas*. In later Latin the word takes on a more concrete meaning, and from being an abstract term, comes to mean the physical reality behind it, hence the Spanish *civitad* and related words in other European languages, including our own 'city'. However, during the earlier Empire, *civitas* was not restricted to urban communities – city states – it could also apply to the non-urban tribal states of the north-west European provinces. As a corollary *civis* means not only a 'citizen', of Rome say, or Athens, but also, in the context of the tribal areas of the Empire, a tribesman, of the Breuci or the Remi for example.

Thus the provinces that comprised the Empire were composed of vast numbers of *civitates*, more precisely *civitates peregrinae*, provincial, or literally 'foreign' states. But whether the *civitates* were Greek city states or Celtic tribes, they had for the most part been free and independent of each other before incorporation into the Empire, and afterwards too, Rome allowed them to enjoy local autonomy. This was not just a case of altruism on the part of the ruler towards the ruled, but a natural consequence of the way Rome had acquired her Empire, the degree of local autonomy depending on a community's initial contact with Rome. Not all contacts had been warlike. During the last two centuries BC, as Rome expanded into the eastern Mediterranean, the Senate had concluded treaties (*foedera*) with numerous Greek city states. Texts of many of these survive in translations into Greek set up on inscriptions in the states concerned, and similar treaties will have existed with some of the tribal *civitates* of the west.

Sometimes the independence of these non-Roman communities within the imperial framework was recognized by Rome although no actual treaty existed between them. This meant in effect that, if Rome decided to violate a state's independence, at least she would not incur the religious sanctions involved in breaking the oaths that would accompany a formal treaty. From Asia Minor come two documents. The first, passed by the assembly of the people (*plebs*) at Rome, and so technically a *plebiscitum*, acknowledged the independent status of Termessus whose beautiful ruins lie high up in the Taurus mountains of southern Turkey. This spells out in detail the areas from which the townsfolk were to be immune from interference on the part of the Roman officials. The second a decree of the Senate (*Senatus Consultum*) dates to 39 BC, though the inscribed copy was actually cut two or three centuries later, and records similar immunity from interference for the city of Aphrodisias, also in Asia Minor (Reynolds, 1982, Document 8). That the title of 'free and immune state' (*Civitas libera et immunis*) was no empty honour can be shown by the successful appeal by Aphrodisias against an attempt by Roman tax officials to levy a tax on nails on the city. As Hadrian concluded in his answer to the Aphrodisians (Reynolds, 1982, Document 15) the city was excluded from the provincial register (*formula provinciae*) and he had written to the procurator of Asia to instruct the contractor for the tax to keep away from their city.

The number of non-Roman provincial communities who enjoyed 'federate' status or 'immunity and freedom' must have been quite insignificant compared to those whose first contact with Rome had been a violent one. This will have been true especially of the western provinces where the tribal *civitates* had all too often been reduced by force of arms into the power of the Roman people, as the inscription recording the victory of Claudius in Britain inscribed on the triumphal arch set up in his honour phrases it. On such enemies who had had the temerity to offer resistance, Rome could impose such terms as she liked. Thus the tribe of the Salassi in the Val d'Aosta leading up to the Great and Little St Bernard passes, defeated by Terentius Varro in 25 BC, were sold into slavery, although a subsequent inscription shows that not all suffered this fate but that some came to live at the newly founded Roman colonial settlement of Aosta (Augusta Praetoria). Converting a defeated enemy into hard cash provided a quick financial return for the state, but in the longer term it was more profitable to turn him into a tax-payer and this is what normally happened. From the word for the payment of what was in effect the annual indemnity that Rome levied on a defeated enemy, *stipendium*, comes the term for the least favoured of all the provincial communities, the *civitates stipendiariae*. Even here however local affairs remained largely in the hands of the individual communities themselves. This is perhaps not surprising in the Greek east with its long tradition of urbanization, where the popular assemblies, councils and magistrates continued to fulfil their old functions, though Rome might curb the more democratic elements of city institutions through the relevant *Lex Provinciae* (Part 6, Chapter 15).

Even in the north-west provinces, where there was virtually no tradition of municipal institutions among the tribal *civitates*, if it existed in embryonic form it was not simply swept away: Caesar (*Bellum Gallicum* I 16.5) mentions annual magistrates called vergobrets among the Aedui, while inscribed Celtic coins of the Lexovii, a tribal state whose territory extended southwards from the estuary of the Seine, show that the same office existed in northern France also. It is interesting therefore to find in the imperial period, vergobrets continuing to function among the Santones, a coastal *civitas* of western Gaul. In fact there is little evidence to show precisely how the tribal *civitates* of north-west Europe came to adopt magistrates and councils on the Mediterranean model. Only in one case is there direct evidence. In AD 47 Corbulo 'imposed a senate, magistrate and laws' on the newly conquered Frisii, an experiment that did not last since the tribe soon rose in revolt.

The diversity that appears from a recent study of how the local administration operated among the Gallic *civitates* (Drinkwater, 1979), suggests that the tribal authorities were given something of a free hand when the time came to draw up their own constitutions, even if *leges provinciarum* provided some check. For such laws after the end of the Republic there is anyway virtually no evidence (Hassall, 1979, 250, note 2). A similar picture of local choice in such matters emerges from north Africa, where a Punic magistracy, the post of *suffes* survived. If the names for magistracies changed from *vergobret* to *suffes* depending on whether one was in the chief town of the Gallic Santones or north African Lepcis, or from *duovir* or *aedilis* in one of the more romanized western Mediterranean provinces, to *strategos* or *archon* in a Greek city-state, it was the male citizen body which elected the magistrates at annual voting assemblies. But the power in each community resided not with assembly or magistrates (the executive), but with the council (the legislative body known by a variety of names in the Latin west: senate, *curia* or *ordo decurionum*, and by the word *boule* in the Greek east).

Before the appearance of Rome, when the city states of the eastern Mediterranean had enjoyed true independence, the council had sometimes been a democratic body, annually elected like the magistrates and sometimes numbering several hundred, and so truly representative. Such a state of affairs was not acceptable to Rome with its tradition of senatorial oligarchical government: the letters written by the younger Pliny, the emperor's representative in the province of Bithynia in north-west Asia Minor, show how the Law of the Province (in this case the *Lex Pompeia*) limited the number of councillors and removed the elective element (Abbott and Johnson, 1926, 76). Councillors were appointed for life and were co-opted from the wealthier members of the community. It was this influential group within the Roman *civitates* which was cultivated by Rome. Its members, like St Paul from Tarsus in southern Asia Minor, were often not only citizens of their own town but also possessed Roman citizenship. Representatives of this class too played their part in the running of the Empire, as officers (*tribuni*) in the legions or commanders of auxiliary regiments.

The Empire, then, of the first two centuries AD consisted of something over forty provinces. Within each province were members of non-Roman communities, *civitates peregrinae*, often city-states consisting of a city with its territory, but sometimes a tribal state whose magistrates met in one of the new urban centres which sprang up in the north-west and Danubian provinces of the Empire (Part 5, Chapter 12). Within each *civitas*, a relatively restricted group, the council, ran local affairs. It is usually assumed in the newly-organized *civitates* of north-western Europe that the council comprised one hundred members, like the 'chartered' towns discussed below, but direct evidence is lacking.

Alongside the *civitates peregrinae*, however, were other communities, where the mass of ordinary people either had 'Latin rights' or else possessed full Roman citizenship. They were the *municipia* and *coloniae*. Under the Republic *coloniae* in Italy could consist either of Roman citizens or citizens who had Latin rights only, but normally under the Empire and in the provinces a *colonia* was a settlement of Roman citizens, and the term will be so used here. To understand the distinction between full Roman citizenship and Latin rights, it is simplest to think of the earliest days of the Roman Republic when Rome herself was just one town in the plain of Latium and a partner with the others in the Latin League. Her citizens were registered in either one of four 'urban' tribes or thirty-one 'rural' tribes, and all Roman citizens continued to be so registered until the early third century AD, even if they had never set foot in Rome or the surrounding countryside. As citizens they had the right of electing magistrates and 'passing' legislation in popular assemblies; the former right was eventually transferred to the Senate under the emperor Tiberius, while the latter rapidly ceased to be of practical importance under the Empire. Those who possessed sufficient wealth and status could also hold office as magistrates and serve in the senate. The citizens of the towns of the Latin League and Rome herself enjoyed certain reciprocal rights in their dealings with each other, such as the right of trade (*ius commercii*) and the right of marriage (*ius conubii*), but they could only stand for election or vote in their own town. The reciprocal privileges were summed up in the terms *ius Latii*, right of Latium, (or *ius Latium*, Latian right or simply *latium*).

As Rome extended her power throughout Italy she came into contact with other towns to whom she allowed reciprocal rights similar to those enjoyed by the cities of the Latin League. And it was natural that as she gained her first overseas provinces, certain towns should be similarly treated, and awarded the *latium*. The process continued under the Empire when there were important changes in both the scale of the grants and the privileges which they entailed, as will be seen below.

Besides binding pre-existing towns in the Italian peninsula to her by the award of Latin rights, Rome also established settlements or 'colonies' of her own citizens at places of strategic importance in a way similar to the fortified townships, *bastides*, later founded by Edward I in Gascony and Wales. One of the earliest of Rome's overseas colonies was at Narbonne in southern France (118 BC). Narbo Martius or Colchester (AD 49) were founded very much as military strong points (Part 5, Chapter 12), but their inhabitants were not only veterans from the legions who might be expected to give a good account of themselves if a military emergency should arise, but they also formed a self-supporting agricultural community, like the settlers on an Israeli kibbutz. Indeed the word *colonia* simply means a body of *coloni* (farmers). The provision of agricultural land, at the expense of the former occupants of the site, was something which the state was expected to provide. There is much information about this aspect of the colonial settlement at Orange in southern Gaul, where the land allotted to the veterans was 'centuriated', rigidly divided up by a grid of access roadways and lanes covering many thousands of hectares, and where, uniquely, fragmentary copies of the map (*forma*), inscribed on marble, have survived (Piganiol, 1962). The veterans of *Legio II* who settled at Orange, not only dispossessed the local tribe, the Tricastini, of the best agricultural land, they also probably enjoyed another great economic advantage that will have been denied to their non-Roman neighbours. This was the right, originally granted by Rome to the towns and cities of Italy, and hence known as the *ius Italicum*, to enjoy freedom from the land tax, *tributum soli*. The occasion for the original grant had been the victory over Macedon at the battle of Pydna in 168 BC, when the wealth of this great hellenistic kingdom had accrued to Rome, but the expansion of the Empire during the later Republic had meant that it had been not only possible to maintain the immunity of Italy from taxation, but even extend the right to favoured cities in the provinces among whom, almost certainly, were the colonies of legionary veterans.

The colonies of Roman citizens resembled, therefore, detached parts of the Roman state: like the citizens of Rome itself their citizens were enrolled into the ancient voting tribes, while like the cities of the Italian peninsula as a whole most may have enjoyed immunity from direct taxation (*ius Italicum*). Similarly the *municipia*, though they had normally existed as non-Roman communities before the grant of the *ius Latii*, were by that grant brought into a similar relationship to Rome as the cities of the old Latin

League. In one technical respect too, both types of town shared something in common that the non-Roman *civitates peregrinae* lacked, which was the possession of a constitution inscribed on bronze tablets defining the way in which the settlement was to be governed. To establish a colony or grant municipal status it had, under the Republic, been first necessary for the popular assembly to pass enabling legislation. This law then empowered an official, which in the case of the colonies theoretically was the founder, the man who 'led forth' the colonists and was hence known as the *deductor*, to give or issue the detailed constitution to the new *municipium* or *colonia*. This document was therefore technically known as *lex data*, literally 'given law', and is conventionally often, if slightly misleadingly, translated as 'charter'.

Substantial parts of four *leges datae* are known from southern Spain. The earliest in date is the charter of Urso, a colony of urban poor from the city of Rome, established on Caesar's instigation shortly after his murder in 45 BC. The other three date to the later first century AD and relate to the creation of three *municipia*, Malaga, Salpensa and Irni. In none of these documents does a description of the actual constitution of the place concerned survive, although it is implied in the detailed series of regulations which are preserved. In all it will have been similar, consisting of the same three elements: popular assembly for the election of the magistrates (minute details for the elections are preserved in the Malaga charter, 51–60), the magistrates themselves and, finally, the all-powerful council which issued decrees and which was not unlike a self-perpetuating municipal mafia.

Section 103 of the Urso charter is of interest in that it refers to three classes of inhabitant of the colony (in the context of arming them in the case of a military emergency). There were, first, the citizens, of the colony itself (who will all have possessed Roman citizenship), second, *incolae*, literally 'inhabitants' but here a technical term meaning 'resident aliens', that is people whose legal abode was some other municipality, and finally the *contributi*. The last were, as with the Salassi at the north Italian colony of Aosta, non-Romans who were legally attached to the colony, just as the local British tribe, the Trinovantes, or at least some of them, may have been 'attributed' to the colony at Colchester. It is uncertain what rights, if any, such people normally had in a colony, but at Trieste the local tribes of the Carni and Catali, who were attributed, could stand for office, and if one was elected to the post of *aedilis*, he had the right of admission to the council, besides being awarded Roman citizenship. In this respect they were in a similar position to ex-magistrates in *municipia* like Salpensa where it is known from its charter that such men, if they did not already possess Roman citizenship, were granted this honour, while if they were already citizens the grant could be made to another member of the family. One final point should be made about the 'chartered towns'. It is usually, and correctly, assumed that the position of a citizen of a colony was preferable to that of a man in a *municipium* who only possessed Latin rights, and that both were at an advantage when compared to the non-Roman member of a *civitas peregrina*.

But paradoxically, the latter was at least subject to his own native laws, and even in a *municipium* like Salpensa, the straightforward process of manumission of slaves and the appointment of guardians to minors were the concern of the chief magistrates while the inhabitant of a colony, as a Roman citizen and subject to Roman law, would have to seek authorization from a Roman magistrate, the *praetor urbanus*, or a pro-magistrate like the governor. From the legal point of view, at a certain level, the non-Roman enjoyed greater autonomy than the normally more favoured Roman.

The numbers of non-Roman communities when related to the chartered towns, whose citizens had Latin rights and Roman citizenship, was not static, and the first two centuries of the Empire saw the steady and sometimes dramatic increase of the latter. Throughout this period large numbers of individual *peregrini* acquired Roman citizenship until finally at the beginning of the third century the distinction between non-Roman and Roman, full Roman citizenship and Latin rights became meaningless with the edict of Caracalla, by which all free born provincials were granted Roman citizenship.

The Social Wars of the early first century BC had resulted in the grant of Roman citizenship to the towns of Italy south of the Po, while Caesar had extended the area as far as Cisalpine Gaul, to include the land between the Po and the Alpine foothills (p. 687). Some of the tribes of the southern Alps whose status was not absolutely clear later had their rights confirmed by Claudius. He, incidentally, showed his liberal attitude by insisting that those Gauls who had Roman citizenship and could meet the necessary property qualifications were eligible for admission to the senatorial order and could hold magistracies at Rome. The controversy over this decision, in AD 48, is recorded by Tacitus with a summary of the emperor's speech to the Senate while the bronze tablet found at Lyon, the capital of the three Gauls, in 1528, gives part of Claudius' actual text. For him at least there were to be no second-class Roman citizens. But the possession of *civitas Romana* was no light honour and Suetonius records that Claudius deprived an important Greek of citizenship because he could not speak Latin, that he actually executed men who had usurped the status, and attempted to prevent *peregrini* from using *gentilicia* (surnames) in the Roman fashion.

Under Nero the *civitates* of the small province of the Maritime Alps were given Latin rights and, perhaps under that emperor, the fifteen *civitates* of the neighbouring province of the Cottian Alps received the same honour. Such wholesale grants pale into insignificance compared to Vespasian's action in giving Latin rights to *all* peregrine communities in Spain. It has been calculated that Vespasian's grant benefited something of the order of 400 towns. The edict by which the grant was made will have been similar in function to the enabling legislation passed by the Roman people under the Republic before a colony was founded or municipal status awarded, and just as under the Republic, will have been followed by the issue of 'charters' (*leges datae*). The charters of Malaga, Salpensa and Irni are but three of the hundreds that had to be laboriously inscribed on bronze, itself no small labour, and sent to the new *municipia*.

Besides block grants to whole provinces, the emperors also created individual new chartered towns. Down to the early second century, colonies of Roman citizens continued to be established, the last two being foundations of Trajan, Sarmizegetusa, which owed its name to the old Dacian royal capital, though a considerable distance from it, and Timgad for veterans of *legio III Augusta* in Numidia. New *municipia* were also created, sometimes by giving Latin rights to pre-existing towns, and sometimes to whole tribal states as with the tribe of the Gallic Lingones near the headwaters of the Saône, who received *Latium* from Otho in AD 69. This was often done as the result of an initiative on the part of the community concerned. A particularly illuminating example relates to the small north African town of Gigthis on the coastal lagoon to the south-east of the Syrtis Minor (Gulf of Gabes). Here an honorary inscription has been found set up to a certain Marcus Servilius Draco Albucianus who had twice undertaken embassies to Rome at his own expense to secure the greater Latin rights and had finally met with success. The greater Latin rights (*Latium maius*) is explained by the second-century jurist Gaius, as the term used when all members of the municipal council gained Roman citizenship, and not only ex-magistrates, as was the case of the Spanish *municipia* like Salpensa. 'Greater Latin rights' were probably first awarded under Hadrian, or certainly existed by his time, as is known from another north African inscription, dated to that emperor's reign, from Thisiduo in the fertile Bagradas valley, on which the councillors (*decuriones*) are simply described as Roman citizens, C(*ives*) R(*omani*).

Just as *civitates peregrinae* could become *municipia* with Latin rights and, from the second century on, greater Latin rights, so *municipia* could obtain the title of colony. To cite one example, Nyon (Noviomagus) was originally a township (*vicus*) of the Gallic Tricastini, part of whose territory had been appropriated when land grants were made to the veterans of the *legio II* at Orange; the township was also the seat of the tribal administration (*caput civitatis*). It became a *municipium* under Augustus, from whom it took its new name of Augusta Tricastinorum, and by the end of the first century was accorded the title Colonia Flavia Tricastinorum. There is no particular reason to suppose that a draft of veterans from the legions was settled in the town at this time to account for the change in name. On the other hand we cannot be certain whether the title also carried with it a grant of Roman citizenship to the inhabitants. Such grants certainly could be made; Marcus Valerius Severus, the son of a man with the Punic-sounding name of Bostar, undertook an embassy to Claudius on behalf of the small Mauretanian town of Volubilis, and won a grant of Roman citizenship for his fellow townsfolk, besides various other privileges. In this case the official designation of the town became, and remained, *municipium*.

While whole communities, sometimes whole provinces, could be awarded Latin rights, and some favoured cities gained Roman citizenship, individuals were also able to achieve this desirable status. There were a number of avenues open to the aspiring citizen, and some have been mentioned already: in *municipia* with the lesser Latin right, candidates for office were awarded Roman citizenship if elected and similarly, at Trieste at any rate, non-citizen *peregrini* 'attributed' to a Roman colony won citizenship if elected to office. With the introduction of *Latium maius*, the whole council, probably normally a hundred men, was given Roman citizenship. Another way in which new citizens were created was by the manumission of slaves. Slaves who were given their freedom normally were accorded the same status as their master, whether he was peregrine, possessed of Latin rights, or full Roman citizen. The only exceptions were freedmen who had been irregularly or informally manumitted, or had been manumitted by a woman who had Roman citizenship; such men had the status of 'Junian Latins', so called from the *Lex Junia Norbana* AD 19 which defined their status. After his manumission a freedman normally took the family name (*nomen*) of his patron which he then in turn passed on to his descendants, and this explains why aristocratic *nomina* are sometimes borne by humble people. It only required the governor of a province to free numbers of his household on leaving office, for holders of his name to remain behind as living testimony of his spell of service.

There were cases where an emperor granted citizenship to the peregrine servants or friends of members of his own circle. Thus Pliny the younger wrote to Trajan on behalf of his Egyptian therapist asking for the emperor to bestow citizenship, adding at the same time a request for a similar grant for two freedwomen of a certain Antonia Maximilla, who, since their mistress was a woman, had only received the status of Junian Latins. The numbers of *peregrini* who acquired citizenship in this particular way will always have been small. Of much greater significance were the two categories of new citizen, both of which had served in the army (Part 3, Chapter 6).

The first were the sons of legionaries who, until a relaxation of the conditions by Severus in the early third century, had been forbidden to marry. Rules, however, and this perhaps more than many, are made to be broken, and it was inevitable that many men who served in the legions and who had to be Roman citizens to qualify for service, married and raised families. The sons of such unofficial marriages were, technically, illegitimate and therefore took the status of their peregrine mothers, but if they chose to follow in their father's footsteps and join the legions, they could expect to be given Roman citizenship on enlistment. Other suitably qualified recruits who were not Roman citizens were also sometimes given citizenship for the same reason.

The second category was that of the auxiliaries. They served in regiments of infantry (cohorts) or cavalry (*alae*) that were recruited from *peregrini* (Part 3, Chapter 6). Those who survived for twenty-five years earned discharge and with it a grant of the coveted Roman citizenship. The process by which the grant was made was as follows: the governors of the provinces in which auxiliary troops were stationed forwarded lists of eligible veterans to the emperor who then issued a decree granting them citizenship. The decrees followed a more or less stereotyped form giving the emperor's full titles and naming the province, governor and all the auxiliary units concerned in the grant, and finally all the recipients, unit by unit. With the exception of two small inscribed fragments, these decrees, which were inscribed on great tablets of bronze and attached to walls of various public buildings on the Capitol in Rome until AD 89, and thereafter on the wall behind the temple of Augustus on the Palatine, have long since disappeared, having been melted down for re-use. But copies in duplicate were made for the veterans themselves, and many of these have survived, some 322, in whole or in part, at the time of writing. The two small fragments of the original decrees in fact only survive because they were reused at a later date, in order to make these copies. The copies were inscribed on two thin tablets of bronze, each about 15 by 13 cm (6 by 5 in.). These tablets were often, though not always, fastened together by two loops of wire which passed through two holes at the bottom corners of one of them and the top corners of the other, so that they could fold like the covers of a book. The word normally used today for the document, *diploma*, comes from a Greek root and means literally 'a doubling', and thus describes the document when the two leaves are folded together. On the inside faces of the leaves was a copy of the imperial decree, theoretically the only omission being the detailed listing unit by unit of all the recipients, instead of which only the name of the recipient concerned, his unit and commanding officer would be given. Once the inner faces of the tablets had been inscribed, the document was closed and a third wire was passed through two more holes which pierced the middle of both leaves, effectively clamping the two bronze tablets together face to face. The duplicate copy was then inscribed on one of the outer faces, and, to certify that both inner and outer texts were true copies of the original decree, the other outer face carried the names of seven witnesses (normal Roman procedure). In Plate 27.1 (see also pl. 11.2 for Syria) it can be seen that, although each of the witnesses had the three names of a normal Roman citizen, the first name (*praenomen*) and family name (*nomen*) were separated from the third name (*cognomen*), because the binding wire passed across the space which, consequently, had been left blank and the seals of the witnesses were affixed at this point, enclosed in a small oblong bronze box.

Diplomas are in effect certificates of citizenship and it is misleading to call them 'discharge certificates' as is so often done, since although they were normally issued to veterans when they were discharged from the service, this was not always so. There is, for example, a diploma issued by Trajan to an auxiliary soldier recruited in Britain, who received Roman citizenship on the 11 August AD 106 along with his fellows in an auxiliary cohort *before* discharge because of courageous service in the emperor's second Dacian war. This diploma is peculiar as, in the preamble, there is no mention of citizenship also being granted to the soldier's children, present or future, together with the right of marriage (*conubium*) for any existing wife or to a future non-citizen wife, provided the soldier married only one woman. This provision is normally a regular feature of diplomas at this date, and the wives and children are also specifically mentioned.

It is clear from this and similar documents that even if the children are ignored, the granting of Roman citizenship to time-expired auxiliaries must over the years have added considerably to the number of new citizens, particularly in a 'backward' province like Britain, where there will have been few Roman citizens, but at fifty the largest number of auxiliary units in any province and about a seventh of the total number in the Empire. It is perhaps worth trying to estimate just how many new citizens would be created annually in this way. To maintain itself, a long established auxiliary regiment of 500 men serving for twenty-five years would have to accept on average twenty new recruits a year to replace the twenty veterans who retired. If we take Britain as an example, there were the equivalent of fifty-seven such regiments (seven of the fifty numbered 1,000 instead of 500) so that theoretically there could have been as many as 1,140 new citizens a year. Even if one assumes that only half survived to discharge, the figure could have been largely made good by children of veterans who benefited at the same time (cf. Roxan, 1981, 276–7 for figures on the proportion of veterans who had wives and for the size of families).

The formulae on the diplomas changed precisely in AD 140. Henceforth children born to a veteran before the grant of citizenship were not included. This change, which on the face of it appears somewhat retrogressive, is usually explained by the theory that, if the sons of veterans already had Roman citizenship, then there would be no inducement for them to join. Margaret Roxan, however, has recently shown (Roxan, forthcoming) that there is more to the change than simply a desire to get more recruits. Indeed there is no independent evidence to suggest that recruits for the auxiliaries were at all in short supply. She suggests that in AD 140 an anomaly was being corrected because the auxiliaries had reached a more advantageous position than legionaries. Both groups of men were, by Roman military law, forbidden to marry, yet the children of the former born before discharge were awarded citizenship while those of the latter were not. She further connects the change in AD 140 with a phenomenon which occurred in the late 160s. A dramatic drop in the number of surviving diplomas suggests that from 140 auxiliary soldiers were brought into line with legionaries in another way. By 140 many recruits to the auxiliary regiments will have been Roman citizens, while those who were not, possibly just the sons of serving soldiers, now received citizenship on enlistment. Thus in 140 Antoninus Pius may have been taking away from the auxiliaries a privilege with one hand, but giving back something with the other. This is precisely what Caracalla did three-quarters of a century later, on an even greater scale.

These then were the roads to Roman citizenship: through the office of magistrate or councillor in a town with the lesser or the greater Latin rights, through manumission by a master who was himself a citizen, or through service in an auxiliary regiment. By the early third century AD there must have been many who had followed them and won the coveted status. The climax came in AD 212 when Caracalla granted Roman citizenship, with minor exceptions, to all free-born provincials. The edict (*constitutio*) by which Caracalla made this grant is generally known today as the *Constitutio Antoniniana*. His motives in making the grant may not have been entirely lacking in self-interest, but one thing is clear; the distinction between Roman and non-Roman, as far as those living within the borders of the Empire were concerned, virtually ceased to exist.

As a mark of this new status, the new citizen formally took a family name (*nomen*) on the Roman model. Sometimes this was based on his own single peregrine name or that of his father. Thus a man called Placidus, the son of Viducus, a tribesman of the Veliocasses north-west of Paris, whose name appears on an inscription from Holland dating to before Caracalla's edict, is attested on an inscription from York dated to AD 221 with the name Viducius Placidus (cf. Bogaers, 1983, 21–4). Others took the *nomen* of their patron Caracalla, Aurelius. The habit even temporarily spread to those who were citizens already and had a perfectly respectable *nomen* of their own (Gilliam, 1965, 86–90), so that, for example, a man known from a series of inscriptions in Rome as Tiberius Julius Balbillus before the edict, occurs after it in AD 215 as Aurelius Julius Balbillus (Sherwin-White, 1973, 387, note 2).

What induced Caracalla to issue his grant, and what practical difference did the grant make to its recipients? A contemporary, the historian Dio, whose work is hostile to Caracalla, while discussing his financial exactions and explaining that these went in increased pay for the army, gives him a financial motive. Roman citizens living in Italy and in many, if not all, of the colonies originally established for legionary veterans were immune from land tax, but there were two minor indirect taxes to which they, unlike non-Romans, were liable. These were the 5 per cent tax on manumissions of slaves and the 5 per cent death duty. The revenues from these two taxes went to the *aerarium militare*, the military treasury established by Augustus as a pension fund for legionaries. Before making all non-Romans liable to these taxes by converting them into citizens, Caracalla doubled the rate of both to 10 per cent! Whatever motives he may have had, there must certainly have been a financial aspect to the *Constitutio* and the one practical difference that it made to the new citizens was that they paid more taxes.

Caracalla's motives are not the only controversial aspect of the *Constitutio Antoniniana*. Much argument surrounds a fragmentary papyrus which either gives the actual text of the edict, or was a measure issued supplementary to it (Lewis and Reinhold, 1955, 427–8 for the text; Sherwin-White, 1973, 380–94). Among other matters, this debate is concerned with the exact meaning of a group called the 'dediticii', who do not appear to have benefited from the grant. The Latin word normally refers to those who had surrendered unconditionally, as had all those non-Roman communities originally defeated in battle, but the term can hardly refer to the *civitates stipendiariae* who were the chief beneficiaries from the grant. Presumably it meant very recently conquered peoples, who had not yet been granted the right of self-government and whom, for various reasons, it might have been desirable to keep apart from the mass of ordinary provincials. Such a group were the tribal warriors defeated by Severus Alexander in some unrecorded campaign in north Britain, whose presence on the Roman frontier in southern Germany, twenty years after Caracalla's edict, is attested by an inscription (pl. 27.2). They remained there as non-Romans helping to defend the Empire whose peace they had disturbed, with perhaps only the remote possibility of eventually becoming full citizens.

When Paul was about to be flogged, he told his captors that he was a Roman citizen and was immediately released. A hundred years later, in AD 153, a veteran of an auxiliary cavalry regiment, Gaius Maevius Apellas, was not so fortunate and was summarily beaten by local officials. It must have been small comfort to him that the beating was illegal, although it was still thought worth lodging an official complaint (*Select Papyri* II 254). After another century, a generation or so after all free men in the Empire had become 'Romans', even the complaint would not have been worth making. In the first two centuries of the Empire a distinction existed between upper-class provincials who were Roman and lower-class provincials who were not. Now all were technically Roman, but the gulf still existed, and by the fourth century was legally recognized. Those whom the second-century orator, Aelius Aristides, in his panegyric to Rome had once defined as Roman 'the more cultured, better born, and more influential' were now known by the simple word *honestiores* ('more honourable'), while the non-Roman rest whom he had categorized as 'vassals and subjects', though now technically Romans, were called *humiliores* (literally the lower classes). And the lot of the *humiliores* compared to their counterparts in the early Empire was bleak, in an age when injustice was rife and corruption endemic.

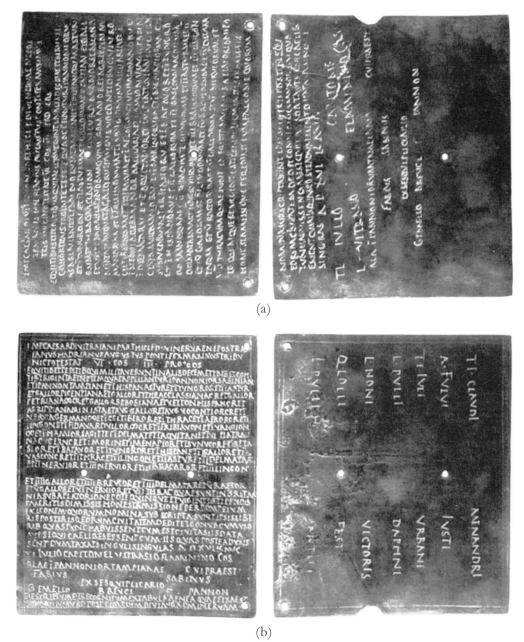

(a)

(b)

27.1 (a) Inner faces of the *diploma* of AD 122 (*CIL* XVI 69) granting Roman citizenship to a Pannonian, Gemellus, the son of Breucus (mentioned in the last line). The preamble lists fifty auxiliary regiments in the army in Britain in which there were veterans who were receiving citizenship at the same time
(b) Outer faces of the same *diploma*, with a second copy of the grant of citizenship inscribed on one leaf and the names of seven witnesses on the other

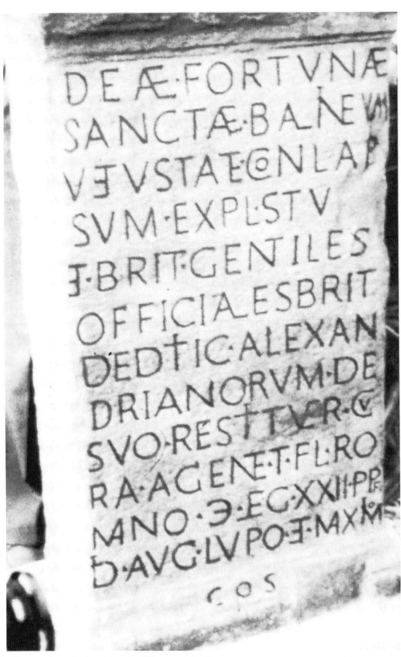

27.2 Dedicatory inscription from Walldürn on the *limes* in southern Germany (*ILS* 9184), mentioning (lines 6–8), the *Britones dediticii, Alexandriani*, a group of irregular soldiers who will not have benefited from Caracalla's grant of citizenship.

CHAPTER 28

·LABOUR·

P. A. Brunt

The economy of the Roman Empire was predominantly agricultural; for the rich land was the safest, and therefore the most honourable investment and most men worked on the fields. The development of trade and industry was hampered by the high cost of transport, especially by land (Part 8, Chapter 23; Brunt, 1971, 179–81, 135, 703–6; Duncan-Jones, 1982, App. XVII but note K. Hopkins, 1983), and by technological backwardness; inventiveness, not marked in the Greek world, diminished under Roman rule. No doubt knowledge which already existed in the more advanced areas was more widely diffused, yet the water-mill, devised in Asia in the first century BC, was not generally used for four centuries, and then only for the grinding of grain (Finley, 1981, Chapter 11). In the absence of large machines there was no advantage in concentrating labour in big factories; industrial establishments will hardly ever have employed more than a score or two of hands (Kiechle, 1969), and in some workshops the master crafts-man would work side-by-side with a few slaves. Wool was often spun and woven in the great households under the eye of the mistress, or by artisans in their own homes.

Transport costs must also have limited the movement of foodstuffs. Even large estates sometimes aimed at self-sufficiency. The cities could only afford imports from beyond their own territories in so far as they could sell their own manufactures or services in return. Except in some favoured regions like the Nile valley the level of agricultural production was probably low. In the first century Columella had the impression that the average return of grain in Italy was fourfold or less (*On Agriculture* III 3,4). He held that most land needed to be fallowed every alternate year. Though the value of manure as a fertilizer was well understood, this practice made it hard to raise enough beasts for the purpose as well as to grow food for the human population. One conse-quence was that the poor can seldom have eaten meat. Famines or scarcities must have been frequent, not to speak of persistent undernourishment and increased susceptibility to disease. Naturally, when prices soared, the poor suffered most. A fourth-century famine at Antioch, one of the largest cities, was alleviated by the extraordinary organization of supplies from districts not more than 50 to 100 km (30 to 60 miles) away (Julian, *Misopogonos* 369); this illustrates how dependent people normally were on the resources of their own neighbourhood. It is no objection that large quantities of food were shipped long distances to Rome, Constantinople and the armies, for in these cases the state paid out of imperial revenues.

Hence the high civilization that the few attained inevitably rested on an unequal distribution of resources; it was secured, and aggravated, by the concentration of political power both centrally and locally in the hands of a small class, who exercised it in their own interests. The general standard of life cannot be gauged from magnificent public buildings or the opulent villas of the rich. Carcopino has given a graphic and documented account of the squalor of the majority in Rome itself (1941, Chapters I–II); here and perhaps in the few other big cities that existed, overcrowding was perhaps an exceptional cause of misery, though it is also revealed in Egyptian towns and villages, (Lewis, 1983, 53 and 158) and probably conditions were no worse than in London or many western cities until fairly recent times, or in some urban agglomerations of other lands in our own day. Most men of course lived in the country, or in small towns, many of whose inhabitants went out daily to till the adjoining fields. At least in Mediterranean lands, land-owners too preferred to live in towns, and they often contributed handsomely to the construction of temples, colonnades, gymnasia, public baths and fountains, theatres, amphitheatres and so forth; these amenities not only ministered to their own pride and pleasure but also benefited the poor who lived in or near the towns, but they were seldom found in villages. The funds needed for these buildings, if not supplied by the magnates, must have come chiefly from the rents of lands owned by the cities themselves, or occasionally from imperial benefactions, that is to say from general taxation or from the rents of imperial domains. In any event, the revenues of most cities were ultimately extracted from the surplus production of rural workers, who must have constituted about 90 per cent of the total population; yet they derived the least advantage from the expenditure. The peasants sometimes lacked local civic rights, and were thus excluded from many benefactions, which provided for distributions of food, wine or cash only to citizens; some charitable foundations also restricted the recipients to those living inside the walls. Galen (VI K 749ff.) tells that in time of dearth city dwellers in Asia would seize all the cereals after the harvest, leaving the rustics to subsist on pulses, tree-shoots, wild roots and grasses (from which they contracted diseases that fascinated him as a doctor). Idylls of country scenes and laudations of the dignity of labour on the land, like Virgil's, were composed by those who never turned a sod.

Some of these and later generalizations cannot be proved, though they may be illustrated, by specific evidence, which is always meagre, but derive from consideration of the basic social and economic structure of the Empire. Numerical data are in particular lacking. Censuses were taken of Roman citizens, and of the inhabitants of provinces, with their property, but figures survive only for the totals of citizens registered under Augustus and Claudius. From the former we can infer that *c*. AD 14 the free inhabitants of Italy numbered about 5 millions; conjecturally 2 or 3 millions of slaves may be added. Under Augustus and Nero the population of Egypt is also said to have stood at about seven millions (Diodorus I, 31; Josephus, *Jewish War* II, 385). If these figures are accepted, the estimate made by Beloch, a master of demography, of 50 to 60 millions for all the inhabitants of the Empire in about AD 1 seems somewhat too low. We have no figures at all to show whether thereafter the population was static, declining or growing, but a decline might explain the apparent shortage of manpower in the fourth century (p. 705); it could be ascribed to the pandemic diseases of the second and third centuries, and to the disruption caused by barbarian inroads after *c*. 250. It is also commonly believed that the importation of slaves diminished (p. 715). Infant mortality must of course have been very high, and it was aggravated by the practice, which the law sanctioned until Christian times, of exposing unwanted children, especially girls. Attempts have been made to calculate the average expectation of life from the numerous tombstones which purport to record the ages of the deceased, but K. Hopkins proved that the data must be unrepresentative and sometimes false: they produce results which are incoherent and impossible in the light of modern statistical evidence; but it may be assumed, on the basis of well-documented material from modern pre-industrial societies, unaffected by advances in hygiene and medicine unknown in antiquity, that with infant mortality about 200 per 1,000 births the expectation of life was below 30; some confirmation comes from the papyrological records of Egypt (Brunt, 1971, Chapters IX–XI; Hopkins, 1966). Naturally the labouring poor had the shortest life span, and they must have composed the immense majority. In Italy substantial citizens with their families will have numbered 350,000 to 700,000 (Brunt, 1962, 71); the remaining 90 per cent or more of the population had to work for their livelihood. It is unlikely that the well-to-do formed a higher proportion of inhabitants of the provinces than in Italy, where riches had been accumulated from the profits of Empire.

These profits had been used in part for the massive importation of slaves. Domestic slavery was ubiquitous in the ancient world, and in the more advanced Greek states slaves had also been extensively employed in the fields, mines and shops, and in the crafts and professions; this continued in Roman times. Galen supposed that in his native Pergamum they constituted a third of the population, but in Italy the proportion may have been higher. The extent to which they were used in most of the provinces is unknown. The elder Pliny ranked Spain next to Italy in many blessings, including the proficiency of slaves (*Natural History* XXXVII, 203). But in Egypt and Palestine most rural and industrial workers were nominally free. For many areas there is no evidence. However, slavery was not the only possible form of legal servitude (cf. Ste Croix, 1981, 147ff. and Jones, 1974, Chapter XIV).

Debt bondage, which still exists today in some parts of the world, and which requires the debtor to render services to a creditor in return for loans he is not able or perhaps intended to repay, was known to Varro (*On Agriculture* I, 17) from Asia, Egypt and Illyricum. He treats it as a thing of the past in Italy, and it is never mentioned by the jurists. However, in Roman law the creditor could take his debtor into custody by order of the court; as he had to provide him with maintenance, this looks like a sanction against the debtor who was able but refused to make payment. Still, some texts suggest that in Italy it might be the means of pressure on an insolvent debtor to work off his debt by an informal agreement of which the law knew nothing. Land-owners could also distrain the personal goods of tenants who failed to pay rent; the threat to do so may have been the means of forcing them to remain in their holdings at times of labour shortage, when it would have been hard to find replacements. Debt was indeed probably a large factor in the growth of large estates: small owners, unable to store much surplus produce in good seasons and hold out for higher prices, could amass no reserves and had to borrow in bad years in order to obtain subsistence and seed, very probably on terms that gave them little chance of ever clearing their indebtedness. A revolt in Gaul in AD 21 was supported by a multitude of *obaerati* who were probably debt bondsmen (Tacitus, *Annals* III, 42): it was directed as much against the Gallic magnates as against Roman rule. And even when peasants were not reduced to debt bondage, they may often have been milked by urban money-lenders. The Jewish rebels in 66 burned the record offices in which the bonds for debt were filed, and in 70 peasants did the same at Antioch (Josephus, *Jewish War*, II, 427; VII, 61).

Serfs, persons nominally free but bound by hereditary obligations of law or custom to work on the lands of others, had been found before the time of Roman rule in for example Etruria, Sparta, Gaul and some eastern regions, certainly not in all; thus serfdom did not exist in Palestine nor in Egypt. It does not seem to have survived under Rome, till recreated in the late Empire. Until that time Roman jurists know nothing of it. They envisage contracts of tenancy, under which the owner may evict the tenant, but the tenant is free to leave. That was clearly the practice in Italy itself. Petitions from tenants (*coloni*) on imperial domains in Asia and Africa reveal that they had been on the same land for generations but that they were not legally restrained from moving. In Egypt too both public and private land was leased; admittedly the government some-times forced men to take up leases of *public* land and debarred them from leaving during the tenancy. Here too the *fellahin* were liable to innumerable taxes and compulsory labour services for the state; the burden was so great that 'flight up-country' resulted in the almost complete desertion of some villages, and the orders given that men should return to their homes for the periodic censuses were probably ineffectual. But wretched as the condition of the *fellahin* was, they were not serfs bound to private proprietors.

It was perhaps Diocletian who introduced a system, progressively developed throughout the Empire, under which *coloni* at least on large estates were bound to the soil, they and their descendants, and to some extent placed under the jurisdiction of the owners. At the same time the owners were forbidden to alienate any slaves they employed on their estates. Thus *coloni* and rural slaves were assimilated to each other. In the same period persons in various other categories who furnished the state with essential supplies, services or revenues, were similarly bound along with their descendants to their respective callings; they included city councillors, soldiers, and those engaged in provisioning the City of Rome (Jones, 1974, Chapter XXI). It seems plausible to suppose that these regulations, which could not in fact be thoroughly enforced, were the consequence of a shortage of manpower. Of course this system prevented tenants from taking advantage of a dearth of labour to better their condition by offering themselves to the highest bidder; that was a gain to the landlords, but the restriction on the movement of rural slaves, which limited their profitable use or sale, shows that the primary motive of the government was not that of favouring their interests.

Debt bondsmen and serfs retained their free status in the eyes of the law. They could acquire and transmit property; in principle the debt bondsman could pay off what he owed. They could contract valid marriages and enjoy a stable family life, though poverty might compel men to expose newborn infants, and even to sell children, when they had no means of maintaining them. If the serf could not legally leave his land, he was at least secured in his tenure; most peasants doubtless desired nothing more. They were not subject to the life-and-death power of a master, and they had access to the courts, though the later *coloni* were barred from impleading their lords, and were liable to be flogged at their order. Not indeed that access to the courts was worth much to any of the poor, who might not know their legal rights, would lack time and money to sue, often in assizes distant from their homes, and could not match the money and influence by which the great could pervert the course of justice; moreover, the successful litigant was usually left to execute for himself the civil judgments of the courts, and the poor man could seldom have had the requisite power (Kelly, 1966; Burton, 1975).

By contrast the slave was in many respects a mere chattel, to be bought and sold like any other animal. Protected against damage by third parties in the interest of his owner, he was in the absolute power of the master, who could put him to death. Some imperial enactments were designed to shield him from excesses of the master's cruelty or lust, but he could not plead his own case in court, and these laws were probably in themselves generally as ineffective as comparable legislation in later slave societies is known to have been; however, they reflect a prevalent opinion in the master class that slaves should be treated with some measure of humanity; Seneca says that savage owners were pointed at in the streets (*de clementia* I, 18). The Emperor Pius justified one such measure by the general interest of owners; the cruelty of an individual, by stirring up general unrest among the slaves, might be injurious to all owners (*Digest* I, 6, 2; cf. Diodorus XXXIV–V, 2ff.). The slave's best protection always lay in the fact that he was a piece of property whose value no sensible owner would wish to impair.

And he was particularly valuable because after all he was a man, a 'living tool' (as Aristotle had said), but a tool of special versatility on account of his human intelligence. The law itself recognized his humanity in admitting his capacity to commit crimes and give evidence, and his potentiality for freedom. Rewards as well as punishments were needed to get the best from him. Thus he might be paid wages or set up in business, rendering only part of his receipts to his owner. What he earned and saved, or obtained as gifts, could form his *peculium*, property which strictly belonged to his owner, but which custom allowed him to treat as his own; it could be substantial. He could not contract a valid legal marriage, and the child of the slave woman was always the property of her owner; but in practice the stable cohabitation of slaves was often treated as if it were a marriage. None the less slaves remained utterly dependent on the master, who could always seize their *peculium*, and break up families by sale, gift or bequest. Manumission too was a reward given at the master's discretion.

No generalizing about the lot of slaves in the Roman Empire is possible. As with all slave societies, there are stories of mutual affection between masters and slaves, or of lust and savagery, reciprocated by hatred and murder; they cannot be made the basis for any general conclusions, if only because it was the minority of slaves in close contact with their owners who were most likely to experience special benevolence or cruelty, not the masses employed in fields, workshops and mines, whose welfare would depend chiefly on the behaviour of overseers. Diodorus (V, 36–8) tells how in the Spanish mines of the late Republic slaves were worked to death in appalling conditions. From the economic standpoint this was rational only because they were exceptionally cheap and because huge profits could be made quickly. Brutality also precipitated the outbreak of the first of three great slave revolts in the Republic, but there were other factors, which cannot be discussed here; no comparable risings are attested in the imperial period, partly no doubt because the government had the means to repress disturbances more promptly; slave revolts have been rare in all times, no doubt chiefly because of the difficulty of organizing them when the power of the state is exerted efficiently. The rebels seem to have sought only to secure freedom for themselves, not to remould the social structure; the same desire for personal freedom explains the flight of slaves, which was probably always frequent, and need not betoken that the fugitives had been ill-treated. Slaves could normally expect food, clothes and shelter, of which the free poor had no guarantee, especially in times of scarcity; the harsh Cato even prescribed grain rations for heavy farm labourers larger than those of the Roman legionary; owners needed to conserve their property and ensure good work.

Slaves were employed not merely in the mines and fields, but in more skilled occupations in trade and industry; they could be teachers, doctors and architects; they performed all sorts of clerical tasks, notably as secretaries and accountants in government departments. In such cases the prospect of freedom was an essential incentive to efficiency. They might 'buy' it by surrendering *peculium* in whole or part, or might receive it as a gift; it is not known which was most common. The freedman might be required to render services without payment in return for maintenance to his old master, now his patron. Some freedmen lived in his household, and the patron might provide in his will that after his death they should be fed and clothed by his heirs as in his own lifetime. But others amassed fortunes, the basis of which was often the *peculium* acquired in slavery; patrons had important but limited rights to inherit from them, but they would often not be his dependants in economic terms. Petronius' novel gives us a picture of vulgar freedmen millionaires in which realism and fantasy are inextricably mingled. Thus economically some freedmen, and even slaves, did not belong to the lowest stratum. It is, however, a ludicrous error to suppose that most slaves could count on manumission. The elder Pliny calls the slave field-workers in Italy 'men without hope' (*Natural History* XVIII, 36). The Roman agronomists assume that even farm managers will be slaves, and such was the condition of most of those commemorated in (the rather few) gravestones. But most slaves must have been engaged in agriculture (and the miners will not have been more fortunate).

It may incidentally be observed that manumission could in some degree promote social mobility in a world that was for the most part structured hierarchically. Tacitus alleges that many senators in the first century were of servile descent (*Annals* XIII, 27). Pertinax, the son of a freedman, became emperor in 193. For the freeborn poor the army, recruited chiefly from the peasantry, presented almost the only means of advancement. A small minority of soldiers could rise from the ranks to the dignity and wealth of a centurion, and a few of these could go still further. In the third century particularly peasant soldiers reached the highest positions and even (it was alleged) the imperial purple.

Even in Italy and still more in the provinces, slaves can only have constituted a minority of the working population. Everywhere the majority must have consisted of peasants who cultivated small holdings, which they either owned or leased by contract or on terms fixed by custom, and who relied chiefly on their own labour and that of their families; of shopkeepers and craftsmen, and of hired labourers, not subject to any form of legal servitude. These people were limited in their freedom by lack of both economic power and political rights, and their standard of living was often no better, and might be worse, than that of chattel slaves. No doubt they included some who worked themselves but were possessed of means sufficient to employ slaves too. Shop-keepers and artisans might have slaves as assistants; army veterans often owned slaves, whom they might have acquired in service, to help in the cultivation of small farms on which they were settled after discharge, and tenant farmers sometimes employed slaves, perhaps hired out to them by the proprietor. It is reasonable to describe the Roman economy, at least in Italy and in some provincial regions, as slave economy, because total production depended largely and essentially on slave labour, and especially that production from which members of the ruling class derived their income. Their slave holdings could be very large. Augustus thought it expedient to forbid men to manumit over a hundred slaves by will. A prefect of the city of Rome murdered by his slaves in AD 61 owned 400 in his town house, and must have had many more on his estates to support this establishment. The saintly Christian lady Melania in the fourth century is credited with possessing among other estates one of sixty-two hamlets near Rome with 400 slave labourers (cf. Jones, 1964, 778–93). By contrast in 1850, when slaves in the Southern States of the USA numbered a third of the population only eleven owners had over 500 slaves apiece. Very probably slave competition held down the remuneration that the free poor could expect for their labour, especially in agriculture and mining; it must, however, be recalled that slaves employed in skilled occupations themselves often received more than the equivalent of a mere subsistence wage, and even rural slaves might be allowed *peculium* in the form of garden plots and farmyard hens.

Extremely little is known of the working population in general, but more of the slaves than of any other section of it. Since slaves were property, they were of constant concern to the jurists, who provide our most valuable information. Domestic and secretarial staff were also in closest contact with their employers, and therefore figure in frequent incidental allusions in the surviving literature. But this literature was almost in its entirety written for, and often by, the elite, who clearly had no interest in the lot of their inferiors for its own sake. Historians and orators had indeed described the discontents of the poor, in times when they had votes by which they could try to enforce their demands or when the soldiery was a civic militia that might reflect their grievances. The Principate extinguished political rights, and organized a professional army in which the soldiers, though recruited from the lower classes, were divorced from the civil population by long service often far from their homes (Baynes, 1955, 307–8). Troops were now available to suppress *émeutes* at an early stage. Detailed historical narratives, moreover, which might reveal the continuance of social discontent, are extant only for short periods of the Principate. Where they exist, they sometimes indicate that it had its part in such risings as did occur. Reference has already been made to those in Gaul in 21, and in Judaea where bandits (*sicarii*) had long infested the countryside before they joined the rebels in 66; Josephus, who often refers to them, treats them as mere criminals, but his evidence shows that in reality most of them combined religious fanaticism with hatred of exploitation by upper-class Jews as well as of Roman rule. Banditry is a well-known symptom of social unrest, and there are scattered allusions to it in various times and places in the Empire. Urban food riots are also known to have occurred. In the late Empire peasants at times combined with barbarian invaders in the delusion that the disruption of Roman power would alleviate their lot (Ste Croix, 1981, 317–21, 474–88; cf. Hobsbawm, 1969).

For Italy of the late Republic and first century AD the agronomists and Pliny's *Natural History* furnish exceptional information on agricultural labour, especially slave labour, but we cannot generalize to the provinces; what is known of one region cannot be assumed to be true of any other in the absence of specific corroborating evidence or arguments. Normally literary works hardly notice the labouring population except when they caused disturbances. This is not indeed true of Christian writers, nor it seems, of Rabbinic texts. In the apostolic age the Christians were 'the weak things of the world' (I *Corinthians* 1, 27); and there is more than a tinge of social protest in the New Testament, for instance in the Beatitudes, which promise blessings to the poor and hungry and retribution to the rich. Later too the Church made its converts, as Celsus complained (Origen, *against Celsus* III, 55) among weavers, cobblers, yokels and other uneducated folk. But Christian writers are naturally concerned chiefly with spiritual themes and allude only incidentally to material conditions.

Where else is there evidence? Thousands of inscriptions survive, although in some regions these too are rare. Moreover, it is certain that the masses especially in the countryside were mostly illiterate and that for centuries few even spoke Latin or Greek, the languages in which most inscriptions were written (Brunt, 1976, 190–2; Balsdon, 1979; Harris, 1983, especially 59ff. and 87ff.). These people had no motive to leave any epigraphic memorial to their existence, even an epitaph, which in itself usually tells little, and especially one affixed, as they often are, to a sculptured gravestone, the cost of which would have been beyond their means (Duncan-Jones, 1982, 80 and 131). It is therefore not surprising that inscriptions of rural workers, whether of small owners, tenants, farm-managers, agricultural labourers, slave or free, are most uncommon, as are those of unskilled labourers like dockers in the towns, as distinct from shopkeepers and craftsmen, who were often perhaps employers of labour. Thus the population known to the epigraphist is no true counterpart of the actual population of the Empire, most of whose inhabitants lived and died without a trace.

In Egypt alone abundant papyrological material illustrates life at every level, though it has not yet been fully and systematically analysed for the specific purpose of determining the condition of the labouring poor. Moreover this uniquely fertile land, 'the gift of the Nile', in which the necessity for centralized control of irrigation had led to the evolution of a system in which the economy was minutely regulated and in which the government itself therefore to a large extent directed labour resources, was so different from every other province that evidence cannot be safely extrapolated for Egypt to other parts of the Empire.

The material remains discovered by the archaeologist may also illustrate the life of the poor, though they were naturally endowed with fewer of the worldly goods which the spade reveals, nor until fairly recent times were archaeologists much concerned with inquiring into their condition, for instance with asking what sort of labour was employed on the estate of which an excavated villa was the centre. Moreover interpretation of the data is speculative. Close to some villas we find living quarters for the farm hands; were they subject to any form of legal bondage, or merely to social and economic dependence on the owners (Part 7; Whittaker, 1980)? Occasional finds of slave fetters may give a conclusive answer: otherwise it is likely to be dictated by some general theory ultimately derived from a conjectural reading of the meagre literary evidence, if not from Marxist dogmas. Doubts may also arise whether any particular site is typical even for its own region, let alone for the Empire at large. What follows will serve in part to show the uncertainties that beset hypotheses which have been widely received.

Numerous inscriptions from all parts of the Empire attest the existence in towns of associations (*collegia, synodoi*) which were formed with the sanction of the state for the celebration of common cults and for social conviviality. Some of them consisted of men engaged within a particular city in the same trade. There was also for instance a *collegium* of shipowners who provisioned Rome. They were certainly capitalists, and it may well be that the members of many other trade associations were employers rather than simple workers; that may be true of the bakers and builders who took some kind of industrial action in Ephesus and Pergamum. They could be required to render public services; the *fabri* (smiths or builders) and *centonarii* (blanket makers) in the west acted as municipal firemen, and in Egypt industrial associations could be made jointly liable for the provision of supplies needed for the army. In the late Empire *collegia* were the instruments for the regimentation of all kinds of services and supplies required by the state. Obviously men in the same business would discuss their common interests and try to further them by concerted action, but there is no evidence that except perhaps in Egypt they had the legal rights of guilds in later times to regulate prices, wages, conditions of apprenticeship or standards of quality. There were also many associations of *tenuiores* (persons of slender means), primarily burial clubs. Men desired a decent funeral and some memorial; if they could make no provision for this, their bodies would be cast into a communal pit. The monthly contributions paid to the club assured them against this fate, but they also covered the cost of monthly feasts. The indigent could not have afforded them. The members could indeed include slaves (who needed their masters' consent to join), but with *peculium* slaves might be affluent.

There was of course no system of social security or of such poor relief as the Church later provided, or the parishes in England from the time of Elizabeth I. Only in Rome and later in Constantinople, as the imperial capitals, did the central government make regular distributions of food and occasionally of cash to a fixed number of regular recipients; in Italy too, which long preserved a privileged position in immunity from direct taxation, it made funds available to the cities from which they could maintain poor children. So far from recognizing any general responsibility to the poor, it imposed a regressive system of taxation; in Egypt the poor were actually liable to poll taxes which the élite were exempted from, or paid at lower rates. Social services were left to the local authorities, and they too did little for the masses. When food was scarce, they might organize supplies and distributions, or try to hold down prices; otherwise there was a danger of riots. They engaged doctors and teachers of literature, rhetoric and philosophy, who also secured from the state valuable privileges such as exemption from taxes and other burdens, but these men charged fees and were often wealthy; they surely served only or principally the members of the upper class to whom they owed their posts. In the east there was heavy expenditure on gymnastics, practised by the youth of the élite. Hardly anything was done for primary education; it is significant that school teachers were denied the privileges granted to those active in higher education. Pagan morality inculcated beneficence, but to one's kin, friends, dependants (including slaves) and fellow-citizens in general, not to the poor as such. By contrast the Christians inherited from the Jewish law and teaching the conception that men had special duties to the poor, and to widows and orphans (Bolkestein, 1939). Whereas the pagan burial clubs gave benefits only in return for subscriptions, in contemporary Christian communities the richer members succoured their indigent brethren. About 250 the Church at Rome was supporting 1,500 poor persons. It may well be that Christian charity did much to promote conversions (Harnack, 1961, Book II). Once Christianity had become the state religion, it had some effect on public policy in this regard. For the first time hospitals, almshouses and the like are found. Constantine authorized grants from imperial funds for the support of children whom their fathers must otherwise have destroyed or sold as slaves out of sheer want. In 451 Christian emperors proclaimed that it was incumbent on their humanity to care for the needy and ensure that the poor did not want food (*Theodosian Code* XI, 27; *Code of Justinian* I, 2, 12, 2; Jones, 1964, 894–910). Legal servitude, however, was accepted and justified by the Church, which itself owned slaves, as part of the curse of Adam.

In Rome and Italy persons engaged in industry and trade are recorded in hundreds of inscriptions besides those of the *collegia*, notably in epitaphs. Here is a random specimen from Beneventum (*ILS* 7667): 'Publius Marcius Philodemus freedman of Publius, plasterer, set up (this tomb) for himself and those who belonged to him (perhaps his freedmen and slaves as well as his family). Here is buried Iucunda, his darling.' Such documents, which individually tell us little, can be used statistically. Long ago Gummerus, not without some conjectural interpretation of many of the inscriptions, was able to tabulate the status of Italian artisans, many of whom were undoubtedly employers, as follows (*RE* IX 1504; cf. Duff, 1958, Chapter VI):

	Freeborn	Freedmen	Slaves
Rome	27%	66.75%	6.25%
Rest of Italy	46.25%	52%	1.75%

But can it be inferred that the proportion of slaves active in industry was so low as the figures suggest at first sight? Clearly not: the freedmen had surely worked in the same occupations before manumission. The statistics show us not the proportions of freedmen and slaves active at any given time, but at best the proportions of those sufficiently successful to leave records, chiefly at the time of death. There is of course much other evidence for the use of slaves in skilled manual work; for instance the fine arretine ware was manufactured, and the Roman aqueducts were kept in repair, by slaves. But was the share of the freeborn in such employment so low as the statistics indicate? Not necessarily, as slaves, trained, financed and often in the end liberated by their masters, may have prospered more than their freeborn competitors and have been better able to bear the costs of commemoration. They may also have taken more pride in the skills by which they had risen in the social scale, and been readier to mention them. The elite certainly despised manual labour, and perhaps communicated this prejudice to the humbler freeborn folk, who none the less had no choice but to earn their living in ways of which they felt ashamed. Caution must also be exercised in supposing that slaves and freedmen had the same preponderance in the crafts throughout the provinces, where our information is less copious; it is indeed certain that most workers in Egypt were of free birth, and this is probable for Gaul and Asia. In Rome and Italy there are no data for unskilled workers.

It has often been held that the extensive use of slave labour explains why there was so little technological advance in the Roman Empire (cf. Finley, 1981). The argument goes thus. Slave labour was so cheap that employers had no incentive to search for labour-saving inventions, while the slaves themselves, working reluctantly, would have been incapable of operating any complex machines. Moreover, the association of manual work with slavery so far lowered its esteem that the best minds would not concern themselves with technology, nor indeed with science, whose progress in later times has often been intimately connected with technical advances. None of this can be proved. It is not known how cheap skilled slaves were. The price of slaves must have varied enormously with their age, physique and special qualifications, and very possibly with variations in demand from one place and time to another. The data possessed are too meagre and scattered to justify any conclusions on mean prices for particular categories of slaves even in monetary terms; to determine their real costs, these prices also need to be related to those for essential commodities, for which the data are equally unsatisfactory, and to take account of the decline in the weight and purity of coinage, gradual in the first two centuries of this era and catastrophic thereafter. This undertaking is impossible. It can, however, be confidently stated that skilled slaves had to be rewarded with *peculium* and often with freedom, and that owners could not extract the entire surplus value of their production; whether in fact they were cheaper than hired free workers is uncertain, because no table of wages can be constructed. Even when money wages are recorded, as in Egypt, it is often unclear whether the employer did not provide subsistence in kind as well as cash. Again, arretine ware furnishes ocular proof that slaves could produce the finest work; it is absurd to assume that they could not as in the United States have operated machines. Seneca actually ascribes to them technical inventions such as translucent glass and shorthand (*Letters* 90, 25). He adds that such inventions were below the dignity of philosophic minds; here is one specimen of aristo-cratic disdain for manual work. But this disdain, if seldom avowed so candidly, has often been felt by the upper and middle classes in non-slave societies. Ancient slavery cannot bear the responsibility for technological stagnation. So far as the Roman imperial period is concerned, it is also apparent, or arguable, that there was a marked lack of originality in literature and philosophy, and even in law and the arts of government and war, as compared with classical and hellenistic Greece or with the Roman Republic and its Augustan aftermath. In these spheres of activity slavery seems irrelevant; some more general explanation of this strange intellectual inertia is needed.

To return to agriculture, Varro in the first century BC and Columella a century later, describe the management of farms of 50–100 ha (125–250 acres), into which large estates were apparently divided, and which might represent the total holding of the average city councillor, as well as of large-scale ranching operations. They assume that the owners will find it most profitable to employ slave gangs, if they can exercise close supervision, and if the habitat is not so unhealthy (no doubt through the incidence of malaria) that the depreciation rate for slaves is not too high; in that case Varro recom-mends resort to hired labourers, and Columella leasing to tenants. Though it is in general impossible to be sure how far owners acted in accordance with their prescriptions, the extensive use of slaves as cultivators and herdsmen in Italy is beyond doubt. But Varro and Columella only had Italy in view, and there is no evidence that the practice was universal or common elsewhere, even though instances of it can be found in some prov-inces such as Africa.

Many modern writers have challenged the correctness of the agronomists' belief that slaves were the most efficient agricultural workers. It is true that ancient accounting methods were so primitive that they may well have had no adequate basis for their opinion, and that agricultural slaves lacked the incentives for good work that operated on urban slaves. However the modern critique was itself founded on the premise that the inefficiency of slave labour had been demonstrated in American plantations, and more modern analysis of the slave economy in the Southern States, even when conducted by scholars hostile on moral grounds to the institution, has subverted, if not refuted, this presumption.

It was certainly uneconomic to rely on the labour of slaves, who had to be con-tinuously maintained, unless they could also be continuously kept at productive work; this was well understood by the Romans. Hence for the harvest and other major seasonal operations which demanded hands additional to a permanent labour force of slaves free labourers were hired. This practice was not peculiar to Italy: a parable of Jesus pictures men standing idle in the market-place waiting to be hired for the vineyards (*Matthew* 20). Small owners and tenants in the neighbourhood would be ready to supplement in this way the insufficient returns of their own holdings (Garnsey, 1980); and there was probably a pool of casual labour in the towns. There too employers would not maintain slaves for work partly or wholly concentrated in some months of the year. Building was to some extent a seasonal operation; large public works, not only at Rome but elsewhere, were constructed only at intervals, and surely gave unskilled employment at least to the free poor. Maritime trade almost ceased in the winter months; the work of loading and unloading cargo, and in some degree of distributing it, was therefore best left to casual free labour (Brunt, 1980; Treggiari, 1980).

To the Greek and Roman elite a man was not truly free if he depended on wages (Johnson, 1933, 301ff.). It is now often supposed that this conception also prevailed in parts of the Empire not yet hellenized or romanized, and that it was imbibed by the poor, and made it impossible for employers to obtain labour, unless they could subject the labourers to some form of servile status. But the poor could not afford to act on this prejudice, any more than on the objection of the elite to manual work, if the alternative was starvation. Moreover, no one doubts that leasing was common; and tenants might be hardly less dependent than wage-earners on land-owners. It is true that allusions to free wage-earners are sparse, but given the general indifference of ancient writers to the lot of the poor, this has no significance. In particular it matters not at all that the jurists hardly ever refer to wage-earners. They are chiefly concerned with legal issues that came to court. But employers engaged free labourers by the day; they would not sue them for damages they could not pay, if they were unsatisfactory, but would just turn them off. And the labourers had no means to sue for breach of contract. The Epistle of James voices complaints of the labourers whose hire was held back by fraud (5,4); these were age-old in Palestine, but surely not confined to that land. It may be repeated that the status of the greater part of the population in most parts of the Empire is entirely unknown.

Varro actually regarded hired labour as the alternative to slave labour in Italy itself, whereas Columella preferred leasing to tenants. This practice was certainly known in the late Republic, and it is apparent that not all tenants were small men; they might own slaves, or at least be able to give security for hiring costly equipment as well as the land itself. But no doubt most of them were poor cultivators, apt to fall into arrears with the rent. More is heard about this class from the Principate thanks to Pliny's letters and the survival of more copious juristic texts from this period (Brunt, 1962, 71f.; Neeve, 1984). It is commonly supposed that as the supply of slaves diminished and their prime cost increased, the great land-owners had to rely more on small tenants. If this be so, where did they find them? Probably among those who had hitherto worked on their lands for hire.

It may, however, be an accident in the transmission of evidence that we now hear more of such tenants. There is in fact no direct testimony for a decline in slave numbers, and the data cannot prove a rise in real costs. The jurists of the early third century constantly presuppose the continued importance of slave labour in every branch of the economy; probably they had Italy chiefly in mind. Jones found little attestation of slaves in the late Empire in the provinces, but in most of them that is equally true in an earlier time; again Italy was, he admitted, exceptional (Jones, 1964, 792–803). Thus a decline in slavery certainly affected Italy least, if at all; and the hypothesis that it occurred rests on argument rather than on documentation or its absence. On the orthodox view it was an inevitable result of the cessation, with a few exceptions, of Roman offensive wars after AD 14.

Slaves were either made or born; it is held that most slaves who were made were war-captives, and that breeding could not have kept up the slave population. The last proposition was inferred from experience in the West Indies, where the unhealthy climate caused exceptional mortality (among whites as well as negroes), and where there was little place for female labour in sugar plantations. By contrast in the United States, where women and children as well as men were much employed in the cotton and tobacco fields and in healthy conditions, the slave population more than reproduced itself. To judge from the Roman agronomists, women and children were not much used out of doors, and the opportunities for female labour in domestic service and household textile work were limited. It therefore seems probable that as a result of a deficiency in women slaves breeding could not have kept up numbers (Brunt, 1971, 144, 707). But the diminution in the supply of slaves who were made can easily be exaggerated. Even in the Republic not all war-captives had been made by *Roman* armies (Harris, 1980; cf. Crawford, 1977). Under the Roman peace slaves could still be bought from warring peoples beyond the frontiers, just as in the past Athenians had bought Thracians and Scythians, and as in the future African tribes themselves supplied the slave markets of America. Moreover, though the freeborn citizens and subjects of Rome were in theory immune from enslavement, in practice exposed children, in Egypt thrown on the dung-heap, could be brought up as slaves; in some areas the sale of children went on, and adults too might sell themselves into slavery; if they 'shared in the purchase price', i.e. if the fictitious vendor gave them part of it as *peculium*, which they would take with them on sale, they could not recover their freedom. With this exception indeed the person born in freedom had a title to recover it, if he could find someone to sue on his behalf and furnish proofs of his birth-right; it is obvious that he could rarely do this, especially if he had been carried off to a place remote from his origin (Jones, 1964, 792–803). It is not known to what extent want forced the poor to abandon or sell their children or even to sell themselves, but it seems to me probable that the supply of slaves from these sources, from the continuance of imports, and from breeding sufficed, not indeed to prevent a decline in numbers, but to make it very gradual, with least effect in Italy, where much wealth was still concentrated.

Granted that there were fewer chattel slaves in the later Empire, it does not follow that as a result the labouring poor were substantially better off. From the second century humble free men had been subjected by the criminal law to servile punishments (Garnsey, 1970, Part II). A great many were now reduced to serfdom, which prefigures and perhaps led on to the feudal villein. It is significant that the very Latin word that denoted 'slave' was to be appropriated to the designation of serfs. As we have seen, serfdom had some important advantages for the victim as compared with slavery, but it offered less hope to a fortunate minority of economic and social advancement. The poor no doubt suffered from the growing anarchy and disruption in the west, and from the general impoverishment. And if slavery was less prevalent than of old, it had not been abolished. In the Byzantine realm it persisted; only in the west did it disappear in a long and mysterious process, which lies beyond our period, and even there not in the Iberian peninsula, whence it was ultimately to be transmitted to the Americas as part of the legacy of Rome.

CHAPTER 29

·SOCIETY·AND·THE·ARTIST·

T. F. C. Blagg

'Qualis artifex pereo', said the Emperor Nero as he contemplated suicide: 'What an artist dies in me' (Suetonius, *Nero* 49, 1; Momigliano, 1934, 741). Our concept of the artist is rather different from what the Romans understood by *artifex*. The effects of the Renaissance and the Romantic movement divide us inescapably from the time when little distinction was made between artist and artisan. To the Romans *artifex* described, not only the creator of an original work of art, as we would call it, but also anyone who practised an *ars*, anyone who did work which 'required a specific technical knowledge and possibly a particular aptitude' (Calabi-Limentani, 1958, 9–15). Furthermore, *artifex* described both the artist who made a living from his art, and one who practised it for pleasure; no explicit distinction was made between amateur and professional, for example, by Pliny in his discussion of various painters. Nero, like several later emperors, practised painting and sculpture; in that sense, he could fairly describe himself as 'artifex', however vain he might have been about his abilities as a performing artist on stage at Olympia and elsewhere.

In other respects, too, Nero's artistic associations can be taken to typify some of the more important recurrent features of the relationship between art and society in the Roman Empire. They include the enthusiasm for Greek art and culture; the role of imperial patronage in the development of new artistic ideas, for example, in the interior design and wall-paintings of Nero's Golden House in Rome; the taste for luxury and magnificence which that building also exemplifies; the image-making of imperial portraiture, from the colossal gilded bronze statue of Nero by Zenodorus which gave the Colosseum its name, down to the careful designs of Nero's coin portraits (pl. 29.1); and the wider public amenities which followed from imperial and aristocratic patronage, exemplified by the well-considered regulations for the rebuilding of Rome after the great fire in AD 64, and by other public buildings: as Martial wrote later, 'What worse than Nero, what better than Nero's Baths?'

The Republican background

The social and political upheavals which led to the establishment of the Principate were accompanied by an equal transformation of Rome's artistic milieu. The deliberate policy of Augustus, assisted in its formulation and execution by Agrippa and Maecenas, was decisive in determining its direction. To demonstrate this, one has only to consider the size of the programme of new building and restoration recorded in Augustus' *Res Gestae*, or the widespread portrait statues of the emperor and the Julio-Claudian family which established the image of the dynasty. In art, as in so many other aspects, the Augustan period established a pattern which was to last until the time of Diocletian and Constantine. In many ways Augustan art was not particularly original, except in the scale of its production and the extent of its diffusion. Several of Augustus' projects were fulfilments of plans initiated by Julius Caesar, to be seen in the context of the artistic activities of late Republican dynasts. However many resources Augustus could draw upon to achieve his artistic policy, its undoubted success was largely based on well-established Republican traditions.

First among them was the essentially public nature of art, particularly in the context of religion (Part 10): cult images of the gods, the moulded terracotta plaques and modelled figures which decorated the temples, the small bronzes and terracotta statuettes which were made for votive offerings. Going back, apparently to the fifth century BC, was the custom of erecting in public places bronze statues, both on foot and equestrian, of those who had deserved honour from the state (pl. 29.2). The triumphs awarded for military victory increasingly became occasions for artistic display. Scipio Africanus' triumph after the battle of Zama (201 BC) included paintings illustrating the campaign, and paintings of other victories were permanently displayed in public buildings in Rome. This taste for narrative depiction of historical events was to find fuller and longer-lasting expression in imperial relief sculpture. By the third century the display of booty in the triumphal parade was no longer just the captured cattle, weapons and armour of the enemy, but included wagon-loads of gold and silver bullion and plate, and the statues of their gods.

Nearly all the artists who made these works remain anonymous. The credit was given to those, normally magistrates of the Republic, who commissioned them: such, for example, as the brothers Cn. and Q. Ogulnius, who as curule *aediles* in 296 BC used the fines paid to the public treasury to have bronze door frames and silver vessels made for the temple of Jupiter on the Capitoline, with a statue of him in a chariot for its roof, and who set up in the Forum the famous statue group of the she-wolf suckling Romulus and Remus (Livy X, 23, 11–12).

The public dedication and display of works of art reinforced the ideology of the state, by honouring its religious and military institutions, and providing a continual reminder to the Romans of their past achievements. At the same time, it reinforced the social position of the governing class, whose benefactions, often inscribed with their names, were in constant public view. It was not until the last century of the Republic that members of this class seem to have become similarly ostentatious in their private lives and possessions. That, at any rate, is the Romans' own literary tradition, which stressed the virtue of frugality and simple manners.

So long as this pattern of life predominated, there was little scope for private patronage of artists, except for religious purposes. The noble Roman family's other respectable artistic indulgence was in its ancestral portraits, first mentioned by Polybius in the mid-second century BC. Originally these were masks of wax, modelled and painted as close likenesses of the deceased, kept in wooden shrines in the *atrium*, and brought out and paraded at family funerals, a physical re-creation of the family and its achievements. From this Roman 'obsession with personal immortality' (Bianchi-Bandinelli, 1970, 90), there developed the realistic portrait busts in bronze and marble (pl. 29.3), and the tombstone representations of the dead so characteristic of Roman art throughout the Empire.

The influence of Greek art

A radical change in the balance between public and private artistic expression, and in the place of art and artists in Roman culture and society, resulted from Rome's conquest of the Greeks. When M. Claudius Marcellus captured Syracuse in 211 BC he brought back for his triumph in Rome many of the most beautiful of the city's art treasures. Later writers saw this as a turning point, and the more conservative Romans did not approve:

> The elders blamed Marcellus first of all because he made the city an object of envy, not only by men but also by the gods whom he had led into the city like slaves in his triumphal procession, and second because he filled the Roman people (who had hitherto been accustomed to fighting or farming and had no experience with a life of softness and ease, but were rather, as Euripides says of Herakles, 'vulgar, uncultured but good in things which are important') with a taste for leisure and idle talk, affecting urbane opinions about the arts and about artists, even to the point of wasting the better part of a day on such things. But Marcellus, far from feeling this way, proclaimed proudly even before the Greeks that he had taught the Romans, who had previously understood nothing, to respect and marvel at the beautiful and wondrous works of Greece (Plutarch, *Marcellus* 21, trans. Pollitt, 1983, 32–3).

During the second century, the conquests of Asia, Macedon and Achaea brought in vast quantities of gold and silver coin, plate, statues, paintings, furniture and textiles.

Greek art and Greek ideas were not completely unfamiliar to the Romans beforehand, particularly in Campania. Now, however, they became much more accessible, and this was not just the result of spectacular triumphal parades. Rome had an extensive area of the Mediterranean to govern and to exploit commercially. The growing interpenetration of the Greek and Roman worlds is well illustrated by the late second- and first-century BC town on Delos, with its portrait statues of Italian, particularly Campanian, merchants, and the mosaic floors and painted plaster walls of its houses, so closely comparable with those of Pompeii. The profitable slave market on Delos is likely to have been the source of many skilled artists and craftsmen of Greek origin who were acquired by Roman masters.

Increasingly, too, there were occasions for artists to travel freely to Italy, as Romans began to commission works from men whose reputations were sufficiently prized for their names to be thought worthy of commemoration. Metellus, the conqueror of Macedonia in 148 BC, erected the temple of Jupiter Stator, the first marble temple in Rome. To build in this new material, experienced masons had to be brought from Greece. The architect was Hermodorus of Salamis. In the first century BC other such artists included Pasiteles (pl. 29.4), from one of the Greek cities of southern Italy, who was a sculptor, a modeller in clay, and who wrote treatises on art; Arcesilaus, who made the statue of Venus for Caesar's forum in Rome, and also worked for the wealthy connoisseur Lucullus, and the sculptor C. Avianus Evander, first brought from Athens to Alexandria by Mark Antony as Cleopatra's art adviser, and subsequently an art dealer in Rome (Pliny, *Natural History*, XXXVI, 33).

With men drawn from so wide an area, the Greek influences upon Roman art were bound to be eclectic. When Augustus set about his great programme of building in Rome, one feature of it was a conscious evocation of the art of fifth-century Athens, very obviously in the copying of the Erechtheum caryatids for the forum of Augustus, more subtly in the ornamental detail which decorated the buildings (pl. 29.5). Contrast with that, the delicate floral scrollwork on the Ara Pacis, which was inspired by second-century Pergamene fashion. Italy could not provide enough marble masons for the enormous quantity of sculpture and architectural detail involved; they could only have come, in considerable numbers, from Greece and Asia Minor.

It was not merely that a market developed for the skills of contemporary Greek artists. There was an equal demand by private collectors for work by famous artists of the past, some of which were sold for enormous sums. The orator Hortensius, for example, paid 144,000 *sesterces* for a painting of the Argonauts by the fourth-century artist Kydias, and put up a shrine especially to house it on his estate at Tusculum. The sum paid would have bought enough corn to have fed 320 families for a year. Prices like that, of course, were memorable because they were exceptionally high, but they indicate a market in which the demand greatly exceeded the supply. This was certainly true of sculpture, and the deficiency was met by extensive copying. Fortunately so, in that many works of Greek sculpture are known to us only through these Roman copies. Since the nineteenth century it has become increasingly difficult not to think of a copy as inevitably inferior to the original, but the ancient world did not place so high a value on creative originality. There was no Roman law of copyright. In any case, authentication was difficult; only a minority of artists inscribed their names on their works, and even these were not signatures in the sense of a unique autograph. Nevertheless, some artists' names did have a commercial value: Phaedrus, writing under Tiberius, remarked how contemporary artists secured higher prices by putting Praxiteles' name on their sculpture or that of Zeuxis on their painting. The demand was not only for direct copies, but also for adaptations, like mirror-image copies to make a pair in the decoration of a room or a garden, and, more creatively, for works which revived earlier styles or were variations on well-known types.

As Greek artistic standards became familiar, and Greek works of art were increasingly sought, both by collectors and by travellers who wished to see them, there developed a considerable literature about Greek art. This brought to Roman acquaintance theoretical writings by such Greek artists and critics as Polykleitos and Xenokrates, and these formed the basis for the way in which Romans themselves thought and wrote about art. It is notable, for example, how many of the technical terms used by Vitruvius in his *De Architectura* are Greek, in addition to most of the ideas about architecture which he expresses. When Latin poets, orators and philosophers wished to typify the artist, they regularly used as their examples, not Romans, but the famous Greeks of the past like the painter Apelles and the sculptor Pheidias (Calabi-Limentani, 1958, 46).

Much of the literature was also concerned with listing masterpieces and what was known about them. Pasiteles, for example, wrote five books on *nobilia opera* and the encyclopedic works of the great scholar M. Terentius Varro (116–27 BC) contained numerous references to artists and their work. Few of these writings have survived, and their contents are mainly known because they were the sources from which the elder Pliny compiled Books XXXIII–XXXVI of his *Natural History*. Pliny, in turn, is an invaluable source of information for us. Without what he wrote about ancient painters, for example, we would know virtually nothing, since none of their work has survived. A few Egyptian panel-portraits, and the evidence of wall paintings and mosaics, can only be faint reflections of those paintings which were of a quality to be worth six-figure sums.

Art collections

The writings of Pliny and his predecessors were produced as a result of the huge number of works of art which were on public display, and of the active market which had developed for the buying and commissioning of works for private collections. For insight into the activities of the connoisseur on the eve of the Principate, Cicero is our most valuable source, unrivalled by any writer of the Principate itself. His prosecution speeches against C. Verres (70 BC) expose a rapacious provincial governor who ransacked Sicily for art treasures; his letters to his friends and family tell us much about his own artistic interests and the building up of his own collection. Verres reveals at their unscrupulous worst the competitiveness and acquisitiveness which can result from the private ownership of works of art. He was accused of obtaining them by forced gift from their owners, by purchase at well below their true value, and by theft, even from temples: for instance, he was alleged to have sent a gang of armed slaves to remove by night and by force the bronze statue of Hercules from the god's temple in Agrigento (Cicero, *Verres* II, iv, 94–5). Several of his acquisitions came from the collections of Greek citizens of the kind which provided the model for Roman private collecting, such as that of Heius of Messina, which included works by Praxiteles, Myron and Polykleitos, which Verres induced Heius to part with for the ludicrous sum of 6,500 *sesterces*. Some of these collections were themselves of recent origin; another of Verres' victims, Sthenius of Thermae, had acquired Delian and Corinthian bronzes, paintings and fine silver plate when in Asia as a young man. Sthenius illustrates a less selfish aspect of collecting, for Cicero tells us that his purchases were not so much for his own pleasure as for that of fellow citizens and friends who were invited to his house (*Verres* II, ii, 83–5). Clearly, Cicero exaggerates the altruism for the effect of contrast with Verres' lack of it, but there were others who were glad for the public to have access and to admire. Thus, C. Asinius Pollio (76 BC–AD 5) a great literary and political figure of the time of Julius Caesar and Augustus, 'being a man of great enthusiasm, naturally wanted his collection to be seen', and we are told of some of the works which it contained (Pliny, *Natural History*, XXXVI, 33).

Unlike Pollio, not every collector was an expert connoisseur, though Cicero need not be taken too seriously when, in his Verrine Orations, he affects an ignorance about artistic matters, to the extent of apparently needing to be reminded of the name of Polykleitos. Here, behind the pretence that it was not proper for a Roman gentleman to know too much about such things, may be detected an unease in Roman society about the opulence and luxury which diehard upholders of traditional Roman virtues, like Cato, considered to be so immoral. It is clear, in fact, that Cicero's taste for and knowledge of objets d'art, and indeed Greek culture as a whole, was particularly well-informed.

Art advisers, agents and dealers, many of them of Greek origin, like C. Avianus Evander (p. 720 above), played a considerable part both in forming taste and in satisfying it. Verres employed a sculptor and a painter from Asia Minor, Tlepolemos and Hieron, as his 'hunting dogs', as Cicero calls them, to scent out objects for his collection. Cicero acquired works of art from Athens through the agency of his friend T. Pomponius Atticus, who lived there. In the early 60s BC he was furnishing his villa at Tusculum.

He asked Atticus to find him sculpture suitable for the *gymnasium*, a colonnaded courtyard which in Greek usage was associated not only with physical exercise but also with teaching. He was delighted when Atticus sent him Megarian statues and herms of Pentelic marble with heads of bronze 'since Hermes is characteristic of all gymnasia', and one of Minerva, the goddess of wisdom, was particularly appropriate for Cicero's conscious desire to evoke Plato's Academy. He also asked for relief carvings to decorate his smaller *atrium*, and for ornamental well-heads. A few years later, he is found complaining to another friend, Gallus, who had bought some statues for him which Cicero felt were exorbitantly priced and also unsuitable for his house: what good was a statue of Mars, the god of war, to Cicero, the man of peace? At the same time, he tells Gallus that he wants paintings to decorate some new sitting rooms, declaring that painting is the art which pleases him most.

It is clear from the way in which Cicero and others wrote, and indeed from excavations at Pompeii and Herculaneum, where art works have been found still in the houses of their owners, that much of the motivation of the Roman collector was inspired, not just by what the object was in isolation, but by how it was to be related to the surroundings in which it was to stand, and to the personality and interests of the owner. Much thought was given to the arrangement of works of art in suitable settings. Vitruvius advised that picture galleries and painters' studios should face north, so that the colours should not be affected by varying sunlight. The Emperor Augustus, who did not much care for private extravagance, preferred his villas to be decorated, not with statues and paintings so much as with natural landscape effects and with old or rare objects like dinosaur bones and the weapons of ancient heroes. In the house of M. Lucretius at Pompeii (pl. 29.6), however, the view from the *atrium* through the *tablinum* led to a little garden with statues of Pan, satyrs, ibises, cupids and dolphins arranged amid the trees and bushes round an ornamental pool, giving the illusion of an escape to a lush mythological landscape beyond the bourgeois walls (Zanker, 1979; Dwyer, 1982).

Public art and display

It was in public buildings and public spaces that works of art were made most widely accessible. Until the mid-second century BC these collections were mainly the spoils of war, dedicated in temples. Under the Empire, many temples continued to be showplaces of art, particularly of sculpture and painting. The Porticus Metelli seems to have been the first building in Rome designed specifically for the exhibition of art; it was built in the 140s BC by Q. Caecilius Metellus Macedonicus, to display the group of thirty-four equestrian bronze statues by Lysippus which portrayed Alexander the Great and the officers who had died at the battle of the Granikos. There were some spectacular temporary exhibitions: Praxiteles' Cupid from Thespiae was displayed in the Roman

Forum as the highlight of C. Claudius' magnificent aedileship in 99 BC and three thousand bronze statues were part of the lavish decoration of the theatre built by the aedile M. Aemilius Scaurus in 58 BC and dismantled a few months after construction.

Public buildings in Rome had already assumed something of the character of museums by Augustus' time, and artistic display was a very important constituent of his building programme. This was not restricted to looted treasure and antiquities, but was often an integral part of the propaganda message which was intended. The Forum of Augustus, for example, contained portraits of the famous men of Roman history, going back to Romulus, on one side, and on the other, portraits of members of the Julian *gens* and kings of Alba Longa, starting with Aeneas. The traditions of the City and the new dynasty were linked symbolically in this forum, which surrounded the temple of Mars Ultor, vowed before the battle of Philippi in vengeance for Julius Caesar's murder. Semicircular *exedrae* in opposite sides were constructed specifically for the display of these statues.

Agrippa's speech advocating the nationalization of all statues and paintings (Pliny, *Natural History*, XXXV, 26) might suggest that there was less available on the antique market than there had been. Certainly, the somewhat eclectic taste of collectors was being replaced, at an imperial level, by something much more deliberate. Contemporary artists were increasingly involved in assimilating the varied influences of the Greek and Italic past to the new needs of the Roman Principate. The process took some time but, by Trajan's reign, in Bianchi-Bandinelli's view (1970, 229), art had become fully Roman, 'since it gives expression to a new and structurally non-Hellenistic society'.

A particularly important aspect of this is the historical narrative subject matter of Roman relief carving. In place of a Greek frame of reference which was mainly mythological or allegorical, the Roman preference was for specific historical depiction. This was first developed in the late Republic. Scenes such as the *suovetaurilia* sacrifice on the so-called Altar of Domitius Ahenobarbus, or the procession of senators and the imperial family on the Ara Pacis (pl. 29.7), prepare the artistic ground for that most original visual record of a historical episode, the spiral relief of the Dacian campaign on Trajan's column.

A key feature of this process of communication from the emperors, through artists, to the people, is the recognizable imperial image. On coins, a triumphal arch with trophies of war and 'DE BRITANN' or 'DE IVDAEIS' could inform the whole Empire of Claudius's triumph (pl. 29.8) over the Britons (AD 43) or Vespasian's over the Jews (AD 70). The latter was made even more specific in the reliefs on the arch of Titus, depicting the triumphal chariot turning the corner of the Via Sacra, and the parade of treasure from Jerusalem, including the seven-branched candlestick, the originals of which could be seen exhibited in the Forum Pacis nearby (pl. 29.9). But even as far away from Britain as Aphrodisias, in Asia Minor, a relief on the Sebasteion showed Claudius overwhelming Britannia (pl. 29.10), represented as a fallen Amazon (Erim,

1982). Claudius appears as a Greek hero, nude save for helmet and cloak, but with a recognizably Claudian face.

As this last example shows, the image conveyed its message in two ways: directly, through the representation of recognizable individuals, objects and surroundings; and symbolically, by the use of mythological or allegorical figures or references.

Roman sculptors thus evolved a mode of expression which had two complementary levels of meaning. Allegory was used to interpret the significance of the real events portrayed. The divine associations claimed by Roman emperors, or accorded to them after their deaths, were conveyed in a similar manner. Sometimes, emperors were portrayed with the attributes of the particular gods with whom they identified themselves; so, for example, a bust of Commodus shows him, rather unconvincingly, in the guise of Hercules, wearing the Nemean lion's skin and brandishing a club (pl. 31.6). A rather more subtle use of artistic representation is recorded by Herodian of the emperor Antoninus Elagabalus, who accustomed the Roman Senate and People to his Syrian dress and his cult of the god Elagabalus, whose high priest he was, by sending to Rome a full-length portrait showing himself wearing that costume, and in the act of sacrifice. The result was that when he eventually arrived in the City for the first time, the Romans were sufficiently used to the idea not to be scandalized, as the emperor's grandmother Julia Maesa had feared that they would be.

Various ideas were current in antiquity about the function of portraiture. In one view, it was to show what a person's nature had been. Plutarch says that he saw a stone statue of Marius in Ravenna 'which successfully conveys his reputedly morose and bitter character'. The imperial image, as officially projected, was often more complicated, and certainly did not remain constant. Augustus successfully established an idealized image of himself and the Julio-Claudian dynasty. Such, presumably, was the image which Suetonius had in mind when he wrote of Nero that 'he did not take the least trouble to look as an emperor should'. In fact, Nero paid very careful attention to his portrait images, but was reverting to hellenistic ideas of how a ruler should appear (Strong, 1976, 45–8 and 64).

Like Nero, Hadrian was a noted philhellene, and his adoption of a beard, in the manner of a Greek philosopher, and the careful styling of the hair in his portraits, reflects the interest of such Greek writers as Dio Chrysostom and Polemon of Laodicea in physiognomy. Hadrian set a fashion which was followed and elaborated by the Antonine emperors. In the late third century the varied types of portraiture of the Tetrarchs, particularly on their coinage, are to be explained as the results of a search for an appropriate new manner of representing the concept of the emperor as *Dominus Noster*, Our Lord. The increasing remoteness and unapproachability of the holders of imperial office was emphasized by Diocletian's introduction of elaborate court ceremonial derived from Persia, and by representations of emperors which paid more attention to the regalia of their office than to the physical characteristics of the individual (pl. 29.11).

A statue conveyed the idea of the physical presence of the person represented. It might indeed be thought of and treated as being that person. For many Greeks, a statue of a god did not just represent the god: it *was* the god (Gordon, 1979, 7–8). Something of this apparent ambiguity persisted under the Roman Empire. After the death of Faustina, wife of Marcus Aurelius, in 175, the Senate decreed that a golden statue of her should always be carried into the theatre when the emperor attended, to be placed in the front seats which she had occupied when alive, and that ladies of the highest rank should surround it, as they had attended her when alive. Conversely, should the memory of an unpopular emperor be officially condemned after his death, as Domitian's was, the posthumous penalty was exacted by erasing his name from inscriptions and defacing his portraits. The arch erected by the *argentarii* of Rome (pl. 29.12) in honour of Septimius Severus and his family, for example, retains the traces of where the figure of Severus' elder son Geta had been chiselled away after his murder. Symbolically he, like Domitian, had become a non-person. The same considerations applied to the statues of any notable. The erection of a statue was a token of honour, and the statue was liable to suffer for the individual's subsequent dishonour. Septimius Severus, feeling that there were rather too many statues of his praetorian prefect Plautianus, ordered that some of them be melted down. This gave rise to a rumour of Plautianus' downfall. That was to happen sometime later, but meanwhile many cities reacted prematurely and demolished his statues, and were punished for doing so.

With this great profusion of works of art on public view, it is small wonder that Pliny complained that there was not leisure and opportunity for the quiet contemplation necessary for their proper appreciation. His references to the considerable number of works by Praxiteles, Skopas and others which were displayed in Rome and were greatly admired shows that then, as now, masterpieces by famous artists were singled out for particular attention. In the second century AD Pausanias wrote a guide to Greece which is full of references to celebrated works of art which were popular tourist attractions. The appreciation of art was not confined to the rich. Even slaves might study paintings intently, though they acquired a bad character by spending their time in doing so (*Digest*, xxi, 1, 65).

Reverent appreciation was not universal. Statues might suffer from the nocturnal urinations of philistine revellers (Juvenal, *Satires*, I, 131; VI, 310). More seriously, they might be stolen, or have the gilt scraped off them. When 900 kg (2,000 lb) of gold was found to be missing from the throne of Capitoline Jupiter in 52 BC the custodian committed suicide in anticipation of the investigation. Temple treasures were normally protected behind strongly bolted doors, and occasionally by guard dogs. Consequently, temples served as the equivalent of bank strongrooms, in which the money and jewels of private individuals were deposited.

In most towns of the Empire, the *aediles* or equivalent junior magistrates were responsible for the care and maintenance of public buildings, and the works of art which they contained. In Rome itself, during the Empire, there were senatorial *curatores* of sacred buildings and public works, with a large staff of assistants (*procuratores* or *sub-curatores*), some of whom were given responsibility for particular buildings (Gordon, 1952, 279–304). A late second-century inscription records a *procurator* for paintings (*a pinacothecis*). Constantine established a *curator* of statues, subordinate to the city prefect. Little is known about what the actual responsibilities of such people involved, and how they were carried out. Pliny and Pausanias tell us about some methods of conservation used in particular cases (Strong, 1973, 261–2). One of the skills of Avianus Evander (p. 720 above) was in restoring damaged parts of famous ancient statues. For more routine maintenance, there must have been many such craftsmen as M. Rapilius Serapio, whose job it was to replace missing glass eyes in bronze statues. For temple collections, daily care was the responsibility of the custodians (*aeditui*), who were normally public slaves.

These custodians had what was no doubt a profitable sideline in telling visitors about the art treasures in their care, and in any town a traveller could expect the attentions of self-appointed local guides to inform them, or misinform them, about the works of art which they could see there. As Pausanias remarked: 'the guides at Argos know very well that not all that they tell people is true, but they say it just the same.' Educated men like Plutarch and Lucian might deplore or satirize the endless patter and the insistent touting of local guides, but it must be remembered that they were the only source of information for most ordinary people, who did not have access to tourist guidebooks or works of scholarship (Casson, 1974, 264–71).

Art and the private patron

Roman art reveals to us in a very direct way the Romans' own view of themselves, both as a society and as individuals. It does so, in particular, through their highly developed and realistic portraiture, and through a taste for the depiction of scenes from daily life in sculpture and painting. The Republican origins of this, as a manifestation of an artistic 'obsession with personal immortality', have been mentioned (p. 718 above). Under the Empire, the opportunities for such private artistic patronage extended well beyond the upper class, and throughout the provinces. They are revealed especially in works commissioned for religious dedication and for the commemoration of the dead.

In the ancient sanctuary of Diana at Nemi, for example, a former slave, the actor C. Fundilius Doctus, erected fine marble statues of his patroness Fundilia, to whom or to whose family he had formerly belonged, and of himself (Poulsen, 1973, 113–14 and pls cxxxvii–cxxxix). Art and religion served both to express the particular social relationship, and also to exemplify the evolution of Roman society which enabled an ex-slave to afford, to commission and publicly to display works of this nature and quality.

The tombstone of another ex-slave, that of Regina at South Shields (pl. 29.13), is an eloquent testimony to the social and geographical penetration of Roman artistic ideas. She was a native British tribeswoman who had been emancipated and married by a Syrian armourer from Palmyra. The sculptor must have come from the same area, for he portrayed Regina seated beneath a Syrian pediment, and added an inscription in Palmyrene script below the Latin (Phillips, 1977, no. 247).

The relief carving on tombstones publicly advertised the lives and achievements of those who could afford them, from senators down to auxiliary soldiers and tradesmen. Sometimes we have simply a portrait of the dead person, dressed appropriately to his or her status: a centurion in armour, with his battle decorations; a citizen in his toga; a woman with her hair dressed to follow imperial fashion or the local style of the region. Reliefs showing the dead person reclining on a couch, with food and drink for the funerary banquet on a table, a servant and often members of the family in attendance, are common from Britain to the Black Sea. They are specific to the ritual of death; what was noteworthy about the life was recorded on the inscription.

One special characteristic of Roman art is its close connection with the realities of daily life (Bianchi-Bandinelli, 1970, 62) and Romans particularly liked their tombs to express what their lives had been. A shipwright in Ravenna is shown adzing a timber for the boat which he is building (pl. 29.14); a miller's tombstone from Narbonne shows the donkey mill and his faithful dog. Tombs of merchants at Igel and Neumagen in Germania (pls 13.12, 13 and 29.15) were carved with scenes connected with the cloth trade: the cloth being examined and transported, and accounts being rendered by men in Gaulish dress (Drinkwater, 1981); and such more intimate scenes as a woman sitting having her hair dressed in front of a mirror.

The care which a patron might take to ensure that his requirements were satisfied is illustrated by an inscription from Langres of a Gaulish citizen, which specifies that his tomb was to be made according to an exemplar already given, with a seated statue in the best marble from overseas, or of the best bronze, no less than five feet high, and that the coffin was to be of the best Luna marble and decorated with the best workmanship (*sculpta quam optume*) (Calabi-Limentani, 1958, 145–6). Such desires might be pretentious, and were wittily satirized by Petronius in describing Trimalchio's instructions for what was to be carved on his tomb, including merchant ships under full sail, and a scene of people enjoying themselves at the public banquet for which he had paid.

Petronius also has the self-satisfied Trimalchio displaying paintings in his house which depicted the stages in his rise to fortune. Normally, however, wall-paintings and mosaics in houses illustrated in a more general way the aspects of the owners' daily lives in which they took pleasure, particularly the gladiatorial games, hunting, erotic scenes and the landscape (pl. 29.16). According to Pliny, Spurius Tadius, in Augustus' principate, was the artist who began the painting of landscapes of varied scenery set with buildings and with nicely observed representations of people travelling through them, fishing, hunting or harvesting grapes. In a very literal way, this was putting into practice the Platonic doctrine that art was essentially an imitation of nature. There was also a taste for paintings of mythological subjects, which told a story. The Elder Philostratus, late in the second century AD, wrote in his *Eikones* descriptions of paintings which, although composed as literary exercises, clearly reflect the sort which we know from Pompeii and Herculaneum, and tell us much about what people looked for in pictures. As his grandson, the Younger Philostratus, tells us in his own *Eikones*, there were also those who sought in art not only the well-observed imitation of the natural world or a narrative entertainment, but also an expression of the invisible underlying reality and psychological insight on the part of the artist (Pollitt, 1983, 213–27; Gordon, 1979, 15).

Whatever the tastes and theories which determined the forms which it took, the function of Roman art was essentially ostentatious. The role of the artist was to produce work through which the owner could display his wealth, culture and importance. High in the scale of luxury was the use of imported marble for the embellishment of houses, first of all in those of late Republican magnates. Lucius Crassus, consul in 95 BC, was the first to have columns of foreign marble (from Hymettos) in his house. Fifty years later Mamurra, who had made a fortune while chief engineer for Julius Caesar in Gaul, had his house walls faced in marble veneer throughout, and columns of solid marble: green-veined Carystian from Euboea, and white from the newly-opened quarries of Carrara in northern Tuscany. The palace at Fishbourne in Britain illustrates the influence of these standards upon provincial architecture. The white and coloured marbles used for wall veneers and flooring came from the Pyrenees, the Garonne, Burgundy, Carrara, the Greek islands and Turkey (Cunliffe, 1971, 1–35). Those who could not afford marble might have the effects of veneer imitated in wall-painting. The coloured mosaics and wall-paintings of the town houses and rural villas of Italy and the provinces were in themselves, independently of their subject matter, an indication of the status of the occupants.

So, too, but at a more personal level, were the products of silversmiths and gemcutters. There was an enormous quantity of silver plate in private possession during the Empire, in contrast with the Republic (p. 718 above), and it was by no means confined to the very wealthy (Strong, 1966, 124–5). Finds like the Boscoreale treasure of 109 pieces of table and display silver (pl. 30.4), or the 118 items found in a chest in the House of the Menander at Pompeii, were the possessions of middle-class Italian provincial families. One was regarded as poverty-stricken indeed not to have any family silver on the table (Suetonius, *Domitian*, 1). Much silver was made for dedication at temples. For many families, the silversmith was probably the type of *artifex* with whom they had the most dealings. Some of the craftsmen signed their pieces: the Boscoreale treasure includes a mirror by M. Domitius Polygnos and a cup by Sabinus.

Chased and engraved gold and silver plate was highly prized, and some metalsmiths achieved reputations as high as those of painters and sculptors. Indeed, there were artists who were skilled in more than one capacity: Pasiteles and Avianus Evander (p. 720 above) were, like the Renaissance artist Benvenuto Cellini, both sculptors and metalsmiths. Two silver cups found at Hoby in Denmark are examples of the high-quality work produced for an aristocratic patron. One shows Priam and Achilles, the other Odysseus and Philoctetes; the name of the maker, Cheirisophos, appears on the former in Greek and on the latter in Latin letters, and beneath them is the name Silius, quite possibly the C. Silius who was governor of Upper Germany in AD 14–21 (Tacitus *Annales*, I, 31; Toynbee, 1951, 52).

The art of gem-cutting, too, was so highly valued that it cannot be considered merely as one of the minor arts. Seal rings, in particular, were items of particular significance to those who wore them; Augustus used three at different times. The last, which bore his own head and was used as a seal by subsequent emperors, was engraved by Dioskourides, a craftsman of outstanding skill (pl. 29.17). Several gems signed by him survive, and also some which were cut by his sons (Pliny, *Natural History*, XXXVII, 8).

Artists and their work

Dioskourides is one of the rare examples of a Roman artist of whom we know something from literature, and of whose work some identifiable examples survive. Altogether, we have the names of about 400 artists (Calabi-Limentani, 1958, 181–93; see also Toynbee, 1951), but in most cases they are known only from an isolated work on which their name appears, an inscription which mentions them, or a reference in literature. Only rarely do these sources supplement one another. It is therefore virtually impossible to reconstruct the way in which the artistic career of any individual developed. More general remarks can be made about the social position of artists and the nature of their working life.

Men of high social standing might practise the arts. Among emperors, in addition to Nero's claims to be an *artifex* (p. 717), Hadrian was an accomplished painter, and if we are to believe Aurelius Victor as a sculptor in bronze or marble he was nearly a Polykleitos or a Euphranor. One senses, however, that while aristocrats might learn such skills as part of a liberal education, they rarely sought or achieved what we might call a professional competence. Nor was it thought respectable or necessary for them to do so. Pliny the Elder considered that his contemporary Turpilius, an *eques* from near Verona, was almost as exceptional among men of his class for painting beautifully as he was for being the first recorded artist to do so left-handed (Pliny, *Natural History* XXXV, 20).

That is not to say that artists in themselves were socially despised, but that they were not expected to be of the highest social rank. They might, indeed, achieve social positions of honour and respect. So, for example, the mosaicist P. Aelius Harpocration, *alias* Proclus, was honoured by the erection of a statue of himself at Perinthus in Thrace, where he had decorated the Tychaeum, where he settled and died, and where his son, also named Proclus and a mosaicist, was a member of the local senate (*CIG* II, 2024, 2025; Toynbee, 1951, 43–4).

Inscriptions do not always specify whether an artist with the *tria nomina* of a Roman citizen was freeborn or a manumitted slave. Among artists of freeborn citizen status, architects form the largest single group, and half of them were associated with the army. Nearly half of the artists known from inscriptions, however, appear to have been *liberti* (Calabi-Limentani, 1958, 38–42). An appreciable number were slaves, some of whom belonged to other artists. Both slave and freedmen artists might be attached to the household of an aristocratic patron of the arts like C. Sallustius Crispus, who emulated Maecenas and who, or whose namesake, possessed as painters the slave Amanus and the *libertus* Aiax. In the *columbarium* of the slaves and freedmen of the Empress Livia, the slaves included painters, goldsmiths, and those concerned with statues, portraits, silver and pearls (some of whom may have been custodians rather than craftsmen). Justinian's *Digest* contains a variety of legal texts which relate to the obligation on the part of the vendor of a slave to demonstrate any literary or artistic qualities claimed for him, which no doubt had enhanced the price (e.g. *Digest* xxi, 1, 19, 4).

The names of many of these artists, both slave and free, indicate a Greek origin. The Greek artists attracted to Italy in the late Republic (p. 720 above) were followed under the Empire by numerous artists who worked far from home, and not only in Italy (Toynbee, 1951, 25–7). Thus, the elder Proclus went from Egypt to Thrace. Criton of Athens, whose name is inscribed on the bull from the Mithraeum at Ostia, must have gone there to carve it, since the marble is Italian. Zenodorus, who made Nero's colossus (p. 717 above), had previously made an equally gigantic statue of Mercury for the Gaulish nation of the Arverni, which apparently took ten years to complete; in Aquitania, he also achieved note by making replicas of two silver cups by Kalamis for the governor of the province.

Nor was the travelling all from the Greek world. A mosaic at Lillebonne, in northern Gaul, was made by T. Sennius Felix from Puteoli and his pupil, who may have come from Carthage. From such immigrants classical artistic skills were learned by the provincials of the western Empire. Annaeus Atticus, buried in the Isola Sacra cemetery in Ostia, was a painter from Aquitaine (Toynbee, 1951, 42). Priscus, whose Gaulish homeland was in the region of Chartres, was a stonemason who dedicated an altar at Bath. The full assimilation of classical traditions by native provincial artists in the west is illustrated by the Jupiter column at Mainz, carved by the Gaulish sculptors Samus and Severus, the sons of Venicarus.

Roman artists were almost invariably men. The one woman of whom we know anything is Iaia, a Greek from Cyzicus, who worked in Rome *c.* 100 BC and who had a high reputation for painting on ivory, mainly portraits of women (Pliny, *Natural History*, XXXV, 147–8). Women might act as artists' models. The painter Arellius was notorious for painting goddesses who looked like his mistresses, and several prostitutes were thus immortalized. But there is little information about the use of models, male or female. That they were usually employed is implicit in Seneca's apocryphal story of how the painter Parrhasius tortured an Olynthian slave to death in order to depict the agonies of Prometheus; we need not believe that this actually happened, for Seneca's point was rhetorical, concerning the use of artistic imagination to achieve realistic effect.

On another occasion, Seneca wrote about the motives of an artist in creating his work: money, if he had made it for sale; glory, if he was working for his own reputation; or religion, if he had prepared a temple gift. To a large extent, the social conditions of artists determined the degree to which they could work for their own satisfaction. Only the very rich, like Sallustius Crispus, could retain artists in their own households to work exclusively for them. Most other artists worked independently, as family groups (Toynbee, 1951, 18–19), like Dioskourides and Proclus and their sons, or in an *officina* or workshop (particularly sculptors: *CIL* VIII, 4779 and 21082; *AE*, 1946, 77 and 90; 1951, 51). Then they might work to contract (*locatio*: cf. *Digest* xix, 5, 5, 2), or produce objects for sale ready-made. And there were those who made works on their own account, to dedicate at temples, like the bronze plaque from Colchester dedicated to Silvanus by the *aerarius* Cintusmus: appropriate returns to the gods for their artistic gifts.

Some great artists, like Dioskourides, achieved a fame which is recorded for us in the writings of their contemporaries. Some sculptors and painters showed their pride in their craft by portraying themselves in action, or the tools of their trade, commemorating their own achievements in the same way as they were employed to commemorate those of their patrons (pl. 29.18). The patron's gratitude might also immortalize the artist. When the freedman metalsmith M. Canuleius Zosimus died at the age of 28, his patron set up his funerary urn, carved with an inscription which praised his surpassing skill as an engraver, his agreeable temperament, his obedience to his master's wishes, and his honesty, despite the tempting weight of precious metals on which he worked (*ILS*, 7695). Nothing is known of the gold and silverware which Zosimus actually made; his epitaph may serve as that of the countless and nameless artists whose work has come down to us, and as an appreciation of the value to Roman society of their achievements and loyal service.

29.1 *Aureus* of Nero

29.2 Bronze statue of Aulus Metellus   **29.3** Portrait of a Roman patrician, Rome

733

29.4 Marble statues: 'Orestes and Electra' from the school of Pasiteles

29.5 Caryatids from the Forum of Augustus, Rome

29.6 Garden of the House of M. Lucretius, Pompeii

29.7 Procession of the Imperial Family on the Ara Pacis, Rome

29.8 *Aureus* of Claudius with a triumphal arch inscribed DE BRITANN

29.9   The Arch of Titus, Rome. Relief showing the triumphal procession

29.10   Relief carving from Aphrodisias showing Claudius overcoming Britannia

29.11 Follis of Diocletian

29.12 Septimius Severus and Julia Domna in a relief on the Arch of the Argentarii, Rome

29.13 Tombstone of Regina from South Shields, Britain. Regina was the wife of a Palmyrene and her memorial was decorated in the eastern manner

29.14   Shipbuilding scene from the tombstone of P. Longidienus, Ravenna

29.15   Scene showing payment and accounting from a tomb at Neumagen, Germany

29.16   Landscape painting from the House of the Small Fountain, Pompeii

29.17   Cornelian intaglio, showing a Trojan scene, and signed by Dioskourides

29.18 Tombstone of the sculptor M. Se . . . Amabilis from Bordeaux

·BIBLIOGRAPHY·FOR·PART·9·

Abbott, F. F. and Johnson, A. C. (1926), *Municipal Administration in the Roman Empire*, Princeton.

Alföldy, E. (1974), *Noricum*, London.

Balsdon, J. P. V. D. (1979), *Romans and Aliens*, London, 116ff.

Baynes, N. H. (1955), *Byzantine Studies and Other Essays*, London.

Bianchi-Bandinelli, R. (1970), *Rome, the Centre of Power*, London.

Bogaers, J. E. (1983), 'Foreign Affairs', in B. Hartley and J. Wadier (eds), *Rome and her Northern Provinces*, 13–22, Gloucester.

Bolkestein, H. (1939), *Wohltätigkeit und Armenpflege in vorchristlichem Altertum*, Utrecht.

Brockmeyer, N. (1979), *Antike Sklaverei*, Darmstadt.

Broughton, T. R. S. (1938), in T. Frank (ed.), *Economic Survey*, IV, Baltimore, 846–9.

Brunt, P. A. (1958), Review of W. L. Westermann, *The Slave Systems of Greek and Roman Antiquity*, Philadelphia, 1955, in *Journal of Roman Studies*, XLVIII.

Brunt, P. A. (1962), 'The army and the land in the Roman revolution', *Journal of Roman Studies*, LII, 71.

Brunt, P. A. (1971), *Italian Manpower*, Oxford.

Brunt, P. A. (1976), 'The Romanization of the local ruling classes in the Roman Empire', in D. M. Pippidi (ed.), *Assimilation et Résistance à la culture greco-romaine*, 170–2, Paris.

Brunt, P. A. (1980), 'Free labour and public works at Rome', *Journal of Roman Studies*, LXX, 81.

Brunt, P. A. (1982), Review of G. E. M. de Ste Croix, *The Class Struggle in the Ancient Greek World*, in *Journal of Roman Studies*, LXXII, 158ff.

Buckland, W. W. (1908), *The Roman Law of Slavery*, Cambridge.

Burford, A. (1972), *Craftsmen in Greek and Roman Society*, London.

Burton, G. P. (1975), 'Proconsuls, assizes and the administration of justice under the Empire', *Journal of Roman Studies*, LXV, 92ff.

Calabi-Limentani, I. (1958), *Studi sulla società romana : il lavoro artistico*, Milan.

Carcopino, J. (1941), *Daily Life in Ancient Rome*, Harmondsworth.

Casson, L. (1974), *Travel in the Ancient World*, London.

Chadwick, H. (1983), *Journal of Theological Studies*, 432.

Cherubini, G. *et al.* (1983), *Storia della Società Italiana*, 2, 95–135, Milan.

Crawford, M. H. (1977), 'Republican denarii in Romania: the suppression of piracy and the slave trade', *Journal of Roman Studies*, LXVII, 119ff.

Cunliffe, B. W. (1971), *Excavations at Fishbourne 1961–1969*, Research Report of The Society of Antiquaries of London, No. XXVI, volume 2, Leeds.

Dill, S. (1904), *Roman Society from Nero to Marcus Aurelius*, London.

Drinkwater, J. F. (1979), 'Local careers in the three Gauls', *Britannia* X, 89–100.

Drinkwater, J. F. (1981), 'Money-rents and food-renders in Gallic funerary reliefs', in A. King and M. Henig (eds), *The Roman West in the Third Century*, British Archaeological Reports S109, 215–33, Oxford.

Duff, A. M. (1958), *Freedmen in Early Roman Empire*, Oxford.

Duncan-Jones, R. (1982), *The Economy of the Roman Empire*, second edition, Cambridge.

Dwyer, E. J. (1982), 'Pompeian domestic sculpture: a study of five Pompeian houses and their contents', *Archaeologica*, 28, Rome.

Erim, K. T. (1982), 'A new relief showing Claudius and Britannia from Aphrodisias', *Britannia*, XIII, 277–81.

Finley, M. I. (1973), *The Ancient Economy*, London.

Finley, M. I. (1980), *Ancient Slavery and Modern Ideology*, London.

Finley, M. I. (1981), *Economy and Society in Ancient Greece*, London.

Frank, T. (ed.) (1933–40), *Economic Survey of Ancient Rome*, Baltimore.

Frederiksen, M. W. (1975), Review of M. I. Finley, *The Ancient Economy*, London, 1973, in *Journal of Roman Studies*, LXV, 164.

Garnsey, P. (1970), *Social Status and Legal Privilege in the Roman Empire*, Part II, Oxford.

Garnsey, P. (ed.) (1980), *Non-Slave Labour in the Greco-Roman World*, Cambridge.

Gilliam, J. F. (1965), 'Dura Roster and the *Constitutio Antoniniana*', *Historia*, 14, 74–92.

Gordon, A. E. (1952), 'Quintus Veranius, Consul A.D. 49', *University of California Publications in Classical Archaeology*, II, 1934–52, 231–341.

Gordon, R. L. (1979), 'The real and the imaginary: production and religion in the Graeco-Roman world', *Art History*, 2(1), 5–34.

Gummerus, H. (1894–), *Realencyclopedie*, IX, 1439.

Harnack, A. (1961), *Mission and Expansion of Christianity*, Book II, Chapter 7, New York.

Harris, W. V. (1980), 'Towards a study of the Roman slave trade', *Memoirs of the American Academy at Rome*, 36.

Harris, W. V. (1983), 'Literacy and epigraphy', *Zeitschrift für Papyrologie und Epigraphick*, 52.

Hassall, M. W. C. (1978), 'Britain and the Rhine Provinces: epigraphic evidence for Roman Trade', in H. F. Cleere and J. du Plat Taylor (eds), *Roman Shipping and Trade*, Council for British Archaeology Research Report, 24, 41–8, London.

Hassall, M. W. C. (1979), 'The impact of Mediterranean urbanism on indigenous nucleated centres', in B. C. Burnham and H. B. Johnson (eds), *Invasion and Response*, British Archaeological Reports, 73, 241–53, Oxford.

Heitland, W. E. (1921), *Agricola*, Cambridge.

Henig, M. (ed.) (1983), *A Handbook of Roman Art*, Oxford.

Hobsbawm, E. J. (1969), *Bandits*, Harmondsworth.

Hopkins, K. (1966), 'On the probable age structure of the Roman population', *Population Studies*, XX, 245.

Hopkins, K. (1983), 'Death and Renewal', in P. Garnsey and C. R. Whittaker (eds), *Trade and Famine in Classical Antiquity*, Cambridge.

Johnson, A. C. (1933), in Frank (ed.) (1933–40), II, 301ff.

Jones, A. H. M. (1940), *The Greek City from Alexander to Justinian*, Oxford.

Jones, A. H. M. (1964), *The Later Roman Empire*, Oxford.

Jones, A. H. M. (1974), *The Roman Economy*, Oxford.

Kelly, J. M. (1966), *Roman Litigation*, Oxford.

Kiechle, F. (1969), *Sklavenarbeit und technischer Fortschritt*, Wiesbaden.

Lewis, N. (1983), *Life in Egypt under Roman Rule*, Oxford.

Martino, F. de (1979), *Storia Economica di Roma Antica*, Florence.

Mócsy, A. (1974), *Pannonia and Upper Moesia*, London.

Momigliano, A. (1934), 'Nero', *Cambridge Ancient History*, X, 702–42.

Neeve, P. W. de (1984), *Colonus*, Amsterdam.

Phillips, E. J. (1977), *Corpus Signorum Imperii Romani I.1: Corbridge, Hadrian's Wall East of the North Tyne*, Oxford.

Piganiol, A. (1962), 'Les Documents Cadastraux d'Orange', *Gallia*, Supplement 16.

Pollitt, J. J. (1983), *The Art of Rome c. 753 B.C.–A.D. 337. Sources and Documents*, Cambridge.

Poulsen, V. (1973), *Les Portraits Romains I: République et dynastie Julienne*, Publications de la Glyptothèque Ny Carlsberg, no. 7, Copenhagen.

Rea, J. R. (1972), *Oxyrhynchus Papyri*, XL, Oxford.

Reynolds, J. (1982), *Aphrodisias and Rome*, London.

Robertis, F. M. de (1946), *I Rapporti di Lavoro nel Diritto Romano*, Milan.

Robertis, F. M. de (1963), *Lavoro e Lavoratori nel Mondo Romano*, Bari.

Robertis, F. M. de (1971), *Storia delle Corporazioni e del Regime Associativo nel Mondo Romano*, Bari.

Roxan, M. M. (1981), 'The distribution of Roman military diplomas', *Epigraphische Studien*, 12, 265–86.

Roxan, M. M. (forthcoming), 'Observations on the reasons for the changes *c*. AD 140', in W. Eck and H. Wolff, *Proceedings of the Colloquium on Roman Military Diplomas, Passau, 1984*.

Samuel, A. E. *et al.* (1971), 'Death and taxes', *American Studies in Papyrology*, 10, Toronto.

Sherwin-White, A. N. (1973), *The Roman Citizenship*, Oxford.

Squarciapino, M. (1943), *La Scuola di Afrodisia*, Rome.

Ste Croix, G. E. M. de (1981), *The Class Struggle in the Ancient Greek World*, London.

Strong, D. E. (1966), *Greek and Roman Gold and Silver Plate*, London.

Strong, D. E. (1973), 'Roman museums', in D. E. Strong (ed.), *Archaeological Theory and Practice*, London, 249–64.

Strong, D. E. (1976), *Roman Art*, Harmondsworth.

Toynbee, J. M. C. (1951), 'Some notes on artists in the Roman world', *Collection Latomus*, vi, Brussels.

Toynbee, J. M. C. (1971), *Death and Burial in the Roman World*, London.

Treggiari, S. M. (1980), 'Urban labour in Rome: mercenarii and tabernarii', in P. Garnsey (ed.), *Non-slave Labour in the Greco-Roman World*, Cambridge.

Walzing, J.-P. (1896), *Étude historique sur les corporations professionelles chez les romains*, Louvain.

Westermann, W. L. (1955), 'The slave systems of Greek and Roman antiquity', *Memoirs of the American Philosophical Society*, Philadelphia.

Whittaker, C. R. (1980), 'Rural labour in three Roman provinces', in P. Garnsey (ed.), *Non-slave Labour in the Greco-Roman World*, Cambridge.

Wiedemann, T. (1981), *Greek and Roman Slavery*, London.

Wilkes, J. J. (1969), *Dalmatia*, London.

Wolff, H. (1976), 'Die *cohors II Tungrorum milliaria equitata c(oram?) l(audata?)* und die Rechtsform des *ius Latii*', *Chiron*, 6, 276–88.

Zanker, P. (1979), 'Die Villa als Vorbild des späten pompejanischen Wohngeschmacks', *Jahrbuch des Deutschen Archäologischen Instituts, Rom,* 94, 460–523.

·RELIGION·AND·BURIAL·

CHAPTER 30

·CLASSICAL·RELIGIONS·

John Ferguson

The nature of Roman religion

There is no Latin word for religion. The closest is the phrase *cultus deorum*, derived from the more concrete *colere deos*, 'worshipping the gods'. *Religio*, from which our English word derives, is itself a puzzle. It may have something to do with a root meaning 'bind'. Its negative seems to be *negligere*, 'to neglect'. Often it means 'superstition'. *Caerimonia*, from which we derive our word 'ceremony', is also puzzling. Its root is unknown, and it is often found in the plural. *Pietas*, the origin of 'piety', has a very different connotation. It stands for a sense of duty, to other members of the family, or within the extended family, or within the state, or within other contractual relations. It is not a religious word except in so far as all those relations are religious, and protected by gods. *Sacer*, our 'sacred', means 'set apart for or by the gods', in blessing or cursing. In a sacrifice, *sacrificium*, the animal or other offering is made over to the gods. There is an early distinction, difficult to analyse precisely, between *sacer*, dedicated to a god, *sanctus*, which is applied to gates and walls, set under divine protection for the defence of those within, and *religiosus*, dedicated to the underworld powers. All are under supernatural protection; a temple is *sacer*, a gate *sanctus*, a tomb *religiosus*. *Fas* has to do with that which is religiously permitted, as *ius* with that which is legally permitted; the ancients derived it from a root meaning 'speak'; it is perhaps thus connected with *fatum*, 'fate'. Days were *fasti* or *nefasti* according to whether they were or were not propitious for public business.

Georges Dumézil in his book (*Servius et la Fortune*, 1943) drew a series of contrasts between the Romans and the Indians, which helps us to identify the nature of Roman religion. The Romans think *historically,* the Indians *fabulously.* The Romans think *rationally,* the Indians *cosmically.* The Romans think *practically,* the Indians *philosophically.* The

Romans think *relatively, empirically*, the Indians *absolutely, dogmatically*. The Romans think *politically*, the Indians *morally*. The Romans think *juridically*, the Indians *mystically*.

Roman religion has to do with action rather than belief, though of course action implies underlying beliefs. There were no credal affirmations. The object of religious practice was to secure the *pax deorum*. *Pax* is our 'peace'; the phrase implies benevolent relations between gods and the Romans; it may be loosely translated 'the favour of the gods'. Roman religion consisted in large part of seeking and observing the signs indicative of the approval of disapproval of the gods, and taking the right steps to secure their approval. The legalism with which this might be carried out is seen in a story in Livy (i, 9, 10). The Romans had been defeated by the Samnites and capitulated shamefully. He advised the Senate to send him back to repudiate the agreed terms. As they reached the Samnite camp he physically assaulted the escorting priest, crying 'I am a Samnite; I have maltreated an envoy in transgression of the law of nations. The Roman will now have the juster cause in making war.' The gods accepted the legal fiction, and in the renewed fighting the Samnites were defeated. The legalism is pervasive. In the rituals of Iguvium any error meant going back to the starting-point of the procession. Rome had once to repeat the whole ritual of the Festival of the Latin League because of an omission of a phrase in a prayer. Divine law paralleled civil law.

Archaic religion

The three great gods of the earliest Roman religion which can be traced are indicated by the precedence of their priests, and by their presence in archaic formulas.

Jupiter is the Indo-European Dyaus and the Greek Zeus with 'father' added. He is certainly a sky-god, though there have been other theories. He is sovereign among the gods. Thunder and lightning are his. He is the guardian of the oath, for he sees all and strikes down the perjurer. The Ides, the day of the mid-month, are his. He presides over the wine-festival of the Vinalia; no fully convincing explanation of this has been given. He was at almost all times the great god of the Roman people.

Mars is clearly the god of war. But he also is found in early agricultural ritual. Whether this is because the soldier-god is the best protector of crops, or because he was in origin a storm-god with a readily understood double function, or because his month of March began both the campaigning and the farming seasons, or for other reason is not clear. His domain is naturally outside the city.

Quirinus may be derived from *co-vir*, men in society; *curia*, the meeting of those taking action for the state, and Quirites, the citizen-body, are probably cognate. Some scholars would have him a kind of doublet of Mars, but his association is with the citizens at peace. Later theorists identified him with the deified Romulus, founding father of Rome.

This triad was replaced, under Etruscan influence, by a new, less masculine triad. Jupiter remained supreme. He was to become Jupiter Optimus Maximus (Best and Greatest), and his great temple stood on the Capitoline Hill. There he gave hospitality to two goddesses. Juno, the Etruscan Uni, is the power of fertility in women who presides over child-birth and over women's festivals. The first day of the month is hers, the rebirth of the moon. But she has other power too. She was brought from Veii as Regina or Queen; as Populonia she blesses the people under arms; as Sispes she protects the state. Minerva, the Etruscan Menrva, is the patron of all arts and crafts.

Two other early deities call for special mention. They are Janus, who comes first in prayers and offerings. His name may be linked with the idea of a gate or passage, and for this reason looks both ways. He is the god of beginnings; he presides over January, the first month of the revised calendar. He has to do with openings and closings; his temple was opened in war and closed in peace. Vesta comes at the end in prayers and offerings. She is certainly the goddess of the hearth, and of the sacred fires of the state.

The antiquarians of Rome distinguished between *di indigetes*, native gods, and *di novensiles*, the immigrant gods. The great German scholar, Georg Wissowa, identified thirty-three 'indigenes', though two of them, the Lares of the estate, and the Lemures of the dead, are plural. The names of ten deities who have priests called *flamines* in addition to Jupiter, Mars and Quirinus are known. They make curious reading: Volturnus, Pales (a shepherds' god), Furria, Flora (the spirit of flowers), Falacer, Pomona (the fruitfulness of autumn), Volcanus (volcanic fire), Ceres (the power of growth in crops), Portunus. They were not, for the most part, the great deities associated with later times; they were pushed aside by the immigrant Greek powers, though no doubt they lingered on in the more conservative countryside.

The religion of farm and home

The religion of farm and home was not identical with that of the state, though the *pontifex maximus* and his colleagues exercised a controlling authority over private cult, maintaining traditions and resisting innovations. The antiquarian Festus defined private cult as pertaining to individuals, households and ancestral families.

The Lares and Penates were at the centre of private cult. The Lares seem to have been spirits of the farmland and associated with the ancestors buried there. The *Lares compitales* were honoured where different estates met. The *Lar familiaris* (pl. 30.5) came into the home with the *familia*, the whole workforce of the estate. The private shrine in the home was called *lararium*. The Penates are spirits of the pantry. To these must be added Vesta, the power of the private hearth as of the public; offerings were made to her at every meal. The Genius was the power of fertility in the male. This was believed to reside in the head of the father of the family, but is sometimes portrayed as a snake, coming from the underworld of the ancestors. The Genius was honoured at family festivals. The *lararium* might contain representations of other deities honoured in the household. In Pompeii the *lararia*, generally of the first century BC or AD, have revealed in painting twenty-seven deities, most frequently Fortuna (12), Vesta (10), Bacchus (8), Amor (7), Jupiter (7), Mercury (6), Hercules (6). Statuettes, apart from the Lares, depict most frequently Mercury (14), Minerva (11), Venus (10), Jupiter (8), Hercules (7); the Egyptian gods also appear. At nearby Herculaneum, with more warning, during the eruption the statuettes were removed to safety.

Private cult was also structured round the great passage-rites of birth, marriage and death. Here is encountered the curious phenomenon of spiritual powers of limited scope, numerous in number and presiding over small operations. They were often called *numina*. So at birth there were different powers looking after the foetus, presiding over the critical ninth and tenth months, guiding parturition, bringing the babe to the light. There was a magical ritual driving away evil spirits with axe, stake and broom, and invoking Cleaver, Staker and Sweeper. Other powers watched over the cradle, induced the first cry, blessed breast-feeding, guided eating and drinking, helped the child to speak or to stand, and guarded the child's going-out and coming-in.

On the farm too, Earth and Ceres (the power of growth) were invoked together with First Plougher, Second Plougher, Harrower, Sower, Top-dresser, Hoer, Raker, Harvester, Gatherer, Storer, Distributor. Spiniensis was responsible for digging out thorn bushes, and Sterculius for manuring. The persistent rituals to Robigus, the spirit of disease in grain, are also known.

These powers were somewhat impersonal. Others, who later became fully fledged gods and goddesses, seem to have affinities with them. Pales, the shepherds' god, is indifferently masculine or feminine. The very name of Venus, a garden-spirit originally, is neuter in form. Names such as Neptunus, Portunus, Saturnus are adjectival in form and seem to relate to functions.

There are some vivid and often beautiful word-pictures of agricultural ritual: the Ambarvalia, a ritual procession of pig, ram and bull round the bounds to purify the land (pl. 30.1); the poet Tibullus too tells us of this holy day and holiday with a stress on purity, cleanness and white. Ovid describes the Terminalia in honour of Terminus, the power of the boundary-stone, with the offerings of lamb and sucking-pig, grain, honey and wine. There is a late record of an ancient ritual for protecting the crops, with a triple invocation of Mars (or Marmar) and the Lares (or Lases). Not for nothing did Vergil write of *divini gloria ruris*, the glory of the gods' own countryside (*Georgics* I, 168).

Priesthood and other religious officials

In the early history of Rome it can be deduced that the king stood as intermediary between the human and the divine. After the establishment of the Republic the *Rex Sacrorum* or King of the Ceremonies maintained the title. The chief religious official was the *Pontifex Maximus* or Supreme Bridge-builder. Most scholars think that this reflects the solemnity and importance of bridge-construction over a turbulent river rather than the more metaphysical bridging of earth and heaven. These priestly officers did not undergo any special training nor hold dogmatic beliefs, nor live in particular sanctity. Julius Caesar, a known unbeliever, became *pontifex maximus*.

There were fifteen priests known as *flamines*, probably 'sacrificers'. The three senior were attached to Jupiter, Mars and Quirinus. The *flamen Dialis* or priest of Jupiter lived a life restricted by tabus. He might not ride that unfamiliar creature, a horse, or see the citizens in military order (not his province), or take an oath (involving an imprecation against himself). He might not wear a closed ring or knots in his clothes, which might bind magic to his person; if a bound person entered his house the bonds must be removed and flung out through the roof. His hair and nails must be cut with bronze (not new-fangled iron) by a free man, and the clippings, which might otherwise suffer evil magic, be buried under a fruitful tree. He might not do or see secular work, and there were objects he might not touch or name. He might not bare his head to the awesome holiness of the sky. He must of course not approach a dead body.

The augurs were three in number in early days, though they grew to be sixteen. Their responsibility was the important task of observing omens, and this was a major part of Roman public ritual. This was not foretelling the future – Cicero, himself an augur, made that clear – it was discerning the favour or disfavour of the gods. Originally the signs were probably given by birds ('auspices' are the observations of birds) but other natural phenomena were used, as was the Etruscan practice of examining the inward parts of sacrificial animals.

The Vestal Virgins were enrolled young and served for thirty years. They had to tend the fire on the holy hearth, make the sacred salt, and participate in various state rituals. During their period of service they had to remain strictly chaste; the penalty for unchastity was burial alive.

One college, which grew from two to ten and then fifteen, was in charge of special rites, especially the Sibylline Books. These were prophetic utterances mysteriously acquired, and consulted in times of national crisis, famine or plague or military disaster. They were much in evidence during the war with Hannibal.

Other groups were called *sodales* or associates. The most important were the fetials, twenty priests who worked in pairs and were charged with international relations, with ancient and carefully prescribed rituals for making treaties or declaring war. Some of these groups were of great antiquity, the Salii or Leaping Priests of Mars, the Arval

Brethren who blessed the fields, the mysterious Sodales Titii, whose concern was fertility.

A religion of observances depends on those who will maintain the observances.

The formation of the later pantheon

As the Romans came into contact with other peoples round about, they brought their divinities into their own cult; Juno Regina was brought from Veii. Another was Diana, a spirit of the wildwood from the Alban Hills, whose priest was called the King of the Grove, and who killed his predecessor and was killed in his turn. Another was Fortuna, an oracular goddess from Antium and Praeneste, and a power of fertility, derived from a root meaning 'to bear', who eventually became Fortune. The Romans thus showed from the beginning their extraordinary capacity for adaptability.

Southern Italy, as far as the bay of Naples, had been a region of Greek colonization, and from an early date there was a powerful cultural influence from the south. The epigram that 'Captive Greece took captive her fierce conqueror' was culturally true. The Romans adopted the Greek pantheon, sometimes forcing their own divine powers into a strange mould. Jupiter was easy; he and Zeus were one in origin. Juno became his consort, the Greek Hera. For Poseidon, god of the sea, the Romans elevated the fresh-water spirit, Neptunus. Demeter found a ready equivalent in Ceres. Apollo remained himself; he was well-known to the Etruscans. His greatest glory was to lie in his relation to Augustus. The crowning victory of Actium had been won under his auspices, and he was the appropriate god of a new age of peace. Artemis, also a power of the wildwood, found her counterpart in Diana. Ares became Mars. Aphrodite, the goddess of love, was identified with the garden-spirit Venus. Hermes, the messenger of the gods, a traveller and trader, was equated with Mercurius, a power of merchantry. Athene became Minerva; they were one in their patronage of crafts, but Minerva had to join the military. Hephaestus, the power of fire on the oilfields of Lemnos and Asia, merged into the volcano-*numen* Volcanus. Vesta was in origin one with Hestia. It will be amply clear that almost all the myths that were told of these deities were taken over lock, stock and barrel from the Greeks.

Others pressed forward, less obviously. Hercules, the Greek Heracles, a demigod in Greece, perhaps even a historical figure, was to the Romans a powerful god of practical success. It is significant that his shrine was in the cattle-market. Castor and Pollux, the Heavenly Twins, were also admitted within the city boundaries, though it was Castor, the horseman, who predominated. They had, unusually, their own Roman myth; they had helped in the Roman victory at Lake Regillus in 499 BC. Dionysus, god of wine and inspiration and nature in the raw, was made one with a power of growth, Liber, whose feminine form Libera was used for the corn-spirit Persephone, whom the Romans mispronounced Proserpina. But Bacchus and Proserpina remained as names in their own right. The healing god Asclepius, whom the Romans mispronounced Aesculapius, was consciously introduced through the Sibylline Books at a time of plague, with his sacred snake, and settled on the Tiber island where his hospital was later taken over by St Bartholomew.

Meantime the old Roman and Italian gods retained something of their power: witness the woodland spirits of Faunus and Silvanus. Faunus was identified with Pan, god of the pastureland, but he remained recognizably Italian. Silvanus never was taken over by the Greeks, but the Romans carried him (with Faunus) as far as Britain.

The calendar

Fragmentary inscriptions enable us to reconstruct the calendar of the main festivals of the Roman year. Each month had three fixed points. The Kalends, the first day, was sacred to Juno; the Ides, in mid-month, to Jupiter. The Nones which fell in between was the day on which the festivals for the month were announced. Throughout the calendar there are standard markings. The most important of these are: F, 42 *dies fasti*, on which civil action was lawful; NF, 48 *dies nefasti*, days on which legal transactions and political assemblies were religiously forbidden; C, 195 *dies comitiales*, days propitious for political assembly. One day, 15 June, is marked Q St DF (*quando stercus delatum fas*); this was the spring-cleaning day for Vesta's Temple, and it was legitimate for business only when the rubbish had been disposed of. Most festivals, except one or two commemorating historical events, fell on odd dates: 'the god loves odd numbers'. The year originally began in March, as the names September to December ('seventh' to 'tenth') remind us, but the switch to a twelve-month year beginning in January must have been early.

March was sacred to Mars, god of war and agriculture, and festivals involving purification of shields and trumpets may have had a twofold function. April was the month of opening. The festivals were mainly agricultural: the Fordicidia involved offerings of pregnant cattle, the Cerealia honoured Ceres of the growing grain, the Parilia was a shepherds' festival, the Vinalia offered the newly broached wine to Jupiter, the Robigalia propitiated Robigus, the power of disease in wheat. May is a month of uncertain meaning, including the Lemuria or Festival of the Dead. June is also of uncertain meaning, with festivals of Vesta, and of an ancient goddess of women, Mater Matuta. July was a period of dangerous heat with miscellaneous and obscure festivals. August was mainly concerned with the corn-harvest and its joyous celebration. September was a period of rest after the intensive August festivals. The gap was filled with a two-week-long Festival of Rome. October saw the vintage and the end of the campaigning system, closing the process begun in March. November was a month of ploughing and sowing with no time for festivals. By contrast December was packed with them – the Agonia of uncertain meaning, which recurs through the year; the Consualia, in honour of Consus, spirit of the harvest-store, perhaps for store-checking; the great Saturnalia, a time of fun and games and presents, which influenced the Christian Christmas; the Opalia in honour of Ops, the power of plenty; the obscure Divalia, something to do with the winter solstice; the Larentalia, perhaps for the ancestors. January, though still a time of winter leisure, did not compete with these. There was another Agonia, and the Carmentalia, in honour of spirits of prophecy and child-birth. February was a month of purification, with six festivals, including the Lupercalia in which two young priests, smeared with blood and wearing the skins of sacrificed goats, went round striking the women with strips of skin for fertility and purification.

There were thus about forty-five major festivals, but some, like the Saturnalia, lasted a week. There were also several minor festivals, and the Ludi, Games or Contests, extended through several weeks of the year. The Romans had no 'week-ends'; their year was structured round holidays which were holy days.

It is interesting to make comparison with a military calendar from the third century AD from Dura-Europos. Two-thirds of the observances honour the divinities of the Royal House, and only Jupiter, Juno, Mars, Minerva and Neptune were left of the old gods.

The religious monuments of Rome and the Augustan reformation

The Capitoline Hill was the inner stronghold and cult-centre of Rome. The great temple, of which nothing remains but foundations, was dedicated to Jupiter Optimus Maximus who shared it with his guests, Juno and Minerva. But there was an even older foundation nearby, to Jupiter Feretrius; the meaning of the cult-title is uncertain, but the temple housed a sacred flint which was used in striking treaties. There was also a lost temple to Juno Moneta, dedicated in 344 BC, which housed and gave its name to the Mint.

Just below, in the Forum, stood the Temple of Saturn (pl. 30.2), perhaps dedicated in 497 BC, and restored by L. Munatius Plancus in 47 BC. It housed the Treasury. But the Forum was full of sacred monuments. The black volcanic stone, called the Lapis Niger, carries the oldest known Latin inscription (*CIL* VI, 36840), hedged round with tabus, commanding detours round it, perhaps sacred to the underworld gods. The Regia was the headquarters of the *pontifex maximus*, containing the sacred shields and spear of Mars, and an altar on which the blood of a horse sacrificed in the Campus Martius was sprinkled. The Temple of Vesta, round like a hearth and always rebuilt to the original plan, the sacred grove, and the Halls of the Vestals, formed a complex of great antiquity and high holiness. The Spring of Juturna (Helper or Immortal?) was naturally sacred from early times. The Temple of Castor (with Pollux) commemorated the victory at

Lake Regillus, and was said to have been dedicated on 15 July 484 BC, being rebuilt in 117 BC and again under Augustus.

Alongside the Forum runs the Palatine Hill, another area replete with sanctity. Here was the cave-shrine of the Lupercal associated with the legend of the wolf suckling Romulus and Remus, and with the purificatory ceremony of the Lupercalia. Here was the Hut of Romulus, preserved as a shrine. Here was a sacred fig-tree. Here also was founded the Temple of the Great Mother, when she was introduced in 204 BC.

It is impossible to mention all the surviving or known monuments even of republican Rome: for example in the Largo Argentina four temples may be seen. Their dedication is unknown, but they go back to the fourth and third centuries BC. Again, the church of S. Nicola in Carcere contains traces of three temples of the third and second centuries BC. Not far away are two exquisite monuments of the late Republic, one round and one rectangular, recently identified as dedicated to Hercules Victor and Portunus, the former built of marble from Athens.

It was the proud boast of Augustus to have found Rome brick and left it marble. In his *Res Gestae* he boasts how in 28 BC he undertook the restoration of eighty-two temples. His greatest foundation was the Temple of Apollo on the Palatine, glorifying the new age of peace and culture. When he celebrated in 17 BC the *Ludi Saeculares* or Festival of the Century, with purificatory ritual and invocation of the gods of the past and gods of the future, and a general sense of rebirth and destiny, Horace's carefully scripted hymn was sung twice, before the Temples of Jupiter Capitolinus and Apollo Palatinus. Other important foundations were to the Divine Julius (a dedication pregnant with much ruler-worship and many temples to come), to Mars the Avenger, and to Concord; the great Altar of Peace, with its sculpture portraying the ancient traditions of Rome records the part played by the imperial family in honouring them, not to forget the Mausoleum for himself and his family. He encouraged others in building too. Agrippa built the first Pantheon (pl. 13.10); Domitian was to rebuild it, and Hadrian again.

There were plenty of new foundations and restorations under the Empire, but Hadrian's Pantheon is in some ways the climax to the religious buildings of pagan Rome. Dio Cassius said, rightly, that with its circular shape it resembled the vault of heaven, or, as Shelley put it, 'it is, as it were, the visible image of the universe'.

Intellectual beliefs

The beliefs which underlay religious practices might sit lightly on some of the upper classes. The Greek historian Polybius praised the Romans for imposing religiosity on the commons to keep them under control; to him religious attitudes were a matter of political expediency. Q. Mucius Scaevola, consul in 95 BC and *pontifex maximus*, expounded a view that gods are of three kinds: the gods of the poets are disgraceful rubbish, those of the philosophers are unsuited to politics, those of statesmen are politically expedient. Cicero, an avowed sceptic about augury, was augur, and Julius Caesar, an unbeliever, *pontifex maximus*.

The leading philosophical schools of the late Republic and early Empire were the Epicurean and Stoic. Epicurus was an Athenian living about 300 BC. He believed that gods exist, in immortal bliss, but care nothing for mankind and neither reward nor punish, though emanations from them may reach those who are attuned to right and truth. The soul is mortal. There is nothing to fear in god; there is nothing to feel in death; good can be readily attained; evil can be readily endured – such is the prescription of salvation. The coming of Epicureans to Rome in 173 BC caused a scandal, and they were banished. But before long the doctrines returned and spread, and were prominent at the end of the Republic, and for three centuries after. The great monuments to the school are Lucretius' astonishing poem *On the Nature of the Universe*, and a huge account of the doctrine put round the city-centre at Oenoanda in Asia Minor by a man named Diogenes for all to see, citizens and 'foreigners', present and to come.

Official Roman policy on the whole favoured the Stoics, though some of the sect ran foul of the first-century emperors. In the second century BC Panaetius had won Scipio Aemilianus to his faith; the first century BC saw the towering magisterial genius of Posidonius. Augustus supported a Stoic court-philosopher. Seneca, effectively regent at the outset of Nero's reign, was a Stoic. With Marcus Aurelius a Stoic reached the throne, though a wistful, half-agnostic Stoic. The Stoics were pantheists. Seneca said that Jupiter is 'governor and protector of the universe, the mind and spirit of the world, the lord and creator of this fabric'. Every name is his – Fate, Providence, Nature, Universe. The Stoics were determinists. We are actors in the divine drama. Our part is determined – but not the spirit in which we play it. Here our will has scope – and the Stoics counselled a spirit of acceptance. The most attractive Stoic of the Roman period was the Greek teacher and ex-slave Epictetus, who called his hearers to a life of praise.

The Stoics, Panaetius and Posidonius especially, had already blended some of Plato's mysticism in with their Stoicism. The Academic or Platonic school had, somewhat oddly, moved into an era of intellectual scepticism, replacing certainty of truth by probability, and in the mid-second century BC their leading spokesman, Carneades, had shocked Rome as much as did the Epicureans. Cicero, who did more than anyone to make the Romans articulate in Greek philosophy, was himself an Academic, much influenced by the Stoics, and wrote a major treatise examining different views, *On the Nature of the Gods*.

But Plato remained powerful in the Greek world under the Empire. Middle Platonists are spoken of loosely – Maximus of Tyre, an unoriginal thinker who lectured in Rome, with a high vision of God, or Numenius who presented Plato with a dose of

Pythagoras, and believed in three gods (roughly an undiminished principle of being, a divine artificer, and a world soul), or Albinus. Christian thinkers, Justin, Clement and Origen, owed a debt to Plato. Then came those loosely called the Neo-Platonists, the rare religious and intellectual genius of Plotinus, who called the ultimate the One, and spoke of the soul's ascent to God as 'the flight of the alone to the Alone'.

The gods from the east

The first impact of Greek religion on Rome came from contact with the Greek communities of Italy. But it has already been seen how the healing god Asclepius-Aesculapius was deliberately introduced from Epidaurus through the Sibylline Books as an answer to the plague of 293 BC. Similarly towards the end of the war with Hannibal, in 204 BC the Books introduced the Great Mother of Pessinus in the form of a black betyl. The information services slipped up; the Senate were horrified at the orgiastic worship and the eunuch priests and promptly clamped down on Roman participation. Catullus' sixty-third poem, a century and a half later, is evidence of the horror and attraction the Romans experienced. From the reign of Claudius a more liberal attitude prevailed. The *taurobolium* or baptism in bull's blood (pl. 30.4), giving new life to the baptized, is recorded from Puteoli in AD 134, and gorily described by the Christian poet Prudentius two centuries later.

Dionysus-Bacchus had his orgiastic worship, and there was a famous scandal in Campania in 186 BC (Livy 29, 10–14; *ILS* 18). Roman participation was thereafter strictly controlled, and assemblies were kept to a maximum of five people. Across the centuries the cult grew again. In Pompeii the Villa of the Mysteries is a marvellous symbolic pictorial representation of initiation presided over by the god and his bride Ariadne (pl. 30.3). In the second century AD there was at Tusculum an association of nearly 500 members headed by a woman, Julia Agrippinilla. The same and the following century saw members of the upper class putting scenes of Dionysus on their sarcophagi, his birth, childhood, awakening of Ariadne, triumph; they portray the lord of life with clear hope of life beyond the grave.

Isis came from Egypt where she was perhaps in origin the land waiting to be fertilized by the flooding waters of the Nile. She became a universal goddess making universal claims, the chief representative of divine femininity in the ancient Mediterranean world. Egyptian religion is attested at Puteoli in 105 BC in the form of Serapis, a god invented to express the universal aspirations of the Ptolemies, and identified in a mystic Trinity with Zeus-Jupiter and Asclepius-Aesculapius. A fine head of Serapis was found in London in the Mithraeum. Tradition said that Isis came to Rome under Sulla. The establishment was uncertain about her, and suppressed her altars. She achieved temporary recognition in 43 BC but Augustus abhorred all things Egyptian, and it was not until Gaius that she was accorded a temple in Rome, and two centuries later that she found a place on the Capitol. Of her popular appeal there is no doubt, and the last book of Apuleius' picaresque *The Golden Ass* is moving testimony to the devotion she might inspire. Her image with her son Horus affected Christian iconography, and her title *Stella Maris* 'Star of the Sea' was taken over by Mary.

Mithras came from Persia, a mediator who, with the Sun, fought for the great god of order and light, Ahura Mazda. He was himself the central figure in a mystery-religion much beloved of soldiers, traders and civil servants. There were seven grades of initiation associated with the seven planets; the worship involved a communion meal; there was a promise of life beyond death. But the chapels (called 'caves') were small (pl. 30.7). There was no question of Mithraism sweeping the Roman world. The religion which for a time did so was Syrian sun-worship, and in AD 274 Sol Invictus, the Unconquered Sun, was established as the supreme deity of Rome. Even with the coming of Christianity to power sun-worship did not wholly lose its grip. Constantine was something of a syncretist between the two cults; Christ was portrayed under St Peter's in the sun-god's chariot, and took over his birthday of 25 December (pl. 30.8).

30.1 A sacrificial procession of a bull, sheep and pig, offered to Mars, a god of agriculture as well as war

30.2 The temple of Saturn, Rome; the existing podium was rebuilt in 42 BC, although the temple was traditionally founded in 498 BC

30.3   The Villa of the Mysteries, Pompeii. The frescoes depict a sequence of
events from the Dionysiac mysteries

30.4   A vessel from Boscoreale depicting the sacrifice of a bull in front of an altar

30.5   Bronze statuette of a *lar*

30.6   Stucco relief of a sacro-idyllic landscape from the Farnesina House, Rome

30.7   The Mithraeum under the church of St Clemente, Rome

30.8   An early fourth-century mosaic under St Peter's, Rome, portraying Christ sweeping across
the heavens in a sun-god's chariot

CHAPTER 31

·RULER-WORSHIP·

John Ferguson

Sacral kingship

The Romans in early days knew all about sacral kingship. The King was a mediator between the divine and life on earth. Servius Tullius traced his descent to Vulcanus, or else the Lar Familiaris. The *rex sacrorum* remained as a ritual priesthood despite the suspicion attaching to the word *rex*. The same office existed in a number of Latin cities. Tradition recalled *reges augures*. The Regia remained as a sacred building, containing shrines to Mars and Ops, and the site for ceremonies associated with the ritual of the October Horse and the worship of Janus. Something of the sacrosanctity attaching to the royal mediator was transferred to the magistrates of the Republic, to the two consuls (by whatever name they were known at first), and to the tribunes.

Sacral kingship, however, is not a precise or immediate model for the later imperial worship, for the very thought of the ancient kings was anathema, and to be a priest and mediator was not the same as to be a divinity.

Julius Caesar

Julius Caesar traced his descent back to Aeneas, one of the divine founders of Rome, himself the son of Venus. When Aeneas died, according to tradition he became Iuppiter Indiges, Jupiter the Ancestor, and his son Ascanius or Iulus built him a temple and initiated a cult. Stefan Weinstock in his remarkable study *Divus Julius* has further argued that the *gens Iulia*, finding their ancestor in Iulus, identified him with Vediovis, the young Jupiter. In one way or another Caesar could claim divine descent.

His birth was reputedly marked by a miraculous sign. The important fact about this story is that, though it cannot be traced before the Civil War, it was certainly in circulation before his death. It is part of the hagiography of a live man.

He was designated *flamen Dialis* by Marius when he was only 13; this office was incompatible with a political career, and he was saved from it by Sulla. He was himself something of a sceptic, tinged with Epicureanism, but he knew the political value of the other priesthoods. He became *pontifex* in 73 and *pontifex maximus* in 63; this title was never omitted from inscriptions in his honour except where he was designated a god.

The issue of Caesar's divinity was first raised after his defeat of Pompey. In 48 statues were decreed to him. In the east these were erected in public places, sometimes accompanied, it seems, by a goddess, Victoria or Roma, with inscriptions designating him a god. In Rome a statue was erected on the Capitol after the battle of Thapsus. The evidence from Dio is difficult and conflicting. Dio says that the inscription contained ἡμίθεος which Caesar caused to be deleted. But what was the word? *Hemitheus* is late Latin only; *semideus* was coined by Ovid; *heros* would have been kept by Dio. *Deo Caesari, Divo Iulio* and *Genio Caesaris* are possible but not certain. By the next year he was *Deo Invicto* even in Rome. About this time some of the ancient divinities become closely personalized to him, Victoria Caesaris, Fortuna Caesaris, Felicitas Caesaris.

These and other honours were awarded to him as victor and to emphasize his superiority to Pompey. After the battle of Munda in 45 he received fresh honours as Liberator, Saviour and City Founder. Liberator was a new title, neither human nor divine. Weinstock, however, has argued that the naming of a month and a tribe after him was conceived in 45 in association with this title. In connection with the title of Saviour, Salus Caesaris and Clementia Caesaris now become explicit. As to his position as Founder his statue was now set up in the Temple of Quirinus-Romulus with the inscription *Deo Invicto*. A further title at this time was *parens patriae*, and in this connection there seems to have been a public cult of Genius Caesaris.

By early 44 fresh honours were decreed: his head on coins; a pediment on his house (a feature of the temples of the gods, and the theatrical palaces of the kings); an empty throne in the theatre. Finally there were temples and altars and a priesthood in his honour, with the title (according to Dio) of Iuppiter Iulius and with Antony as his priest.

Not everyone will accept Weinstock's reliance on the late authority of Dio, or his deductions about early observances. What we must accept on the evidence is that there was in his lifetime a movement towards the divine honours he undoubtedly received after his murder.

Appian's account of Antony's funeral speech tells that he chanted a hymn declaring Caesar a god. The people spontaneously took up the bier with the aim of cremating Caesar and setting the ashes in the Capitoline Temple of Jupiter. This did not happen, but there arose an improvised cult where the pyre stood. The great comet further helped the belief that a new god had appeared. The consecration of the new god took place in the senate on 1 January 42 (*status dei cuiusque in senatus aestimatione pendebat* – Tert. *Apol.* 13,30), being confirmed by the people (*ILS* 72). The name Divus Iulius had been in use since 44. The people were not always consulted later, but in general the precedent was followed: the Senate decreed the deification, acclaimed the new god, and pronounced the organization of the cult.

The struggle for power

In the jockeying for political power in the decade that followed religion played its part. Octavian was Caesar's adopted son – Antony remarked bitterly that he owed everything to his name – and with this inheritance, at least after the pact of Brundisium, he began to call himself *Divi filius*. Suetonius tells us of a banquet of the gods in which he took the role of Apollo. The story is dubious: whom did he allow to play Jupiter? But, Octavian certainly had Apollo as his peculiar protector long before Actium, and the god's symbols appear on his coins. It was perhaps now that he allowed the story to get about that Apollo was his father, having come to Atia in the form of a snake. There were plenty to see in Vergil's *tuus iam regnat Apollo* a reference to Octavian himself.

Sextus Pompeius, remembering how his father cleared the sea of pirates, and realizing that his own hopes depended on sea-power, proclaimed himself Neptune's son, wore a sea-blue cloak, put Neptune on his coins, and offered extravagant sacrifices to Neptune; Horace called him *Neptunius dux*. The very image of Neptune in a procession led the people of Rome to demonstrate in favour of Sextus.

Antony was the first of them to receive divine honours, but he was of course operating in the east. He was greeted as Dionysus incarnate. Plutarch describes his arrival at Ephesus:

> 'Women attired like Maenads, and men and boys like Satyrs and Pans, went in front of him clearing the way. The city was full of ivy, thyrsus wands, harps, pipes and flutes. The people greeted him as Dionysus, Beneficent Giver of Joy.'

This identification did not depend on Cleopatra. When he was in Athens with Octavia he banqueted in a Bacchic cave in the theatre of Dionysus. The Athenians set up inscriptions to him as the new Dionysus, renamed the Panathenaea the Antonaea, and gave him Athene to wife with a dowry of 1,000 talents. When he returned to Cleopatra this religious dimension was intensified. Their twins were already Alexander Helios and Cleopatra Selene, harbingers of a new age. Cleopatra herself was the new Isis, Antony Dionysus-Osiris. Their portraits were painted as such; the Athenians set up statues to them as such. But in the end Dionysus abandoned his human incarnation.

Augustus

Octavian was faced with dangerous precedents. Deification was associated with the oriental divine kingship which the Romans feared and repudiated. Yet in some sense deification was a necessity of power.

In Egypt for practical purposes he had to be the divine king, the inheritor of the divine titles of the Ptolemies and, before them, of the Pharaohs. His statue was arguably in all the temples. To the Egyptian Greeks he was identified with Zeus Eleutherios; his name was invoked in oaths; he received the temple Cleopatra had prepared for Antony, and other temples too.

Elsewhere he was more cautious. The Greek states of the east tended to be fulsome in flattery. They had established societies (*koina*) for a variety of purposes, and these proved adaptable to ruler-cult. The initiative came in 29 BC in Asia and Bithynia. There were precedents in the honours accorded to proconsuls. But he was canny; he would not let Roman citizens worship him as a god on earth. In general he did not encourage the dedication of altars or temples to himself alone; his name must be coupled with Roma, or the Lares, or, as in Cilicia, with Poseidon. About 27 BC at Mytilene a decree conferring privileges on him left room for future additions; the whole object was 'that he may be deified as much as possible'.

At Rome and among Romans his chief title was *Divi filius*; here the example of Hercules might give hope of future deification. The Roman establishment went beyond his own overt wishes. The Senate made his birthday a public holiday, and named a tribe after him, following the precedent established by Julius. The inclusion of his name among the gods honoured in hymn by the Salii was going further; whatever his public policy he was privately pleased, as he recorded years later in his *Res Gestae*. They also, even before his return, decreed that a libation should be poured to his Genius at every dinner, public or private, setting him among the founding fathers. Vergil in an earlier poem called him *deus*, but that was hardly more than an Epicurean echo of Lucretius. Now, in a semi-official poem with which he greeted the ruler's return, he did not call him a god, but indicated that he was marking out his road to Olympus, and dared to suggest that deity did not need to wait for death. Horace, slightly oddly, identified him with Mercury incarnate, though the identification is found also in an inscription from Cos.

The ruler himself was circumspect. He demonstrated his piety with a temple to the Divus Iulius who was the foundation of his own religious position. He restored the broken-down shrines, later boasting that there were eighty-two of them. He saw that honour was paid to Victory and Peace. He dedicated the new Temple of Apollo on the Palatine to vie with the temple of Jupiter on the Capitol. His act in having his own statues melted down to enrich the new temple is ambiguous because it in some sense identified him with Apollo. Further he actually permitted one of the statues of

Apollo in the temple surrounds to bear his likeness. Still, he had no place in the temple cult. When his political sagacity led him to a nominal restoration of the Republic the speech which Dio recorded linked his act with Caesar's renunciation of the crown. Were he to be killed like Caesar, he would like Caesar attain divinity. He was not immortal, but looked forward to divinity as a reward for service.

Three days later by a stroke of genius he took the title Augustus. At first he wished to take the name Romulus, which was actually proposed, declaring him unequivocally the second founder of Rome. But it was too blatant. 'Augustus' had all the religious overtones; Rome, said Ennius, had been founded *augusto augurio*; it had the associations of *augurium, augere* and *auctoritas*. Livy explained the word as 'superhuman'. Now a month was named after him, and a golden shield honoured him in association with Virtus, Clementia, Iustitia, Pietas. Horace at times called him a present divinity. More generally Horace and Vergil used the parallel of Hercules, and Livy stressed the parallel. Augustus would not let Agrippa consecrate the Pantheon to his present divinity. The expectation of apotheosis is seen in the appearance of the eagle on coins: no more. The climax of this period was the inauguration of a new age in the *Ludi Saeculares* of 17 BC.

The pressures mounted. From 12 BC, when he became *pontifex maximus*, the emperor's Genius was the object of a formal state-cult and formally recognized in oaths between Jupiter Optimus Maximus and the Di Penates. The Lares Augusti also were publicly recognized. Concordia Augusta, Pax Augusta, Salus Augusta, Fortuna Augusta were honoured in the west. It was in 12 BC that Drusus at Lyon (Lugdunum) dedicated an altar to Roma and Augustus built by sixty tribes from the three Gauls; the cult was administered by an annual gathering of delegates. There was a similar altar, of uncertain date, at Cologne (Oppidum Ubiorum). At Narbo in AD 11 an altar was dedicated to Numen Augusti, perhaps a variant on Genius Augusti, but a significant one. In the east enthusiasm could hardly be controlled. Augustus was called Zeus Eleutherios in a number of inscriptions from varying sites between AD 1 and 3. At Mytilene at the same time there was a priest of Roma and Sebastos Zeus Caesar Olympios: Sebastos is the Greek for Augustus. Livia and Julia were called goddesses. A dedication to the *Theoi Sebastoi* presumably included Livia with Augustus. Julia was called the new Aphrodite or identified with Venus Genetrix. At Puteoli in AD 14 some sailors from Alexandria made a spontaneous act of veneration.

The expectation was fulfilled. After his death, on 17 September 14 the Senate decreed that the Divine Augustus be accepted among the gods of the State. In other words, Augustus was not among the *di Manes* in the underworld, but among the *di superi* above; a senator claimed to have seen him bodily ascending, and an eagle was released from the pyre. The structure of heaven reflected the structure on earth; there was imagined a kind of celestial super-senate with co-option on the basis of merit. Hercules labouring for mankind was the model, and Tiberius drew the parallel at Augustus' funeral. A rescript based the emperor's divinity on 'the magnitude of his benefactions to the whole world'. Tiberius authorized a temple to Divus Augustus in Tarraconensis in AD 23, and thereafter the cult spread widely.

The Julio-Claudians

Augustus had a flair for success, and he set a workable pattern which only megalomaniacs departed from. Tiberius, who was in the obvious senses a far abler person but who notoriously lacked his touch, tended to follow his example. He accepted sacrifices and oaths to his Genius, but rebuked a courtier who called his duties sacred, preferring 'laborious' (as Hercules). He told the people of Gythium that divine honours should be confined to his father; he was content with human rewards. Of necessity he was, like Augustus more flexible in the east than in the west, but he adhered to precedent. He allowed the people of Asia to dedicate a temple to him, Livia and the Sacred Senate, taking as model the Temple to Augustus and Roma at Pergamum. But he would not accept a temple in Spain. Tacitus places a speech of some nobility into his mouth:

'Conscript fathers, I call you to witness and I desire future generations to recollect that I am a mere mortal, fulfilling the duties of a man, satisfied if my actions are worthy of my high calling. Men will give my memory enough – more than enough – if they account me worthy of my ancestors, with a providential care for your interests, unflinching in danger, undeterred by enemies I encounter in my service of the State.'

Germanicus in Alexandria in AD 19 deprecated anything tending to deify himself; it was his father who was saviour and benefactor. At most he experienced the reflection of the divinities of Tiberius and Livia. But that was Egypt (pl. 31.1). Some of the official propaganda of the reign emphasizes qualities with divine overtones – *providentia*, for instance, and *liberalitas*. There can be little doubt that Tiberius lived in the expectation of a deification after death which he did not in fact receive.

With Gaius we come on the first of the megalomaniacs. The day of his accession was called the Parilia and treated as a second founding of Rome. In 38 he had his dead sister Drusilla consecrated and granted a priesthood. A senator declared that he had witnessed her ascension and she was given the name Panthea. Livilla was honoured at Pergamum. He himself appeared in various divine guises, as Dionysus, Mercury, Apollo, Mars, Neptune, Juno, Diana, Venus and one of the Dioscuri. He made the Temple of the Dioscuri a vestibule to his palace. He invited the Moon to share his bed. He was greeted as Jupiter Latiaris; he ordered his head to be placed on the statue of Zeus at Olympia; he scandalized the Jews by ordering a statue of Zeus with his own head to be placed in the temple at Jerusalem. At Rome he instituted one or even two temples to his own godhead. At Miletus an association of Lovers of Augustus consecrated a temple to him.

The admirable Claudius redressed the balance. Only in Britain did he accept a temple in his honour. This, as Lily Ross Taylor remarked, was simply a means of insuring the loyalty of a region which had no relations with the earlier *divi*. Elsewhere in the west it was his Genius which received honour. Claudius actually deprecated the offering of divine honours in Alexandria, though the governor in publishing the refusal called him 'Caesar our god'. His consecration of Livia in 41 was in accord with precedent, and an altar to Pietas Augusta no doubt acknowledged this. Seneca called him a Saviour and spoke of his *divinae manus*. However much the Senate might resent the authority of upstart freedmen controlling the civil service, however tragic his private life might be, there was appreciation of his wise care of the State, and he duly received deification after death, though Seneca is said to have jested at his 'pumpkinification' and a satire (perhaps by Petronius?) survives on the apotheosis. It parodies the official procedure with the witness to his ascension and the debate in the Senate. A temple to him was begun; there were *flamen* and *flaminica* and Sodales Augustales Claudiales.

With Nero megalomania returned, and as early as 54 the Senate voted a large statue in the temple of Mars Ultor. But his own ambitions were slow to develop, and as late as 65 he vetoed a proposal for a temple to Divus Nero; it was ill-omened as anticipating his death. His consecration of Poppaea and their dead child did not go beyond precedent. His naming of April Neroneus however showed the trend in his mind. In Egypt the month Pharmuthi became Neroneios Sebastos. Caesarea Philippi was renamed Neronias, Artaxata Neronei, and there seems little doubt that he intended to rename the Peloponnesus as the Neronesus, and even Rome Neropolis. On coins of Asia Minor he was called 'god', and at Sicyon identified with Zeus. More frequent was the identification with Hercules, as on coins of Patrae, or Apollo, as in an inscription from Athens. He was greeted on his return to Rome in both identities. Above all there was his identification with the Sun-god in inscriptions from Acraephiae and Sagalassus, in his representation on coins with the Sun's radiate crown, in his depiction on theatre-hangings driving the Sun's chariot through the sky, and in a colossal statue of the god with his own features.

The Flavians

After the traumas of the assassination of Nero and the Year of the Four Emperors, the Empire settled back into sanity with the accession of the blunt soldier Vespasian. But he was a usurper, and had to establish his claims in which the capture of Jerusalem was a part. Dedications to Pax Augusta or Vespasian's Victory are known, and coin-types also deal in semi-divine abstractions. He gave short shrift to flattery of his own person.

He was a man among men, a servant among servants; that he personally helped to shift the rubble from the Capitol was typical of his attitude. Yet he knew he had served well, and his words as he felt the approach of death 'Vae! puto deus fio!' ('Oh dear! I think I'm becoming a god!') were only half in jest. Vespasian saw in his reign the centenary and the reenactment of Augustus, and it was appropriate that he succeeded Augustus and Claudius, whose temple he completed, among the divinized emperors.

Vespasian, against the views of Stoics and traditional Romans, had insisted on dynastic succession. Rome feared his son and successor Titus for his ruthlessness, and his fondness for oriental splendour. He belied their fears. He was proud of being a Benefactor, and if a day passed without his conferring a benefit he would cry 'Friends, I have lost a day!' His premature death was greeted with sincere and spontaneous mourning, and he, the son of a god, was also admitted to the ranks of the gods.

His brother Domitian was of a different temper. Brought up under the shadow of his father and brother, he showed the megalomania of a Gaius or Nero. Suetonius and Dio both tell that he demanded to be addressed as *dominus et deus*. There is no record of this on inscriptions, but Martial as early as 89 speaks of *edictum domini deique nostri*, and the remarks of Pliny and Dio of Prusa confirm the same thing. Some people think that the words put into the mouth of Thomas in the Christian gospel *According to John* were intended as a counterblast to Domitian's claims; Jesus, not the emperor, is the true Lord and God. Domitian's claims were dangerous; as god he belonged to a different plane from his subjects; as *dominus* he could treat them as slaves. In fact, though Domitian persecuted the senatorial class, he did not undo the government of his predecessors; only, in Charlesworth's words, 'he paraded absolutism, giving to the imperial position the airs of divinity and the pomp of a despot', and he met the assassin's knife.

The five good emperors

The period which followed the assassination of Domitian was accounted by Gibbon the happiest in the history of mankind, though his ironical detachment noted that it was essentially unstable. Whether by deliberate policy or through the accident of childlessness the pattern grew of the adoption of the best successor by his predecessor.

The general practice with respect to deification was a return to Augustus. Trajan deified Nerva. He did not seek worship for himself, and refused it when offered. When his sister Marciana died in 112 he had her deified together with his own natural father. He was doubly *Divi filius*. Hercules was his patron deity; he instituted the *ludi Herculei* at Rome, and Hercules appears frequently on the coins. The analogy with the emperor labouring for his people could not be missed, and Dio of Prusa was one of those to draw it. The expectation of divinity was there (pl. 31.2), and it was fulfilled by Hadrian who dedicated a temple to Trajan and his wife Plotina in 125. More, his memory was long-lasting. In the fourth century they prayed for an emperor to be *felicior Augusto, melior Traiano*. The Slavic god Trojan, worshipped in early Russia, seems to be nothing more than the divinized Trajan mediated through the Dacians. Even Christian Europe had a legend of the admission of Trajan to heaven at the instigation of Gregory the Great.

Hadrian began in the same way, deliberately recalling Augustus, and in 126 refused the divine honours formally offered by the Achaean League, though divine titles were sporadically attached to him in dedications. But from the winter of 128 a new attitude appears. In consecrating the *cella* of the huge temple of Zeus Olympios at Athens he dedicated an altar to himself outside. Shortly after, a coin commemorating his visit to Ephesus proclaimed that the emperor was identified with Zeus Olympios in person. The Athenians, who dedicated 95 known altars and 47 known statues to him, did not call him Zeus and simply kept the title Olympios, but the 174 altars and 107 statue bases known from Asia frequently identify him with Zeus or, sometimes, with other gods (even the God of the Underworld), and the colossal temple at Cyzicus showed him in the guise of Zeus. He was Zeus Panhellenios calling the Greeks to their inheritance. On official coins he is sometimes portrayed with an aureole. At Antinoopolis he was entitled Saviour of the World and received the cult-names of Zeus. The new name for Jerusalem – Aelia Capitolina – pointed in the same direction. When he travelled to Miletus he was greeted as Olympios. At Patara they called him Zeus and Sabina Hera. In the Serapeum at Alexandria he installed a chapel to his own divinity. In Egypt they called him the glorious god.

This is the necessary background to the deification of his beloved Antinous, drowned in the Nile. This was not directly part of the imperial cult; yet it was part of the same pattern as the imperial-divine will. And it caught on. Half a million pilgrims brought offerings to Antinoopolis. Coins and inscriptions proclaimed the dead boy 'Antinous the God'. He was inevitably identified with Osiris, and with Hermes, Silvanus, Pan. Over thirty Greek cities issued commemorative coins. At least 2,000 statues were produced in eight years and at least forty cities venerated him; twelve had cults and seven had festivals in his honour. And it lasted. His statue at Antinoopolis stood till 375, and, even later, medallions were issued proclaiming him a god. At Delphi the statue, thrown down in an invasion from the north, was carefully replaced. In Italy his statues were meticulously shielded from Christian iconoclasm or barbarian assault.

So Hadrian's divine status lived on, despite the opposition of the Senate. Aelius Aristides in addressing Antoninus Pius declared that the mere mention of Hadrian's name was enough for people to rise and worship him. Zeus brought order out of chaos, and Hadrian, Zeus-like, had done likewise. 'Confusion and strife came to an end, and universal order entered as a brilliant light over the private and the public affairs of men.' He received temples in the Campus Martius, and at Puteoli games, *flamines* and a Sodalitas Hadrianalis.

His successor T. Aelius Antoninus insisted on the consecration, earning for himself the titles of *Divi filius* and of Pius. He liked the shortened name Antoninus Augustus Pius, and reverted to the full spread of his names only for the dedication of the temple to his predecessor. Where Hadrian had travelled throughout his empire, Antoninus sat in Rome; like a spider in the middle of his web, said one historian. No longer was the emperor Zeus Panhellenios. The very cult of Roma was in decay in the provinces, though in Rome he dedicated a temple to Roma Aeterna and Venus Felix. There was praise of Victoria and Pax and Felicitas and Fortuna, associated with the emperor. In Alexandria he was honoured as Pantheos, Helios-Zeus-Ammon, Ruler of the Universe, a power of light after what some saw as the dark days of Hadrian. Or he might be seen as Hercules. The comparison remained potent, and he too received his heavenly reward (pls 31.3 and 31.4). The temple which he had dedicated to his wife Diva Faustina, in honouring her after her death, now became a temple to them both (pl. 31.5).

So we come to Marcus Aurelius, the half-agnostic philosopher-king, a figure of tragic pathos. He was no judge of men. He took his brother L. Verus as his equal colleague, but Verus was unworthy of his confidence. Verus liked titles; after his exploits in the east he styled himself first Armeniacus and then Hercules Pacifer. Marcus took the hint, and, on his death from apoplexy, had him deified; perhaps the burden of Lucius dead and divine was lighter than the burden of Lucius alive and human. When the younger Faustina died the Senate deified her; who knows what Marcus would have done left to himself? Marcus pursued his lonely human course to the bitter end. As his death approached on a campaign far from Rome they asked him for the password. He said: 'Go to the rising sun; my sun is setting.' It was an ambiguous and half-religious answer. The rising sun was Commodus, another example of his ill-judgment of people; the epigrammatist said that the only harm he did was in being a father. His sun set, and he too passed among the gods, though to the Stoic part of himself the divine spirit was already within him, and nothing to do with his imperial status.

From Commodus to Aurelian

With Commodus we are back in the realm of megalomania. As early as 175 he had taken the *toga virilis* on the very day when Romulus had become a god. At first his actions were merely undignified and offensive to Roman tradition. Eastern cults were growing in strength at Rome; he took the gods of the east as his protectors. His Felicitas and Salus and even Hilaritas were honoured at Rome; Pietas and Libertas too. But his ambitions were expanding. Interestingly his self-identification was with Hercules (pl. 31.6), but not with Hercules labouring for mankind in the hope of further divinity, but Hercules already a god, his labours over. He was Hercules Romanus, the new founder of Rome, ruling at Jupiter's side; Romulus was pushed out. Nero's colossus was to be turned into a statue of Commodus as Hercules. The twelve months were to be named for all time Lucius Aelius Aurelius Commodus Augustus Herculeus Romanus Exsuperatorius Amazonius Invictus Felix Pius. He was, wrote Weber, lord of the world, of space and time, of mankind and its happiness. He fell to a palace revolution, to rise again as Divus Commodus at the hands of Septimius Severus.

For, by the time of the Severi, it was clear that the Empire had no focal point of spiritual unity except in the *divina domus*. So Severus claimed continuity with the Antonines, deified Commodus and Pertinax, and began to emphasize the divinity of the ruling emperor, and his house. The emperor was *numen praesens*, the gods his partners, even advisers (*comites*). Emperor-worship was strong in the military camps. In an altar on the Raetian frontier the members of the imperial house are named before the other gods; so too at Lambaesis. In the calendar of military festivals from Dura the imperial divinities from Julius onwards have ousted the Olympians except for Jupiter, Juno, Minerva, Mars and Neptune. A typical entry is that for 7 May: 'For the Birthday of the Divine Julia Maesa, an act of prayer to the Divine Julia Maesa.' On coins too Septimius and Caracalla are compared to the Sun-god, the *rector orbis*. Geta appears with the rayed crown of the Sun-god. The empress has the attributes of the Moon-goddess, Julia Domna is portrayed as Cybele with the ambiguous title *Mater Deum*, or seated on Juno's throne; so too Julia Mamaea.

The extraordinary career of Elagabalus was thus only an exaggeration of what was already implicit. A priest of the Sun-god of Syria, whose black betyl he brought from Emesa to Rome, he was identified with his god, an identification made easier by his radiant beauty. He married a Vestal Virgin in a ritual enactment of a heavenly union. Rome could not stomach his oriental extravagances and he succumbed to a palace revolution.

It was in the second half of the century that Aurelian brought a decisive change. He abandoned the theory of *Gottkönigtum* for the Mazdean doctrine of rule by the grace of God, though, paradoxically, he was himself honoured as *dominus et deus*, as was Carus after him. To the Mazdeans and to Aurelian god was the Sun-god. For the remainder of the century the divine favour was shown sometimes by the Sun, sometimes by Jupiter or Mars or even Hercules. In the reorganization of Diocletian the senior emperor was under the protection of Jupiter, the junior under Hercules.

The way was prepared for the Christian Empire. Constantine was something of a syncretist between the Sun-god and the god of the Christians. But though he might invest his statue at Constantinople with the attributes of the Sun-god, and though the emotions appropriate to the divine monarch might still be directed to the monarch who ruled not as god but as his god's vice-gerent, Constantine's resting-place was set not among the thrones of the twelve Olympians, but among the cenotaphs of the twelve apostles.

The neocorate

The imperial cult flourished in the Asiatic provinces. A city which received authority to be a centre of the provincial cult was styled temple-warden or *neokoros*, and the neocorate was an object of some contention.

It was at Smyrna that Roma was first recognized as a goddess. By 10 BC the assembly of the *koinon* was meeting there. Under Tiberius the cities of Asia applied to set up a temple to Tiberius, Livia and the Holy Senate. Smyrna was assigned the temple with the title *neokoros*. In the second century Smyrna was granted a temple to Hadrian and a second neocorate, and a third in the third century.

Pergamum was the first meeting-place of the assembly of the *koinon*. It had a temple of Augustus and Roma, a festival Romaea Sebasta, and the neocorate. In the second century it received a temple of Trajan and a second neocorate.

At Ephesus the representatives of Asia joined in calling Julius god manifest. There was a city cult of Augustus, and of Gaius and Lucius, and under Tiberius a priestess of Livia as Augusta Demeter, a priest of Tiberius' twin grandsons, and a dedication to Tiberius by the Roman settlers. But it was not till Claudius that the title of *neokoros* was granted. A second title was granted for a temple to Domitian, withdrawn by Trajan because of Domitian's unpopularity, and restored for the new temple of Hadrian Olympios and the festival Hadrianeia Olympia.

Tarsus was twice *neokoros*, once under Hadrian, and once under Commodus. Sardis had the neocorate for a temple of Hadrian as Dionysus with a Sacred Hadrianic Stage Guild of actors. Philadelphia, though a centre of imperial cult, did not receive the neocorate till Caracalla. Tralles received the title without a temple. At Magnesia-on-the-Maeander there were Asiarchs in Nero's reign and, later, a festival of Roma. At Laodicea the *koinon* held meetings and the emperor's names were added to the Festival of Zeus. So too with the Festival of Apollo at Thyiateira, where there was a shrine to Trajan and Hadrian was honoured as Zeus Olympios. At Caesarea the temple of Augustus and Roma dominated the city, and there was a shrine to Tiberius dedicated by Pontius Pilate.

The climactic period of the neocorate was about AD 200. The possession of a temple was not enough; Nicaea never received the title. This was granted under the Julio-Claudians to Ephesus, Pergamum, Smyrna, Ancyra and probably Tarsus, in the second century to Ephesus, Pergamum, Smyrna and Tarsus again, Cyzicus and Laodicea, and under the Severi to Ephesus for the third time, Perinthus, Sardis and Mazaca-Caesarea. But there were other grants at unknown dates. We know of provincial cults at Tomi, Philippopolis, Thessalonica, Nicomedia, Amasia, Neocaesarea, Nicopolis, Synnada, Tralles, Anazarbus, Perge, Side, Tripolis and Syrian Laodicea, and cults of some sort at Juliopolis, Hierapolis, Aegae, Neapolis, Teos, Acmonia, Nysa and Abila-Leucas. Besides the festivals at Pergamum and Ephesus, the Hadrianeia were celebrated at Cyzicus and Smyrna, the Commodeia at Tarsus, and the Severeia at Perinthus, Cyzicus, Sardis, Caesarea in Cappadocia and Laodicea in Syria.

The process of apotheosis

The main symbols of apotheosis were the eagle and the wreath (pl. 31.7). We have imaginative representations of apotheosis in sculpture. A relief from Ephesus (now in Vienna) shows Trajan rising to heaven in the chariot of the Sun, leaving Earth behind. A panel in the Capitoline shows the apotheosis of the empress Sabina, in the presence of Hadrian, attended by a winged spirit representing Eternity and bearing the truth of eternal light. The Vatican Apotheosis shows Antoninus and Faustina (pl. 31.3), identified with Jupiter and Juno, swept upwards by a winged spirit with eagles on either side and the goddess Roma and god of the Campus Martius watching. A coin of 176–9 shows the younger Faustina, with a sceptre in her hand and her veil forming a nimbus, translated to heaven on the back of Juno's peacock.

Conclusion

Behind the imperial cult were three major impulses.

For the imperial subjects in the east it was an expected tradition and a spontaneous reaction. After all the Greek gods had not been morally better than men, only more powerful, and the Roman emperor exercised wider power than any human had ever possessed. It is notable that the Greek cities went beyond the measures encouraged by the more moderate rulers, and that Romans in the east were assumed to respond differently.

For the emperor it was a means, an extreme means, of attaching to himself sacrosanctity and an extra dimension of authority. For the more moderate it offered a goal and aspiration; a Tiberius, a Claudius, a Vespasian, really did strive to merit posthumous glory. But it was a dangerous weapon in the hands of those who suffered from an inferiority complex or were in other ways unbalanced.

For the Roman government the object was political. 'The emperor was god,' said Fustel de Coulanges, 'because he was emperor,' and Havet called the apotheosis 'merely one form of the adoration which Rome exacted for herself'. So, by a curious paradox, it was more readily introduced in the newer or more backward provinces of the west, Britain and Germany for instance. Indeed it has been argued with some weight that Vespasian began by combining political resettlement with a provincial cult of the emperor in Narbonensis, Baetica and Africa. Jupiter-Zeus could unite the Romans and Greeks, and the Capitoline temple was prominent enough in north Africa, but he did not ultimately offer a focus of unity. Much later, Aurelian tried to find a unifying symbol in Sol Invictus, but by then it was too late. Roma, an abstraction devised by the Greeks, did not excite the provincials. But Augustus and Roma did, or rather Augustus did in association with Roma, or faintly disguised under his Genius or his *numen*. The emperor was the focus of unity for the Empire, and in a world where religion was simply a dimension permeating the whole of life, this was expressed through ruler cult.

31.1 The apotheosis of Germanicus on a cameo now in the Bibliothèque Nationale, Paris

31.2 The apotheosis of Trajan on the Arch of Trajan, Benevento, dating to AD 115

31.3 The apotheosis of Antoninus Pius and Faustina

31.4 A *sestertius* of Antoninus Pius depicting the temple of Faustina, who died in AD 141

31.5 The apotheosis of Antoninus Pius and Faustina portrayed on an ivory diptych, and dating perhaps to some three centuries after the event

31.6   A statue of Commodus as Hercules, his favourite identity

31.7   Coin of Claudius II: *obv.* DIVO CLAUDIO; *rev.* an eagle and CONSECRATIO

CHAPTER 32

·PROVINCIAL·CULTS·

Miranda J. Green

Introduction

Roman divinities were introduced to their provinces at the time of occupation, were adopted, absorbed and adapted to indigenous taste. Different reactions of native to Roman religious influences may be seen in different areas: in some regions Rome, at least overtly, swamped native religious culture. In others, the indigenous element clearly shows through. One sharp division may be recognized. It is only in the western, Latin-speaking areas that the Roman pantheon was adopted in any real sense. In the hellenized east, Greek divinities were firmly established and it was to them that indigenous divinities remained linked rather than to the later intrusive religion of Rome.

The Danubian and Balkan provinces

Noricum and Dalmatia possess similar evidence for patterns of belief. Official Roman deities are represented in both; both saw an upsurge in the adoption of eastern cults like those of Mithras and Dolichenus, possibly in response to a need for the comfort of personal commitment after a time of political instability in the later second century. A *Dolichenaeum* was erected at Virunum in south Noricum in AD 189; there were *Mithraea* around Arupium and Cavtat (Epidaurum) in Dalmatia in the third century. In both provinces Roman and native divinities were conflated; Minerva Flanatica may be cited, a local goddess of Flanona in Istria, Jupiter Uxellinus and Mars Latobius, who were topographical *genii* of Noricum. Latobius had a shrine near St Margarethen in the Lavant Valley. The Celtic Belenus, identified with Apollo, was popular in Noricum; and we know of Noreia, patroness of the province (pl. 32.3), who had a shrine at Hohenstein. Some native deities did not have Roman equivalents; Sentona of Tarsatica in Dalmatia was an independent goddess.

In Pannonia native deities took shape only within the outward religious framework of Rome and, unlike the main Celtic provinces, the stimulus of Roman traditions of physical representation and epigraphy did not lead to expression of native beliefs. Even local *genii*, like Danuvius (of the Danube) were artificially created by foreigners. Roman cults abound; in the mid-second century statues to the Capitoline Triad were set up in Szombathely (Savaria) and Sopron (Scarbantia) in western Pannonia. Under army influence Mithras and Dolichenus appear in the second century, at Ptuj (Poetovio) and Carnuntum. The Egyptian pantheon was honoured in some towns. Under the prosperity of the Severan Dynasty, there was renewed religious activity; most important seems to have been the cult of Silvanus. He possibly masks a local rural god, and his popularity was as a domestic, personal fertility power, represented by dedications, not shrines, attached to private small-holdings in the Danube frontier-regions. In summary, the main characteristic of Pannonian religion was its lack of synthesis; notwithstanding underlying beliefs, everything was expressed in Roman terms. Moesia paints a similar, somewhat colourless, picture; the only really local god recorded is Andinus who appears once.

One major cult shared by the main Danubian provinces of Pannonia, Moesia and Dacia was that of the Danubian Rider-Gods. Its *floruit* was the third century; it is expressed usually by small marble or lead plaques, and its basic iconography is that of one or two riders trampling a vanquished enemy and accompanied by a goddess (pl. 32.4). A complex mythology and liturgy are implied, suggesting mysteries of initiation, death and rebirth, chthonic and cosmic forces.

Before the conquests of Thrace and Dacia and their division into separate territories, the indigenous religions of modern Romania and Bulgaria were in some respects homogeneous. Both worshipped Bendis, a Mother-Goddess, and Zalmoxis, an underworld deity, who are represented in open shrines, for example at Hunedoara (Sarmizegetusa). The Thracians were horse-lovers and, like the Dacians, expressed this in their religion. In Thrace the main god was a Rider-Hunter; he had no name and on dedications he was simply 'the Hero'. More than 3,000 pre-Roman and Roman reliefs to him survive. He represents the hunting prowess of the horse-owning Thracian aristocracy; indeed, the hunting symbolism is so strong that Roman votive tablets here portray Apollo and Dionysus as horsemen. The Thracian Horseman should never be confused with the Danubian Riders who were a totally separate phenomenon not developed until the late second century.

In Dacia and Thrace Graeco-Roman and Oriental gods had their following. The variety present is exemplified by the Severan hoard of twenty-four sculptures from Constanţa (Tomis) on the Black Sea. In Thrace, the main Graeco-Roman divinities were Dionysus, as Lord of life and vegetation, and the Healers Aesculapius and Apollo.

Asia Minor and Syria

In this culturally Greek area, Greek religion predominated. Though the main construction of the great temple to Artemis at Ephesus was hellenistic, her fame remained undiminished in Roman times, and the cult obviously masks that of a local goddess. Sardis has similar evidence for Artemis. The oracular cults of Apollo at Claros and Didyma were patronized by Roman emperors until at least the third century. Aesculapius was worshipped at Pergamum from the archaic period, but great rebuilding activities took place in the second century AD. Zeus was everywhere adopted; Tyche or Fortune was important as protectress of cities.

Certain cults are especially distinctive. At Xanthus the Sanctuary of Leto, the national deity of Lycia, may be noted; Comba was the centre of a specifically Lycian cult, that of the 'Twelve Gods', represented by a homogeneous group of reliefs. Other Anatolian religions, like those of Cybele and Sabazius, spread to the west, and there became more important than in their homeland.

Although Syria and Arabia possessed a hellenistic tradition, they had also strong indigenous cults which were adopted and conflated both with Greek and later Roman religious concepts. Sun- and sky-gods were particularly important and religion was dominated by various Baals or celestial high gods. At Baalbek, the home of the great Syrian sun-god, Baal was identified first under the Ptolemies with Helios and then with Jupiter; so he is frequently invoked as 'Iuppiter Optimus Maximus Heliopolitanus'. The main sanctuary, begun under Augustus, occupied 2.7 ha (6.7 acres). Baal was associated here with the great Syrian fertility goddess Atargatis, to be discussed below. At Palmyra two major triads may be identified. Bel, a sky-god linked with Jupiter, was associated with the local deities Iarhibol and Aglibol. Baal Shamin, another lord of heaven, was linked with Aglibol and Malakbel. The temples of both Bel and Baal Shamin (pl. 32.5) at Palmyra were especially splendid and most building activity took place during the first two centuries AD. Baal Shamin is depicted sometimes in Roman armour, with sky-symbols, thunderbolt and corn-ears, showing his multifunctional character as god of sky, rain, protection and fertility. At Dura Europos, where Palmyrene troops were present, a temple-fresco displays the cohort's tribune sacrificing to a Palmyrene triad of gods dressed in Roman armour; this can be dated to the earlier third century AD.

Dea Syria (Atargatis) was the patroness of the Syrians. She was essentially a fertility-deity and was associated with Baalbek's sun-god. She was worshipped in the province of Arabia, where the Nabateans called her Allat; indeed the Arabians had a strong and interesting religious tradition of their own. Two sites concern us here, Petra and Khirbet Tannur. At Petra, Allat-Atargatis was associated with the local life-giving natural springs. She was represented in anthropomorphic form associated with lions and leopards, but the Arabian Dusares was generally portrayed in the old Nabatean manner, represented by a block of stone, as in the main shrine at Petra of Kasr-el-Bint, built in late Nabatean times in the late first century BC (pl. 32.1). At Tannur, a hilltop shrine south of Petra, the visible remains are of second century AD date. Here Atargatis is depicted with fertility emblems of pomegranates and grain-stalks, in company with Dusares and a thunder-god Hadad. But here she is associated also with dolphins, perhaps linking her with Aphrodite but possibly symbolic instead of a deity who protected travellers (the dolphin being a fair-weather symbol). It is interesting that Atargatis sometimes appears not with dolphins but as a fish-goddess (possibly a fertility-motif). As such she had a sacred pool at Hierapolis, and Lucian describes her fish-connections and her cult in general.

Egypt and North Africa

In Egypt, under the Ptolemies, Egyptian religion was thoroughly hellenized. In the Greek-settled cities the main Egyptian gods received Greek names: for instance Isis = Aphrodite; Ammon = Zeus. The importance of animal-symbolism decreased; the cult of Serapis, created by Ptolemy I, from the old Osiris/Apis cults, had major sanctuaries at Memphis and Alexandria. In the Roman period Serapis was popular primarily as a saviour-god of healing and fertility, with oracular properties. The Romans did little to alter the essence of Graeco-Egyptian religion, though official dedications, like that to Jupiter Capitolinus at Arsinoe, are known. In theory the emperors were heirs of the pharaohs and Egyptian temple-carvings depict them in the Egyptian iconographical tradition. Official patronage is indicated clearly in upper Egypt, where a series of great Nile temples, begun by the Ptolemies, were completed or embellished during the first two centuries AD. Dendera, dedicated to Hathor, was begun in the second century BC and completed in AD 60. But the great sacral complex of the Nile-island of Philae is of greatest interest for our period. Situated at the beginning of the first Cataract, it is covered with temples and monuments; the main sanctuary, dedicated to Isis and Harpocrates, is Ptolemaic in origin but the presence of Roman involvement from Tiberian times is much in evidence; Trajan, Hadrian and Marcus Aurelius are all depicted in company with Isis and other native gods. Philae was still visited by devotees from the Roman Empire until the fifth century.

In Africa, Roman religion was introduced to a land with a strong indigenous tradition. Of pre-Roman deities the Punic Tanit of Carthage and Baal Hammon were the most prominent. Roman and native gods co-existed to an extent, but phenomena peculiar to Africa may be observed. The numerous urban *capitolia* may be due partly to accidents of preservation; that at Sufetula (Tunisia) is noteworthy in having separate buildings for each of the Capitoline Triad with the largest to Jupiter. But whilst the official Graeco-Roman pantheon was readily accepted by romanized Africans, there is evidence of conflation and overtly classical representations were sometimes merely a veneer for the old Phoenician gods. The bloodthirsty Tanit, who in Carthage demanded the human sacrifice of children burnt alive, survived as Caelestis, frequently identified with Juno. A Severan temple to her survives at Thugga (Tunisia), alongside a Hadrianic complex of shrines to Concordia, Frugifer and Liber. At Thuburbo Maius (Tunisia), Aesculapius was equated with Punic Eshmoun; at Gigthis, Hercules was identified with Punic Melqart. Liber, the African Shadrapa, had a Severan dedicant at Lepcis Magna with a Punic name, Boncarth.

Despite the multiplicity of their gods, to only a few of whom allusion has been made, north Africans appear to have tended towards monotheism, in which one syncretistic cult seems to predominate: that of the high god Baal, identified not with Jupiter but with the obscurer Italian Saturn, presumably because the latter's fertility function as *numen* of sowing made him the appropriate Roman equivalent. Of the numerous sites attesting to the cult, Bou Kournëin (Tunisia) is a typical Baal-Saturn sanctuary; there is no built temple but a *locus consecratus* was situated high up and yielded hundreds of inscribed and sculptured dedications. Epigraphic material dates to the mid-second and early third century; the god is portrayed bearded, with radiate crown, whip and *patera*. At Tiddis near Cirta (Algeria) Baal-Saturn was again worshipped in a high place, at the topmost point in the town. Hippo Regius (Algeria) had a shrine with three *cellae* and, as at Tiddis, the deity was invoked on numerous stones. Lambaesis produced nearly 200 Saturn-stones in the vicinity of a mid-second century shrine to Aesculapius.

Romano-African religion is ambiguous; romanization was thorough, but the popularity of Baal-Saturn indicates that it was not total. Saturn was an ancient Italian god, comparatively rare in the Empire outside Africa, and his appearance here must indicate deliberate choice by the indigenous population to worship their own wholly African deity of heaven and fertility, under the guise of a Roman god.

Spain

It is sometimes assumed that indigenous beliefs (Blázquez, 1977; 1983) were overlain by those of Rome almost to the point of obliteration (Wiseman, 1956, 99ff.). Although this seems frequently, though not always, to have happened in Lusitania and Baetica, in north-west Tarraconensis (Galicia) where the mountain tribes were not finally subjugated until the late first century BC, native cults were preserved and are in evidence epigraphically throughout the Roman period; these will be dealt with more fully below.

Deities of Roman or Oriental origin occur all over Iberia (Vazuez, 1982) especially in the romanized towns. Thus Venus Victrix is found at Merida (Emerita Augusta) in Lusitania; Victory at Santiponce (Italica) in Baetica and Minerva at Coruña (Clunia) in Tarraconensis. Mithras and Cybele were worshipped at Chaves (Aquae Flaviae) and

Emerita, and a woman, Fabia Fabrana, set up a statue to Isis at Guadix in the south.

Jupiter was dominant; about a hundred dedications come from Galicia alone, where many different aspects of his cult may be observed. In the Bracara and Asturica areas official dedications appear in the state-run mining lands, with Jupiter Municipalis invoked at Aquae Flaviae. But, at a personal level, Spaniards equated the Roman sky-god with their own high mountain gods, like Jupiter Candeidus ('brilliant') worshipped by an Asturian. Mars was conflated with local protectors of rural territory. In Spain, unlike Gaul, Mercury was not readily adapted to native cults. In the north-west, the Roman tutelary *numina* were popular, and *lares* are found with local names attached, for example Lar Sefius at Braga (Bracara); it is as if Roman divine protectors of the home were considered suitable for adaptation to local, domestic worship.

In Galicia, where recent detailed studies have been made, the most interesting results lie in the discovery of numerous gods with local, native names, not linked with Roman gods and pre-dating the occupation. Of these some were popular and presided over several localities; others appear only once or twice and were tied, like many Celtic gods of Gaul and Britain, to specific places. The Celtic origin of the devotees may be inferred from many of the names. Thus, the Suleae Nantugiacae ('nantu' is Celtic, referring to water) at Condado were invoked by a local, Flavinus; the Suleviae were Celtic mother-goddesses known in Britain and Gaul and associated, at Bath, with a therapeutic spring sanctuary. Bormanicus, at Caldas de Vizela, was also a spring-deity, turning up as Bormanus and Bormana in Gaul. The importance of water-gods in the mountains of northern Spain is likewise indicated by the presence of *genii loci* occurring perhaps no more than once under a given name. Tameobrigus was honoured at the confluence of the rivers Douro and Támega.

Evidence for the dominance of several native divinities is provided by multiple dedications in given regions within Tarraconensis. Around Bracara Augusta, Bandua, Nabia and Laraucus were popular local powers. Laraucus had a small shrine at the foot of a high mountain near the modern village of Perdizes; two altars, dedicated to Laraucus and Jupiter respectively, suggest identification of a local mountain god with the Roman sky-father. Native cults, like that of the Lusitanian underworld god Endovellicus, are sometimes found outside the north-west.

In Spain, as one might expect, it is in the remote areas that native deities are dominant (Blázquez, 1983), on mountains, on the sites of rivers and springs, in small shrines or worshipped at home, and this is echoed in Gaul and Britain. While towns and mining regions received the full impact of Roman religion, in some country districts only the presence of epigraphy and the use of Roman lettering betray the existence of intrusive influence.

Gaul, Britain and Germany

Here Roman religious traditions were superimposed on peoples whose cults, like those of Spain, were largely aniconic and anonymous. There is evidence of Classical and Oriental cults entirely free from Celticism. Several Provençal towns, like Nîmes and Arles, knew Cybele and Isis; Serapis was worshipped in the Lower Rhône Valley; Mithras and Dolichenus occur at Tournes and Marseille respectively (Clébert, 1979, 256–62). Further north, Cybele was established in Lyon by AD 160. Mithraism was important in the Rhineland, Koenigshoffen being just one of the known *Mithraea*. In Britain, London was the main centre for eastern cults in the south; Mithras was the most prominent, but Serapis, Isis and Cybele all had followers (Harris and Harris, 1965; Green, 1983, 17ff.). The frontier-zone of Hadrian's Wall too has rich evidence for Mithras, with Dolichenus also attested.

Roman religion flourished particularly in the major cities of Gaul and Britain. Each urban centre would have had a *capitolium*. Jupiter Optimus Maximus was prominent on Hadrian's Wall, and such sites as Birdoswald and Maryport in Cumbria have each yielded more than twenty altars affirming the continued fealty of the troops. Mercury, Mars and the other major Roman deities are well-represented iconographically and epigraphically (Green, 1976, 10–36; 1983).

Caesar lists various deities encountered in Gaul in order of popularity – Mercury, Apollo, Mars, Jupiter and Minerva (*de Bello Gallico* VI, 17). He writes as though the gods were Roman, but all the divinities on Caesar's list underwent celticization to some degree (Thévenot, 1968). Thus Jupiter was identified both with a Celtic Thunderer Taranis, attested from Chester to the Rhineland, and with a Celtic solar god whose emblem was a wheel. Mercury's popularity, alluded to by Caesar, is endorsed by a wealth of archaeological evidence, but he is often linked with local Celtic spirits, like Mercury Dumias at Puy de Dôme and Arvernus among the Arverni. Other non-Roman features include Mercury's depiction as an old man at Lezoux, triple-headed among the Remi, and with a Celtic consort, Rosmerta, in Gaul and western Britain. Mars too had Celtic names attached, implying his identification with local protectors, as with Vesontius at Besançon. Mars was called Lenus, a healer, at Trier and Caerwent. In Britain, Minerva was conflated with a local healer, Sulis, who presided over the great sanctuary at Bath. Apollo's greatest Gaulish role was also healing, and associated with spa-shrines, as at Aix-la-Chapelle and in the Vosges where he was called Grannus. But in the Nettleton (Wiltshire) temple Apollo was a hound-lord 'Cunomaglus'.

Cults which are totally alien to the classical world are present, the only intrusive influence being physical representation and endowment with names (Green, 1986). Triplism was important, and the potency of 'three' is illustrated by the triplication of several deities including the Matres and Genii Cucullati (pl. 32.6), the hooded *numina* of prosperity. The Deae Matres were worshipped widely; they are portrayed side by side with loaves, fruit or children, as at Bonn and Cirencester. A local mother, Nehalennia, whose emblem was a dog, was invoked in Holland; Epona was a fertility goddess associated with horses; Sucellus was a hammer-god, and his name means 'the Good Striker'. Deities like these were popular and known over wide areas. Others, like Sequana of the Seine and Abandinus at Godmanchester, Cambridgeshire, were tied to specific localities.

The importance of animal-symbolism is striking; Epona and Nehalennia show this. But sometimes the theriomorphic element is stronger, and anthropomorphic gods sprout horns. The Brigantes of north Britain favoured horned divinities. In Gaul Cernunnos ('Horned One') is associated with stags and himself bears antlers. Bulls, boars, horses and birds are abundant in iconography. Composite, monstrous animals occur also; the triple-horned bull and ram-horned serpent represent the Celtic habit of enhancing symbolism by addition and multiplication (Green, 1977). Animals, like most divine forms of Celtic origin, reflect the religious emphases of a rural people whose livelihood depended on fertility of crops and the reproductive capacity of beasts, both wild or domestic.

32.1 The temple Kasr-el-Bint at Petra: the shrine of the Nabatean deity Dusares

32.2 Early fourth-century relief of the Genius or Spirit of Salona

32.3 Statue of Isis Noreia from Virunum

32.4 A lead plaque from Romula depicting the Danubian rider deity in duplicate

32.5   The temple of Baal Shamin at Palmyra

32.6   Relief of *Genii Cucullati* from Cirencester

CHAPTER 33

·THE·RISE·OF·
·CHRISTIANITY·

Jill Harries

The first five centuries of Christianity pose problems both of history and historiography. For Christian historians prospering under the fourth century Christian Empire, the workings of providence were far from inscrutable. The growth of Christianity from the time of the birth of Christ into a world united by Augustus so that the new religion could spread, to the conversion of Constantine in 312 was, for them, pre-ordained. It was also a demonstration of the power of God over the multifarious gods of the pagans in a world in which power, *potentia*, was to be found in many forms, and Christian writers were quick to combine explanations of the divine will with attacks on pagan interpretations of the past. Orosius, for example, in his *History against the Pagans*, written in 417, argued that the world was far worse off before the birth of Christ, under pagan gods, than it had been since. This polemical or apologetic purpose of Christian historiography inevitably coloured interpretations of the Christian past.

Nor were Christian historians exempt from the characteristics of the time when they wrote. The 'avenging sword' of imperial legislation which punished evil-doers had its Christian counterpart in an avenging God. For the writer of the treatise *On the Deaths of the Persecutors*, Lactantius, the grim fates that befell most members of the Diocletianic Tetrarchy were appropriate ends for persecutors of Christians; the gory and disgusting details of the death of the arch-persecutor Galerius in 311 underline what enemies of Christianity could expect. True, Christians themselves differed over how far they should employ or adapt themselves to the classical literary conventions prevalent in the world at large: Cyprian of Carthage in the 250s took a more purist line than did Tertullian fifty years before, or Lactantius fifty years later; Jerome agonized over the imputation that he was more a Ciceronian than a Christian. In practice, however, lettered Christians after Constantine could not escape contemporary literary usages, although they were modified, sometimes brilliantly, as by the great Spanish Christian poet Prudentius, to

Christian ends. Thus it became possible to turn the pagans' own weapons against themselves. When in 384 Symmachus, the pagan senator, based part of his argument for the restoration of the Altar of Victory to the Senate-house on the early history of Rome – 'these sacred objects drove Hannibal from our walls, the Gauls from the Capitol' – Ambrose of Milan, in his counterblast to the emperor, used the identical *exempla* to prove the opposite. This cultural and religious milieu common to Symmachus and Ambrose governed their approach both to the literary 'conflict' between Roman paganism and Christianity and to their shared history.

By the time of Ambrose, Christians had already evolved their own form of 'church history', a genre of which the founder was Eusebius, bishop of Caesarea. Few researchers were more painstaking than he who, in the late third century, bravely embarked on establishing a chronology for early Christian history in his *Chronicon*. From this followed his *Church History*, which broke new ground both in subject-matter and in its incorporation of original documents unearthed in archives from Alexandria to Edessa. But, pioneer though he was, Eusebius' interpretation of his material was based on several misconceptions. He believed that from the beginning Christianity was prosperous and respectable; hence he accepted uncritically the story that Christianity had found favour with Tiberius (II.2) and, although aware of the problem of forgery, incorporated as authentic the apocryphal personal correspondence between Christ and Abgar, King of Edessa (I.13). His preconceptions about imperial policy affected his chronology (Barnes, 1981, 140ff.); and he viewed heresies as diabolical infiltrations of the Christian body from outside. Most important, Eusebius failed to signal the landmarks or the turning-points in the development of Christianity and his history therefore serves as a quarry for facts rather than as a guide. The modern historian, who seeks to analyse Christianity in the context of Roman imperial society (Judge, 1979), may resort to unevenly distributed earlier sources, but has still a long way to go before a connected narrative of the rise of the Christian Church in Roman society becomes possible.

In the reign of Tiberius, a Jew called Jesus was crucified by the Roman authorities outside the remote and troubled provincial city of Jerusalem. No official, non-Christian, source recorded the event but, by the end of the century, four separate accounts of his teaching, miracles, death and resurrection had come into being, an exceptional number of '*Lives*' for a single teacher. The fact that the founder of Christianity was an historical personage at once distinguished that religion from the host of others that jostled for the allegiance of the subjects of the Roman Empire: unlike the myths on which most mystery cults relied, the story of Christ had really happened.

From the small group of witnesses of Jesus' life and death in Jerusalem and Galilee, the news that the promised Messiah had come was spread to Jews of the Diaspora in other cities of the Empire along routes used by traders and pilgrims. For Peter and James, the leaders in Jerusalem, the main task was to preach the risen Christ to Jews subject to the rigorous demands of the Jewish Law, and many early Christian communities took root among Jewish minority groups in cities and were doubly suspect, both to fellow-Jews as members of an heretical splinter group and to society at large as part of an alien minority. However, the spread of Christianity by these means was rapid: the Christian community in Rome, for example, existed before Peter or Paul ever set foot there. Later Christians, detecting the Divine Purpose in the unifying of the Roman world under Augustus to coincide with the birth of Christ, acknowledged that a common political order, two common languages, Greek and Latin, and easy communications had facilitated the spread of the world-religion. And that religion also spread eastwards to the Euphrates and the colourful mixed communities in the border zone between the Persian and Roman empires: Damascus itself, to which Paul set out to restore a Christian group to the orthodox Jewish fold, lay on the trade route from Jerusalem to the Euphrates.

The background of Paul of Tarsus, an orthodox Jew and Roman citizen, born in a Greek city famous for philosophy and education, equipped him in language and thought as the 'apostle to the Gentiles'. Whether Christianity would have remained as Peter and James envisaged it, a Jewish splinter group, if Paul had not experienced what he did on the road to Damascus cannot be known. As it was, his missionary journeys through Galatia and Asia, Macedonia and Greece resulted in the founding of new churches (*ecclesiae*) strong enough to hold their own when Paul moved on, although occasionally liable, as Paul's letters to the church at Corinth show, to spiritual pride, misunderstanding and schism. The Pauline letters reveal the practical difficulties of setting up a unified organization at a time when there was no recognized central authority, problems which continued to affect the early churches. At the same time, the letters show the development of Paul's ideas, the rejection of the way of the Law for that of faith, the fulfilment of the prophecies of the Old Testament in the coming of Christ, all expressed in the language of the Septuagint to a non-Jewish as well as to a Jewish audience. More than any other individual, Paul gave to the early Church the beginnings both of its organization and its theology.

In the early decades of Christianity, little thought was given to the morrow: the end of the world was too imminent to allow for long-term future planning. But as time went by and the apocalypse failed to materialize, the need for a durable cultic organization grew more apparent. Given the haphazard nature of the spread of Christianity, it is not surprising that initially organization seems to have varied from city to city, consisting of groups either with a single head or a committee of elders: these two main types probably co-existed for a time before episcopal rule by a single head or 'overseer' (*episcopus*) came to prevail. The letters of Ignatius of Antioch, written on his way to martyrdom in *c.* 115, laid emphasis on the respect due to clergy, and especially bishops, and may have accelerated the trend. The prominence of the bishop may also have arisen from the nature of early cultic organization, although little, as yet, is known of this. The material wants of early Christians were few but the emphasis on charity, initially financed by offerings (*oblationes*) in a liturgical context, and the need for house-churches large enough to be viable meeting-places may have supplied opportunities for patronage for wealthier Christians, as was the case with some pagan cults. Such patrons may even have become bishops and then kept the office in the family; episcopal dynasties are attested in early Christianity, becoming more prominent later.

The early churches were tiny scattered enclaves, inviting by their enthusiasm and their physical distance from each other the dangers of disunity and schism. These were partly avoided by the rise of regional leading churches, Jerusalem, Antioch and Ephesus in the first century, later joined by Rome and Alexandria, which foreshadowed the great ecclesiastical metropolitans of the fourth and later centuries. Their hegemony was probably of a loose and informal nature to start with and, even in the third century, the primacy of Lyon in Gaul seems to have rested on a similarly vague foundation and failed to last into the fourth century. Inevitably, inter-city church organization became more formal and, by the fourth century, its provincial structure reassuringly mirrored that of the secular Empire, with the provincial metropolitan bishop being based, as a rule, in the secular provincial capital. This association of metropolitan bishop with provincial capital simplified matters but did not allow either for the occasional provincial reorganization or for fluctuations in the fortunes of some cities: the rises of the new holy city of Jerusalem and of the new imperial capital of Constantinople after Constantine and the struggles of their bishops for recognition and supremacy are cases in point.

Heresies were the most obvious threat to the precarious unity of the infant churches. It is easily forgotten that, in the absence of any agreed central authority for the defining of doctrine, 'heresies' often originated from the need of Christians to define and explain their beliefs to themselves and others, to take account of contemporary forms of Gnosticism, or to respond to St Paul's own acceptance of the value of the prophetic gift. The emphasis of the Apostolic Age on prophecy with its apocalyptic overtones had obvious drawbacks as the prospect of the millennium receded: individual inspiration, if unchecked, would destroy the core of belief essential to the unity of the world-religion. Hence the self-appointed spokesmen of the early Church outlawed the prophetical extravagances and personal vision of the Phrygian Montanus and his starry-eyed lady followers; attempts to redefine the nature of Christ as God or man, or to deny that the God of the Law and the Prophets was the father of Christ were likewise adjudged beyond the pale. The authority with later generations, who preserved them, of such works as the *Against Heresies* of Irenaeus of Lyon, written in Greek in the late second century, can obscure the fact that, at the time, the differences between heresy and orthodoxy were not clear-cut. In Carthage in the early third century, the abrasive and eloquent Tertullian espoused Montanist beliefs and turned against his local church organization, yet his works achieved a wide Christian readership. Even in the more structured world of the early fifth century, another African, Augustine, had difficulty in convincing contemporaries that the doctrines of Pelagius, which argued that salvation was possible through the human will, thus excluding the action of divine grace, should be classed as heretical.

Thus the spread of the early Church went wide, especially in the east, but not deep. Threatened as they were with fragmentation from within, the Christian communities had also to contend with hostility and persecution from outside. Within Judaea itself, the Christians of Jerusalem might have been tolerated at the outset, but for public attacks made by such hotheads as the deacon Stephen on the Jewish Law and the opposition of generations of Jews, as he claimed, to the workings of the Holy Spirit. The first to suffer for his faith, Stephen's status as the 'first martyr' was not fully exploited before the miraculous discovery of his relics at Caphar-Gamala in 415 and their subsequent dissemination over much of the Mediterranean world. In respect of cult, his recognition was somewhat belated compared with that accorded Peter and Paul, who as martyrs and as joint apostolic founders of the Roman Church, were in the fourth century accorded a status analogous to that of Romulus and Remus.

Legend ascribed the deaths of Peter and Paul to the first imperial persecution of Christians, initiated by Nero in and after AD 64. Christians were already perhaps associated in the minds of the authorities with civil disturbances among the Jews and Nero, with his fanciful interest in eastern affairs, may have perceived the Christians as socially subversive religious dissidents, unsanctioned either by antiquity or by their own people. In his need to find scapegoats for the Great Fire of Rome, Nero turned on the Christians in Rome and subjected them to such spectacular cruelty – some were made into human torches in the public gardens – that popular dislike for them was converted into sympathy. But Nero, however eccentric personally, was emperor and his actions could be deemed to have the force of law: thus his persecution of Christians could have set a legal precedent for future emperors.

Christianity, along with Druidism (which had Celtic nationalist implications), stands out as the only persecuted religion in the otherwise tolerant Roman Empire. The legal ground, apart from the Neronian precedent, has been much debated (Ste Croix, 1963 and 1964) but both the Christian apologists and the famous exchange of letters between Pliny as governor of Bithynia and Trajan (Pliny, *Letters* X, 96 and 97) confirm the centrality of the 'name of Christian' (*nomen Christianum*) to any accusation or conviction for adherence to the sect. Pliny informed his emperor that he had investigated allegations of *flagitia* (disgraceful practices) levelled at Christians but had found nothing; willingness to sacrifice and curse Christ was accepted as proof of 'innocence', that is non-adherence to the *nomen*. Moreover, as Trajan reminded Pliny, Christians were not to be hunted out: in other words, they did not fall into the category of dangerous criminals whom it was a governor's duty to pursue. Conversely, stiff-necked would-be martyrs on trial before often bemused governors would assert the *nomen* as their own, 'I am (a) Christian'. Indeed such court records as that of the trial of a Christian group in the small African town of Scillium in 180 (Musurillo, 1972, 86–9) make Pliny's confusion understandable: however well-intentioned the governor, communication between him and the defendants was virtually impossible.

The constancy and suffering of martyrs was exploited to encourage the survivors. The celebration of martyr cults began in a small way in the second century and accounts of martyrdoms were lovingly preserved. The tone was set by the letters of Ignatius of Antioch, described by Streeter (1930, 165) as 'a man of abnormal psychology', with their ecstatic anticipation of martyrdom in the arena at Rome. 'I am ground by the teeth of wild beasts that I may be proved true bread of Christ,' he wrote, evoking the ideas associated with the central secret rite of full Christians, the Eucharist. Open letters between churches recorded the persecution at Smyrna in the mid-150s, where the mob howled for the blood of the aged bishop Polycarp, and of the daughter-churches of Smyrna at Lyon and Vienne in *c.* 177 (Eusebius, *Church History*, V.1–2). As at Scillium, the most effective testimony of faith might be that offered in the course of interrogation: the confrontation between future martyr and judge or governor could provide considerable scope for drama and rhetoric, the more elaborate as the realities of persecution receded in the generations after Constantine. But the most striking document to survive from a period of persecution is the record of the experiences of a Carthaginian woman catechumen in 203, who became a mother in prison and whose dreams, as recorded in the *Passion of Perpetua*, have the ring of psychological truth. Such descriptions served to stiffen the resolve of Christians but were also an expression of a more general feeling among Christians of piety towards their dead, which was also shown in gatherings in graveyards commented on unfavourably and distorted by pagan contemporaries. Martyrs were not yet the foci of spiritual power and heavenly patronage that they were to become in the fourth century but the early concern shown for preserving the relics of the dead – the Lyon martyrs were cast into the Rhône to prevent this – provided the foundation for later developments.

Faced with this bulk of laudatory evidence, it is hard to realize that many Christian communities in cities in the second century may have been preserved from persecution simply by their obscurity. The casual attitude of the Pergamene physician Galen (born in 130), who may have been hazy as to the differences between Jews and Christians, may be typical of pagan indifference in general. For Galen, Moses was interesting because he had something to say, with which Galen disagreed, on the function of the divine in connection with the question of why hair grows and needs to be cut, while eyelashes do not. On Christians specifically Galen commented in passing that their pursuit of justice was in no way inferior to that of 'true' philosophers, a somewhat backhanded compliment which hardly implies profound knowledge of, or interest in, Christianity. The fact was that the average Pergamene would have been more interested in the great local shrine of Asclepius, a centre for pilgrimage which formed the base for a flourishing tourist industry, than in a fringe group. Yet such indifference need not have entailed hostility and the Pergamene protests recorded at the martyrdoms of their fellow-citizens Carpus, Papylus and Agathonice may well have been genuine.

Thus many Christian groups survived unmolested, protected by their obscurity and pagan tolerance, as a rule, of religious eccentricity. But at times of disaster or unrest, Christians were an obvious scapegoat. Popular prejudice, which was combated strenuously by the apologists, ascribed to Christians the practice of incest and cannibalism, accusations based respectively on misunderstandings of Christian brotherly love and of the eating of the 'body of Christ' in the Eucharist. Moreover, and perhaps worse, the Christian religion excluded the worship of other gods and this could be interpreted as 'atheism', which the offended gods were liable to punish by visiting their wrath on the whole community. At such times informers grew more active, the city mob was roused and the governor, as at Smyrna and Lyon, was obliged to take action. But such outbreaks were not imperially initiated and the emperor was involved only in that he might be appealed to if the fates of Roman citizens were at stake.

Despite Christian praises of martyrs and the inspiration for conversion they may have supplied, persecution was not welcomed by Christians in general. The aim of apologists for Christianity was to explain Christian belief and practice and, insofar as they were read by non-Christians, to break down the misunderstandings which threatened Christians. The growing wish on the part of some Christians to make themselves intelligible and acceptable to contemporary intellectuals can be shown both in individual cases, like that of Tertullian who couched his message in the language of the Second Sophistic (Barnes, 1971), and in broader developments, such as the founding of a school of Christian learning in Alexandria by Pantaenus in 180, that was to nurse the talents of Clement of Alexandria and Origen. Such men as Tertullian both celebrated martyrs and, through their explanations of Christianity, sought to undermine the hostility that was one cause of persecution. The same complex of attitudes can be found in Eusebius who, while a devotee of martyrs, nevertheless saw the Great Persecution as an evil, ascribing it to the anger of God at his lax and quarrelsome Church, and accepted that a bishop's duty to keep his congregation together at a time of crisis might be more important than ensuring his personal place in heaven through martyrdom. One of Eusebius' heroes, Dionysius of Alexandria, was, in the mid-third century, kidnapped by friends concerned for his safety and stranded in a desert until the danger was past, while Cyprian of Carthage in 251 withdrew from the city to avoid arrest, although six years later, under Valerian, he chose to stay and suffer for his faith.

The Decian persecution of 250–1 was the first imperially-initiated attack on Christians on an empire-wide basis. It stemmed from an edict which compelled all subjects of the Empire to sacrifice to the traditional gods of Rome and was clearly an attempt to regain the favour of the gods for the troubled Empire. Only when it became apparent that Christians would not do so (and might therefore offend the gods) were they singled out for special treatment. Decius himself died in battle in 251 but persecution was renewed under Valerian in the late 250s and continued sporadically thereafter.

It was ironic that emperors intervened precisely at the point when Christianity had become socially acceptable in many cities. By the late third century, public churches, like the one at Nicomedia opposite the imperial palace, were taking the place of house-churches and the charity of some Christian communities was extensive and munificent, as at Rome, where widows and other recipients of charity numbered fifteen hundred. While Christian organizations remained, it seems, comparatively unaffected by the social and economic difficulties of the third century, which may have dried up the sources of support for some publicly-financed pagan cults (Geffcken, 1978, 25–30), their leaders were also poised to play a part in the intellectual, philosophical flowering of the time. That they were by now treated seriously is demonstrated by the famous attack of Plotinus' pupil Porphyry on the Christians; his arguments were to be reused by the emperor Julian in his own assault on the 'Galilaeans'. Persecution of Christians may now have required the intellectual justification that it was given by the publications of some Diocletianic philosophers (Barnes, 1981).

Persecution culminated with the edicts of Diocletian and Galerius against Christians in February 303: churches were to be destroyed, the scriptures banned and known Christians were to lose office, if they held it, and be imprisoned; a further edict stated that Church officials were to be put in prison and made to sacrifice (Eusebius, *Church History* VIII.2; Lactantius, *On the Deaths of the Persecutors* 12). The approach was similar to that of previous emperors: those who sacrificed were to be let off but the Christian group identity was to be destroyed by the loss of meeting-places, sacred books and community leaders. The fact that the Bible could be looked down upon because of its unconventional style did not alter its importance as a mainstay of Christian belief in the eyes of persecutors and persecuted alike.

Although the persecution proved unworkable because of the sheer numbers of clergy, who filled the prisons and left no room for real criminals, it was still terrifying to its victims at the time and many simple souls, confronted with the harsh apparatus of a police state, would have succumbed (Dix, 1945, 24–6). Just as in the 250s Cyprian and others had confronted the problem of those who had lapsed through fear and later begged readmittance, recommending leniency, so too in the sequel to the Diocletianic persecutions Christians had to decide on the fate of the lapsed and of those who had handed over (*traditores*) sacred books to search parties of soldiers. At Rome in the 250s, leniency had sparked off the Novatian schism, when followers of Novatus refused to accept repentance as a reason to be readmitted. Similarly in Africa in the early years of Constantine the Donatists refused to recognize the consecration of a bishop of Carthage, in which an alleged *traditor* was one of the consecrating bishops, and proved so successful in establishing themselves as a 'Church of the Martyrs' that they formed virtually an alternative Church in Africa throughout the fourth century and required stern measures, spearheaded by Augustine of Hippo, to put them down (Frend, 1952; Brown, 1967, 330–5).

Historians from the time of Constantine onwards have seen the conversion of that emperor as inaugurating a new era for Christianity. Given that imperial edicts, however unenforceable they may sometimes have been, nevertheless had considerable social implications, and that an emperor's religion might well become that of many of his followers for reasons of convenience, Constantine's adherence to the new faith is rightly regarded as a watershed, but the break with the past can be exaggerated. As we have seen, the growth in the wealth of some churches, like that at Rome, the increased social and intellectual importance of Christianity and the growth of Christian willingness to communicate with pagans in their own terms predated the conversion of Constantine. Lavish imperial and senatorial donations under Constantine and his successors rapidly increased the assets and thus the social and economic importance of churches in the cities of the Empire but the charitable (and building) purposes for which Church funds were administered and held 'in trust' by the bishops and clergy remained unaltered. And just as Tertullian or Origen had employed the language and thought of the contemporary world to explain their case and refute their opponents, so aristocratic Christian literati of the fourth and fifth centuries justified themselves and sought to convert pagan friends through cultivated citations of, and allusions to, Cicero, Vergil, Horace or other classical authors: despite qualms of conscience that afflicted such purists as Jerome or the ascetic Gallic senator-turned-priest Paulinus of Nola, most Christians felt they communicated most effectively through the medium of the literary exercises fashionable at the time. Thus although imperial and aristocratic patronage was to change the face of Christianity, its evolution progressed on lines already established before 312.

The effect of imperial legislation in isolation on paganism is hard to assess, because of the varying social contexts in which it was, or was not, implemented. Certainly, repeated legislation by the successors of Constantine gradually ate away at the social and financial supports of the public pagan cults, but some laws may have been more bombastic than effective. In 341, for example, Constantius II declared, 'Let superstition cease. Let the madness of sacrifice be rooted out'; yet in Rome itself in 359, the prefect of the City, Tertullus, publicly sacrificed to Castor and Pollux for the safe arrival of the grain ships. For the followers of *all* religions, the indispensable feature of state offerings to the tutelary deity was that they were publicly subsidized; hence Constantine's insistence that the clergy should not be distracted from their full-time duty, which was to conduct divine service for the good of the state. This belief underlies the efforts of the pagan senator Symmachus in the 380s to have the Altar of Victory, removed by Gratian in 382, restored to the Senate-house and to have pagan cults publicly subsidized. Symmachus and his like-minded friends could well afford to make sacrifices on their own account but no one, however rich, was empowered to offer on behalf of the state from his own resources, the use of which could guarantee only his individual welfare. The edicts of Theodosius I against paganism in the early 390s (*Theodosian Code*, XVI.10.10 and 10.12), a short-lived usurpation in the west (392–4) characterized by a very limited pagan revival (O'Donnell, 1978) and the final removal of subsidies by Theodosius spelled the end for state paganism. With the state cults departed the protection of the state gods and thus, wrote the pagan Byzantine historian Zosimus, 'the Roman Empire gradually declined and became the home of barbarians' (*New History*, IV.59.3).

But legislation, as the expression of an emperor's standpoint, had social repercussions which partly depended on pre-existing conditions. The accession of the pagan Julian in 361 immediately sparked off riots in Alexandria, where the controversial bishop George was lynched: but it was the peculiar combination of the Arian controversy, long-standing racial disharmony, and the provocative utterances of the bishop against pagans in Alexandria itself which led to his destruction (in which Christians opposed to him may also have joined). Likewise the strongly pro-Christian attitudes and legislation of Theodosius I and his western colleagues coincided with widespread destruction of pagan shrines, such as those engaged in by the monk-bishop Martin of Tours in the Gallic countryside. Thus the emperor's will became a factor in local affairs, lending strength to one side or the other in pre-existing internecine struggles between Christian and traditional pagan groups, which occasionally erupted into violence against temples, often the objects of anti-pagan legislation, or, from the other side, against bishops as the main foci of Christian power and authority.

In the cities of the Empire, and in the imperial consistory, the pagan-Christian conflict was a reality, expressed through direct physical action and the making of laws. In the field of literature, however, it has a shadowy and one-sided quality. Attacks were made on the morality of the old Olympian gods through stories that few pagans now took literally and arguments were adduced from Tertullian and other long-dead Church fathers; but these modes of expression, to us unconvincing, were the product of the traditionalism of methods of argument among the cultured of the Roman world. More significant for the relationship of literature with reality is that a number of polemics against pagans were associated with events in the wider world: the unpleasant little pamphlet, *A Poem against the Pagans* with perhaps the death of the great pagan senator Praetextatus in 384; or Prudentius' *Against Symmachus* with the Roman victory over the Goths at Pollentia in northern Italy in 402. On a vastly different level, Augustine's monumental *City of God* grew out of his thoughts on the Fall of Rome in 410 and conclusively dissociated the assertion of the power of God from the survival of the ephemeral Empire. For thinkers like Augustine, Providence and the place of God in history were central Christian preoccupations; but they also derived from Christian interpretations of the contractual relationship of god with man which was basic to ancient religious experience. The bargain on both sides must be seen to be kept.

For in fact, despite Christian assertions to the contrary, pagan and Christian beliefs were, throughout antiquity, rooted in the same religious soil. Monotheism, for example, was not unique to Christians; the soldier Ammianus, who had little time for certain types of philosopher, casually accepted that human affairs were governed by a 'divine power' (*numen*) and that the decrees of fate were inescapable; among more sophisticated thinkers, too, general assumptions were made as to the existence of a supreme deity, who stood at the head of a variety of philosophically invented divine hierarchies, and had features in common with the figure of the emperor, who was progressively and publicly raised through display and ceremonial above the heads of his Roman subjects. Among philosophers, Christianity battled with, and took over, many features of Neo-Platonism: the conversion of the Neo-Platonist Marius Victorinus in the late fourth century and to some extent of Augustine, was a natural outcome of the merging of the two worlds. Such men, pagan and Christian, who were prepared to adapt their message in order to explain it, contrast with the uncompromising Julian, whose edicts as emperor undermining Christianity and promoting his idiosyncratic Hellenic form of philosophical paganism were not favourably received: even his ardent supporter Ammianus disapproved of Julian's edict forbidding Christian teachers to teach the pagan classics. Moreover, Ammianus was obviously worried by the last pagan emperor's addiction to the theurgic rites and beliefs espoused by the 'magician' Maximus of Ephesus and saw the failure of Julian's Persian expedition as bound up with his ignoring of divination and omens of a traditional kind and excessive devotion to 'philosophers'.

Christians therefore both adapted themselves to current religious usages and challenged them. Mystery cults, with their obvious similarities to Christianity, were an embarrassment and in the 340s the convert Firmicus Maternus proclaimed that the ritual aspects of mystery cults were a diabolical parody of the true faith. In the streets of the cities of the Empire, the processions of Isis, featured in Apuleius, and other pagan gods (MacMullen, 1981) were gradually replaced by the liturgical progresses of bishops and the remains of saints (although Isis was still publicly celebrated in Italy in the early fifth century); and pagan pilgrimages to such sites as the Asclepeium at Pergamon were superseded by the new tourist attractions of the holy sites in Jerusalem and Judaea associated with the life of Christ and promoted by Constantine and his mother Helena (Hunt, 1982a). Finally, Christianity was in tune with the prevailing moral tone of the fourth century, austere, even self-righteous, virtuous and grandiloquent, the language alike of Christian apologetic and of imperial legislation. Moral uprightness was common to virtuous pagan and Christian alike: the epitaph of the pagan *senatrix*, Fabia Aconia Paulina, 'nurse of modesty, bond of chastity . . . gift of the gods who bind our marriage couch with friendly and modest ties', could almost be that of any Christian matron.

Thus the strength of Christianity in the fourth century lay in its ability to harness the diverse trends of society to the service of the universal religion. In so doing it inevitably was affected by contemporary language and ideas of a non-Christian, and even a non-religious, kind. Imperial patronage was acknowledged in fulsome panegyric in the language of the time, sometimes, it is thought (Kee, 1981), to the detriment of Christian integrity. The splendour and power of God were envisaged in the visual and literary terms associated with the emperor, his court and the senate on earth; thus martyrs were adlected into the 'heavenly senate' and Christ was depicted enthroned with his apostles in the manner of Roman court painting. On a less obvious level, benefits similar to those achieved by cities through the physical presence (*praesentia*) of emperors were also ascribed to the *praesentia* of saints (Brown, 1981). Likewise, the acts of public patronage and munificence by the rich which had sustained the workings of society for centuries, retained their old lavish splendour, albeit in Christian guise; in 396, the wealthy senator Pammachius distributed food to the poor in St Peter's in the traditional manner of scattering largess to the masses. Pammachius was one of several senators to make a much publicized renunciation of worldly wealth and status – with the assurance of continued 'noble' and 'senatorial' standing in the hereafter.

Language and visual display were only the superficial signs of the means by which the Church was not only adapting to society but was also coming to perform important social functions – although such display was a necessary concomitant of real power in late Roman society. As patrons of their congregations, bishops could be more power-ful in their cities than many a secular magnate, not only through their control of church finance but also through the network of episcopal connections open to every bishop and many a prominent cleric to exploit. The letters of Augustine, Ambrose, Paulinus of Nola and Synesius of Cyrene, to name but a few, repeatedly document the workings of patronage, the rendering and receiving of favours for clients often employed as post-men, and the genteel arm-twisting that transcended provincial and religious barriers. In the episcopal courts first recognized by Constantine, the jurisdiction of the bishop was independent of the state, faster (some secular cases could take more than thirty years) and far less expensive. Enlightened bishops saw their role in terms of reconcili-ation rather than judgment and were resorted to as righters of wrongs rather than as pursuers of the guilty. In an age of brutal punishments, in which torture and burnings alive were commonplace, the Christian method of justice offered a humane and welcome alternative.

As always, social influence was linked to and backed by economic power. The enormous wealth of the Roman Church, already well off in the third century, dated from the donations of Constantine and as late as the sixth century was administered on traditional secular lines, with *conductores* in charge of the organization of ecclesiastical lands and the collection of revenue. To fourth-century pagans, the wealth of the Roman Church was notorious: Praetextatus, whose unpopularity with such Christians as Jerome may have stemmed from his refusal to take them seriously, once joked, 'Make me Bishop of Rome, and I'll become a Christian right away.' Naturally, provincial churches also benefited from pious donations, most welcome when in the form of antiquity's best investment, land. However, the haphazard nature of such gifts must have created inequalities of wealth between the churches of different cities. Certainly some bishops perceiving the chance of a donation may have brought discreet pressure to bear on a possible benefactor: the comment of a fifth-century Gallic bishop to the donor of

an estate to the Church, that God had rewarded him for his kindness by allowing him
to inherit a larger one, shows the confusion of values that could result, as well as the
bishop's ability to recommend piety in practical terms. For, like their secular land-
owning counterparts, bishops, while devoting much of their revenues to obligatory
charitable work, nevertheless ran their affairs on hard-headed and, by ancient standards,
commercial lines. In a year of famine in the 470s the bishop of Lyon fed much of the
Rhône corridor and Aquitaine from corn out of his personal resources, but in normal
years he would have sold it. Tax advantages and exemptions granted to the Church
and its agents further underlined its economic power (Whittaker, 1983).

Thus gradually as patrons, land-owners, judges and city magnates, Christian
bishops adapted themselves to the secular structure of the Roman state. Yet this identification had its dangers. Imperial generosity was liable to lead to imperial control and
bishops, while claiming to associate with emperors without fear, were in practice often
cowed. From Constantine at Nicaea in 325 through to the involvement of the eastern
emperors Theodosius II and Marcian in the Monophysite controversy, bishops were
pressurized and virtually controlled by their imperial sponsors, even on matters of doctrine. The most conspicuous exception to this rule, Ambrose of Milan, asserted his will
over the young emperors Gratian and Valentinian II in the 380s and brought Theodosius
I to his knees in 391, but when Eugenius, backed by prominent pagans, seized power
in 392, Ambrose beat a hasty diplomatic retreat to Florence and waited there to ascertain
the mood of the new administration. Ambrose's control of emperors was based largely
on his control of a loyal and excitable congregation in an imperial capital, combined
with his own forceful and at times ruthless personality; the removal of the imperial
court to Ravenna five years after his death denied similar opportunities to his successors.

Prosperity brought other dangers. Land-ownership by bishops, who personally
controlled a quarter of their church's total revenues, could be seen as a contradiction
of their role as champions of the poor and needy, to whom the wealth of the churches
properly belonged. Episcopal chairs came to be sought by undesirable candidates for
the wrong reasons. At Rome in 367 riots broke out between two contenders for the
papal chair, Damasus and Ursinus, and their followers, which were quashed by the intervention of the City Prefect, Praetextatus; Ammianus looked with disfavour on their
ambition and the lavish displays which ran counter to the modest behaviour and humility
of provincial bishops, which alone, to Ammianus, 'is pleasing to God'. But even the
provinces were not exempt from electoral corruption. In the small port town of Chalon-
sur-Saône in the 460s, the episcopal chair was sought by a degenerate noble, an owner
of kitchens who promised his partisans free food, and a third character who promised
a redistribution of church lands; all three were rejected by the metropolitan bishop,
Patiens of Lyon, who was called in to settle the affair. Such worldly preoccupations,
and the pressures of lay patronage locally exercised, could well have rendered bishops
little more than mitred offshoots of the Roman state. Indeed, when a group of Gallic

bishops in 386 acquiesced in the execution by the secular power of the Spanish heretic leader Priscillian and his noble lady followers, some were convinced that the Church was already the prisoner of the state and that the hour of the Antichrist was at hand.

Chief among the opponents of the execution of Priscillian was Martin of Tours, one of the founders of western monasticism, who established monasteries at Ligugé and Marmoutiers before being controversially elected bishop of Tours in 373. Because Martin, Jerome and others in the late fourth century questioned the values of the organized Church, the monastic movement itself can be interpreted as a reaction against ecclesiastical corruption and involvement with the state and temporal concerns. Thus Jerome repeatedly urged friends and disciples to abandon the bustle of the city for a monastic life, while Martin was convinced that by becoming a bishop he had diminished his personal holiness.

But monasticism did not originate as a movement of protest. The pattern was set early in the fourth century by Antony in Egypt. Having imbibed ascetic ideas and practices from holy men already living on the fringes of cities, Antony withdrew deep into the desert, as none had done before him, but not to solitude. The desert world of Antony was as thickly populated with demons as was a city with people and, so far from being a withdrawal from the world, Antony's desert sojourn was a confrontation with its profoundest spiritual dangers and the strength that he derived from the struggle enabled him to fill a role closely related to the needs of contemporary society. For Antony had to cope not only with demons but also with a constant stream of visitors, petitioners and even philosophers, with whom, despite his lack of literary learning, he successfully disputed. Nor were his visitors in search only of advice or spiritual counsel: Antony also acted as arbiter in matters of litigation, giving wise advice to judges and military commanders alike. Athanasius' biography of Antony, written after Antony's death in 356, might be thought to project on to the saint a respectability that he did not in fact have, but an Egyptian papyrus shows that a monk, Isak of Karanis, was an acceptable witness in an assault and battery case before the prefect of Egypt as early as 324.

Athanasius' biography of Antony publicized his achievement in both east and west, and was read at the imperial court itself. In Egypt, Syria and Palestine, hardy souls took to a life of fasting and prayer in the desert, in solitary caves (Jerome's in Syria was large enough to house his library), in gatherings of huts which allowed for both solitude and communal life, and, as time went on, in more organized communities. Inevitably the merits of the solitary, or eremitic, and communal, or coenobitic, modes of life were compared and a body of monastic literature evolved, establishing rules and justifying monastic modes of life (Rousseau, 1978). Such works present an idealized picture, although problems were not glossed over, and it should be remembered that monasticism too had its darker side. Jerome in the 370s was disillusioned by the squalor and arrogance of the Syrian monks and the monks of Nitria were notorious for violence and rioting. Such notable bad examples were, however, isolated and less potentially damaging, perhaps, for the future of monasticism than attempts by Jerome and his like to keep separate the roles of monk and member of the organized, city-based, clergy.

For in fact church and monastery needed each other. True to form, bishops like Ambrose and Augustine were quick to harness the spiritual energies of monasticism to the service of the churches they headed. Such bishops, often in concert with lay patrons of monks, brought monastic communities into cities, or just outside their walls, and thus more closely under the episcopal eye. Conversely, the strict anti-materialism of monastic ideology, whatever its realization in practice, was a reminder of Christian values older than those of Constantine. Such values could be given a new twist in a fourth-century setting: display based on sackcloth and ashes could be as potent a force as that based on gold vestments and splendid carriages. Thus the great monastic houses, particularly in the west, became nurseries for future bishops and it became something of the fashion for scions of local and senatorial notables to have a spell of training at such centres as the island monastery at Lérins, off Cannes, founded by Honoratus in c. 410. Products of this training went on to occupy episcopal chairs and combined the abilities, and the aristocratic assumptions, of noble or administrative families with the spiritual powers of servants of Christ.

Ultimately, the rise of Christianity depended on the assertion of power and on its definition, or redefinition, in contemporary terms. The dispensing of wealth through charity and other forms of conventional patronage could be no more than a back-up to the exercise of authority over the spirit world, which was of immediate practical relevance on every social level. Most obviously, this authority was demonstrated in the working of miracles, the casting out of demons, healing of the sick, raising of the dead. The true miracle was proof of sanctity, of God working through his authorized instrument, and the false miracle-worker was liable to be painfully confounded. But the power of sanctity to work miracles lay not only with the living but with the holy dead, with saints whose bones and shrines became the objects of international pilgrimage and devotion, and of local piety. Augustine, initially a sceptic, went to some trouble to collect miracles attested for his relics of St Stephen, brought to Africa by Orosius from the east after their discovery in 415.

Such saints were more than wonder-workers: they were patrons, protectors and, for some, friends. Their special relationship with their cities guaranteed their intercession with God for their clients and, on occasion, their intervention to protect their people from enemies: Alaric and his Visigoths, the sackers of Rome in 410, are supposed to have been turned back from Nola, near Naples, by a miraculous appearance by the local saint, Felix. For Christians successfully to assert that former human beings could act as heavenly patrons was itself a revolutionary achievement and a mark of the effect of Christianity on ancient belief. For it owed something to Christian assertion of a 'God made man'; to Christians' traditional devotion to their dead as shown in the grave-feasts so suspected by pagans of the second century and in the preservation, where possible, of the relics of their martyrs; to the 'friendship' with the divine felt by Christian and pagan philosophers; and to the unsettled state of the late Roman world, even in the fourth century, which rendered the more urgent the need for a friend at the heavenly court (Brown, 1981). The patronage of saints was more effective if the saint was physically present in the shape of relics, either locally owned or discovered, or begged, acquired or stolen from elsewhere. Failing the presence of relics, association with the life or death of past martyrs was enough to ensure their protective interest, and beyond the local saints were the great international patrons, Peter and Paul, or Stephen, the first martyr, who had their proper places in liturgical calendars.

Christianity rose to become the dominant religion of the Roman Empire in a world conscious of the manifold workings of *potentia*, of power both material and spiritual. In the beginning it was without obvious power, suffering from disunity, from the inherent paradox of being 'in the world but not of it', from heresies and from persecution. The survival of many churches in the second century must have been often precarious. Yet Christians turned these drawbacks to their advantage, obedient to the state yet keeping their distance, outlawing heretics, yet profiting from the intellectual vitality and questioning of which they were a symptom, venerating their martyrs and advertising their sufferings as 'witnesses' to their faith, and thus paving the way for the flowering of the cults of the saints in the fourth century. The conversion of Constantine brought with it recognition and freedom from fear, economic advantages and enhanced opportunities for the exercise of episcopal and clerical patronage, and of power in a secular sense. Yet at the same time the Church was drawn more closely into the deadly embrace of the state. Once again, however, the balance was, in the long-term, rectified: the otherworldly values of monasticism, or of the City of God, were reasserted and western bishops relied on them, and on their authority in their respective cities, as Roman political rule in the west crumbled in the fifth century. In the early sixth century, Caesarius of Arles commented apropos the Crucifixion that God could not simply have exercised his *potentia* against the Devil without further ado because such an act would have been devoid of justice (*iustitia*). The assertion of that principle, too, had ensured that the Church survived the ending of emperors in the west.

CHAPTER 34

·BURIAL·CUSTOMS·OF·ROME· ·AND·THE·PROVINCES·

Richard Jones

In the end all Romans died. It is fitting then to look, in this last section on religion and beliefs, at how they died, how their remains were disposed of, and how they were commemorated. In doing so, our most immediate contact is made with the individuals who lived in the Roman World. The remains of people and the residues of those ceremonies they used to take them through the universal experience of death are dealt with directly. Yet as in so many aspects of the study of the Roman World, care must be taken in the use of the different kinds of evidence that are available. In particular, the abundant literary and artistic evidence for funerary practices must be handled with caution. Literary works, fine bas-reliefs, or even tombstones were all made for the relatively prosperous upper classes of Roman society and were themselves expressions of Roman traditions. As such, they cannot be taken automatically as indicators of the meanings of what was done in the burials of the masses of the population. The only information to be gained about the humble people who made up most of the population of the Roman Empire is to be found in the archaeology of their burial-places. There the interpretation of what archaeologists have discovered has more in common with the approaches of prehistoric study than of classical literature or art history. Nevertheless, one of the greatest assets to the study of Roman burial is that there is a substantial amount of information about the rituals which surrounded the burial of the remains which survive for the excavator. Even though such evidence and what is known about ideas on the after-life may both relate to a classical Roman ideal of what was supposed to happen, it is interesting to see what can be found to tell how far these ideals were followed and how they related to the local native traditions in the provinces.

Most of the evidence for burial rituals comes from occasional references in the classical authors and bas-reliefs showing scenes from the ceremonies. These have been brought together in a clear account by Professor Jocelyn Toynbee (1971, 43–64). When death was thought near, the family gathered. The closest relative gave a last kiss to catch the dying person's soul, which was thought to leave the body with the last breath, and then closed the eyes. The close relatives then shouted their grief and called the dead person's name. The body was washed, anointed, dressed and laid out for the lying-in-state, probably with a coin for Charon's fee placed in the mouth. Many tomb-stones and other reliefs show the body lying on a couch, often surrounded by mourners (e.g. pl. 34.1). After the lying-in-state, which might last for only one day, but sometimes extended to a week, the body was carried to the cemetery in a procession of relatives and friends of the deceased wearing black. An elaborate funeral procession is shown on a relief from Amiternum in Italy (pl. 34.2). There the procession is accompanied by pipers, a trumpeter and horn blowers as well as hired professional mourners, a Roman practice that followed Etruscan traditions. These arrangements in upper-class funerals were organized by professional undertakers, called *libitinarii*. It seems that poorer people's funerals followed the same kind of pattern. Certainly all corpses had to be taken outside the town or city for disposal, a rule laid down in the early Roman law, the Twelve Tables, and quoted by Cicero (*On the laws*, 2,23,58): 'the dead shall be neither buried nor burnt in the city'. It was this ruling which was rigorously followed through-out the Empire and brought about the characteristic topography of the Roman town, whereby the roads leading to the town were lined with cemeteries. What was true of Rome itself and Pompeii in Italy was true of Canterbury in Britain or Trier in Germany (pl. 34.3; figs 34.1 and 34.2). The peculiarly 'Roman' nature of this practice can be over-emphasized, since it is such a frequent custom of most societies to separate formally the places of the living from those of the dead. It makes for a healthier way of living and is also influenced by various ideas on the spiritual 'pollution' associated with the dead. Given these factors, and the fact that urbanized life in general in the Empire was given a Roman shape, it is hardly surprising that burial places conformed to a common standard.

Once in the cemetery, during the early Empire the body was normally burnt, usually in a place set aside for cremations, called the *ustrinum*. Sometimes the cremation took place at the spot where the ashes were to be buried, normally over a grave already dug. This style of cremation was known as a *bustum* grave. Gifts and personal possessions of the deceased were sometimes put on the pyre for burning with the body. When the corpse was burnt, the fire was put out with wine and then the remains were collected from the *ustrinum* and normally put into some sort of container, which could range from a gold casket or marble chest to a simple pottery jar or cloth bag. The container was then placed either in some kind of built tomb-structure, or buried in the ground, often with more objects to accompany the remains into the after-life.

After the funeral itself, there was a series of rituals to be followed to confirm the grave legally and to purify the relatives. A funerary meal, the *silicernium*, was eaten on the day of the funeral at the grave; another, the *cena novendialis*, took place to mark

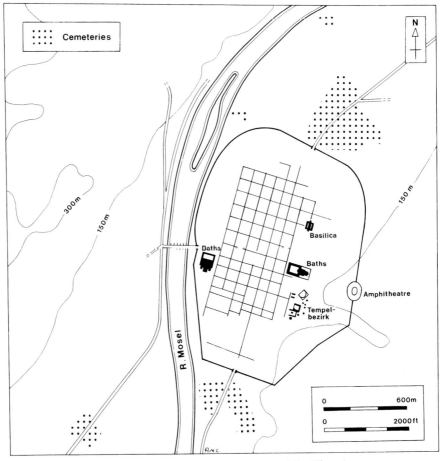

Figure 34.1   Trier with cemetery areas (*after Thomas*)

the end of full mourning after nine days. The dead continued to be remembered, on their birthdays, and more generally in two important religious festivals the *Parentalia* and the *Lemuria*. At the *Parentalia* people visited the graves of their dead relatives, took small gifts, perhaps food or flowers, and had a meal at the grave. Some more elaborate tombs included a kitchen and a well for these functions. These were far from being solemn occasions. Tomb inscriptions encouraged the living to enjoy themselves, but sometimes they may have become more lively than might be expected: some early Christian writers criticized pagans for getting too drunk at such gatherings.

These ceremonies are known from references which largely date to the late first century BC and the first century AD. Strictly the information applies only to this period and to the most romanized, upper sectors of society. However, the archaeology suggests that the picture created can also be applied rather more widely, but it must not be thought

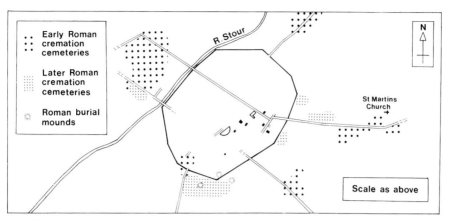

Figure 34.2 Canterbury with cemetery areas (*after Canterbury Archaeological Trust*)

that ideas and customs of burial were static and universal. They varied from place to place and were constantly changing over time, sometimes rapidly. Archaeology has discovered both general trends and some curious and exceptional practices.

At this point, it is worthwhile to give a brief typology of the actual kinds of Roman grave most often found. Stated simply, there are cremation graves and inhumation graves. The cremations can be split between those burnt at an *ustrinum* and subsequently buried elsewhere and *bustum* graves (p. 813 above). Where the human remains were taken from the *ustrinum*, they may or may not have been put in the ground with some of the ashes from the pyre. Many cremation graves were furnished with grave goods, often unburnt in the pyre. Most commonly these were pottery vessels for food and drink, such as bowls, flagons and beakers, but lamps, brooches and small perfume flasks were also included, as well as an enormous variety of other things which occasionally turn up in graves and must have had some special significance for the deceased (pls 34.4 and 34.5). Inhumations which were most common in the late Roman period were provided with grave goods markedly less frequently than cremations, though the practice survived. The main area of variance in inhumations is in their grave structures and orientation. Sometimes the body was protected by an arrangement of roof-tiles or stones or a broken amphora, or the grave was lined with stones. A wooden coffin was also used quite frequently (fig. 34.17). In fact all these types followed traditions already used for cremation graves. It is easy to distinguish whether or not the burials in an inhumation cemetery followed a system of regular alignment.

However, beyond the normal range of burials, there were some unusual and even bizarre practices. At the site of Skeleton Green in Hertfordshire in Britain, Calvin Wells's study of the cremated remains showed that there were quite clear variations in the presence of particular bones in the urns buried. Skull bones were missing surprisingly often, suggesting that fragments may have been kept by relatives (Wells, 1981). Unfortunately, since cremations have rarely been studied in such exemplary detail, there are few other examples of such practices. Inhumation graves allow the easier recognition of anomalous practices. In Britain, decapitated skeletons have been found from more than fifty sites of the Roman period, as well as from another thirty Anglo-Saxon sites. The detached head is usually found towards the feet. Many suggestions have been made to explain this phenomenon: was it to stop the dead from walking, to lay the ghost; was it to sacrifice an 'expendable' member of the community or was it to execute a criminal? However, there is as yet no explanation with more claims to be believed than any other (Harman, Molleson and Price, 1981). If from time to time, unusual things were done to the human remains, there are also practices in the choice of grave goods which have attracted attention. Normally the carrying of weapons by civilians in the Empire was forbidden, but there are graves containing weapons known in many places in northern Gaul and Germany and some from the Roman period in Britain. It seems unlikely that they were all soldiers and more likely that the continuity of a pre-Roman Iron Age custom is being observed, perhaps with the change that the deceased might have claimed that the weapons were for hunting and therefore legal (van Doorselaer, 1967, 185–99).

A common thread which links all that has so far been said about funerary ceremonies, both the commonplace and the exceptional, is that they express ideas about an after-life. Such ideas are often linked with religion, but the exact nature of how religion and burial were linked in the Roman world needs some clarification. Undoubtedly, attitudes to the dead and to some kind of after-life are profoundly religious in a general sense. They are part of how people see themselves fitting into the world and how they seek to explain the great mysteries of life and death. What is more difficult is to argue that in the Empire specific religions required specific funerary practices. It can be said that Roman paganism included the system of ideas on an after-life which found expression in the furnishing of the grave for the comfort of the deceased (pl. 34.5). There is very little evidence for particular cults having any influence on burial ritual, except in the sense that a faithful follower of a deity might have a cult object such as a figurine included in their personal possessions put into the grave.

The religion most often thought to have influenced ancient ideas about the dead and their treatment was of course Christianity. It has frequently been asserted or assumed that the rise of Christianity was directly responsible for the change of burial practice from cremation to inhumation. However, it was conclusively demonstrated many years ago that inhumation became popular significantly earlier than Christianity. The wholesale shift from cremation to inhumation was a cultural upheaval of striking proportions. In the later second century the overwhelming majority of people were cremated; by the late third century most were inhumed (fig. 34.3). All members of society took part in this phenomenon, from the provincial aristocrat to the rural peasant. There were always exceptions to the general rule, and the rites were practised at the same time

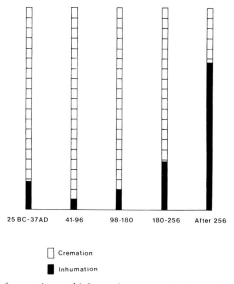

25 BC-37AD	41-96	98-180	180-256	After 256

□ Cremation

■ Inhumation

Figure 34.3   Histogram of cremation and inhumation cemeteries in northern Gaul, by period (*after van Doorselaer*)

in the same cemeteries. Nevertheless, there is no questioning the clarity of the general picture of change, nor is there any easy explanation how it spread so thoroughly and so quickly in the ancient world, without the aid of legal pronouncement, and certainly without mass media. The mechanisms of how the ideas spread are surprising for their efficiency, but elude attempts to understand exactly how they worked. It is easy to see how the rise of Christianity has been seen as an attractive explanation. However, the religious historian Arthur Nock showed in 1932 that inhumation became fashionable among prominent people in Rome as early as the end of the first century AD, perhaps because people were tempted by the opportunities for ostentation provided by using *sarcophagi*. He also pointed out that the early Christians inhumed their dead not because they saw cremation as a denial of the resurrection of the flesh, but because they followed Jewish custom, being part of the Jewish tradition. Nock argued that the spread of inhumation was essentially carried by the forces of fashion (Nock, 1932). The many excavations of cemeteries in the half century since Nock wrote have confirmed his central point, that inhumation became popular before Christianity (Jones, 1981). It is less clear why people were so receptive to the new ideas. Nock was adamant in seeing the shift in burial practice as no hint of a broader change in religious thought, but many others have tried to suggest that the rise of inhumation was one aspect of a changing view on the world which was widely experienced and provided the background for the eventual acceptance of Christianity. That Roman cemeteries played a role in the development of Christianity will be seen later.

It is from the archaeological remains that most can now be found out about burial

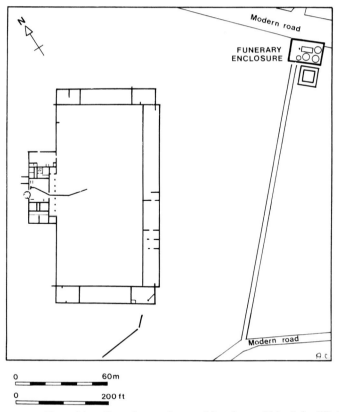

Figure 34.4 Plan of the villa and mausoleum at Newel, near Trier (*after Wightman*)

customs. To do this, the full range of burial forms must be understood. The burials of the upper classes, perhaps accompanied by the musicians and professional mourners described already, have left an impressive series of major funerary monuments and mausolea. Such structures tended to follow their own patterns and are sometimes to be found in urban cemeteries and sometimes in the countryside on the estates of the deceased's family (Toynbee, 1971). Some were very grand, such as the tomb of the Scipios near Tarragona (pl. 34.9), or the mausoleum of the Julii at St-Rémy-de-Provence (Glanum), which followed an Italian style (pl. 34.6). Others were eccentric like the pyramid of Gaius Cestius and the tomb of the baker, Marcus Vergilius Eurysaces, both at Rome. All date to the late republican or early imperial periods, as do the more modest tomb-gardens at Pompeii (pl. 34.3), which add a further dimension to the understanding of these monumental tombs and walled enclosures (Jashemski, 1979). Of rather later date, but still on an imposing scale, is the mid-fourth-century mausoleum at Centcelles, near Tarragona in Spain (pl. 34.7), with a surviving dome decorated with a painted frieze showing biblical figures and a hunting scene: it was clearly built by a rich and

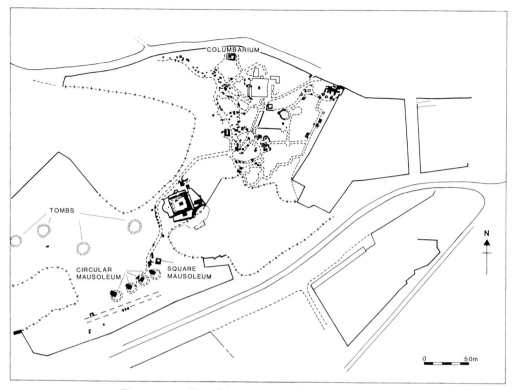

Figure 34.5   Plan of the cemetery at Carmona (*after Bendala*)

important Christian, perhaps even for Constans I, who died in 350 (Toynbee, 1971, 161–3; Gorges, 1979, 411–12; Fernández Castro, 1982, 59 and fig. 21). The Centcelles mausoleum was an integral part of a much larger villa complex and is a very grand example of the villa mausoleum. More simple versions can be found at many sites such as Newel near Trier (fig. 34.4). All these monuments followed classical architectural traditions, but this was not always the case. In particular there was a series of barrow burials which has been recognized in northern Gaul and south-eastern Britain, as well as some further east in Noricum and Pannonia. These were imposing earth mounds covering elaborate burials, and dating in some cases as late as the third century (Jessup, 1959; Amand, 1960; 1965). They shared with monuments in more classical forms the quality of impressing the onlooker with the importance of the person buried there (pl. 34.8).

Most of these monumental tombs of the rich tend to survive in isolation, at least outside places like Pompeii or Ostia in Italy. However, at the town of Carmona in southern Spain a very large and well-preserved cemetery contains hundreds of more or less monumental tombs, surrounded by many more humbler graves (fig. 34.5). Unfortunately little has been done there beyond recording some of the more important monumental tombs and their decoration, but the potential of such a site is enormous. It could be made to reveal a fascinating picture of the burials of the whole spectrum of the town's society (Bendala Galán, 1976).

It is more normal in urban cemeteries for the majority of whatever monuments were there to be lost, leaving perhaps few traces among the burials of the masses of the population. However, it is by studying the large cemeteries attached to towns that it is possible to make some progress in understanding the trends in burial custom which were expressed by most of the urban population. The full extent of the problem of trying to understand the character of urban cemeteries is rarely appreciated. The weight of numbers is perhaps the most striking point. A modest provincial Roman town might have had a population of 2,000. That figure is inevitably a guess, as must be estimates of mortality and life-span, but they are guesses informed by what evidence there is for the demographic patterns of the ancient world and of more recent pre-industrial societies. If therefore the adult mortality rate was about twenty-five per thousand per year, this provincial town would have been burying some fifty people each year making a total in excess of 15,000 over the whole Roman period. A figure of this order of magnitude for a small provincial town makes the idea that a sample of fifty graves

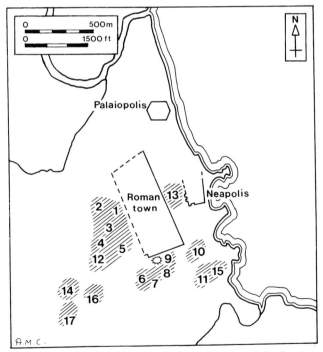

Figure 34.6 Plan of the cemeteries at Ampurias (*after Jones*)

excavated could be in any way representative of the whole cemetery unduly optimistic. It is laughable at major cities like Lyon, Arles or Trier, not to mention the extreme of Rome itself, where the population at its height has been estimated at one million. It is therefore crucial that urban cemeteries are examined on a large scale. The few cases where this has been done have revealed the potential for such work, but it is apparent that to draw useful conclusions at least hundreds of graves must be excavated, and preferably thousands.

At the site of Ampurias in north-east Spain, many graves were excavated in the 1940s covering all periods in the development of the place from the Greek colony in the sixth century BC to the late Roman settlement of the fifth century AD and beyond (Almagro, 1953; 1955). The cemeteries spread around the main foci of settlement, the Greek town (Neapolis) next to the sea and the Roman town on a hill overlooking it (fig. 34.6). The Roman period cemeteries were situated mostly to the west and south of the Roman town. There appeared to be an extensive cemetery west of the town, mostly of cremations, but it was excavated and recorded in the parcels of land of the modern field system. Detailed analysis of the graves and grave goods has however shown that there were major variations of practice from one zone to another within that large cemetery (Jones, 1984a). The individual cremation burial areas in all the cemeteries could be split into two groups of richly-furnished and poorly-furnished graves (fig. 34.7). The difference of provision was very marked and occurred even between adjacent fields,

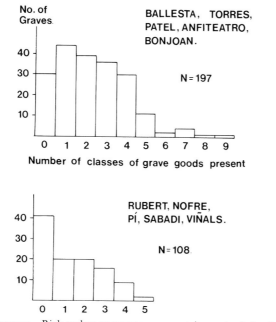

Figure 34.7   Rich and poor cemetery areas at Ampurias (*after Jones*)

where the style of burial might have been expected to be consistent. There were similar differences among the inhumations, though here expressed in grave form, as there were few grave goods as such. There were significant differences in the proportions of graves protected by a tile structure, burials under *amphorae*, and plain graves, both between individual cemeteries and between those cemeteries containing both cremations and inhumations and those exclusively for inhumations (figs 34.8 and 34.9). The interpretation of these variations is rather more difficult than their observation. Few of the graves have been dated individually, nor have the human remains been adequately studied. It is hard to assess the influence of date and the age and sex of the deceased. Only the difference between adult and child inhumations could be identified on the basis of the length of the skeleton, but that did allow a link between amphora-burials and child burials to be established (fig. 34.10). The nature of the forces determining the other variations in burial custom can only be surmised, whether they be social and economic, or religious or ethnic. What is important here is to stress that Ampurias shows how

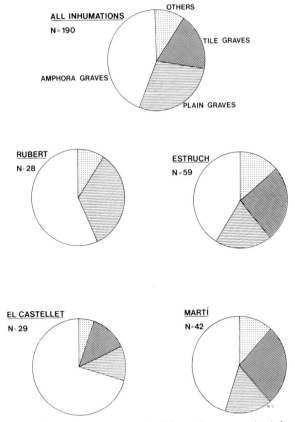

Figure 34.8   Ampurias: grave types in inhumation cemeteries (*after Jones*)

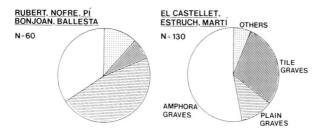

Figure 34.9 Ampurias: grave types in mixed rite and all-inhumation cemeteries (*after Jones*)

much difference in pattern there may have been in the various cemeteries around a Roman town, and within what seem to be single cemeteries. It emphasizes that now we can only really report on work in progress, since the systematic study of Roman cemeteries in this sort of way has only just begun.

Despite that, much work will still depend on observations made long ago. Another site where there is a good picture of the cemetery topography is York, but there most of the information comes from the records of nineteenth-century observers of building work as the town expanded. The collection of that work, coupled with the excavation of one part of a large cemetery, has served York well in terms of its cemetery archaeology (RCHM, 1962; Jones, 1984b). It is possible to see, for example, how there were two main cemeteries at The Mount and the Railway Station on the south-west side of the river Ouse, and another on the other side of the river around Bootham–Clifton, but that there were also many other smaller cemeteries scattered around the outskirts of

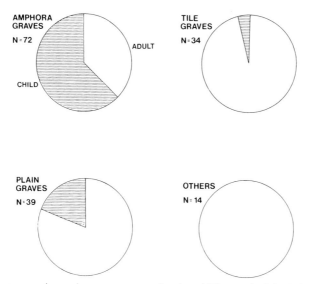

Figure 34.10 Ampurias: grave types related to children and adults (*after Jones*)

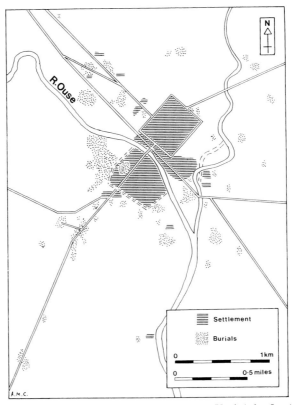

Figure 34.11   Cemeteries and settlements at York (*after Jones*)

the city and fortress (fig. 34.11). It was also the case that of these smaller cemeteries, the earlier ones tended to be farther from the main areas of settlement than the later ones, suggesting that the early limits of settlement were defined too widely, in an area that was never completely filled. There was also a curious pattern found in the Trentholme Drive area, at the south-western limit of The Mount cemetery. There burials were very densely packed and intercut in a most haphazard fashion. Burials disturbed even very recent earlier interments. Moreover, males outnumbered females by about four to one (fig. 34.12). A somewhat similar style has been found in the sector of a cemetery excavated at Cirencester in Britain. Again the burials were not aligned neatly in rows, although they were not as dense as at Trentholme Drive, and again men outnumbered women markedly, this time by five to two. No satisfactory explanation has been suggested for these two curious cases. The idea of a strong military presence at either or both sites, on a scale sufficient to cause the sex imbalance does not seem plausible for the later Roman period, nor would it account for the lack of alignment of the graves. The two sites must be seen in their wider local contexts, when new excavations on

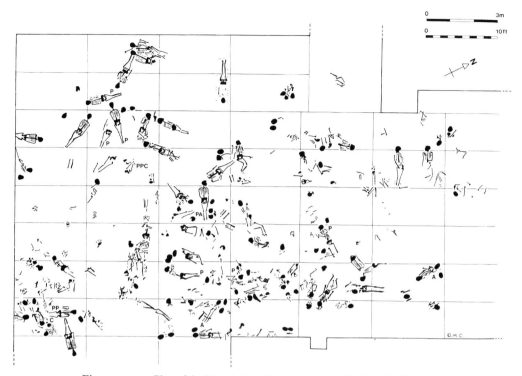

Figure 34.12 Plan of the Trentholme Drive cemetery at York (*after Wenham*)

other parts of the cemeteries may reveal how typical or how anomalous they are in the cemeteries of York and Cirencester.

They were certainly not typical of the late Roman cemeteries of Britain as a whole, nor of the rest of the western Empire. The normal pattern was of orderly rows of inhumation graves, such as at the Lankhills site at Winchester (fig. 34.13). Similar lay-outs are familiar from all parts of the western Empire: Tarragona in Spain, Tours in France, Nijmegen in the Netherlands, Xanten in Germany or Colchester and Dorchester in Britain. One of the main issues raised by these late Roman inhumation cemeteries is the presence or absence of Christian influence. It has already been argued that the change from cremation to inhumation was in no way caused by Christianity. On the other hand, following the conversion of Constantine the Empire's official religion was Christianity and inhumation burial did conform to what is thought of as Christian practice and what certainly was Christian practice in some places. In many cases it is hard to find explicit evidence for or against Christianity in fourth-century cemeteries, but sometimes there is positive evidence. The clearest example is that of the Catacombs in Rome where there is abundant Christian imagery in the decoration (Stevenson, 1978). Similar underground burial chambers are found in other parts of the central Mediterranean as well as further

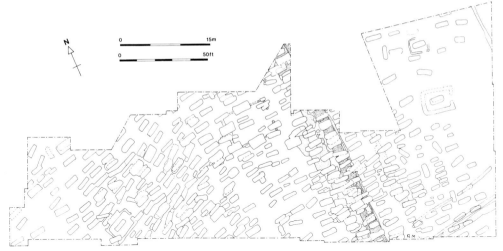

Figure 34.13   Plan of the cemetery at Lankhills, Winchester (*after Clarke*)

east, but they were exceptional in the west, where the open cemetery was everywhere
the norm. At the Poundbury site at Dorchester in Britain, many burials have been found
covered in gypsum plaster, which is widely considered an early Christian practice. Furthermore, some graves are surrounded by small buildings which were decorated with
painted wall plaster portraying figures perhaps praying. These structures are best interpreted as small shrines marking the graves of several early Christians, perhaps even
saints (pl. 34.10). In some cases much more substantial buildings were eventually constructed to supersede such simple shrines. These basilicas were often imposing buildings
decorated with mosaics. The outcome of the process was the development during the
early medieval period of a major church in the middle of what had been the Roman
cemetery. Often this led to a shift in the centre of settlement, as probably happened
at St Albans in Britain. At Tours in France (fig. 34.14) a second focus of settlement
was created around the basilica of St Martin in the Roman cemetery area to the west
of the other early medieval centre, which was established inside the late Roman defences.
The Christian connection with the sites of the late Roman cemeteries has therefore had
a marked influence on the development of urban topography in Europe.

   If urban cemeteries lend themselves most readily to modern archaeological
approaches simply because of their size, the rural population must not be overlooked.
They must always have outnumbered their urban neighbours heavily, but because they
tended to bury their dead near their settlements, the cemeteries tend to be small. The
western provinces abound with small groups of graves sometimes found apparently
in isolation, sometimes quite clearly associated with a farming settlement, but always
presumably serving some rural community. The small towns and villages had their
cemeteries beyond their settlement areas, mirroring the cities, but individual farms also

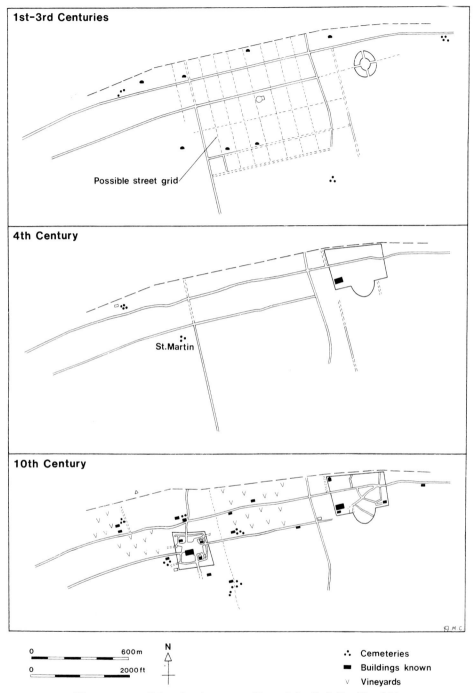

Figure 34.14 Urban development at Tours (*after Galinié and Randoin*)

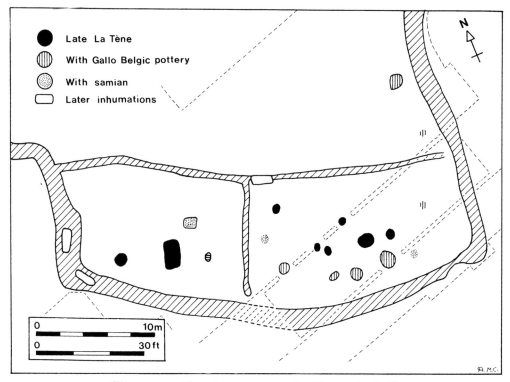

Figure 34.15 Plan of the cemetery at Owslebury (*after Collis*)

had their own burial areas. Several recently excavated examples of such sites show that the small cemeteries probably served the extended families working peasant farms, perhaps about ten people living there at any one time. In Britain at Owslebury in Hampshire and at Lynch Farm near Peterborough (figs 34.15 and 34.16) there were well defined cemetery areas with neatly arranged graves, as well as isolated graves dug in the field ditches of the farm. With only seventy graves excavated at Owslebury, spanning in date the whole Roman period, John Collis was still able to show how varied were the burial customs and to use them to suggest the social composition of the people using the cemetery. At Lynch Farm, burials were confined to the later Roman period but showed a marked difference between those in the ordered part of the cemetery and those disordered. Most of the graves in the ordered part were carefully aligned east–west and were respected by later burials. One grave, however, turned out to contain the successive burials of six adults and a new-born baby (pl. 34.11). We can only speculate on the reasons behind such behaviour, when apparently there was no shortage of space for graves. It is worth noting that although we might expect burial practices in the countryside to follow local pre-Roman traditions more closely than those of the towns, there is little evidence for it.

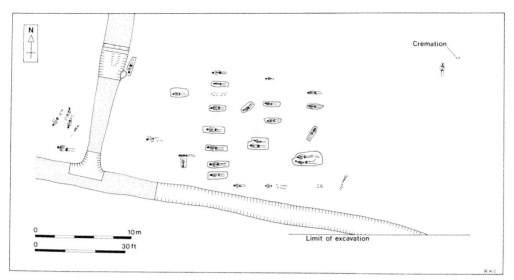

Figure 34.16 Plan of the cemetery at Lynch Farm (*after Jones*)

If burial practices can be seen as cultural artefacts, urban and rural cemeteries have much to tell us about patterns of society in the Empire. There were three levels of cultural integration quite clearly discernible. Overall there was a quite astonishing degree of conformity. In most places, whatever had been the practice before, within a generation or two of an area being incorporated into the Empire, and mostly by the end of the first century AD, the normal burial practice was cremation, usually with the remains collected from the pyre, and placed in the ground accompanied by a variety of grave offerings. Then, mainly during the third century came an even more thorough shift of practice as cremation was replaced by simple inhumation, establishing a pattern of burial practice which was to be consistently followed into modern times. In both early and late Roman periods, the exceptions were insignificant when set against the dominance of the rule.

However, within this overall homogeneity, a second level of patterning was working at regional level. Certain similarities of practice can be defined in provincial terms, or sometimes even in smaller units, such as a river basin or a city. These groupings were expressed in the method of cremation and collection of the remains, as in the Schelde Valley; or in the provision of small monuments as in north Africa, or in the types of grave goods as around Cimiez in southern Gaul. They no doubt sometimes related to continuing pre-Roman ideas and sometimes to the objects generally available in circulation to be used as grave goods. Nevertheless they show the definition of clear local identities in at least one sector of cultural behaviour (cf. Jones, 1982; forthcoming).

Third, within individual cemeteries there was often a wide range of practice. Most commonly, this can be seen in the degree of complexity of the funerary provision:

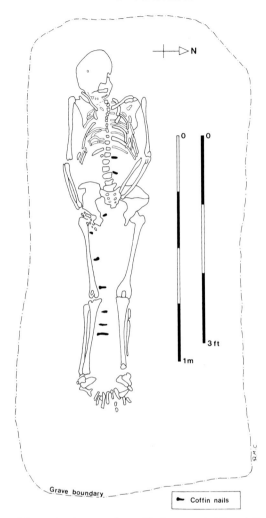

Figure 34.17 Inhumation in a wooden coffin (grave 31) at Lynch Farm (*after Jones*)

elaboration of the grave structure or the richness of the grave goods. This seems to have been the normal situation in cemeteries throughout the western Empire. There were other types of variation within cemeteries, but these are more difficult to understand (cf. Jones, 1984a).

In all these aspects of patterning in funerary behaviour, we are dealing essentially with the outward forms of burial, rather than explicit beliefs. Of course, even then there are only those aspects of the form of burial which survive into the archaeological record. Despite the limitations of the evidence, burial does offer hints on the way the cultural systems of the Empire worked. In burial at least can be seen a part of how people defined themselves and their membership of groups in society. The threefold split into empire-wide, regional, and specifically local systems is worth pursuing into other areas of cultural behaviour in the Roman Empire.

Yet it must not be thought that these systems were static. Another characteristic of burial practice is rapid change. Considering the limited means of communication, it is remarkable how quickly the empire-wide changes came about. As in so many aspects of Roman life, a Roman time-traveller from the first century who visited the late fourth would only have recognized a small part of what was happening around him.

Beyond the Roman period itself, the large late Roman inhumation cemeteries took on a considerable importance in the transition to the medieval world. In many places cemeteries were still used for centuries after the political end of the Empire. This is true of places around the Mediterranean like Tarragona, where such things have come to be expected, and Frénouville in Normandy. Where the cemetery continued in use it must be likely that the community using it continued as well.

Conclusion

Studying Roman burials can yield a catalogue of ancient quirks. It can also give a special perspective on the workings of ancient society. That is the direction where advances can be expected in the future. The developing techniques of research on the human bones themselves offer exciting new insights not only on the health and living conditions of the ancient populations, but also of the funerary rituals by which people were dis-patched from among the living (cf. Manchester, 1983; Wells, 1981; McWhirr, Viner and Wells, 1982). As new work is done on pathology and nutrition, anthropology and demography, the questions which can be asked of the burial evidence will be transformed.

While it is exciting to look ahead to the fruits of new work, it is worth remembering that the greatest potential seems to lie in ways of understanding ancient living conditions, or of identifying cultural patterns in living societies. Although the forms of chosen burial can be observed, what they really meant about how those people thought about death is still elusive. That is just as true of the 'normal' burial as it is of the exotic decapitation. When we encounter such a practice, it should give pause to those who become too intoxicated with the 'civilized' achievements of the Roman Empire. The people who chopped off their neighbours' heads in the fourth century probably drank water brought to them in an aqueduct. The surface of Roman high culture should not persuade us too easily of a special difference between it and contemporary non-Roman societies. Roman civilization had its own barbarities, no less than others.

34.1   Relief of a dead girl on a couch, mourned by her surrounding family

34.2   Relief of a funeral procession from Amiternum, Italy: the deceased is carried high on a bier and
is accompanied by musicians, hired mourners and relatives

34.3 Street of the tombs, Pompeii

34.4 Cremation groups *in situ* at Chichester, Britain

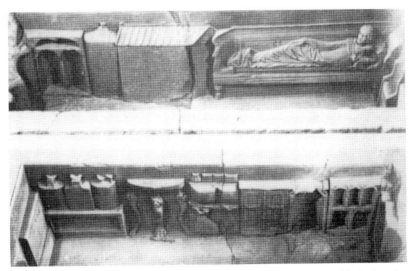

34.5 The Simpelveld Sarcophagus, Holland; the tomb of a wealthy woman, with the interior of the sarcophagus carved to resemble a room with furniture

34.6 Monument of the Julii at Glanum (St-Rémy-de-Provence)

34.7 Mausoleum at Centcelles, near Tarragona, Spain

34.8 The Bartlow Hills, Essex; a group of Romano-British barrows

34.9 Tomb of the Scipios, near Tarragona, Spain

34.10 Poundbury cemetery, Dorchester: graves and a mausoleum

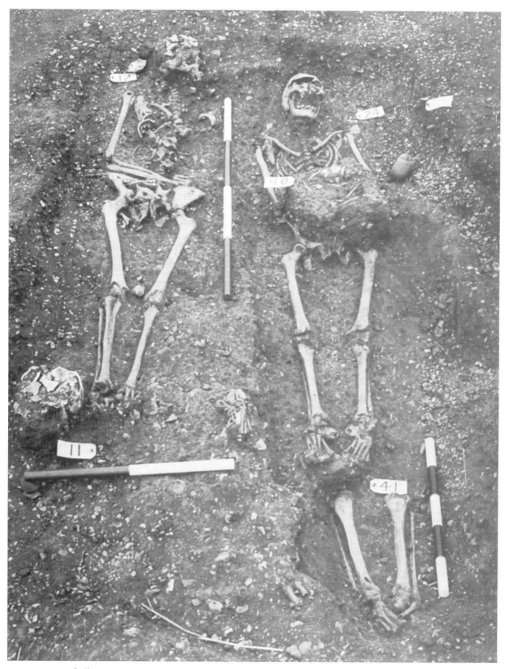

34.11   Collective grave, in all containing the remains of six adults and a baby, at Lynch Farm,
near Peterborough, Britain

·BIBLIOGRAPHY·FOR·
·PART·10·

Aartsen, J. van (1971), *Deae Nehalenniae*, Leiden.

Abaecherli, A. L. (1935), 'The institution of the Imperial Cult in the Western Provinces of the Roman Empire', *Studei materiali di storia delle religioni*, 11, 171–87.

Akurgal, E. (1973), *Ancient Civilisations and Ruins of Turkey*, Istanbul.

Almagro, M. (1953), *Las Necrópolis de Ampurias I: Necrópolis Griegas*, Barcelona.

Almagro, M. (1955), *Las Necrópolis de Ampurias II: Necrópolis Romanas y Indigenas*, Barcelona.

Amand, M. (1960), 'Roman Barrows in Belgium', *Analecta Archaeologica: Festschrift Fritz Fremersdorf*, 69–81, Köln.

Amand, M. (1965), 'Les tumulus d'époque romaine dans le Norique et en Pannonie', *Collections Latomus* 24, 614–28.

Amo, M. D. del (1979), *Estudio critico de la necrópolis paleocristiana de Tarragona*, Institut d'Estudis Tarraconenses Ramon Berenguer IV, secció d'arqueologia i historia, 42, Tarragona.

Bailey, C. (1932), *Phases in the Religion of Ancient Rome*, Berkeley.

Barnes, T. D. (1971), *Tertullian. A Historical and Literary Study*, Oxford.

Barnes, T. D. (1981), *Constantine and Eusebius*, Harvard.

Bauman, R. A. (1976), *Impietas in Principem*, Munich.

Baynes, N. H. (1931), *Constantine the Great and the Christian Church*, Oxford.

Bean, G. E. (1966), *Aegean Turkey*, New York.

Bean, G. E. (1978), *Lycian Turkey*, New York.

Bell, H. I. (1954), *Cults and Creeds in Graeco-Roman Egypt*, Liverpool.

Bendala Galán, M. (1976), *La Necrópolis Romana de Carmona (Sevilla)*, Publicaciones de la Excellentissima Diputación Provincial de Sevilla, historia, series Iª, X I, Seville.

Benjamin, A. (1963), 'Altars of Hadrian in Athens and Hadrian's pan-hellenic programme', *Hesperia*, 32, 57–86.

Benjamin, A. and Raubitschek, A. (1959), 'Ares Augusti', *Hesperia*, 28, 65–85.

Beurlier, E. (1891), *Le Culte impérial, son histoire et son organisation*, Paris.

Blázquez, J. M. (1977), *Imagen y Mito : Religiones Mediterráneas e Ibéricas*, Madrid.

Blázquez, J. M. (1983), *Primitivas Religiones Ibéricas II : Religiones Preromanas*, Madrid.

Bloch, R. (1958), *The Etruscans*, London.

Bober, P. P. (1951), 'Cernunnos: origin and transformation of a Celtic divinity', *American Journal of Archaeology*, 55, 13–51.

Bouché-Leclerq. A. (1879–82), *Histoire de la divination dans l'antiquité*, Paris.

British Museum (1969), *Introductory Guide to the Egyptian Collections*, London.

Brogan, O. (1953), *Roman Gaul*, London.

Brown, P. (1967), *Augustine of Hippo : a Biography*, London.

Brown, P. (1971), *The World of Late Antiquity*, London.

Brown, P. (1972), *Religion and Society in the Age of St Augustine*, London.

Brown, P. (1981), *The Cult of the Saints. Its Rise and Function*, London.

Browning, I. (1974), *Petra*, London.

Browning, I. (1979), *Palmyra*, London.

Browning, I. (1982), *Jerash and the Decapolis*, London.

Buschner, W. (1888), *De Neocoria*, Gissen.

Cameron, A. (1977), 'Paganism and literature in late fourth century Rome', in *Christianisme et formes litteraires de l'antiquité tardive en occident*, Entretiens Fondation Hardt XXIII, 1–40, Geneva.

Cerfaux, L. and Tondman, J. (1957), *Le Culte des Souverains dans la civilisation gréco-romaine*, Paris.

Chadwick, H. (1967), *The Early Church*, London.

Charlesworth, M. P. (1935), 'Some observations on Ruler Cult', *Harvard Theological Review*, 28, 8ff.

Clarke, G. (1979), *The Roman Cemetery at Lankhills, Winchester Studies 3 : Pre-Roman and Roman Winchester, Part II*, Oxford.

Clébert, J.-P. (1979), *Provence antique : 2. L'époque gallo-romaine*, Paris.

Collis, J. R. (1977), 'Owslebury (Hants) and the problem of burials on rural settlements', in R. Reece (ed.), *Burial in the Roman World*, Council for British Archaeology Research Report 22, 26–34.

Conductu, E. and Daicoriciu, C. (1971), *Romania*, London.

Cook, A. B. (1914–40), *Zeus*, Cambridge.

Cunliffe, B. W. (1969), *Roman Bath*, Society of Antiquaries of London Research Report, No. 24, London.

Cunliffe, B. W. (1975), *Rome and the Barbarians*, London.

Dix, G. (1945), *The Shape of the Liturgy*, London.

Dodds, E. R. (1965), *Pagan and Christian in an Age of Anxiety*, Cambridge.

Doorselaer, A. van (1967), *Les Nécropoles d'époque romaine en Gaule Septentrionale*, Dissertationes Archaeologicae Gandenses X, Brugge.

Dudley, D. R. (1967), *Urbs Roma*, London.

Dumézil, G. (1970), *Archaic Roman Religion*, Chicago.

Duval, P.-M. (1957), *Les Dieux de la Gaule*, Paris.

Eitrem, S. (1936), 'Religious calendar concerning the Imperial Cult', *Papyri Oslôenses* 3, 77.

Etienne, R. (1970), *The Religions of the Roman Empire*, London.

Ferguson, J. (1970), *The Religions of the Roman Empire*, London.

Ferguson, J. (1980), *Greek and Roman Religion: A Source-Book*, Park Ridge.

Fernández Castro, Mª. C. (1982), *Villas Romanas en España*, Madrid.

Fink, R. O., Huey, A. S. and Snyder, W. F. (1946), 'Feriale Duranum', *Yale Classical Studies*, 7.

Fishwick, D. (1961), 'The Imperial Cult in Roman Britain', *Phoenix*, 15, 159–73 and 213–20.

Fishwick, D. (1964), 'The institution of the provincial cult in Africa Proconsularis', *Hermes*, 92, 342–63.

Fishwick, D. (1978), 'Provincial ruler worship in the west', in H. Temporini (ed.), *Aufstieg und Niedergang der römischen Welt*. 16.2, 1201–53, Berlin/New York.

Fol, A. and Marazov, I. (1977), *Thrace and the Thracians*, London.

Fowler, W. W. (1899), *The Roman Festivals*, London.

Fowler, W. W. (1911), *The Religious Experience of the Roman People*, London.

Frend, W. H. C. (1952), *The Donatist Church. A Movement of Protest in Roman North Africa*, Oxford.

Frend, W. H. C. (1965), *Martyrdom and Persecution in the Early Church*, Oxford.

Gage, J. (1955), *Apollon Romain*, Paris.

Galinié, H. and Randoin, B. (1979), *Les Archives du Sol à Tours: survie et avenir de l'archéologie de la ville*, Tours.

Geffcken, J. (1978), *The Last Days of Graeco-Roman Paganism* (trans. S. MacCormack), Amsterdam, New York, Oxford.

Glover, T. R. (1920), *The Conflict of Religions in the Early Roman Empire*, London.

Glueck, N. (1965), *Deities and Dolphins*, New York.

Goodenough, E. R. (1928), 'The political philosophy of the hellenistic kingship', *Yale Classical Studies* 1, 55–102.

Gorges, J. G. (1979), *Les Villas Hispano-Romaines: inventaire et problématique archéologiques*, Publications du Centre Pierre, 4, Paris.

Grant, F. C. (1959), *Ancient Roman Religion*, New York.

Grant, R. M. (1978), *Early Christianity and Society*, London.

Green, C. J. S. (1977), 'The significance of plaster burials for the recognition of Christian cemeteries', in R. Reece (ed), *Burial in the Roman World*, Council for British Archaeology Research Report, 22, 46–52.

Green, M. J. (1976), *A Corpus of Religious Material from the Civilian Areas of Roman Britain*, British Archaeological Reports No. 24, Oxford.

Green, M. J. (1977), 'Theriomorphism in Romano-British Cult-Art', in M. Henig and J. Munby (eds), *Roman Life and Art in Britain*, British Archaeological Reports, 41, 297–327, Oxford.

Green, M. J. (1983), *The Gods of Roman Britain*, Aylesbury.

Green, M. J. (1984), *The Wheel as a Cult-Symbol in the Romano-Celtic World*, Brussels.

Green, M. J. (1986), *The Gods of the Celts*, Gloucester.

Griffe, E. (1964–6), *La Gaule chrétienne à l'époque romaine*, Paris.

Gsell, S. (1920), *Afrique du Nord : IV*, Paris, 171–220.

Hammond, M. (1959), *The Antonine Monarchy*, Rome.

Harman, M., Molleson, T. and Price, J. L. (1981), 'Burials, bodies and beheadings in Romano-British and Anglo-Saxon cemeteries', *Bulletin British Museum (Natural History, Geology)*, 35(3), 145–88.

Harnack, A. (1904–5), *The Expansion of Christianity in the First Three Centuries* (trans. J. Moffat), London and New York.

Harris, E. and Harris, J. (1965), *The Oriental Cults in Roman Britain*, Leiden.

Horsley, G. H. R. (1981), *New Documents illustrating Early Christianity*, Macquarie.

Hunt, E. D. (1982a), *Holy Land Pilgrimage in the Later Roman Empire, A.D. 312 to 460*, Oxford.

Hunt, E. D. (1982b), 'St Stephen in Minorca. An episode in Jewish-Christian relations in the early fifth century A.D.', *Journal of Theological Studies*, XXXIII, 106–23.

Jashemski, W. F. (1979), *The Gardens of Pompeii*, New Rochelle, New York.

Jessup, R. (1959), 'Barrows and walled cemeteries in Roman Britain', *Journal British Archaeological Association*, third series, 22, 1–32.

Jones, R. F. J. (1975), 'The Romano-British farmstead and its cemetery at Lynch Farm, near Peterborough', *Northamptonshire Archaeology* 10, 94–137.

Jones, R. F. J. (1981), 'Cremation and inhumation – change in the third century', in A. King and M. Henig (eds), *The Roman West in the Third Century*, British Archaeological Reports S109, 15–19, Oxford.

Jones, R. F. J. (1982), 'Cemeteries and Burial Practice in the Western Provinces of the Roman Empire, to AD 300', unpublished Ph.D. thesis, University of London.

Jones, R. F. J. (1984a), 'The Roman cemeteries of Ampurias reconsidered', in T. F. C. Blagg, R. F. J. Jones and S. J. Keay (eds), *Papers in Iberian Archaeology*, British Archaeological Reports S193, 237–65, Oxford.

Jones, R. F. J. (1984b), 'The cemeteries of Roman York', in P. V. Addyman and V. Black (eds), *Archaeological Papers from York for M. W. Barley*, 34–42, York.

Jones, R. F. J. (forthcoming), *Burial and Society in the Roman West*, London.

Judge, E. A. (1979), 'Antike und Christentum: Toward a Definition of the Field. A Bibliographical Survey', in H. Temporini (ed.), *Aufstieg und Niedergang der römischen Welt, II, 23.1*, 3–58, Berlin/New York.

Kee, A. (1981), *Constantine versus Christianity*, London.

Kelly, J. N. D. (1975), *Jerome. His Life, Writings and Controversies*, London.

Kornemann, E. (1901), 'Geschichte der antiken Herrscher-Kulte', *Klio*, 1, 51–146.

Krascheninnikoff, M. (1894), 'Über die Einführung des provinzialen Kaisercultus den römischen Westen', *Philologus*, 53, 147–89.

Lambert, R. (1984), *Beloved and God*, London.

Latte, K. (1967), *Römische Religionsgeschichte*, Munich.

Lengyel, A. and Radan, G. T. B. (eds) (1980), *The Archaeology of Roman Pannonia*, Kentucky/Budapest.

Liebeschuetz, J. H. W. G. (1973), *Continuity and Change in Roman Religion*, Oxford.

Lohmeyer, E. (1919), *Christuskult und Kaiserkult*, Tübingen.

MacKendrick, P. (1969), *The Iberian Stones Speak*, New York.

MacKendrick, P. (1975), *The Dacian Stones Speak*, North Carolina.

MacKendrick, P. (1980), *The North African Stones Speak*, London.

MacMullen, R. (1981), *Paganism in the Roman Empire*, Yale.

MacQuitty, W. (1976), *Island of Isis: Philae, Temple of the Nile*, London.

McWhirr, A., Viner, L. and Wells, C. (1982), *Romano-British Cemeteries at Cirencester*, Cirencester Excavations II, Cirencester.

Magie, D. (1950), *Roman Rule in Asia Minor*, Princeton.

Manchester, K. (1983), *The Archaeology of Disease*, Bradford.

Matthews, J. (1975), *Western Aristocracies and Imperial Court, A.D. 364 to 425*, Oxford.

Matthews, J. (forthcoming), *The Roman Empire of Ammianus Marcellinus*, London.

Mattingly, H. (1948), 'The consecration of Faustina the Elder and her daughter', *Harvard Theological Review*, 41, 147–51.

Mattingly, H. (1957), *Roman Imperial Civilisation*, London.

Metcalf, W. E. (1974), 'Hadrian, Jovis Olympius', *Mnemosyne*, 27, 59–76.

Millar, F. (1967), *The Roman Empire and its Neighbours*, London.

Mócsy, A. (1974), *Pannonia and Upper Moesia*, London.

Musurillo, H. (1972), *The Acts of the Christian Martyrs*, Oxford.

Nock, A. D. (1928), 'Notes on Ruler Cult', *Journal of Hellenic Studies*, 48, 21ff.

Nock, A. D. (1930), 'A Diis Electa', *Harvard Theological Review*, 23, 266–8.

Nock, A. D. (1932), 'Cremation and burial in the Roman Empire', *Harvard Theological Review*, 25, 321–67.

Nock, A. D. (1933), *Conversion*, Oxford.

Nock, A. D. (1938), *St Paul*, London.

Nock, A. D. (1949), 'Roman army and religious year', *Harvard Theological Review*, 42, 187ff.

Nock, A. D. (1972), *Essays on Religion and the Ancient World*, Oxford.

O'Donnell, J. (1978), 'The career of Virius Nicomachus Flavianus', *Phoenix*, 32, 129–43.

Ogilvie, R. M. (1969), *The Romans and their Gods*, London.

Oliver, J. H. (1949), 'The Diui of the Hadrianic period', *Harvard Theological Review*, 42, 35ff.

Palmer, R. E. A. (1954), *Roman Religion and Roman Empire*, Philadelphia.

Pease, A. S. (1963), *M. Tulli Ciceronis De Divinatione*, Darmstadt.

Pettazoni, R. (1959), *La Regalita Sacra*, Leiden.

Piana, G. la (1927), 'Foreign groups in Rome during the first centuries of the Empire', *Harvard Theological Review*, 20, 383–403.

Picard, G. (1964), *Carthage*, London.

Pilet, C. (1980), *La Nécropole de Frénouville*, British Archaeological Reports S83, Oxford.

Pleket, H. W. (1965), 'An aspect of Emperor Cult: Imperial mysteries', *Harvard Theological Review*, 58, 331ff.

Poultney, J. W. (1969), *The Bronze Tablets of Iguvium*, Baltimore.

Price, S. R. F. (1984), *Rituals and Power: the Roman Imperial Cult in Asia Minor*, Cambridge.

Ragette, F. (1980), *Baalbek*, London.

Raubitschek, A. E. (1945), 'Hadrian as the son of Zeus Eleutherios', *American Journal of Archaeology*, 49, 128–33.

Raven, S. (1969), *Rome in Africa*, London.

Reynolds, J. (ed) (1976), *Libyan Studies: Select Papers of the late R. G. Goodchild*, London.

Rose, H. J. (1926), *Primitive Culture in Italy*, London.

Rose, H. J. (1948), *Ancient Roman Religion*, London.

Ross, A. (1967), *Pagan Celtic Britain*, London.

Rostovtzeff, M. I. (1928), *Mystic Italy*, New York.

Rousseau, P. (1978), *Ascetics, Authority and the Church in the Age of Jerome and Cassian*, Oxford.

R.C.H.M. (1962), Royal Commission on Historical Monuments (England), *Eburacum: Roman York*, London.

Ste Croix, G. E. M. de (1954), 'Suffragium: from vote to patronage', *British Journal of Sociology*, V, 33–48.

Ste Croix, G. E. M. de (1963), 'Why were the Early Christians persecuted?', *Past and Present*, 26, 6–38.

Ste Croix, G. E. M. de (1964), 'Why were the Early Christians persecuted?', *Past and Present*, 27, 28–33.

Savory, H. N. (1968), *Spain and Portugal*, London.

Scott, K. (1934), *The Imperial Cult under the Flavians*, Stuttgart, Berlin.

Scullard, H. H. (1981), *Festivals and Ceremonies of the Roman Republic*, London.

Sherwin-White, A. N. (1964), 'Why were the Early Christians persecuted? An Amendment', *Past and Present*, 27, 23–7.

Stein, A. (1927), 'Zu sozialen Stellung der provinzialen Oberpriester', in *Epitymbion H. Swoboda*, Reichenberg.

Stevenson, J. (1978), *The Catacombs*, London.

Streeter, B. H. (1930), *The Primitive Church*, London.

Strong, E. (1915), *Apotheosis and After-Life*, London.

Sweet, L. M. (1919), *Roman Emperor Worship*, Boston.

Taylor, L. R. (1931), *The Divinity of the Roman Emperor*, Middletown.

Thévenot, E. (1968), *Divinités et Sanctuaires de la Gaule*, Paris.

Thompson, L. and Ferguson, J. (eds) (1969), *Africa in Classical Antiquity*, Ibadan.

Toutain, J. (1907–20), *Les Cultes païens dans l'empire romain*, Paris.

Toynbee, J. M. C. (1971), *Death and Burial in the Roman World*, London.

Tranoy, A. (1981), *La Galice Romaine: Recherches sur le nord-ouest de la Péninsule Ibérique dans l'antiquité*, Paris.

Tudor, D. (1969), *Corpus Monumentorum Religionis Equitum Danuviorum*, II, Leiden.

Vanderlinden, S. (1946), 'Revelatio Sancti Stephani (B.II.L. 7850 6)', *Revue des études byzantines*, IV, 178–217.

Vazuez, A. M. (1982), *La Religion Romans en Hispania: Fuentes epigráficas, arquelógicas y numismáticas*, Madrid.

Vermaseren, M. J. (1956), *Corpus Inscriptionum et monumentorum religionis Mithriacae*, The Hague.

Vermaseren, M. J. (1963), *Mithras, the Secret God*, London.

Vries, J. de (1963), *La Religion des Celtes*, Paris.

Walzer, R. (1949), *Galen on Jews and Christians*, Oxford.

Wardman, A. (1982), *Religion and State-craft among the Romans*, London.

Wedlake, W. J. (1982), *The Excavation of the Shrine of Apollo at Nettleton, Wiltshire 1956– 1971*, Society of Antiquaries of London Research Report 40, London.

Weinstock, S. (1971), *Divus Julius*, Oxford.

Wells, C. (1981), 'Report on three series of Romano-British cremations and four inhumations from Skeleton Green', in C. Partridge, *Skeleton Green: a late Iron Age and Romano-British site*, Britannia Monograph 2, 277–304, London.

Wenham, L. P. (1968), *The Romano-British Cemetery at Trentholme Drive, York*, London.

Wheeler, R. E. M. (1964), *Roman Art and Architecture*, London.

Whittaker, C. R. (1983), 'Late Roman Trade and Traders', in P. Garnsey, K. Hopkins and C. R. Whittaker (eds), *Trade in the Ancient Economy*, London, 163–80.

Wightman, E. M. (1970), *Roman Trier and the Treveri*, London.

Wilkes, J. J. (1969), *Dalmatia*, London.

Wiseman, T. P. (1956), *Roman Spain*, London.

Wissowa, G. (1911), *Religion und Kultus der Römer*, Munich.

PART 11

·POST-SCRIPT·

CHAPTER 35

·POST-SCRIPT·

John Wacher

The end of the Roman Empire in the west is traditionally placed in AD 476, when the last of the western emperors, Romulus Augustulus was deposed. But the west had been beset by serious difficulties long before that, and many of the internal changes in the structure of the Empire can also be detected before they came to fruition in the fourth and fifth centuries.

One of the most critical changes was the final separation of the civil administration from the army (Part 3, Chapter 7 and Part 6, Chapter 17), which in some ways can be seen as starting under Hadrian, when the career structure of civil servants was separated from that which had hitherto covered all officers, both military and civil, who aspired to imperial service. The style and mode of operation of the emperors also changed, so that by the fourth century most resembled absolute monarchs, and any final republican trappings, carefully fostered by Augustus and the early emperors, had been discarded. Administratively also, from the fourth century onwards, the Empire was divided into two parts, the West and East.

The stresses to which the frontiers were subjected, when combined with the restructuring of the army, also caused many changes (Part 4). The succession of barbarian invasions, which over-ran much of Gaul in the third century, led, by the early fourth, to the abandonment of all territory across the Rhine and upper Danube. In consequence, fortifications were added along the lines of both rivers, and the new styles of defensive architecture, which can be seen in use in many of them, were simultaneously extended northwards and eastwards to the mouths of both rivers; Dacia was abandoned at the same time, although a new province of that name was carved out of land south of the Danube. In the east, there was the third-century interlude of Palmyra entering the power vacuum left by the breakdown of the frontier defences, and the later return, for a short time, of Diocletian's army to Mesopotamia. The replacement of a weakened Parthia by Persia led to a consolidation of fortifications, again in the new styles, along the traditional line of the Euphrates and thence stretching south through Syria and Arabia to the Red Sea and westwards across to the Mediterranean through the modern Negev. Pressures were also building along the extensive boundaries in Africa, and, as elsewhere, more troops were deployed, often in small fortlets of the type which is so characteristic of Africa and the east in the later Roman period. Chief among the changes, though, was the recognition that linear barriers and boundaries were generally inadequate to bar a determined invader, leading to the establishment of a number of mobile field armies, which tended to become the elite troops of the Empire.

By the fourth century also, most urban sites (Part 5) of any merit not already fortified received walls and, as such, came to play an increasing part in imperial defence, providing a series of centres which not only protected the organs of the administration, but also acted as refuges for the local inhabitants, their livestock and harvested crops. In many of the frontier provinces small fortified road stations were constructed along major routes between principal towns and cities. Quite often when defences were erected for the first time around these sites, only a fraction of the settlement area was enclosed, suggesting either a considerable reduction in population, or a concentration on those buildings and functions which really mattered. Internally many towns changed also, with migrations of wealth to and from the countryside.

Naturally, the insecurity felt in the countryside in some provinces, particularly in the west, in consequence of breaches of the frontiers, produced some profound changes (Part 7). It has, for instance, been argued that the quite exceptional growth of large villas in Britain during the fourth century was caused partly by a flight of capital from Gaul and Germany.

The effects of these changes on the economy of the Empire (Part 8) were patchy. Insecurity was bad for the transport of goods, both by road – due to brigandage – and sea – due to piracy. Surprisingly trade continued at a fairly high level of activity, until the ultimate destruction of the western markets in the fifth century brought about its virtual termination. Other factors to affect it were severe inflation, intermittently from the third century on, and the exhaustion of some of the principal mines in Spain, whence had come much of the Empire's gold and silver. Closer control was also exercised over some industries, such as clothing, to secure supplies for the army.

Society also changed radically (Part 9), partly owing to the grant of Roman citizenship to all free-born inhabitants of the Empire in the early third century, which removed one of the chief divisions between social classes. But new ones appeared, notably that between the so-called *honestiores* and *humiliores*; the latter were much more harshly treated with regard to legal processes, invariably being questioned under torture, while the former were more leniently treated. The peasant class became more and more bound to the land, usually through debt, and although ostensibly 'free' were, in fact, little better than slaves. In many occupations, including the curial class, families found themselves in hereditary employment. Attempts to elevate themselves into a higher class must often have led to bribery, which became rife in many of the Empire's affairs, so chipping away at morality and the fabric of society.

In religion, the fundamental change came with the adoption of Christianity as the official religion of the Empire in the fourth century, following the personal conversion of the Emperor Constantine (Part 10). Some attempts were made to restore the 'old order', notably under Julian, and there is little doubt that pagan cults and practices lingered on in some rural or remote areas, although subjected to increasingly severe measures by the early Church.

The Roman Empire survived as long as it did, which was longer than most other empires known to history, because its chief strength lay in 'government by consent', backed, in the last resort, by overwhelming force. This meant that by far the highest proportion of the population was probably content to be so ruled, taking advantage of the peace and protection which the *Pax Romana* ensured. Conditions within the Empire would generally have been far superior to those existing beyond the frontiers. So long as these conditions lasted, all was well. But the combination of internal disorder, external threat and economic disarray in the third century threatened the Empire's survival. On that occasion it did not prove fatal, but the Empire which re-emerged from it had changed fundamentally, while the increasingly repressive methods which were introduced to bolster its crumbling structure can have appealed to few; the consent had become divorced from the government. Morale was sapped, and the Empire began to lose its self-respect; it relied more and more on lower-grade citizens, recruited from beyond the frontiers and settled within them, to do its fighting. Consequently, when the massive attacks from central Europe were mounted against the very heart of the traditional Empire – Rome itself – there was little power of resistance left and Rome fell in 410 to Alaric. Disintegration was not even then immediate, although effective overall political control was lost in the west. Fortunately the seat of real government had already left Rome, with the division of the Empire into two parts, and from the middle of the fourth century Constantine's great city of Byzantium – renamed Constantinopolis – became the power centre, with its marked eastward shift. Not surprisingly, the eastern Empire was more successful in repelling invaders and containing internal strife, and its separation from the west ensured its survival, much changed – even in name – for a further thousand years, until Constantinople finally fell to the Moslem invaders in 1453. Although the Byzantine Empire was very different from the Roman Empire, it nevertheless inherited many of the customs and traditions of Rome and maintained that inheritance into the Middle Ages.

·INDEX·